State and Society in Post-War Japan

State and Society in Post-War Japan

BERNARD ECCLESTON

Polity Press

First published 1989 by Polity Press in association with Basil Blackwell

Editorial office:
Polity Press, Dales Brewery, Gwydir Street, Cambridge CB1 2LJ, UK

Marketing and production:
Basil Blackwell Ltd
108 Cowley Road, Oxford OX4 1JF, UK

Basil Blackwell Inc.
3 Cambridge Center,
Cambridge, MA 02142, USA

ISBN 0 7456 0165 0
ISBN 0 7456 0166 9 (pbk)

British Library Cataloguing in Publication Data

A CIP catalogue record for this book is available from the British Library.

Library of Congress Cataloging in Publication Data

A CIP catalogue record for this book is available from the Library of Congress.

Typeset in 10 on 11½ pt Ehrhardt by Photo-graphics, Honiton, Devon
Printed and bound in Great Britain at
The Camelot Press Ltd, Southampton

Contents

List of Figures and Tables

Figures

Tables

List of Abbreviations

DSP	Democratic Socialist Party
EPA	Economic Planning Agency
EPI	Employees' Pension Insurance
EA	Environment Agency
EEC	European Economic Community
FTC	Fair Trade Commission
FEER	*Far Eastern Economic Review*
FT	*Financial Times*
FILP	Fiscal Investment and Loan Programme
FPC	Foreign Press Centre
HLC	Housing Loan Corporation
JCP	Japan Communist Party
JEcJ	*Japan Economic Journal*
JEdJ	*Japan Education Journal*
JFN	*Japan Foundation Newsletter*
JSP	Japan Socialist Party
JTW	*Japan Times Weekly*
LDP	Liberal Democratic Party
MITI	Ministry of International Trade and Industry
NP	National Pension
NIC	Newly Industrializing Country
NLC	New Liberal Club
NYT	*New York Times*
OECD	Organization for Economic Cooperation and Development
OPEC	Organization of Petroleum Exporting Countries
PAB	Public Advisory Body
QC	Quality Control Circle
SDF	Self-Defence Forces

Preface

One of the most challenging aspects of working with adult students in particular is the way the questions they raise force us to move across what at times appear to be rigid subject or discipline boundaries. When I agreed to contribute a section on Japan for an interdisciplinary course at the Open University called *The State and Society*, I was confronted with a fairly clear division of labour between anthropologists, economists, political scientists and sociologists who had specialized in writing about Japan. My initial attempt to forge links across these specialist studies made me aware of the inadequacies of my previous work on Japan which had been based within departments of economics and economic history. The reaction of students and tutors to my Open University publication was encouraging enough for me to attempt to expand it into a book which is designed to offer those interested in the Japanese experience a general introduction from which they can then deepen their contacts with some of the more specialist publications.

I have based this study on sources that have been published in English using books and journal articles that are widely available in college, polytechnic and university libraries or that are accessible through loan schemes with specialist centres of Japanese studies. I would also recommend that contact be established with the Information Section at Japanese Embassies because this is an invaluable source for translated summaries of official reports and survey results. This emphasis on references accessible to those who do not read Japanese is quite deliberate because the book is intended for those who may be intrigued by various aspects of Japanese society to a depth which does not require familiarity with the language. My intention was not for the reader to become totally absorbed in another society, but to raise questions about Japan that derive from wider debates about economic, political and social change in Western societies.

In the context, for example, of debates on how to maintain high rates of economic growth, Japan's experience is clearly more impressive than most and therefore arouses immediate interest. Among the factors involved are the higher levels of industrial investment in Japan and the apparent ease with which new sectors and methods of production are introduced. Chapter 2 explores some of the consequences of an industrial structure which paradoxically combines a high level of competition between Japanese firms with a certain degree of interdependence. In particular this chapter examines why large numbers of small firms acting as subcontractors continue to play such an important role in Japanese production when a buoyant small firm sector is not normally expected to remain a feature of an advanced industrial economy.

Linked to the relative ease with which the focus of production can be shifted goes the commonly held belief that employment in Japan unlike the West, has not been subject to the same degree of variability. Not only has the rate of unemployment remained especially low, but even in declining sectors Japanese firms profess an ability to shift into newer sectors without enforced redundancies among their labour force. However, though the long-term growth of the Japanese economy has been very rapid, this has not precluded periods of recession. Chapter 3 therefore takes as its central concern the paradox of a commitment to lifetime employment and at the same time the need to have a labour force flexible enough to accommodate periodic fluctuations in output. In addition to considering just how many Japanese workers can expect the guarantee of a lifetime's employment with one company to be fulfilled, we will also look at the way the formation of enterprise unions was coordinated by the state to produce a segmented labour market. One can then see how a core of permanent employees is complemented by a much larger number without any such expectations.

In the construction of a flexible structure of employment and production, the Japanese state played a vital role as it attempted to reconstruct an economy devastated by the Pacific war. However in recent years there has been a trend among commentators to argue that the economic role of the state has been exaggerated. This tendency in part reflects the re-emergence throughout the West of a free market ideology which insists that state intervention should be constrained. In part too it reflects the gradual liberalization of economic control in Japan since the 1960s after which the continued growth of the economy is used to show what can happen if market forces predominate. Chapter 4 addresses this debate directly by arguing that it is not the size of state spending *per se* that is crucial but the relative shares of public investment and current spending on public services. Additionally, the Japanese state continues to play an important part in managing consultation among representatives of private business. In other words a small state in terms of public expenditure and revenue totals does not necessarily exercise less influence over economic relations.

Despite the erosion of certain of the state's more formal powers there exist elements of continuity in the involvement of the state not least, for example, in the persisting pattern of personnel movement from the bureaucracy into leading private firms or into the ruling conservative party. A related aspect of this continuity is the remarkable fact that public officials have for 40 years been able to look forward to working with governments elected from representatives of the same party. Chapter 5 examines the reasons why Japan has not seen the alternation of elected governments formed from different parties that has characterized most other liberal democracies. In many ways this chapter explains the conservative hegemony as much in terms of the weaknesses and fragmentation of opposition parties as in the claims of the ruling conservatives that they are the party of government because they truly reflect the spirit of collective national purpose for which Japan is said to be renowned.

For many this strong sense of collective identity is underpinned by the belief that the material benefits of the economic miracle have been so widely dispersed that Japanese society is either classless or much less socially divided than in other capitalist countries. While there is consistent evidence from self-assessed social surveys that 90 per cent of those interviewed consider themselves to be middle class, Chapter 6 argues that this may give only a superficial representation of an egalitarian society. For women, members of minority groups and the elderly, there continue to be predictably different life chances which the state has done little to alter and arguably has helped to perpetuate.

It is important then to keep in mind several dimensions of continuity in the development of Japanese society since 1945. But it is also vital to recognize that the representative institutions of a liberal democracy were bestowed on Japan during the US Occupation, and that government could not continue to ignore pressures for social change. Chapter 7 uses several examples to illustrate how the Japanese state and society at large has responded to pressures for change. Divisive internal issues such as the demand for Equal Opportunity Legislation and widespread environmental protest or the external pressure for economic change prompted by the substantial appreciation of the yen in 1985, will be explored to suggest how social consensus has been managed.

Each chapter therefore has as a part of its rationale the comparative notion that the Japanese experience is very different from other industrial societies in the West. At various points I do argue that some of these perceived differences are more apparent than real, but there does seem to me to be a general tendency for writers to approach their study of Japan looking for uniquely different features. In some ways this reflects Japan's position as the first non-Western industrial society with a cultural and historical heritage that was more likely to encourage people to forego private interests for the sake of collective goals. Hence most of the literature implicitly assumes a greater propensity for social consensus.

Chapter 1, which serves as an introduction to the whole book, attempts to trace how our images of Japan have been shaped by the expectation

that consensus rather than social conflict is the norm. In particular this
chapter examines the influence of Japan's cultural and historical background,
and how the institutions of liberal democracy established during the US
Occupation were supposed to prevent the re-emergence of the coercive
regimes of pre-war Japan.

Acknowledgements

The accumulation of source materials for this book has been assisted by a number of people from various institutions in whose debt I remain. Through the Information Section at the Japanese Embassy in London I have been given access to an enormous number of Foreign Press Centre translations which has kept my research more closely in touch with current affairs in Japan. The good offices of the Japan Foundation also ensured that I received complimentary copies of the *Japan Times Weekly*, the *Japan Foundation Newsletter* and the *Japan Educational Journal* thus fulfilling their objective of facilitating the work of all foreign students of Japan. John Allen, Colin Bamford, John Crump, Sue Himmelweit and Yoshio Sugimoto were kind enough to supply me with references, offprints and press cuttings.

In 1984 several people offered criticisms of my work on Japan for the Open University course after Polity Press suggested that I might develop this publication into a book. John Crump, Tetsuro Kato and Ross Mouer challenged my account in various ways and their comments were extremely helpful as was the report from an anonymous Reader contracted by Polity. Even though I have tried to accommodate their criticisms, they will no doubt still disagree with a number of my arguments.

During three lengthy spells of research leave colleagues in the Yorkshire Region of the Open University mitigated the effect of my absence on our students and tutors. John Barrett, Elizabeth Chaplin, Savita de Sousa and Jackie Wootton helped to keep my desk covered as did Diana Carroll who also helped to compile the bibliography. Chris Nicholls in the Social Science Faculty at Milton Keynes was unfailing in her willingness to share with me her expertise of word processing with an Apple Macintosh and her intervention saved me many hours of 'manual' studying.

David Held at Polity Press has kept faith with this project throughout its prolonged period of production and his consistent encouragement has been a source of inspiration.

Finally, saving the most important person until last, it is no exaggeration to say that Julie Eccleston has shown undiminished powers of patience and tolerance during the four years that it has taken to produce this book. I only hope that the final product compensates in some way for the time she has had to spend listening to me rehearsing some of the ideas that sprang to my mind at all hours of the day or night.

Bernard Eccleston
Boltby, North Yorkshire

1

Conflict or Consensus: Competing Images of Japan

Initially at least, most of us find our thinking about Japan grounded in the differences we perceive between our own society and Asia's New Giant. In the process we may fall back on an idealized view of our own society, or take our cue from generalized impressions of 'Western' experience. Despite these dangers, there is a widespread belief that Japanese society differs from Western societies because of the greater willingness of the Japanese to conform and defer to group consensus.

Japan's superior economic performance has been a major focus of interest, concern or envy, but alongside the contrast in economic performance has gone fascination with Japan's system of industrial relations. These two themes of rapid economic growth and workplace harmony are often connected as cause and effect to produce a neat and tidy contrast. As we shall see, this connection although appearing neat is certainly not tidy because in many ways Japanese industrial relations are not nearly the radical contrast with the West that they first appear. Nevertheless, our view of Japanese society is often supported by an underlying assumption that a tendency towards social consensus rather than social or class conflict, is what makes Japan different.

There are, to be sure, competing and contradictory images most clearly seen in militarized public demonstrations, but these are frequently and misleadingly labelled as the activities of student radicals or Red Army factions. Thus this type of conflict is treated as an isolated exception against the backdrop of assumed consensus. In recent years as Japanese competition penetrates ever deeper, Western media coverage of Japan has been much more concerned with economics and trade than with conflict inside Japan. Not only are Japanese products now highly visible in our shops, but also Japanese companies are equally visible as employers in their overseas plants.

Nowhere is the idea of harmony and consensus so sharply fastened in Western minds as in our perceptions of Japanese employment practices.

In explanations of fewer days lost through strikes, in comment on superior quality products or in the relative ease with which robots are introduced into factories, workplace harmony is a common thread. One well publicized feature of harmony and cooperation in Japanese companies can be seen in the removal of the outward signs of distinction between workers, whether these are based on dress, working hours or canteen facilities. Working together for the good of the company transcends the need to distinguish production from office or staff employees on the basis of the colour of their collar.

Harmony and collective company effort is portrayed as a reciprocal bargain. Labour gives total commitment in return for a promise of job security; management assures long-term employment and receives positive support for any workplace changes that enhance productivity. Various institutional arrangements both support and reproduce cooperation such as continuous consultation with the union and the practice of delegated decision-making. Most unions are single enterprise units extending membership to all regular employees, but what appears unusual from a Western perspective is the amount of administrative support given by the company in collecting union subscriptions or in providing organizational help for union officials. Another difference is noted in the way union and management negotiators often move across the negotiating table: a chief union official one year, a management representative the next. Such an interchange is identified as crucial for maintaining the cooperation that appears absent in adversarial Western systems.

Decision-making is also supposed to be different in Japanese companies as power is pluralized in consensual mechanisms such as *ringi-sei*. This involves the channelling of policy initiatives upwards from lower levels so that as proposals move through the company they gather support leaving the final decision-maker with the simple task of confirming the agreed consensus. As a process, this presents a stark contrast to Western models which stress the rights and prerogatives of senior management.

A commitment to power sharing, company loyalty and group harmony does not mean the complete absence of differences in pay and status within the company. Differentials do exist between blue- and white-collar workers, but they appear to be narrower than in most Western companies, and they are seen to be justified by different educational qualifications. Pay scales, for example, are determined in part by the length of an individual's educational career. Another important component of pay is related to the length of service with the company which produces an escalating reward for loyalty. Taking these two elements together then, pay differentials are considered as only proper because someone with better qualifications and a longer service record may be expected to contribute more to the company.

Hierarchies certainly exist within Japanese companies, but with extensive consultation and the higher entry qualifications of management personnel, the structure of authority appears fair and legitimate. In a sense, such clearly defined ground rules are said to reduce the alienation of labour from management, and provide a secure base for corporate harmony.

Reducing the sources of internal division within the Japanese company allows the focus of collective effort to be directed externally towards rival companies in the market. Extensive interest is promoted in the relative perfomance of Japanese companies in league tables based on output, exports, or profits, and company commitment binds employees towards the main goal of improving league position. Such a high level of identification with one's company is reinforced outside normal working hours in the provision of collective leisure facilities for employees and their families; by company-based health, education and welfare schemes or by the provision of company housing or housing subsidies. In addition, employees share the proceeds of company success either through general productivity bonuses or bonuses attributed to their particular section. Therefore group effort on behalf of the company is reflected not only in working hours, but also in voluntary overtime clubs or quality control circles that meet outside regular working hours.

When we focus on differences between Japan and the West it has been common to paint pictures based to a large extent on our general impression of how relations at work offer such sharply contrasting attitudes to work. However, these general impressions run the danger of stereotyping both Japanese experience and the idealized Western contrast. In later chapters we will probe the image of harmony in some detail to question whether all Japanese companies display such a high degree of harmony, cooperation or power sharing. There are questions to be raised specifically about the coverage of job security guarantees, especially for women, the amount of independence unions have and the extent of delegation as opposed to ritualized consensus formation. Equally, there are dangers in suggesting that all Western economic ills are explained by militant labour or autocratic managers, thereby downplaying differences in the quality and quantity of capital equipment used. Similarly, we might consider whether educational qualifications or length of service are not also components of pay scales in Western companies. Simply because Japan appears to be different we should guard against reversing the image by suggesting that none of the standard elements of Japanese work practices is present in the West, and that workplace conflict is rare in Japan. Chapter 3 will question whether the novelty of labour management in Japan has been exaggerated, but it is important to recognize how the stereotypical view of workplace relations is regarded as one manifestation of the general characteristics of Japanese society. So diminished status differentials in private companies is said to reflect the existence of a more egalitarian society where leadership is based on personal merit. Collective effort for the good of one's company is seen as one example of the willingness of the Japanese people to sacrifice private interests in favour of the collective good.

1.1 A uniquely consensual society?

The tendency for distinctions between labour and management to appear less overt connects with the widely expressed view that class consciousness is not important to the Japanese. Public opinion surveys undertaken by the Prime Minister's Office have, over the past two decades, shown that 80–90 per cent of Japanese consider themselves to be middle class. There are some serious shortcomings in this sort of opinion polling, but there are nevertheless, connections between this majority middle-class identification and trends in income inequality. By some measures incomes are more equally distributed in Japan than in the West, and in 'employment income . . . Japan's degree of equality parallels that of some of the socialist countries of Eastern Europe' (Boltho 1975 p.163). Problems abound in measuring income distribution and although there has been a reversal in equality trends since the mid-1970s, middle-class identity in Japan is more closely related to earning middling incomes than attachment to class specific values. One implication of phenomenal rates of economic growth can be seen in rising incomes leading to an enormous increase in the ownership of consumer durables, although it is debatable whether incomes have risen as fast as GNP. Thus, relative to other generations and to other societies, the Japanese certainly feel more prosperous and some of the more outward signs of affluence are widely spread.

The company loyalty bargain which exchanges labour cooperation for job security also has a wider significance if we think about the amazingly low national unemployment figures recorded by the Ministry of Labour. Even in the decade following the 1973 oil crisis, official unemployment rates have never exceeded 3 per cent, compared to the double figure levels in the EEC or the US. International comparisons of unemployment rates are as notoriously difficult as measures of income distribution, and the Labour Ministry in Japan, as in other countries, has its own idiosyncratic style of creative statistical construction. There are studies by Japanese labour economists which suggest that if the US definition of unemployment were used in Japan, the unemployment percentage would at least double (Tominomori 1985). The common issue in disputing the accuracy of unemployment statistics concerns the under-recording of women who wish to take paid employment but do not register. There will be a more intensive look at this problem later, but for now all that concerns us is that the job security component of the company loyalty is reflected at national level in official unemployment rates.

Management delegation and consultation within companies has its wider reflection in the institutions of Japan's democratic polity. Japan's 1947 constitution, drawn up by the US occupying authority, widened the franchise to all adults and the frequent national elections since then have, technically at least, given citizens the opportunity to express their preferences. More important perhaps for regular consultation are the vast array of interest and pressure groups that coordinate opinion on separate issues, or who are consulted continuously in permanent opinion gathering bodies, or who are asked to participate in Advisory Commissions on specific issues like Public Administrative Reform. In many ways this array of interest groups is not peculiar to Japan, and the usual debate exists about whether some groups rather than others have more access or influence. These debates are particularly acute when the level and regularity of consultation with large business corporations is compared to consumer groups, women's organizations, non-unionized labour or minority groups. Such a list though, would hardly be out of place elsewhere.

One debate focuses on the power and influence of elites within Japanese society, and obviously any book on the Japanese state must have this as a major element, and indeed it does. Before we plunge into that debate we ought to recognize that recruitment to elite positions in the public and private sectors is said to be highly meritocratic. We have already seen how authority within companies is deemed legitimate when it is based on educational achievement and length of service; attitudes towards public sector bureaucrats who occupy high office are likewise framed by the priority given to individual merit displayed by educational status. With one of the highest rates of college and university entry in the world it appears that those who get to elite positions, do so through individual effort, and merit is thus properly rewarded. So educational achievement rather than nepotism offers a background to the respect, status and deference accorded to elites. There are competing views which see family income as the key determinant of access to the top universities from which elites are recruited into large companies or the bureaucracy. Competiton for places in high status universities is so enormous that after-school attendance at expensive private crammer schools is virtually compulsory. While this tendency towards the importance of supplementary education has grown significantly since the 1960s, the enormous priority given by the Japanese to education underpins the significance of meritocratic ideals.

One other feature which is said to distinguish Japanese society from the West concerns their greater propensity towards collective effort for the good of the nation. A parallel is drawn between the direction of a Japanese company's collective effort against outside competitors, and the ability to mobilize national effort. This has been illustrated by comparing the Japanese reaction to the two oil crises in the 1970s. At the same time as OPEC massively increased oil prices in 1973–4, Japan was experiencing high and accelerating rates of inflation, there was an internal political crisis for the ruling LDP party as their support inside and outside the Diet fell in the face of corruption scandals and popular pressure for tighter controls on environmental pollution. In this context Japan's overwhelming dependence on imported oil set off the most severe economic recession since World War II and GNP actually fell by 1 per cent in 1974 after growing at an average rate of nearly 10 per cent in the previous six years. Not only was the economy fragile and exposed, but also was the domination of the LDP.

By the time the second oil shock hit Japan in 1979–80 the rate of inflation had been brought under tight control by a sharp reduction in the level of wage increases, energy-saving technology had been introduced, stricter pollution controls were enacted and LDP support had revived. The short-term reaction to the second oil price increase on GNP was much less severe, and Japan went into the 1980s with higher growth rates relative to other Western economies, though well below the rates achieved before 1973. This relatively smooth response to the second oil shock has been interpreted as a united, collective effort to resolve the severe crisis of the mid-1970s which had exposed Japan's energy vulnerability and her fragile political consensus.

Many factors were involved in the national response to economic crisis, but the belief that Japan can produce a greater sense of collective purpose was a key theme in a general shift of attitudes towards the lessons that Japan can offer the West. Up to the mid-1970s, the focus of the debate on lessons from the Japanese experience was related mainly to the problems of underdeveloped countries in achieving rapid industrialization. It is true that there had been a steady erosion to the pre-war image of Japan as a cheap labour economy producing shoddy goods, but the 1970s saw an explosion of interest in what lessons Japan could offer advanced industrial societies.

The main thrust in the 'Learning from Japan' movement came from the United States which dominates the literature on Japan published in English, and there are two main areas of interest. First, a fairly narrow area concerned, initially at least, with management practices and connections between company collectivism and higher productivity levels. Here, attention is focused on the possibility of transplanting institutions like Quality Control circles or delegated authority mechanisms into Western companies. However, where such transplantation has been attempted, the results as far as productivity is concerned have not been as dramatic as management academics had expected (Cole 1980). When the reasons for the disappointing response are explored, we find that the emphasis is placed on the unique social and cultural values of Japanese society. At this point in the analysis the more narrow focus on production merges with a second broader area of interest. This too includes analysis of employment practices, but attention is broadened to include a wide range of social trends such as lower Japanese crime rates, a preference for private family-based welfare, income equality, middle-class identity and the responsiveness of democratic institutions.

Vogel's book entitled *Japan As Number One* (1979) is the epitome of this trend, as he sets a scenario in which he not only predicts that the Japanese economy will be the biggest in the world before the end of the century, but also that Japanese society should henceforth be *the* model for post-industrial societies. Special prominence was given to the value of community policing within densely populated areas, the value of widening entry to higher education, the meritocratic recruitment of elites, the role of harmony in companies and the Japanese welfare system of 'security without entitlement'.

In social welfare, Vogel touched on a very topical issue when he praised the advantages of a minimal welfare state for holding down tax levels and maximizing individual incentives. Such a theme was, and still is, at the centre of debate throughout all Western societies, but what was really surprising for the Japanese to read was the clear attribution, from a Westerner, that a limited state role was one of the most important reasons why Japanese was destined to be the 'Number One'. It is easy to exaggerate the impact of a single book although when published in Japanese the book was itself the number one bestseller. Vogel was actually pulling together a good deal of social science research and his approach was not too dissimilar from many others, except in its more explicitly laudatory style. What was perhaps vital was that Vogel's view of the causes of Japanese prosperity echoed the statements of many of Japan's leaders.

In the context of a smoother short-term response to the second oil shock and a higher long-term economic growth path than in the West, there was an acceleration of interest in the notion of Japan's uniqueness not in the vein of inferiority or economic fragility, but in the context of superiority and independence. So when comparing economic performance, it appeared that Japan had avoided the endemic Western problems of alienation and social conflict particularly in economic organizations. A new disease was identified which had the symptoms of workplace disunity, low productivity, poor quality products. It was named variously as the English, British, European or Western disease – presumably a contagious disease! The importance of this emphasis on Japanese uniqueness and immunity to the new disease, cannot be underestimated in the contemporary political debates that surround the appropriate role of the Japanese state in the society of the 1980s and beyond. At another level it raised confidence in national identity and gave support to social science studies of Japan which stressed the way its unique cultural heritage underpinned economic success.

It would be an exaggeration to imply that Vogel's views have been slavishly followed by Japanese or Western writers. There is a very strong critical tradition within Japan which has stressed the need to consider the other side of the economic miracle whether this concerns the social costs of pollution and congestion, gender and racial inequalities, repressive police methods, the inadequate provision of housing, the lack of proper attention to the elderly or sick. Publications in English do not in any sense reflect the strength of this critical approach, mainly because it is associated with Marxism, and in a US-dominated publishing market for Japanese studies this is hardly surprising.

Research on the implications of American dominance of Japanese studies in English has been limited, although Dower (1975) Kawamura (1980) and Mouer and Sugimoto (1986) have offered a useful start. This is not the place to consider the role of research funding bodies or US universities in constraining the careers or publications of academics, but we should recognize that the bulk of publications in English are drawn from writers whose work is 'conceived in terms congruent with idealizations of US democracy' (Boyd 1985). Such a recognition is doubly significant in Japanese studies because the Japanese polity was reconstructed by the US occupation in the 1947 constitution along the lines of their own system. Therefore writing on Japan in English operates, to a significant degree, within an agenda set by a liberal democratic tradition involving a commitment to private property, the role of market competition, citizenship rights and representative democratic institutions.

Where democratic institutions were ineffective as in pre-war Japan, it was all too easy for a collectivist tradition to be used to mobilize support for an authoritarian regime. Vogel and others argue that Japan only became the model to follow once constitutional safeguards of individual rights harnessed a cultural preference into a force for the good of society as a whole. What was it about Japan's history that limited the pursuit of individual self-interest and gave precedence to the collective community?

1.2 Collective identity in pre-war Japan

Explanations of Japan's unique cultural tradition have as their base then, a belief in the vital place of liberal democratic institutions in the post-1947 era. What has intrigued many Western observers however, is the absence of the strong sense of individualism that usually distinguishes the 'liberal' element in liberal democratic societies. Using the work of social anthropologists and social psychologists to get closer to an understanding of the unique parts of Japanese culture, great play has been made of the primacy of group over individual interests. Individuals in Japan are said to find their true self-identity only through membership of, and intimate participation in, group activity. This approach was popularized by Nakane (1973) who, building on Benedict's earlier study (1946) among others, stressed the preference for group identity in Japan as a clear contrast to Western characteristics of self-assertive individualism.

In the open acknowledgement of group interdependence, conformity to group objectives is based on respect for, and loyalty to, the leadership provided by senior members. Emphasis is placed on reciprocity in the sense that leaders listen to the wishes of all group members whereupon group activity is designed to reflect the consensus. Seniority is itself based on the length of service to the group as in the classic statement of Japanese company practices; authority is legitimated by its long record of commitment and respect for seniority is therefore justified. Vertical loyalties within groups are taken to be the common base for the preservation of conformity as each individual knows their place and takes on a role consistent with that place.

The connecting mechanism between local groups and Japanese society as a whole, runs along the traces of a common commitment to the nation. So, the acute sense of collective identity that the Japanese display in language and culture prevents the rivalry of separate groups deteriorating into serious internal conflict. National leadership, with legitimate authority, binds local group interests into collective Japanese interests.

This kind of analysis sees Japanese uniqueness begin from the basic subversion of individualism into collectivism and traces the implications in cultural patterns which are distinctively different from Western ones. This contrast is used to explain why the Japanese are said to feel less class conscious than Westerners because vertical loyalties within companies, say, are more important than horizontal relations with other people who occupy the same position but who work for different companies. This single example shows how powerful the ideal of collectivism can appear, as it seems to connect in a very real way with commonsense ideas, in this case about Japan as a classless society. Equally it is often used to explain why national leaders are better placed to mobilize collective effort in the national interest such as in the response to the second oil crisis in 1979.

When we consider the dominance of collectivism as an explanation of what makes Japanese experience unique, we do need to emphasize that this is not simply a characteristic of Western or American writing, but many Japanese social scientists have echoed this explanation in their attempts to identify the sources of consensus in Japanese society. In the debate about uniqueness, a growing minority of writers have raised many problems about the way the connections between collectivism and social conformity vastly understate the importance of social conflict and overstate the level of voluntary conformity to group or national objectives in Japan. There is also concern that in efforts to provide a contrast with the West, anthropologists have reduced differences within Western experience to derive a convenient comparative stereotype. But the critics of collectivism face a formidable task because collectivism does seem to fit so well with commonsense ideas about Japan, and the identification of unique cultural values offers a convenient residual 'black box' which can be used to explain away those aspects of Japanese experience which don't quite fit with social science models.

It is generally agreed that Japan possesses many of the institutional characteristics of other capitalist societies, but these institutions do not produce the same degree of impersonal alienation because subordinates are regularly consulted and authority is 'soft' and legitimate. Explanations of the contrast are framed by the tradition of group loyalty and consensus formation. A tradition implies continuity, and the historical origins of collectivism have been traced in a variety of ways. Perhaps the most common explanation compares the modern version of group identity to the communal basis of rural rice cultivation in pre-industrial Japan. In common cause against the elements, each rural community would have mobilized collective effort when planting and harvesting rice, or constructing irrigation systems. Village meetings would possibly have reached consensual decisions on the order in which crops were to be worked, under the leadership of elders. Another variant of rural communality in Japan concerns environmental determinism: given the frequency of earthquakes or typhoons collective human effort was essential to survive the ravages of nature.

Rural collectivism is one theme, but the continuity of subordinate loyalty may also be explained by the divergent style of Japanese Confucianism. Morishima (1982) has identified a major difference between Chinese and Japanese Confucianism, in that while the former stresses humanistic benevolence, the latter places much more emphasis on loyalty and duty to seniors in the hierarchy of authority.

Thus collectivism has historical roots in religious or intellectual ideals, and in communal social practices. However it is not at all clear to what extent religious ideals were widely shared, or to what extent communal cultivation was an agreed voluntary process. An alternative explanation of collective agricultural work could very plausibly stress the degree of compulsion by landlords on landless peasantry. Compulsion could then have been justified in Confucian teachings without there being widespread acceptance of its moral codes. In raising such questions, the intention is to lay warnings about tracing the origins of voluntary collectivism in selected traditions.

Many more questions have been raised about the adequacy of such historical antecedents, but in a sense it is more pertinent to ask how such ideas and practices have survived the rapid changes that went with the industrialization of Japan after the 1870s. It is somewhat easier to see how a rurally-based tradition of collectivism could have survived in pre-industrial Japan, especially in the 250 years of isolationist rule which lasted until the mid-nineteenth century. In that period of decentralized feudalism, one clan (the Tokugawa) usurped the authority of the Emperor and ruled over other clans within a structure which prohibited almost all contact with the outside world. With strict control over the internal movement of people inside Japan, and a strictly enforced system of social hierarchy, it is not difficult to see how the identity of groups at a local level might be maintained.

This isolated existence was ended in the 1850s when external pressures from Western powers forced Japan to re-open diplomatic and trading links. In many ways the Japanese response to the external threat was undermined by the internal erosion of Tokugawa authority and its economic weaknesses. When the Emperor was restored in 1868 national leadership concentrated on centralizing authority in order to foster a national drive for industrialization. Only through industrialization would independence from the West be maintained, as the internal weaknesses of China and its consequent loss of territory had shown.

Some of the important mechanisms in Japanese industrialization will be examined in other chapters, but the question of continuity in cultural traditions must address the survival of collectivist ideals in the face of the rapid changes associated with industrialization after the 1880s. Not only were rural communities drawn forcibly into expanding the scale of agricultural production, but also urbanization increased and a compulsory system of education and military conscription brought social contacts that were impossible under Tokugawa feudalism.

It is possible to exaggerate the speed with which industrialization transformed Japan, partly because economic change was not insignificant in Tokugawa times, and partly too because industry was based primarily in the rural areas until well into the twentieth century. Nevertheless, the vastly expanded social contacts removed a shield of isolation from village life. Rural communities were still the main focus for most Japanese, but even rural communities had to cope with the exigencies of the drive to industrialize. Voluntary group participation may have existed in the era of Tokugawa isolation, but how was collectivism maintained thereafter?

Analysis of the maintenance and reproduction of collectivism is divided over whether the tradition of collectivism encourages the voluntary conformity of individuals, or whether the sanctions on non-conformity are so great that individuals have no alternative. Even in the work of Nakane (1973) and Vogel (1979) we find acknowledgement that collectivism is a perishable commodity that needs nurturing. Nakane's work has a more voluntaristic approach, but even she writes about the assertive techniques that management uses to build up company identification of workers. She also makes it clear that if labour attempts to leave one large company for another, such mobility is taken as evidence of unreliability. Labour will then find it difficult to get an equivalent job elsewhere because they have 'soiled their *curriculum vitae*' (Nakane 1973 p.111). Vogel too, emphasizes the way company uniforms, badges or songs are used to reinforce worker loyalty and he suggests that wider social conformity and 'homogeneity is created and maintained by social and educational policy' (Vogel 1979 p.180). But there does seem to be tendency to see the symbols or institutions of collectivism as mere reminders of the values in an otherwise 'collectivist social order accepted voluntarily' (van Wolferen 1982 p.121).

It is on the issue of how far people *willingly* forego individual interests that much controversy rests. In particular, with the imposition of liberal democratic institutions after 1947 it is widely felt that 'the Japanese *have elected* to forego the assertion of the right to the expression of untrammeled personal freedom in the. interest of maintaining public order and the common good' (Smith 1983 p.124). The dominant view on the crucial place of Japanese tendencies towards group consensus, rests very heavily on the structural changes that were enshrined in the constitutional apparatus.

Collectivism is thus given a very positive image when linked to constitutional guarantees of individual rights. But this very positive image is almost the exact opposite of the prevailing view about conformity before 1945. In this era, it is widely accepted that collectivism was an ideal cultural trait which could be harnessed to the growth of aggressive nationalism. As the post-war years are the golden age of Japanese liberal democracy, so the pre-war years were a 'dark valley' (Hein 1984) for the Japanese people. Militaristic fascism in the 1930s is seen as the inevitable outcome of an increasing use of nationalistic ideals to force people to conform to the goals of independence through industrialization.

Between industrialization and the end of World War II, we find emphasis placed on the way vertical loyalty to the nation took precedence over, and shaped, the absorption of individuals into local groups. In the absence of deep-rooted democratic institutions which could have held back the force of aggressive nationalism, local groups took the form of mere channels through which the idea of the nation as an integrated family could be reproduced. Instead of village communality channelling loyalty to leaders of provincial clans, each local group whether it be based on a factory, an army unit, a common landlord, a school, or a community organization now channelled loyalty to the central state. At the head of the state was the Emperor, the patriarchal head of the national family and all Japanese were to follow his authority as they would follow patriarchal authority in their own families. Being able to trace the divine origins through centuries of Imperial continuity, allowed the Emperor's authority to be treated as an untouchable prerogative.

Within this context of the nation as a family, the actions of individuals were expected to be based on selfless service to their immediate group, and thereby to the state. Self-assertive behaviour at whatever level was labelled as a dangerous, anti-social and deviant trait which transgressed the conformist thrust of national familism. Individuals were guided towards the ideals of service and loyalty through a centralized system of compulsory education and military conscription, but for those whose individualism survived these processes, a comprehensive local police force used repression to eradicate dissent.

The all embracing structure of the nation as a family headed by the Emperor, made it impossible to challenge particular aspects of the social order without calling into question the ultimate authority of the Emperor. During the 1920s the Japan Communist Party attempted to organize opposition in a movement which asserted the primacy of individual democratic rights. However in attacking the failure to ensure adequate political representation for labour, any opposition group, let alone the Communist Party, had to face repression on the grounds that they were challenging the entire fabric of the Emperor system. This dilemma eventually led, in 1932, to the JCP accepting that the only way to alter institutions of exploitation such as in the landlord system or in industry was indeed to dismantle the entire structure of the state as an Imperial family. Thereafter, the authorities had the evidence from the JCP's own objectives to justify the suppression and extinction of opposition by labelling it Marxist.

Even anti-Marxist political parties were constrained by the need to frame their objectives in terms consistent with the need to prove loyalty and commitment to the nation as the ultimate expression of collective cohesion. In the three decades that followed the issue of a new constitution in 1890, elected party members gradually increased their occupation of cabinet posts. But the constitution itself was explained as a gift from the Emperor as a reward for the loyalty of the restricted numbers that were enfranchised, and its whole ethos was rooted not in the rights of individuals but in their duties as obedient subjects. This limited degree of representation was in an important sense imposed from above, rather than actively won through struggle from below, in the same way that the 1947 Constitution was imposed by the US occupation.

Making parliamentary representation conditional upon loyalty to the Emperor system, formally narrowed the freedom for party initiatives. Elected party members may have increased their role in cabinet, but key decisions had to meet with the approval of the Emperor and his personal advisors at Court. The two main political parties took a generally conservative line and were distinguished more by personal attachment to the leading personalities of each party than by any basic differences in ideology. What they did have in common, was a relatively poor organizational base among eligible electors and financial dependence on the leaders of industry and finance.

Japan's economic structure has, for the last century, been distinguished by the continuing existence of a limited number of very large producers and a very large number of very small producers. In the promotion of rapid industrialization, the Japanese state fostered the growth of large organizations which would be better placed to resist the intense competition of Western companies. These large organizations combined industrial, financial and trading activities around a central holding company and were known as *zaibatsu*. Given a severe shortage of expertise in production, finance or marketing the state used the *zaibatsu* as instruments of national policy by, among other things, offering preferential contracts for state orders, by selling state factories to them cheaply and by building national financial and trading institutions around *zaibatsu* companies. By the 1920s, the *zaibatsu* had come to dominate the newer manufacturing sectors like steel, machinery or shipbuilding but they also dominated the financial sector, owning two-thirds of banking and insurance institutions. The four main *zaibatsu* were more than able to supply the financial needs of the two main political parties, but in return they expected state support to continue. Herein lay a grave source of weakness for the attempt of elected politicians to assert their right to take a greater share of power.

It was all too easy for opponents of the move towards greater political party involvement in national leadership to label the activities of politicians as corrupt, self-seeking, individualistic and anti-social. In a society where service to the state was a paramount requirement, the close association of political parties with wealthy financiers and industrialists was a serious liability. Personal corruption was seen as symbolic, by military officers in particular, of a trend to sacrifice Japan's rural sector for the benefit of the expanding industrial dominance of *zaibatsu* capitalists.

Throughout the 1920s Japanese silk and rice producers faced severe competition from Asian producers, some of whom were based in territories that had been incorporated into the Japanese Empire. Matters were made worse by financial policies which kept Japanese export prices high and the declining rate of rural productivity improvement meant that the rural sector was severely affected. To some extent the blame for rural distress was attributed to the fluctuations in world markets, but as the *zaibatsu* did not appear to be suffering to the same extent, rural discontent was increasingly directed towards the alliance between politicians and industrial financiers. Junior military officers played an important part in orchestrating rural opposition within a movement which, in reasserting the ideal of service to the state, took on an anti-capitalist tone. While it is clear that politicians and *zaibatsu* groups were the object of a more aggressively nationalist movement in rural areas, there was also some strong anti-landlord sentiment. In general, links between impoverished peasants, landlords whose rent incomes were falling and junior officers were based on common opposition to the 'anti-social' actions of the *zaibatsu* and their allies.

The role of the military in the transition to ultranationalist authoritarianism in the 1930s remains controversial. However, junior officers upholding the sanctity of Japan's rural heritage led the physical attack on politicians and *zaibatsu* leaders in a series of assassinations. Senior officers may or may not have been involved, but they certainly made public their opposition to party politicians who had held back the growth of military expenditure in budget balancing financial policies. Senior officers were generally resentful of the attempts of politicians to interfere in military affairs and in the organization of the Empire, which was almost a military fiefdom. Rivalry between the army and *zaibatsu* did not prevent the *zaibatsu* from taking a full part in the production boom of the 1930s. Where their profits were associated with service to the Empire, their operations reverted to the nineteenth century 'tradition' of patriotic capitalism.

There is also great uncertainty about the role played by the Imperial bureaucracy in the 1930s. In the immediate post-war years there was an attempt to absolve the bureaucracy of responsibility for externally aggressive and internally repressive policies, by pointing out the ways in which bureaucrats had tried to hold back military excesses. But as far as political representation was concerned, the bureaucracy was unable, or unwilling, to uphold the power of elected politicians relative to military cabinet members. For the bureaucracy, allegiance to the Emperor came before democratic representation. When faced with the seemingly inevitable growth of military authority backed up by frenetic ultranationalism and repression of those who opposed Japanese imperialism in Asia, the Emperor system provided the core values to justify collective effort and sacrifice.

1.3 The US Occupation: rights versus duty

This speedy review of pre-war Japanese history is a necessary scenario against which to assess the motives and methods of the reform policies of the US occupation after Japan's unconditional surrender in 1945. In preparing the reform and reconstruction of Japanese institutions, there was a conviction that 'what went wrong' in the 1930s was the way the traditional commitment of the Japanese to a group identity had been diverted all too easily into collective militaristic nationalism. An era of ultranationalism had withered the fragile plant of democracy whose seed had been sown in the 1890 constitution, and the 1930s was interpreted as a period of aberration in Japan's progress towards a democratic society. The idea of the 1930s as an interruption in the development of latent democratic tendencies, has been the dominant one, and seen in this light, US reforms were based on the need to destroy the weeds that had stunted democratic growth, and provide liberal doses of fertilizer.

In contrast to the pattern of sharing the administration of occupied territories in Europe, the US took almost exclusive control of occupied Japan. After disbanding the Japanese military, releasing political prisoners and legalizing opposition political organizations, the US set about the task of writing a new constitution. Their aim was, to quote a directive from the Joint Chiefs of Staff, the 'elimination of ultra-nationalism ... the strengthening of democratic tendencies in governmental, economic and social institutions ... the encouragement and support of liberal political tendencies in Japan' (Ward 1968 p.480). All of these objectives were enshrined in a document written at great speed within six months of the Japanese surrender, and enacted in the following year, 1947.

To correct the negative tendencies of Japanese collectivism, the new constitution gave fundamental priority to individual civil and political rights. Free speech and free political association were to be backed by an extension of the franchise to all adults over the age of 20, a formal extension of the power of the elected legislature (the Diet) and guarantees of judicial independence from both the executive and the Diet. Alongside national changes went directives aimed at increasing the power of elected local authorities, especially in education and police administration where the power of central bureaucrats was too dominant. Civil rights were to include the freedom to join labour unions, the right to strike and the right to expect equal opportunity in employment irrespective of gender, race or creed.

As most of these changes conflicted with the pre-war stress on duties and loyalty to the Emperor, the role of the Emperor was redefined. After 1947 the Emperor was relegated to a constitutional symbol of the state and his supernatural attributes were denied: sovereignty now passed to the will of the Japanese people. Other lethal dangers to the fragile democratic plant were to be displaced by formalizing the permanent demilitarization of Japan in the unique Clause 9 statement that 'land sea and air forces will never be maintained. The right of belligerency of the state will not be recognized'. In addition, military elites were to be purged along with other bureaucratic, political, industrial and intellectual leaders of Japan's route through the 'dark valley' of the 1930s.

Within this spirit of democratic evangelism, the US occupation followed up their constitutional provision with other reforms designed to implant liberal economic structures which would encourage market competition, and equalize the ownership of private property. The *zaibatsu* were to be dissolved as interlocking corporate entities and the US model of monopoly control established. Financial and business leaders were already on the list of personnel to be purged, but anti-monopoly controls were needed to prevent the re-emergence of conglomerate dominance. Therefore a new agency, the Fair Trade Commission, was established to act as an independent guardian of market competition.

Land reform was an equally vital commitment if the 'semi-feudal' foundations of Japanese rural society were to be undermined. Tenants were to be transformed into owner-occupiers and thereby be given a property stake in the new society. At a stroke, this would neutralize the long experience of rural discontent between tenants and landlords, it would remove the over-bearing power of landlords in village communities and in the process eliminate one source of support for the ultra-nationalist movement.

Throughout all of this 'experiment with externally planned and controlled political change' (Ward 1968 p.483) the US occupation was acutely aware that attitudes and social practices had to change, as institutional change alone would not be sufficient to maintain the substance, as opposed to the form of liberal democracy. In some ways, this explains why education was an important initial target for reform. Not only was the administration of education to be decentralized, but also the curriculum was to be revised to eradicate the transmission of ideas about the deferential *duties* of citizen subjects, which were to be altered to stress individual *rights*. Secondary education should not be the preserve of men, and the curriculum should not have a gender specific bias based on expected household duties.

It is in this context of how far US reforms affected the substance of attitudes towards liberal democracy, that we uncover the origins of the positive view of Japan's unique culture so widely publicized by writers like Nakane and Vogel. Their approach, put crudely, says yes there was a change in basic attitudes following institutional reform, and modern Japan is therefore an uncommonly equal, consensual and meritocratic democracy.

The survival of the 1947 constitution without major change since the US occupation ended, is taken as evidence of how well it fits with the attitudes and expectations of contemporary Japan. Such a sweeping interpretation can be challenged by distinguishing between the formal acceptance of reform institutions from their operation in practice.

Even before the ink was dry on the main elements of reform, 'there is no doubt that the relative emphasis and priority accorded to democratization appreciably diminished from late 1947 onward or that this was regarded as a betrayal or serious dilution of earlier objectives' (Ward 1968 p.503). What was the significance of this reversal for the democratization of Japanese collectivism?

Two aspects of the shift in emphasis accorded to democratic reform need to be distinguished. First, the specific areas of 'betrayal or dilution', and secondly, the very fact that the US found it necessary to alter its stance at all. As the constitutional reforms were to a very great degree imposed on the Japanese, the lead given by US authorities on interpreting the reforms was going to be crucial to post-Occupation Japan. Learning how to apply alien Western ideas is supposed to be a special Japanese attribute and the US provided practical lessons of democracy in action down to 1952. These lessons were contained in revisions to the constitution and in the explanatory legislation that codified its clauses. In both processes, the US occupation 'commited flagrant violations of normal democratic procedure' (Moore 1979 p.727) in a wide range of areas from direct intervention in Japanese politics through a reinterpretation of labour rights to a revival of educational control.

There is a danger of assuming too much agreement within the US personnel who were supervising the occupation. While MacArthur had enormous power as the supreme commander, there were noticeable differences among his advisors especially on the general issue of the strength of 'latent democratic tendencies' in Japan. While the first year of occupation was marked by a firm emphasis on the need for liberal democratic reforms to avoid a revival of militarism, by 1947 it seems that the need for an anti-military government was not taken to imply an anti-conservative one. In the turmoil of the two years after the Japanese surrender, catastrophic inflation at triple digit rates coupled with an explosion of labour and political activity culminated in mass protest and plans for a general strike on 1 February 1947. When MacArthur banned the strike his action symbolized the feeling that Japan was not yet ready for the complete freedoms contained in the labour reforms.

In the following years the US occupation eroded labour rights even further by initiating proposals to remove the right to strike of public sector employees, by supporting the establishment of enterprise unions as opposed to inter-company trade unions and by leading the purge of radical employees in the public and private sector. Within a context of 'de-politicizing' labour affairs, local control over education was constrained by a prior national need to confront the radical teachers union, and the liberal emphasis on decentralizing curricula control was checked.

At the time these changes were justified by the need to maintain social order and the 'violations' of individual rights were explained as purely temporary expedients. But, in the two areas of labour rights and educational control, it is not at all certain that the temporary reversal of constitutional guarantees has ever been restored.

A common explanation of the reversal of US reform policies relates the changed priorities to the wider context of Asian politics, and in particular the victory of communism in China. There is no doubt that the US needed a relatively stable ally and that reconstructing the Japanese economy took precedence over nurturing democratic ideals. But, it is equally vital to recognize that the reversal of reforms began well before Mao's victory in China in 1949, indeed, it appears that one section of the US occupation was anticipating a reversal almost as the constitution was being drafted. Certainly MacArthur's economic advisors were horrified to find on their arrival from the US, that the need for liberal competition was being used to justify a purge of thousands of business leaders, and they viewed the dissolution of the *zaibatsu* as a threat to the whole fabric of Japanese capitalism. There is controversy over the extent to which the *zaibatsu* were actually dissolved, but there is some agreement that fewer business leaders were purged than originally intended, that many pre-war industrialists re-appeared in key positions during the 1950s and that their banks largely survived intact.

When it comes to the separation of powers and the system of checks and balances that the constitution asserted, it is also clear that the bureaucracy was given a much more equal share than either the Diet or the Judiciary. To some extent this was inevitable given the US decision to operate through a civilian Japanese administration rather than through the US military command. But once again this 'temporary' extension of power and influence has lasted a long time, and the relative weighting of Diet, Cabinet, Bureaucracy and Judiciary remains a debated issue.

So even before the US occupation ended, the Japanese had learned that the form of the constitution did not totally determine the substance of its application. With independence, came freedom to assess the appropriateness of the US constitutional model which had been imposed on Japan. There was some consultation with Japanese leaders during the drafting of the constitution, but this was largely concerned with how to redefine the role of the Emperor and at most the consultation was with reluctant partners. In no way were the reforms 'of the Japanese people, for the Japanese people by the Japanese people' (Iida 1970 p.62). Like the changes following the restoration of the Emperor in 1868 or the 1890 constitution, the new structure was imposed from above. It is arguable that the feeling of external imposition weakened commitment not just to the formal provisions of the new structure, but to the spirit within which these provisions are applied.

While it is true that no major changes have been made to the constitution, this is not through want of trying. Conservatives have long held the view that there is too much emphasis on individual rights and not enough on duties, especially when they rail against the self-interested, Westernized attitudes of modern Japanese youth. Clause 9 renouncing the right of belligerency, has been contested throughout the post-war era and remained an objective of the 1986 Prime Minister Nakasone.

Taking a lead from the US Occupation's reversal of the substantive operation of the constitution, there are many instances where either reform reversal has taken place, or where constitutional provision has proved ineffective. Some of these changes relate to the way the US ideal model of liberal democracy was said to sit uneasily with Japanese experience so some refining was necessary to render them more effective. But the difference between refining and reversing is a slippery one, so it is not surprising to find those who write in terms of refining, generally say much less about reversing. Refining, especially among those writers who stress the uniqueness of Japanese collectivism, is part of the democratic process of responding to a consensus of opinion. Those who stress reversal see the process as one that has been led from the top, using the need to accommodate the reforms to Japan's particular social system in order to legitimate the changes.

1.4 Liberal reforms refined or reversed?

Much greater detail on specific examples is contained in later chapters, but a few examples may establish more clearly the framework of the debate. If we consider the independence of the Judiciary, the Supreme Court has the right to determine the constitutionality of all legislation. In practice this power has been rarely used, and only with the greatest reluctance. Explanations from refiners would suggest that this is because the Supreme Court has confidence in the Diet, regards the legislature as the main expression of popular sovereignty, and that the Japanese tradition is to settle disputes by negotiation which, in the case of controversial legislation, is adequately done in the Diet. So here Japanese trust in consensus formation through the Diet makes US-style Supreme Court intervention unnecessary. Those who are inclined towards reform reversal, place much more weight on the way the long dominance of the Conservative LDP party allowed it to pack the Supreme Court with its own nominees, so that the independence of the.Judiciary is a myth. Or alternatively, that the Judiciary fears that too much intervention in the area of protecting individual rights, may result in a revival of pre-war encroachment by the executive in legal affairs. So keeping a low profile avoids getting embroiled in political controversy, which is the proper province of the elected Diet.

If the absence of active Judicial intervention is to be explained by confidence in the Diet's ability to represent electoral consensus, we can see how Japan could manage without the fierce watchdog role that the constitution envisaged for the Supreme Court. But is such confidence in the Diet warranted? Arguably not, because until recently most political scientists saw the Diet as an institution which merely gave symbolic ratification to legislation handed down by the executive. Some writers (e.g. Krauss 1984) argue that this power imbalance between the Diet and the executive was just a temporary phase which reflected the obstructionist tactics of Diet opposition groups who did not follow the rules of the parliamentary game. So from the later 1960s when intra-parliamentary negotiation replaced outright confrontation, the Diet has been a much more equal partner. In this scenario, the Diet took a subordinate role only until the socialist and communist parties accepted the system of liberal democracy and spent less time arguing for an alternative.

Executive dominance is still evident though, particularly through the power of non-elected bureaucrats who have exceptionally close links with the majority LDP party. Few writers deny that the bureaucracy is very influential, but most go on to suggest that this influence waned from the later 1960s as the Diet and the LDP cabinet took a more positive role. Besides, even if the bureaucratic elite is more influential than in the West, their high status as permanent guardians of the national interest is said to be justified by their personal merit. This stress on meritocratic leadership also justifies the regularized coordination of discussions between bureaucrats, LDP cabinet members and the leaders of big business.

Leaving aside for now the question of whether big business in modern Japan is really the reincarnation of the *zaibatsu*, there is no doubt that business leaders have preferential access to the political process through a variety of channels. Just how far they influence policy outcomes is contentious, but the level of consultation is reinforced by the regular recruitment to private companies of bureaucrats who retire early from public office. In economic terms, the continued strength of large companies may be contrasted with the relative ineffectiveness of the anti-monopoly agency. At times the FTC appears to spend much of its time worrying about how it can control the anti-competitive actions not of private business but of fellow bureaucrats who are busy promoting cartels. So in this area, the attempt to impose US guidelines on competition were reversed. An alternative explanation though, would say that the US model is not appropriate for Japan because it is based on the ideal of atomistic competition between a large number of small firms. Is it not more important to ensure the survival of important large firms, while at the same time promote fierce competition between them? That is, replace the model of atomistic competition with one of competitive oligopoly which may be more suited to Japanese conditions.

If fierce competition between large firms is the 'Japanese way', it also explains the background to the promotion of enterprise unions as the mechanism through which collective effort at the company level can be focused against rival companies. If in the process there is less stress on individual labour rights than the constitution proposed, then this merely reflects its inappropriate model of industrial, general or trade unions. Is not the excessive stress on labour rights unnecessary in Japan given the tradition of reciprocal labour/management relations? If women are not treated equally either in pay or promotion prospects, it is either because absolute equality has to be refined to incorporate differences in education or productivity, or because the constitution ignores the wish of Japanese women to give priority to their household duties. Women's productivity is lower, in this argument, because their employment hours are legally restricted and menstrual leave is guaranteed. Therefore their child producing role has been protected and inequality in employment is compensated by a superior role in the family where men concede control of finance and child rearing. Refining individual labour rights is then merely adjusting the ideal model to Japanese social practice.

One final illustration concerns defence. While military spending was constrained by the renunciation of belligerency, this does not mean that defence expenditure is insignificant. A Self-Defence Force was established in 1954 to act as a permanent source for disaster relief and as a force capable of defending Japan's borders. In essence this appeared to reverse the commitment not to maintain land, sea or air forces, but as the stress was placed on self-defence the SDF was said not to contradict the spirit as opposed to the letter of the constitution. As an extremely well-equipped force, the SDF have been at the centre of political controversy in Japan because of the difficulty of assessing the basic needs of a force that is there purely to defend. To protect the spirit of demilitarization, a convention has been followed that defence spending will not exceed 1 per cent of GNP, and although this ceiling has been broken on a few occasions, the 1 per cent target has a symbolic significance. However 1 per cent of a very large and expanding GNP produces a significant total, making Japan the world's ninth biggest military spender. With a very vigilant peace movement reflecting a wide spectrum of opinion, the existence of the SDF is publicly justified less by its military role and more by its value for disaster relief. Given Japan's history of earthquake and typhoon devastation, refining the military role means stressing the unique need for a permanent relief organization.

1.5 Liberal democracy in Japan: issues and perspectives

Many aspects of the issues involved in refining or reversing US reforms, are reflected in debates throughout the West, whether these are concerned with the distribution of political power, labour rights, gender inequalities or defence spending. Indeed it is from the comparative studies of how different societies have reacted to these issues, that the view of Japan as a model to follow has emerged. As I indicated earlier, not all writers think it advisable or possible for the West to import Japanese practices. Research on the negative side of the Japanese miracle has been undertaken by Western writers with experience of Japan or in collaboration with Japanese social scientists. This work has given a close insight into problems of pollution, congestion, intense company group pressure, sexism and racism. But in much of this work there is a tendency to imply that the Japanese system is flexible and responsive enough to correct the negative features, although the response may take longer in some cases than others. Liberal democratic institutions, it is argued, have been grafted onto a society which places a high value on social consensus, but there are opportunities for groups to press for change. For example, while some companies may have been able to ignore the social protest of individuals who suffered the effects of industrial pollution, they found it more difficult to resist organized groups of citizens whose opposition accompanied a marked decline in support for the LDP.

When interest group activity is added to electoral pressure, the 'shame' attached to being held responsible for social dissensus, lead to changes which may have been a voluntary response or have been supervised by a state responding to legitimate protest. The underlying assumptions of this view are clearly associated with commitment to the pluralist model of how liberal democracies work with its emphasis on electoral accountability and open access for interest groups to a state which has an arbitrating role. As this approach dominates US political science, and as the US model was transplanted into Japan during the Occupation, it is, in some ways, not surprisingly the dominant perspective. The debate about reversing or refining US reforms has illustrated that there are differences between ideals and practices, and US writers have not ignored them. But, they do seem to stress the way the changes in democratic practices were merely responding to the need to adapt the US model to Japanese values as though there were a collectively agreed set of values to call upon. When it comes to the question of who initiated changes in the emphasis on labour rights or anti-monopoly legislation for example, answers focus on bureaucrats, cabinet ministers or elected Diet members who were able to represent the national interest or consensus. The emphasis then is placed on a responsive state, interpreting change in terms of majority preferences.

In economic studies, similar weight is given to the state as guide or guardian within a liberal democratic Japan where the relatively small size of the public sector is seen as an important indicator of the limits to state economic control. Without a significant amount of public ownership therefore, a liberal market system gives companies independence. Competition may not follow the perfect model, but fierce large company rivalry should have the same outcome in lower prices and rapid technological change.

Within the general emphasis on political pluralism and competitive markets, various qualifying terms are used to take account of Japanese deviations from ideal models. So 'bureaucratic' pluralism has been used by some in recognizing the more important role of Japanese civil servants; this has been further qualified as 'bureaucratic-inclusionary' pluralism to suggest that the widest possible range of citizen consultation is used to assess the national interest. Others, who deny the breadth of consultation, prefer 'bureaucratic-exclusionary' pluralism or 'authoritarian pluralism' (Fukui 1984 p.486). Economists likewise vary in their labelling: from 'sponsored capitalism' (Lockwood 1965 p.487) to 'market oriented . . . not market dominated' (Khan 1973 p.5) or MITIs own label of a 'planned market'. The perennial problem is how to express market coordination, guidance or indirect nurturing without undermining the host of implications that derive from liberal freedoms. G.C. Allen, the doyen of British Japanologists, put it this way 'although government fostered growth in Japan . . . it certainly did not and could not *prescribe* the policy to follow' (1981 p.192, italics added).

Allen's comment is typical of the general approach to the role of the state and two aspects are interesting. First, his emphasis on the word 'prescribe' indicates an inability and/or unwillingness to coerce. So, a relatively small public sector in the economy is added to a pluralist arbitrating role for the state, to deny the state the power or authority to command. The state can encourage, foster or guide, but not force producers or consumers to do what they prefer not to do. The other, not unrelated aspect, is use of the term 'government' rather than state, an interchange that is not at all untypical in studies of the political economy of contemporary Japan. I cannot claim to have undertaken a comprehensive content analysis of the literature, but it is very unusual to find systematic analysis of the 'state' as such in works on Japan written in English. There are a few exceptions which I will come back to later, but generally 'government' is used interchangeably with 'state'. Even Johnson (1982), who untypically devotes a whole chapter to Japan's 'developmental state', changes to 'government' on the page following his first mention of the 'state'.

This interchange between terms, is significant because it implies the equivalence of 'state' and 'government'. This assumed equivalence is related partly to the notion of a responsive, arbitrating state in pluralist models of liberal democracy. But in Japanese studies this tendency is compounded by the way contemporary Japan is starkly contrasted with the 'dark valley' of the 1930s. Analysis of pre-war Japan is not at all characterized by the absence of attention to the state, quite the contrary. Labour repression, military violence, the all-embracing ideology of service to the Emperor and the spirit of ultranationalism are all explained as instances of a domineering state. In studying this period writers have tended to use 'government' to refer to elected party or civilian cabinets, whose position is eroded in the 1930s as the state became even more totalitarian. When we move to studies of post-war Japan however, we discover pluralist writers have 'denied the state a theoretical niche' (Boyd 1985 p.11).

Tight definitions of the state and clear conceptual distinctions between state and government remain enormously contentious, but in European social science at least there has been a lively debate. This is not generally reflected in work on Japan published in English where the debate, if it is mentioned at all, seems to be based on the early works of Marx and a selective version of Weber. It is Weber's emphasis on the state's monopoly of the legitimate use of violence, that, it seems to me, gives overtones of coercion which encourage a narrow approach to the state in contemporary Japan. While coercion may have been appropriate enough before 1945, the plurality of power in a representative system makes it inappropriate thereafter. Using 'government' instead of 'state', carries important trigger connotations of accountability to electors that are missing from the coercive feel of the term 'state'.

Weber did qualify his emphasis on the coercive methods through which the state maintains order and compliance, 'force is certainly not the normal or only means of the state' (Weber 1972 p.78). But this interplay between coercion and consent has been underemphasized in pluralist analysis by focusing only on the inadequacy of the coercive dimension. Such a narrow focus on state coercion had led to limited, superficial and largely sterile debate about the notion of *Japan Incorporated*.

The presentation of the Japanese economy in terms analogous to a business corporation, seems to have been popularized initially in describing the constraints that foreign business was likely to find when selling goods in Japan. Close consultation between business and the bureaucracy was likened to the internal organization of large corporations, except that *Japan Inc.* was a national unit headed by public officials. Even when the central board of directors was expanded to include business and political elites as well as bureaucratic leaders, it never offered much depth in an analytical sense. Yet, it has been consistently used as a straw model which could easily be knocked down to deny the existence of centralized power centres in Japan.

Disagreement over economic policies between the buereaucracy, the LDP and big business is well documented across a range of issues from anti-monopoly controls through rationalization cartels to state subsidies for rice producers. Equally there has been disagreement within the LDP, business groupings or the bureaucracy, such that policy making is not the smooth process implied in *Japan Inc.* Instead of the central board of directors foisting decisions on unwilling parties, policy formation reflects endless bargaining between diverse competing interests.

Identifying divisions of interest does not by itself provide an adequate rejection of the claim that elites are very powerful in Japan. To take an outlandish illustration: do divisions between the army, the politburo and industrial managers in the USSR over the allocation of resources between weapons and consumer goods, imply that pluralism is alive and kicking? Or let us not forget that research on Japan in the 1930s has revealed conflicts of interest between and within the military, *zaibatsu*, politicians and the bureaucracy. Clearly the difference for contemporary Japan in the pluralist approach, lies in the framework of a representative democracy with intense interest group activity.

While it is clear that an enormous range of interest groups exist in Japan, few would argue that small firms, non-unionized labour (who make up over 70 per cent of the total), minority groups or the elderly have the same continuous access to the state as do large companies. Leading business representatives have access through many different channels being members of the Employers' Federation, trade associations, industrial associations or public advisory bodies, not to mention regular contact through LDP research groups. Has this extensive network of connections nothing to do with the way contentious issues like discrimination against women or minorities pollution, state welfare, or housing costs were kept from the political agenda for so long? We need therefore to qualify the existence of pluralist interest group activity by asking about differing degrees of influence and this is one of the main themes in Chapters 4 and 5.

The existence of powerless groups has been highlighted even by those who extol the virtues of the Japanese commitment to consensus. Nakane for example, writes about 'the cruelly heavy handicaps facing the powerless and socially inferior' (1973 p.155). This leads to questions about why these groups miss out, why their inferiority does not result in social disorder and more generally what barriers exist to prevent the mobilization of action to correct their 'cruel handicaps'? I will argue later in Chapter 6 that powerless groups are not a small minority especially when we realize that the cherished pattern of lifetime employment applies to barely 30 per cent of labour, within which there are only a tiny percentage of women.

It is misleading to dismiss arguments that focus on the unequal distribution of power in Japanese society simply because there are some examples of disagreement among dominant groups. There is general agreement between leaders of the LDP and business over the need to reduce state spending so that taxes can be lowered to allow private initiative to flourish. I will argue later, that by treating state financial deficits as 'failures' in the drive to promote a vigorous self-reliant welfare society (Kumon 1984 p.161), big business has supported the agenda within which the state has managed conflicting attitudes to public welfare spending.

The debate about social welfare is but one example of the way even the multi-dimensional negotiation is organized around the general commitment to preserving Japan's existing social priorities. This has usually meant giving precedence to private sector economic growth rather than other priorities such as social welfare. Economic priorities are given the status of a nationally agreed consensus, especially by those who stress the unique willingness of the Japanese to forego individual interests for the benefit of the group. It would be foolish to ignore the historical roots of self-sacrifice or deference to group leaders, but we do need to avoid the danger of assuming that cooperation is always given voluntarily.

Voluntary cooperation and consensus formation is not simply a matter of agreeing national objectives, it relates to the display of consensus in everyday activities. Are individual Japanese so decidedly group orientated by cultural tradition or is it that 'in many cases they are loyal to their groups because it pays to be loyal' (Befu 1977 p. 87)? In other words, might not loyalty in large companies be bought by promises of job security? For those without such guarantees, there may be no alternative to pragmatic acceptance of their lot. There is a danger of assuming that the Japanese have not rejected the contemporary institutions of collectivism because they are accepted as ideal. Collectivist tendencies, while an important outward feature, may reflect apathy, the lack of alternatives or instrumental acceptance of material rewards, as I will argue in Chapter 3. We should not ignore collectivism, however, because it is so often used by the state in Japan to mobilize the support of those who have not benefited as much from the economic miracle, or by company leaders to exhort yet more effort from employees. In either case collectivism is an important rock on which attempts to coordinate opposition to growth-first policies have foundered.

In relating everyday experience of consensus pressures to the overarching priority of economic growth, we find that it is not only the state that constructs their operation. Private sector employers, university entrance authorities, unions and arguably men in general, play their part in maintaining differences in 'an individual's access to four types of social resources: income, power, information and status' (Sugimoto 1982 p.17). These inequalities are managed through the activities of interest groups, market competition, educational institutions, enterprise unions and the state as they participate in constructing the national interest. Hence we need to consider the mechanisms through which compliance is secured in a system of structured inequalities.

There is a tendency in some pluralist analysis to view the state as an independent public entity outside society acting as guardian of the national interest. But the division between public and private is very ambiguous and cannot be drawn simply by examining the size of the public sector in the economy and assuming this defines the limit of state influence. As experience in the US or UK during the 1980s shows, a small state is not necessarily a weak state despite the rhetoric of claims that a limited state sector restores individual freedom and personal initiative. The Nakasone cabinet in 1986, like the Reagan or Thatcher governments, was deeply involved with issues that are ostensibly private to individuals or families. For example, in underlining the need to reduce public welfare provision in the long term, the state upholds the family as the alternative centre of provision, with consequent implications for women's domestic role in the care of children and the aged. So efforts to facilitate a painless reduction in one sphere requires the state to assist in the maintenance of the other.

Reactions by pluralists to Marxist analysis of the Japanese state have rarely been characterized by rigorous argument. Although Marxism is very influential in Japanese social science, this is poorly reflected in work published in English. Even the work published in English by people like Norman, Halliday, Moore or Steven is often ignored or treated as misguided. One crucial reason for this lies in the way only one element of Marxist work on the state is used by pluralist critics. In a similar fashion to the narrow interpretation of Weber on state coercion, most responses to Marxist work focus on the state as the agent of monopoly capitalism. 'The notion that modern state power is merely a committee that manages the common business of the bourgeoisie is one of the least adequate generalizations that Marx ever made' (Nettl 1968 p.571). What is missed by those who follow Nettl's view, is that a number of Marxists would probably agree, in the sense that the idea of the state as *merely* an agent distorts the observed contradictions within the bourgeoisie, and assumes a purely passive role for the state in capitalism. Despite these qualifications to the degree of state dependence on monopoly capital, pluralists frame their response to Marxist ideas almost as though more recent developments in Marxism did not exist.

In my view it is just as vital not to ignore Marxist work because it contains one inadequate generalization, as it is not to ignore pluralist work because it is based on an idealized view of liberal democracy in Japan. The sterile debate about the contemporary Japanese state has, in. my opinion, emerged from the failure to confront the deeper arguments of both perspectives.

Pluralist accounts of the Japanese state for example underestimate the ambiguity of the division between public and private when they imply that individual rights in a liberal democracy confine the scope of the state to exclusively public spheres. Neither is it acceptable to see the state as entirely dependent on monopoly capital as some Marxists still suggest. Rather the state is the central site for the negotiation of conflict over a whole range of issues, in which the state is a participant though not necessarily a consistently dominant or united one. While many of the negative aspects of compliance in Japan have been highlighted by Marxists, there are non-Marxist critics of voluntary or spontaneous collectivism. Taken together this work sees Japan as 'one of the most politically centralised societies in the world . . . [But] . . . Japan is also characterised by contradictions similar to those found in developed capitalist nations' (Kawamura 1980 p.58). This emphasis on centralization with contradictions, helps to avoid overestimating the unity of elite interests or treating the state as a monolithic entity. As a site for negotiation between divided interests, the state aims to secure support for the long-term survival of Japan's capitalist society by, among other things, absorbing the legitimacy of the elected government into the process of constructing the national interest. If the state can relate the manifesto of the majority party to policies which emerge from negotiation between interest groups, then these policies can claim to represent both the consensus of individual electors and views of organized pressure groups.

This, in some ways, explains the attraction of using state and government interchangeably because the outcome of negotiation can be expressed in terms of the representative electoral process. If instead we use 'government' to mean the majority party, the government becomes one power centre participating in the formation of state policies. Even in this sense as Chapter 5 will show, the LDP has hardly been a united force, with the cabinet and Diet members divided into personality factions and at odds with bureaucrats or business on some issues. There is not, of course total disagreement, but contradictory positions are present, even if they do not radically affect the priority to be given to economic growth.

In what follows the state will be considered as a set of institutions including the Diet, judiciary, police and the bureaucracy but not simply as the location of public employees or officials. Managing contradictory interests involves active participation and negotiation with other representatives of civil society. In the process of negotiating conflict all the participants help to set the framework of ideas within which conflict is managed and a crucial dimension of this framework is that the Japanese people are characteristically said to defer to the national consensus. Many writers have gone on to argue that such consensual preferences became even stronger once post-war reforms ensured a more representative structure through which citizens could contribute to the formation of a national consensus.

This chapter has suggested that it is common to find exaggerated accounts of Japan's position as the model of an unusually successful and harmonious capitalist society, in particular that compliance may be involuntary and that social inequalities are not as insignificant as they may appear. There seems to be little doubt that the liberal reforms of the US occupation did attempt to safeguard basic individual rights and reinforce the institutions of a free market economy. But in practice the spirit of these reforms has been refined to undermine part of their intended outcome. The general case for amending the ways in which the reforms operated in practice, involved adapting imported principles to meet particular interpretations of Japan's national interest. One such example concerns the way a prior need to reconstruct a war-damaged economy required the model of competition to be adapted so that the advantages of inter-firm rivalry could be retained alongside a degree of interdependent affiliation between Japanese companies. As Chapter 2 demonstrates the structure that emerged in no small way explains the impressive record of productivity growth among private firms in Japan.

2

An Economic Structure of Interdependent Rivals

The transformation of the Japanese economy over the past 30 years has been highlighted by its stunning record of growth in output, productivity and exports. Inevitably, attention has focused on very high levels of capital investment in advanced technology, pioneering innovation and the constant search for new sectors to maintain the rapid rates of industrial growth. This record though, has not at all reduced the importance of output and employment in small units of production.

In total, some 55 per cent of the labour force worked in units that employed less than 30 people in the mid-1980s and that aggregate was not dramatically different from what it was 30 years before. What had changed was the distribution of employment so that although Japanese farms are very tiny, the threefold decline in agricultural employment to about 10 per cent of the labour force means that non-agricultural sectors now provide the bulk of small-firm employment. Adding together the numbers of self-employed, family workers and labour in firms of less than 30 employees in non-agricultural work for 1984 gives a total of about 25 million people, of which it appears that one-third (8.2 million) work in units of less than five people (*JTW* 1/2/86).

Of course it is true that construction, distribution and services are often very labour intensive sectors even in the West, but in Japan not only are these three sectors more labour intensive, so also is manufacturing industry.

International comparisons of the proportionate employment share of 'small' firms are bedevilled by variations in classification categories. However, if we concentrate on broad comparative trends rather than statistical precision, Figure 2.1 highlights the middling position Japan occupies between the West and other Asian economies when we measure the proportion of manufacturing employment in firms with less than 100 workers.

Neither is there much evidence that the share of the small firm sector

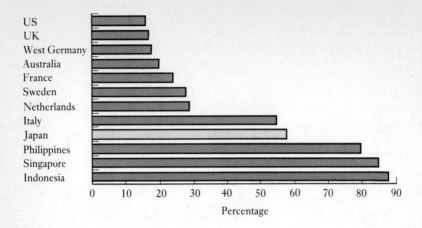

Figure 2.1 The share of manufacturing employment in firms with less than
100 employees: an international comparison
Source: Storey (1983)

is falling as the Japanese economy becomes more mature: over the 1970s
the share actually increased from 51 per cent to 58 per cent. Equally, there
was no reduction in the share of small firms in total shipments of
manufactured goods or in total value-added as firms with less than 100
workers contributed fairly constant shares at around 35 per cent and 40
per cent respectively. These broad comparisons do conceal some interesting
short-term changes which I will come back to, but at a very general level
Japanese manufacturing industry is twice as dependent on the contribution
of small firms than other leading members of the OECD. While it would
be misleading to suggest that small firms are important across all
manufacturing industries, it is also incorrect to assume that small firms are
confined to traditionally labour-intensive industries like textiles, clothing,
furnishing or ceramics. Ganguly (1982) attempted to disaggregate the
manufacturing totals and although his criterion for a small firm was 20–199
employees, his data illustrate well the higher employment share taken by
small firms even in industries like metal goods, vehicles and electrical or
mechanical engineering. In each of these four industries, as in total
manufacturing, the share of small Japanese firms was about twice as large
as that in the UK, US or West Germany.

Of all the major Western economies, Italy offers the closest comparison
to Japan in terms of aggregate employment distribution and firm size. But
the duality of Italian production is much more regionally defined with small
firms concentrated in the submerged South and large firms in the prosperous
Northern cities. In contrast to the Italian pattern of 'independently orbiting
systems with poor levels of technical and spatial contact' (Tuffarelli 1981

p. 765), Japan's system is based on cohesive co-existence. Instead of pitting the small firms against large firms, specialization by technique or process in a pervasive network of subcontracting forges a partnership which seems to have maintained the widely dispersed structure.

The extent to which Japanese manufacturing firms rely on outside orders for intermediate materials, parts or fittings is illustrated in Figure 2.2, and confirms the importance of subcontracting for firms of all sizes. It is the case that smaller firms are more reliant on subcontracting in its narrowest form: processing materials supplied by firms who purchase the bulk of their output. But the wider definition of supplying mainly to other producers, indicates that subcontracting is not the exclusive preserve of very small firms. For example, in a survey of the Iron and Steel Industry during 1979, it was found that over 90 per cent of subcontracting companies employed over 300 workers (Mesatoshi 1980 p.51).

There is nothing especially unique about the presence of subcontracted parts suppliers because all manufacturing firms rely to an extent on the purchase of components from outsiders. What is remarkable is the extent and persistence of subcontracting relations. In two of Japan's leading export items, colour TV sets and motor vehicles, it is estimated that only 25 per cent of the value-added in production is generated internally by the company that sells the final product in contrast to 50 per cent in the UK or US.

Industrial production in Japan then, differs from many other advanced economies in the continuing reliance on the contribution of small firms, which is surprising given the economies of scale that large firms can reap by expanding their output. In most other countries those firms employing over 1000 workers have substantially increased their share of output and employment over the past few decades, so why is Japan different? One crucial reason is that large and small firms in Japan operate with a greater degree of interdependence than is suggested in conventional models of competitive markets. In addition to the expectation of continuity in subcontracting partnerships, larger companies share semi-permanent trading agreements and are often stockholders in rival firms.

In what follows I will argue that there are specific financial advantages for Japanese firms which compensate for the presumed loss of efficiency that accompanied the shift away from the model of atomistic competition proposed in the reforms of the US Occupation. Continuity in subcontracting allows parent companies to diversify the risks of specialization and promotes the exchange of technological information so that the quality of inputs is ensured and delivery schedules guaranteed. Affiliative links between larger firms enhances the procurement of materials and smooths their pattern of marketing while inter-group stockholding prevents unwanted takeover bids and allows management to concentrate on long-term performance rather than short-term profits distributed to stockholders. This longer run perspective is a feature of Japanese business and is greatly helped by the

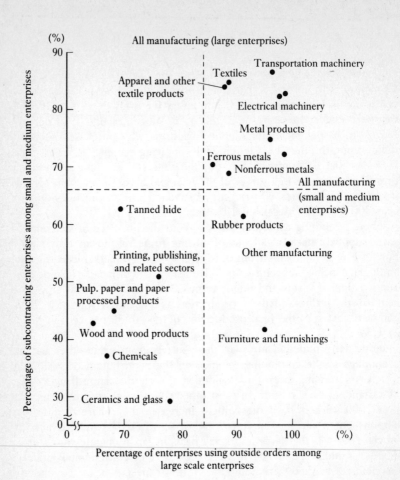

Figure 2.2 Enterprises in Japan depending on outside orders (subcontracting) by industry

Source: Ministry of International Trade and Industry, 'Kogyo Jittai Kihon Chosa' (Basic Survey of State of Industry), 1976

Notes: 1 Percentage of enterprises using outside orders = number of enterprises using outside orders/number of large enterprises × 100

2 Percentage of subcontracting enterprises = number of subcontracting small and medium enterprises/number of small and medium enterprises × 100

existence of lead banks within affiliated groups that ensure access to loans even in periods when bank credit is restricted.

As we shall see the unequal power relations between parent companies and their subcontractors does mean that the burden of adjusting output in a recession can result in smaller firms going out of business. In such circumstances the state has sought to mitigate the consequences of recession on small firms although it seems to have acted more effectively when the existence of a larger company is threatened. Equally, the state has helped to maintain the structure of capital markets which promote closer relations between financial and industrial capital.

In the rest of this chapter we will consider how state policies have reaffirmed the financial advantages that derive from the continuation of a dual structure of production.

2.1 Affiliated subcontracting and flexibility in production

The experience of other advanced economies would lead us to expect the increasing dominance of larger manufacturing firms who can benefit more from economies of scale as the level of output and capital investment increases. One underlying reason for the expected shift in firm size is related to the higher transaction costs that are involved in using outside suppliers relative to greater in-house production. Where the purchase of processed or partially processed inputs is outside the direct control of firms there is greater uncertainty about their quality and delivery schedules. Such uncertainty can be reduced by strict contractual agreements, but the danger, for example, of late deliveries interrupting the flow of production is still greater than it would be if the firm expanded in-house production. In periods of expansion, the time involved in negotiating contracts can be lengthy as suppliers look for long-term guarantees and may try to play one buyer against another.

Transaction costs have encouraged firms to expand their own internal capacity in preference to extensive reliance on outside suppliers. However where demand is known to be variable, for example if a large share of output is exported, any major internal expansion carries the danger of periodic over-capacity with consequent higher average costs just as the market is weakest. Hence the higher transaction costs of using outside suppliers have to be balanced against the dangers of under-utilization before a final decision is made about the scale of internal expansion. This balance is particularly important for several of the industries that have been at the heart of the Japanese economic miracle like motor vehicles, electrical consumer goods, watches or cameras. These industries export well over 50 per cent of the output and any exogenous change in foreign exchange rates can have a dramatic effect on costs, relative prices and therefore sales.

One way out of the dilemma has been for larger Japanese companies to reduce transaction costs with outside suppliers by promising continuity in their subcontracting arrangements. Continuity is idealized as a family relationship and is symbolized in terms such as parent company or child subcontractor. Indeed the hard and fast distinction between firms becomes very blurred when we find some supplier companies located within the plant of the parent firm, when the smaller company is managed by ex-employees of the larger one or when the bulk of the small firm machinery is handed down in second-hand sales from their principal buyer. This symbolic, familial structure of affiliation between firms of very different sizes makes it difficult to identify the exact extent of independent control especially where subcontractors supply the bulk of their output to one buyer.

Close affiliative relations between firms are not confined to single level subcontracting but are typical of a hierarchical network of connections at several stages removed from the largest firms. Primary subcontractors will therefore transfer personnel, equipment and ideas about organization to their own subcontractors who in turn do likewise right down to the level of the single-person firm. Neither is subcontracting confined to Japan, as many electrical goods producers, for instance, buy in parts from subsidiaries in South East Asia. Figure 2.3 illustrates a production flow in the TV industry with just three stages, but these would have to be extended many

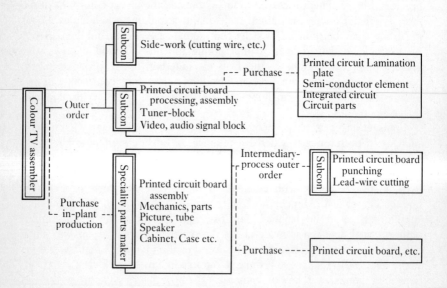

Figure 2.3 Conceptual subcontracting framework (colour TV)
Source: *White Paper on Small and Medium Enterprises*, 1980, p. 161.

times to include all the firms involved. One important feature to note, is
the way some processes, like printed circuit board assembly, are common
to both partners. This gives the parent firm a measure of independence
but with the flexibility to expand output when necessary by giving more
orders to outside suppliers.

Although it is tempting to trace the historical antecedents of subcontracting
to the pre-industrial 'putting-out' system, the crucial impetus came from
the very rapid expansion in manufacturing output from the later 1950s.
Surprising as it may seem in the 1980s, there was great uncertainty both
within Japan and outside about how long the boom would last. Large firms
attempted to expand production levels but tried to avoid incurring heavy
fixed-cost burdens on their own plants in case the boom was only temporary.
It was not simply a matter of avoiding the dangers of under-utilizing capital
equipment, but also avoiding any unnecessary increase in the recruitment
of regular labour. Until the early 1960s temporary and seasonal labour was
used to supplement the workforce, but thereafter the relative share of
temporary labour employed in larger firms began to decline as the role of
external subcontractors increased.

There are significant differences in the terms and conditions of regular
relative to temporary labour, not simply in terms of wages but involving
housing and welfare expenses, which can mean regular labour costing up
to 50 per cent more. When these higher costs are related to the expectation
of lifetime employment for regular workers, there was a real incentive for
large firms to stabilize their own labour force. Labour supply in the early
1960s was elastic not least because of a massive decline in the share of
agricultural employment, so cheaper subcontracted labour was used in
preference to any expansion of regular labour.

Thus the expansion of larger manufacturing firms was designed to give
them the opportunity to expand output with protection from fluctuations
in demand given by avoiding any excessive accumulation of fixed costs. In
order to expand output quickly Japanese firms did invest heavily at over
twice the rates of their competitors, but this increase in their own capacity
did not result in the demise of the small firm, rather subcontracted orders
offered an expansion path based on interdependence. With promises of
continuous association, transaction costs can be reduced especially when
subcontractors are heavily dependent on one source of orders. Equally,
uncertainties over delivery timing can be drastically reduced when
subcontractors are located close to the parent and the Japanese obsession
with inventory control can easily be extended to suppliers.

Studies of Japanese management practices have highlighted many peculiar
features among which is the *kanban* system of ordering components.
Although *kanban* is highly developed in Japan, the system reflects a
universal desire of management to reduce production costs by treating
inventories as 'the root of all evil' (Hayes 1981 p.59). Therefore the
underlying aim is not unique, but the power of large Japanese firms is

extensive in enforcing systematic inventory reduction.

Kanban when translated as 'just in time' neatly captures the essence of the system. Delivery of components to particular plant sections must be smooth enough to prevent delays and at the same time reduce stocks of surplus materials. Final output targets are determined at the outset and input requirements are calculated precisely for each stage of manufacturing, including those bought from outside subcontractors. Not only have the supply of components to be of perfect quality and in the exact quantity, but they have to be delivered in small batches at very specific times. These times are increasingly denominated in daily or hourly units, thus a motor vehicle survey in 1982 reported that 82 per cent of parts are delivered to hourly or daily schedules (Y. Sato 1984 p.17). Parent companies can thereby keep under tight control the capital they have tied up in idle stocks and make substantial savings on fixed outlay in storage or warehousing.

Focusing on the novelty of Japanese inventory control can however divert attention from the fact that *kanban* is 'primarily a method of achieving process change and only secondarily ás a method for controlling the flow of materials' (Lee, Sang and Schwendinan 1982 p. 149). Thus small batch deliveries at regular intervals are essential in minimizing the change-over time in the assembly of different models which is critical in the production of differentiated consumer goods. The system also allows parent firms to concentrate on more capital intensive processes. Reorganizing the lay-out of the production process can therefore permit the much greater automation of final assembly processes if robots, for example, can be programmed to perform different operations for different models almost to the exact moment the components arrive.

Kanban reflects the drive to speed up a flexible system of production, and success, in terms of productivity, is dependent on the ability of parent companies to guarantee prompt and regular delivery of components. Attempts to introduce the system in Japanese plants overseas have frequently been thwarted by the inability of component suppliers to meet quality and timing schedules. When Kawasaki began operations in their US plant at Nebraska they found it preferable to import components from their subcontractors back in Japan who could even at that distance, guarantee weekly deliveries.

Within Japan, larger firms have a tremendous advantage because there are so many small component suppliers who rely extensively on subcontracting for their existence. Very recent figures on the precise extent of subcontracting are difficult to obtain but the *Fifth Basic Survey of Industry* (1979) showed that over 60 per cent of small and medium-sized firms (i.e. up to 300 employees) were dependent on orders from other firms. While it is fair to assume that the smaller the firm the greater the degree of subcontracting, even 50 per cent of firms with 100–300 workers were acting as suppliers to larger firms. As Table 2.1 shows the degree of dependence for small firms increases substantially when we recognize that

Table 2.1 The framework of subcontracting in Japanese manufacturing, 1979

Size of firm (no. employees)	% engaged in sub-contracting	% materials supplied free or bought from 'parent'	% using 'parents' trademark	% sales to three largest customers
1–9	63	62	21	75
10–19	54	52	25	64
20–99	51	50	28	57
100–299	51	53	34	51

Source: *Fifth Basic Survey of Industry*, MITI 1979.

for many of them the bulk of their orders come from a narrow range of just two or three customers. Similarly, small firm independence is eroded by the fact that over half of the raw materials to be processed are obtained from the buyer and nearly one-third of subcontractors use the buyers trademark. Not only then is subcontracting widely practised but the small firms are so dependent on a limited range of buyers that they have little alternative but to accommodate to tight *kanban* schedules.

These indications of the importance of small firm production and the extent of subcontracting make it vital to recognize the place of a differentiated structure of production in assessing the causes of Japan's rapid economic growth. Small producers have provided larger companies with an important cushion against fluctuations in demand by allowing them to use outside suppliers as shock absorbers. So for example, as demand falls in-house production takes a greater share to protect employment for regular workers but at the expense of labour in smaller suppliers. Equally the burden of financing surplus stocks of materials is transferred along a chain of those subcontractors who face reduced orders. Hence the promises of continuous affiliation with parent firms have to be weighed against variations in the quantities of orders given to child companies.

Apart from using supplementary outside orders as a flexible cushion in recessions, large firms can also maximize the gains from small-firm specialization where production need not be capital intensive. So for motor industry parts like door handles, plastic fascia or springs, there may be cost savings to be had from the simple labour intensive pressing operations of smaller firms.

The contrast in the relative proportions of labour and capital used in production is clearly reflected in productivity when this is measured in terms of the value added per worker. While the Japanese record of

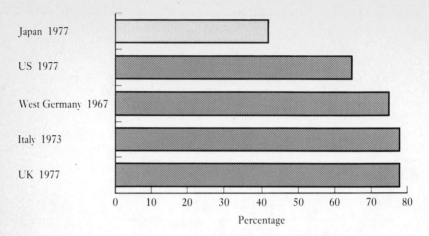

Figure 2.4 The differentials in value-added in manufacturing between large and small firms in five economies
Source: A. Lessandrini, 1979.

productivity improvement has been remarkable, aggregated data masks substantial variations according to firm size which tend to be more marked than in most other advanced economies. Figure 2.4 offers a broad international comparison which highlights the consequences of much higher levels of capital equipment per worker in large Japanese firms for the size of the productivity gap. As we will see in Chapter 3, the gap in wages runs parallel to productivity to give the two quite distinct units of production and employment that characterize the Japanese economy.

2.2 Group affiliation among large firms

The extensive network of subcontracting is one important mechanism which preserves dualism in Japan and in the process cushions the impact of market fluctuations on larger companies. However in industries like shipbuilding, oil refining or chemicals, production is so capital intensive that it restricts the possibility of transferring the burden of adjustment to small firms. In these sectors the organization of Japanese industry into loosely affiliated groups provides additional sources of protection for large firms.

Research on the level of concentration in Japan usually emphasizes the smaller share of output taken by large companies whether this is measured by the size of the top 100 companies or the share of the three or four biggest firms in each industry. These quantitative measures though, do not reflect the impact of the extensive coordination that takes place between formally independent firms nor the importance of affiliation through subcontracting. Inter-company transactions in Japan are more numerous within the umbrella of federations of industrial, financial and trading companies. The problem of assessing the impact of these conglomerate groupings lies in the loose, amorphous nature of the connections because in few of the federations is there an obviously dominant leader.

Coordination between affiliated firms takes various forms but inter-company stockholding is one of the most obvious. Although there are over 20 million individual shareholders in Japan they only account for a quarter of the total shares held. The bulk of the remainder are held by companies who show a strong preference for holding the stock of companies with whom they have important trading connections. In some cases this is mediated through the bank that handles the business of both parties, and the banks themselves are also stockholders in their clients' companies. New issues of stock are frequently allocated to major trading partners through a common bank, which reduces the uncertainties and underwriting costs of new issues. Since the mid-1970s the proportion of stock held by non-financial companies has risen partly because of the constraints placed on stockholding by banks and financial institutions. As a result, this has produced a 'tightening of intra-group financial reins' (Shonfield 1984 p.81), both between companies of equal size and between parent companies and their subsidiaries.

It is difficult to measure the extent to which stockholding influences decision-making, but taken together with the interchange of personnel through interlocking directorships, trading connections are most certainly cemented through financial channels. Once joint prospects are more securely fastened, even more preferential trading terms can be secured. For example, a company manufacturing pressed steel cabinets for washing machines clearly benefits from conglomerate connections with suppliers of the basic materials and with those firms who assemble the branded final product. In such cases trading may be done through reciprocal dealing or swapping arrangements, with trade credit provided by a common bank or trading company.

Marketing itself tends to be a more specialist operation organized through trading companies who act as agents for manufacturers. These trading companies handle about half of all Japanese exports and approximately 65 per cent of imports which means that they can arrange the purchase of raw materials from abroad, organize the export of finished goods as well as marketing within Japan. Although the operations of trading companies are not confined entirely to specific conglomerate groups, a certain degree of 'mutual favouritism' exists in supplying shipping, insurance, freight, storage and credit services. At the point of final sales too, trading companies coordinate the activities of group members in retail distribution.

Intra-group connections then, cover the whole spectrum from the source of raw material right through to consumer purchases. More informal links, which are by no means unimportant, occur through the voluntary exchange of information between companies and regular meetings of the Presidents of leading members.

None of these connections necessarily implies any reduction of competition between firms that produce similar goods because of the intense efforts that are made to increase market share even at the expense of rivals within the group. There are as we shall see, problems for consumers at the retailing stage in the sense that distribution is notoriously complex and subject to a variety of restrictive practices, but this is a common feature of the domestic market that applies to all consumer products whether Japanese or foreign. What the close connections do achieve is a general diversification or sharing of the risks inherent in constantly changing market demand and product development.

New ventures that embody a high degree of risk, for example in high-technology areas, are often undertaken by newly formed companies financed by the allocation of stock to group members. Should the venture fail, the debts can be shared among several companies; if it succeeds not only does the value of the stock rise but group companies can reap the rewards of the innovation in their own production facilities.

Unwanted takeover bids for troubled companies are relatively rare in Japan because intra-group stockholding reduces the availability of stock in companies to outsiders. In many ways the motive for holding stock in related companies has less to do with short-term dividend prospects and much more to do with group cohesion and stability that is vital for securing material supplies or finding markets. Equally, group affiliation provides a source of mutual support for companies in financial trouble when group banks take responsibility for coordinating rescue packages. On the other hand, in periods of expansion the financial muscle of the group can be mobilized to provide preferential loans and credit terms.

One related consequence of mutual support expectations among affiliated companies is to allow operations to be managed within longer term horizons. Sales maximization and market share objectives are said to be preferred in Japan to short-term profits, although the two strategies are not necessarily mutually exclusive. If there is any more pronounced preference in Japan for the long-term view, then part of the reason is surely connected to the expectation that managers are less likely to be rejected on the basis of short-term dividend performance. Overall group needs and mechanisms of mutual support provide the institutional stability that allows a more long-term orientation.

The general umbrella term 'grouping' in practice covers a range of different organizations, and much of the comment on their influence has been focused on how much collective power they exercise. In particular, the question of whether the largest groups, known as *keiretsu*, are merely pre-war *zaibatsu* in a different guise. Certainly the size largest *keiretsu* have at their centre very influential banks, who in some cases, managed to deflect the attempts of the US Occupation to dismantle their organization.

Certainly too, the size of the big six is significant as they own the equivalent of a quarter of total corporate assets, return a quarter of corporate profits and provide a sixth of national sales (Sasaki 1981 p.98). But there are differences in that they are not owned by family dynasties, are not as rigidly organized through central holding companies and do not appear to be as dominant in specific industries.

What appears to be of more significance for the role of *keiretsu* in Japan's economic growth is their objective of diversifying their interests in the widest possible range of activities throughout manufacturing industry, construction, finance and the service sector. Each *keiretsu* has representative companies in all these areas and pursues new growth sectors with relentless enthusiasm. As a result, the whole group through its loose but multifarious connections, can reap the benefits of a conglomerate structure without apparently suffering the organizational disceconomics of large companies. Adjustment to market variation is never painless, but the advantages of diversification were clearly evident when from 1979–82 Mitsubishi's surplus shipyard workers were temporarily transferred to sell motor cars for the Mitsubishi Motor Company. Like the subcontracting system, group affiliation provides an important adjustment cushion which helps to explain why *keiretsu* profits are much less variable, if not necessarily higher, than other firms.

A slightly different format for group affiliation exists in single industry organizations that dominate many of the sectors producing consumer goods. Companies like Toyota, Nissan, Sony, Hitachi, Honda or Matsushita concentrate on narrower product ranges but their operations involve an extensive array of horizontal and vertical relationships with affiliated firms. It is in these groups that subcontracting is especially strong, and their organization is more heavily centralized around the parent firm than is the case in the *keiretsu*. Even though some single industry groups are less directly connected to banks and financial companies, they are still deeply involved in interlocking shareholding arrangements with their suppliers. Aoki (1984 p.15) has shown that the ratio of investment in subsidiaries to total paid-in capital in all Japanese industry more than doubled from 1966–81. In manufacturing industry this trend was even more evident as the ratio increased from 11 per cent in 1966 to 35 per cent in 1981.

2.3 Industrial strategy, priority sectors and the favoured few

Links between ostensibly independent firms in Japan thus encompass both subcontracting relations and networks of affiliation between firms of relatively equal stature. Mutual support mechanisms have helped to maintain the drive to diversify into new growth sectors and have facilitated a commitment to long-term market expansion. The prime movers in developing this structure have been larger firms who can expect favoured treatment in times of expansion, and can transfer adjustment burdens along a chain of subcontractors in recessions.

In essence, the initiatives taken by larger companies were a consequence of the radical economic strategy which was promoted by the Ministry of International Trade and Industry (MITI) from the early 1950s. Not without opposition from other sections of the bureaucracy especially those in Finance ministries, MITI argued that long-term self-reliance for Japan would be delayed or even undermined by following its apparent comparative advantage into labour intensive sectors. Despite grave shortages of capital and an infrastructure devastated by US bombing, MITI saw the route to sustained economic expansion in sectors that would offer the maximum possible productivity growth. Heavy industry not toys or low quality textiles, was targeted as the driving force for development, and a vast array of incentives and restraints were applied to ensure that the strategy was implemented.

Several criteria were used to identify priority industries. First, they should have significant input/output linkages so primary energy sectors for example, would lower fuel costs across the economy, and steel expansion would generate external economies in shipbuilding or motor vehicles. Secondly, in order to maximize the use of scarce capital resources, industries were selected that could utilize the backlog of technological change that had been developed in the Western economies. Purchasing patents would make significant savings on initial research costs and adapting or improving known techniques would increase the speed of development. Thirdly, targeted industries should have markets that were known to be price and income elastic and would offer long-term growth, in contrast to the low value-added products that were the usual sources of stagnation in Asian economies.

To guarantee the survival of these industries and to speed their rate of expansion, the home market was secured behind protective trade barriers. The need to foster rapid growth in a drive towards reducing Japanese reliance on US financial support, encouraged MITI to concentrate policy incentives on large capital intensive firms. This renewed the nineteenth century tradition of favouring selected producers in the interests of national strength and independence but with one important difference. When the state sold off its industrial interests or sponsored new ventures in the 1880s, it favoured the *zaibatsu* who tended to accumulate specialized industrial holdings, rather like the more recent French strategy of creating large firms as sector leaders. MITI's approach was to favour several large producers in the manner of an elite squad, and then to encourage rivalry between them so as to avoid the dangers of complacency in single firm monopolies. Each of the elite firms would, it was hoped, be able to spread the benefits of concentrated but competing favouritism throughout Japanese industry by the increased level of activity among related companies.

By the middle of the 1960s, MITI's strategy was paying handsome dividends in a wide range of industries where output, productivity, exports and profits were expanding rapidly. The more important contribution of large firms in terms of investment or technical change was evident, but large and small firms alike shared in the remarkable growth of output. The years from 1966 to 1969 saw real GDP growing in excess of 10 per cent annually and, with growth at twice the level of Japan's competitors, it was confidently expected that the substantial differences in productivity levels between large and small firms would be eroded.

Marked differences in efficiency and factor proportions between firms in the same industry are usually associated with periods of transition to a fully industrialized economy. With rapid and sustained economic growth more capital becomes available to finance investment in labour saving machinery, and higher labour rewards in the advanced sector of industry are thought to encourage the mobility of labour away from the small firm sector. The advantages of scale for larger firms are expected to lead to lower product prices and an increase in market share relative to smaller producers. In sum, the small firms are squeezed out by losing the advantages of labour intensive production as output becomes concentrated in larger companies.

There is some evidence that from the mid-1950s the average size of firm in manufacturing was growing as the employment share of firms with less than 100 workers fell from 60 to 50 per cent. The proportion of both total output and value added in production from these same smaller firms also fell, and wage differentials began to close. Taken together, these trends encouraged the view that 'duality in the economy is approaching its term' (Allen 1965 p.114). With hindsight the confidence with which the demise of dualism was predicted appears to have been premature. Throughout the 1970s the share of employment, value added and output taken by firms with less than 100 workers has grown in an unexpectedly resilient fashion. Employment is back to 60 per cent of the total, wage differentials between large and small firms have widened and the share of small firms in total value-added and shipments of manufacturing output is back to the level of the later 1950s.

The role of subcontracting and the increasing rate of investment by large companies in their subsidiaries has already been highlighted as one factor involved in the resilience of the small firm sector. There are several other processes which maintain and reproduce the structure of dualism.

2.4 Differentiated cooperation between finance and industrial capital

Small firms in all economies face severe problems raising finance to expand, or even maintain, their scale of operations. These difficulties contrast with the relative ease with which larger firms can obtain investment funds and in Japan the differential access to sources of finance is very significant.

For small firms the cost of raising capital through public stock issues is prohibitively expensive, but in Japan this is not the main problem as firms are significantly less reliant on equity finance. Although firms are more dependent on external fundraising, the proportion of shareholders equity in total assets is lower than in other advanced capitalist economies. During the 1970s for example, this proportion was around 19 per cent for manufacturing firms representing half the West German and about one-third of UK or US levels. The traditional external source of funds has been bank loans, and despite some recent reduction in bank dependence as internal reserves or retained profits have increased in importance, higher levels of bank debt is still a characteristic of Japanese company finance.

Bank loans carrying fixed interest payments over specific periods, are thought to be more constraining in contrast to the flexibility gained by varying stockholders dividends in line with company performance. The ability to alter dividends is said to give companies more freedom relative to the external dependence on banks who may impose unilateral changes in interest rates or loan allocation. However as we have already seen, there can be disadvantages for companies who rely extensively on equity finance if any fall in expected profits leads to unwelcome takeover bids. Experience in the UK and US especially, indicates how long-term strategies can be undermined by the need to confront the uncertainties of takeover at the whim of large institutional investors or ambitious competitors. The objective of long-term stability in Japan's conglomerate groupings does explain their preference for durable stockholders who place group cohesion ahead of short-term dividend gains.

There are also questions to be raised about the supposed disadvantages of excessive dependence on bank loans which relate to their classification as external sources. Where bank affairs are closely tied to the fortunes of their leading customers through shared group affiliation, the lending bank and the borrowing company are bound to the same fate which makes unilateral changes in loan terms much less likely. So in allocating loans, banks are especially committed to the expansion of their more important customers and preferential terms are offered through lower interest rates or more flexible borrowing limits. Companies that are heavily involved in foreign trade, or whose markets are seasonal, can expect their banks to be responsive to variations in liquidity and generally act as financial advisers. This frequently involves coordinating the exchange of marketing information and the organization of trade credit with trading companies. In short the level of cooperation between banks and their more important customers is much more extensive in Japan, thus mitigating the problems of depending on external loans.

Commercial banks have generally been able to provide the finance necessary to support the huge increase in investment because they have collected substantial deposits from savers. The level of personal savings is particularly high in Japan at over twice the rate in Western economies, and as the majority preference is for assets with a lower risk, over two-thirds are kept in bank deposits. Those banks that offer services to affiliated groups benefit from deposits taken from related companies, especially as group employees tend to deposit their savings with the bank most closely associated with their company.

Mutual cooperation between banks and their larger customers is rooted in their common interests. Banks have a vested interest in the growth of the firms to whom they lend most, not least because their profits are dependent on regular interest payments. Larger capital intensive firms equally benefit from the reduced levels of uncertainty surrounding their future investment plans.

Although bank loans are a vitally important source of finance, this is not to the complete exclusion of equity issues. Here also banks play a crucial role in advising on the scale or timing of issues but perhaps even more important in the Japanese context, in assisting the allocation of shares. Until the mid-1970s, additional equity finance was obtained through rights issues to existing stockholders at par rather than market share values making this a less attractive option for corporate borrowers. In placing stock with other affiliated companies, the banks played a key coordinating role. Even though new issues are increasingly being offered at current market values, the banks continue to facilitate the accumulation of stock within related groups of companies.

Not all of Japan's leading companies are members of groups that have particular banks at their centre. Yet they all certainly benefit from the much closer coordination of industry and finance, whether this is through preferential interest rates from a number of different banks or through the advisory functions of their main lenders. Large companies in particular, have received extensive support when markets were expanding but they can also rely on financial support in less prosperous years. Just as banks have a vested interest in the growth of their main customers, they have a clear role to play in limiting the damage that recession can bring especially where the failure of a leading company will affect many of their other customers.

A classic example of this process came in the wake of the huge losses made in 1974–5 by the Toyo Kogyo Co. who produce the Mazda motor car. Unfortunately for Mazda, the introduction of the powerful Wankel rotary engine coincided with the massive increase in oil prices which spelt disaster for an engine with high fuel consumption. Enormous bank debts and large stocks of surplus parts encouraged the biggest creditor, Sumitomo Bank to place five of its own executives onto the Mazda board to rescue the company. To avoid the damage to company status that would have accompanied widespread redundancies, many regular production workers were transferred to marketing jobs, including door-to-door selling, while

Sumitomo officials reorganized the company. Models were rationalized, a *kanban* system of inventory control was introduced and within five years a leaner and fitter Mazda emerged. The importance of Mazda to Sumitomo meant that they could 'never seriously consider the possibility of letting Toyo Kogyo go under' (Salamano 1980 p.65).

It would be misleading to imply from the experience of Mazda that all large companies have immunity from bankruptcy. What really influences the incidence of rescue operations is partly the extent of danger to related companies, but also the degree of previous cooperation with group objectives which incur debts of gratitude for past favours. Unlike Mazda the bankruptcy of the Sanko Steamship Co. in 1985 did not stir any great sympathy because the company management had a previous record of arrogance 'likened to that of a rowdy lone wolf refusing to line up with other shipping firms' (*JTW* 31/8/85). In this case the company's record was instrumental in the failure of the usual support mechanisms despite the presence of an LDP Cabinet Minister on the board. Mutual support in troubled times then, is seen as a reciprocal reward for cooperation over the long term.

If there are disadvantages to higher levels of reliance on bank loans, they are clearly counterbalanced for those large firms that are considered too important to fail. It is not possible though to find similar priorities for long-term survival where small firms are concerned. Despite the very high savings ratios, the demand for funds from capital intensive firms has been so enormous that small firms are regarded as marginal prospects and the vast bulk of loans have been allocated to large firms. In a sense large firms are supposed to act as financial intermediaries for their related suppliers through for example the provision of trade credit or through the re-sale of capital equipment.

Even for small firms closely affiliated to leading companies, preferential interest rates are rare. More importantly, when credit is tight they find available funds rationed to large borrowers. Such rationing is determined partly by the rank or importance of companies and is related to the level of deposits that they keep with the bank. Compensating deposits or balances are usually demanded as collateral before loans are allocated and this is one reason why corporate savings are also higher in Japan. The interrelation between deposits and loans 'thus become another form of reciprocal dealing: an increase in either the amount in deposit or the amount on loan is inevitably linked with an increase in the other' (Okamura 1982 p.58).

Needless to say, small firms are less able to maintain high levels of bank deposits and they are not given the priority accorded to the privileged class of borrowers among large companies. Small firms are consequently forced to rely much more on trade credit to finance their operations. The payments that small firms receive from their sales tend to be divided in roughly equal proportions between cash and credit notes that delay payment for periods from three to six months. Credit notes can be exchanged before they mature but this does involve the deduction of a premium. What is more disturbing for small firms is the propensity of large companies to increase the length of credit notes when their own liquidity is tight, thereby transferring part of their financial burden onto suppliers. In a similar fashion large companies frequently reduce the cash element or where they supply materials to be processed by subcontractors, increase the prices they charge for these materials.

Small firms then may have to pay more for their materials, receive less cash for their output and have to wait longer for their credit notes to mature. These financial burdens are magnified in the absence of other important sources of finance, and it is hardly surprising to find 99 per cent of the total number of firms going bankrupt located in the small firm sector. This high level of mortality stands in stark contrast to the operation of support mechanism for large companies and was highlighted vividly during the recession of the mid-1970s. Between 1975 and 1980 the share of firms employing less than 300 workers in total bankruptcy debts rose from 75 to over 90 per cent. For those small firms that managed to avoid failure, the extent of their fall in profits was proportionate to the extent of their involvement in subcontracting. Surveys in 1975 and 1980 show that dependent subcontractors in household electrical goods and motor parts, experienced a 30 per cent greater fall in profits than independent small firms (N. Sasaki 1981 p.102 and Steven 1983 p.73).

2.5 The state as financial guardian for large firms

It could be argued that inadequate finance and higher mortality rates among small firms is a reflection of the way market forces allocate scarce capital according to long-term growth potential. For large companies in Japan, however, the free market has been controlled in various ways so as to 'mitigate the unfettered ravages of a market economy' (Saxonhouse 1979 p.320). One way in which this operates is through the coordinating role of banks who can organize a protective safety net during periods of acute financial distress. This safety net is itself a response to the attitude of the state towards the need to safeguard the position of leading companies.

Much of the debate surrounding the role of the state in financial markets has centred on power of the central monetary authorities over Commercial Banks who frequently overcommit themselves when financing the growth of investment. As large companies are heavily dependent on bank loans, and with banks tending to lend beyond their means it was crucial for the Bank of Japan as final guarantor to support the banking system. There appeared to be a chain of dependency from private companies to the state with the Commercial Banks acting as 'merely a channel through which the Central bank fed industry with funds' (Allen 1981 p. 50). Through this chain of dependency, it is argued, the state could exercise control over the policies and practices of the Commercial Banks, and through them Japan's leading firms.

There is some agreement that, down to the late 1960s at least, the state did encourage overborrowing by firms and overlending by banks through its commitment to rapid growth. There is also evidence to show that by keeping interest rates artificially low in boom years, the state forced banks to allocate credit by rationing quantities and this favoured large borrowers. But we do need to be wary of inferring too much central direction, partly because this implies that banks or companies were forced into compliance. As the record shows, the preference given to large companies and the support they receive from their bankers has led to rapid growth in output with consequent effects on the profits of banks and their leading customers. So there is a sense in which both companies and banks have found the financial system mutually beneficial. It is also important to recognize that several of Japan's most well-known companies like Honda, Sony or Toyota have relied less on bank loans and have therefore been able to follow fairly independent policies. Since the 1970s the reduction in dependence on bank loans has been a more general feature, especially among manufacturing firms who are able to finance more of their investment out of retained profits or accumulated reserves. If we place too much weight on direct financial controls it is all too easy to miss other less visible ways in which the Japanese state has systematically supported the position of large companies.

Corporate taxation policies for example, have greatly favoured capital intensive firms and thus helped to widen the productivity gap between large and small companies. Rates of company taxation may be high, but what is also significant is the proportion of profit that is non-taxable. Special purpose tax-free reserves include allowances for bad debts, reserves to cover the impact of exchange rate fluctuations and the accumulating half-yearly wage bonuses. Employee retirement funds are also included as special reserves, but up to one-third can be used for investment at the discretion of management.

None of these allowable deductions is 'uncommon in other countries but they are more wide-ranging in Japan than is generally the case elsewhere' (Elston 1981 p.515). Tax-free depreciation allowances are also in common use, but in Japan they have been more selectively applied. So in addition to standard depreciation allowances, certain designated sectors can write off another 25 per cent of the investment against tax in the first year, while in energy saving or robotic investment the rate has gone as high as 60 per cent. Selected industries have also been able to secure extra depreciation in proportion to any increase in the share of exports in their total sales.

In these and other ways the state has favoured those companies who have displayed very high rates of investment, and this almost by definition excludes most small firms. Where tax-free reserves are so closely linked to capital investment, the small firm finds a greater proportion of profits subject to tax and may therefore be subject to a higher marginal rate of taxation. These policies of tax forgiveness have the added advantage of making the sharing of risk between companies and society less visible than would be the case if all assistance were given as direct subsidies in identifiable budget items.

Direct participation by the state in the allocation of savings to industry has been important in both qualitative and quantitative senses. Just as Commercial Banks have collected deposits from the public so also has the state through the Postal Savings system, where savers can accumulate several tax-free accounts by using fictitious names. These funds have been used to finance the work of specialist quasi-public financial institutions in a range of activities from overseas projects to long-term loans for the purchase of specialist equipment. Although the share of state borrowing in total company finance has recently been relatively small at about 10 per cent, in a qualitative sense even a small loan by a state institution carries a seal of approval that enormously enhances the standing of companies with their banks.

In equity finance, the state has allowed the lower dependence of Japanese firms to continue by treating loan interest as tax deductible in contrast to dividends. This practice is also not unknown elsewhere, but the preferential treatment for corporate dividend receivers where the effective tax rate is 'close to zero' (Aoki 1984 p.238), has been a clear incentive to inter-company stockholding. In perpetuating a financial structure which offers tremendous advantages to large firms, it is as important to consider the role of the state in maintaining the idiosyncracies of the financial system as it is to debate the extent of state control over commercial banks.

State agencies have also played a formative role in limiting the damage recessions impose on large firms. MITI has a long record of concern with the dangers of excess capacity for capital intensive sectors. Specific measures in 1978 allowed tax credits to be accumulated if capacity was reduced in industries like shipbuilding where world demand had slumped dramatically. More generally, MITI has been a consistent promoter of recession cartels which would facilitate an 'orderly' reduction in excess capacity.

The organization of cartels runs directly counter to the anti-monopoly legislation bestowed by the US occupation, and this has produced a prolonged struggle within the bureaucracy between MITI and the Fair Trade Commission. In some cases this has led to the formation of unofficial cartels often with the tacit support of MITI, but the whole process has led to a 'systematic undoing of the American-inspired anti-monopoly legislation both in letter and spirit' (Yamamura 1982 p.81). Large firms have the expectation that prolonged recession will provoke assistance from at least some parts of the bureaucracy. What is equally well known is that the orderly reduction in capacity will be proportionate to existing market shares. This expectation adds further pressure on companies to capture bigger shares when markets are expanding when banks and companies have an informal assurance that the state will provide assistance if markets deteriorate.

2.6 Birth and death rates among small subcontracting firms

Japan's financial structure offers large companies significant advantages in access to funds to finance rapid expansion, and offers substantial support for them to survive periodic recessions. The risks involved in entering new markets, new sectors or using new processes can be externalized or shared within conglomerate groups or underwritten by the state on behalf of society. In some ways it is surprising that smaller firms have survived at all, let alone increased their share of manufacturing employment. As we have seen, the ability of large firms to transfer financial problems to suppliers has led to high rates of bankruptcy among smaller companies. Yet what distinguishes the structure of Japanese industry is not only the high death rate of companies but the fact that even in the severe recession of the mid-1970s, the birth rate of new small firms exceeded the number of bankruptcies by 50 per cent.

In recognizing the relationship between size of firm and the likelihood of failure it is important to point out that, even in recent years, the failure rate in manufacturing was approximately one in every 100 incorporated firms. It is widely accepted that the rate increases as firms get smaller as liquidity burdens are passed along in a ripple effect from the very largest firms through lengthening credit notes. Those firms that rely heavily on subcontracting though, do have a vested interest in offering at least some protection to their main suppliers and this is one reason why the small firm sector has survived.

With, for example, a greater use of *kanban* inventory control, parent companies have to weigh the advantages of lengthening credit notes against the need to preserve the existence of their primary suppliers. These more favoured subcontractors, however, gain a greater degree of continuity at the expense of wider variations in profits. In the lower levels of economic activity since 1973, the extent of competition between subcontractors has allowed parent companies greater bargaining power over delivery schedules, quality specifications and prices. Survival in business gives little option to small firms but to concede to these demands, especially as larger manufacturers are increasingly using overseas suppliers in Asia where wage costs are significantly lower than in Japan.

While large firms have continued to increase their capital/labour ratios thus widening the productivity gap with smaller firms, this has certainly not prevented them from persuading their suppliers to improve the quality of their equipment. In one sense Japanese subcontractors are being pushed away from the most labour intensive processes where overseas plants have the advantage. Demanding higher levels of technical efficiency from domestic suppliers is directly related to the need to standardize and improve the quality of inputs that are used in later stages of manufacturing, where closer physical location to the main plant is crucial. Some of the new investment is financed by parent companies, as is shown by the growing share of investment in subsidiaries, but the resale of less up to date equipment to subcontractors is also a common practice.

Entirely new ventures, especially in areas of very advanced technology like microelectronics, have frequently been pioneered by small firms spinning off as satellites from parent companies. As well as confining the risk of such projects to expendable subsidiaries the new firms enable large companies to transfer surplus labour from their regular payroll. In the decade up to 1982 employment in firms with over 1000 workers fell by over a quarter and the establishment of affiliated companies provided a vehicle for shedding labour. New ventures are one way to solve the problem of promotion bottlenecks for middle managers whose prospects are constrained by slower rates of industrial growth. Such vertical moves 'became a standardized system for technology transfer as employees of large firms with advanced technological knowledge, as well as employees of subcontracting firms, split off and formed their own businesses' (Y. Sato 1984 p.21). By creating a new but related company, the parent firm gains a partner with recent experience of its working practices and, as wages are related to seniority, removes an expensive element of labour cost.

Technological improvement has also been an objective in state policies for the small firm sector. Legislation in 1970 was designed to raise the quality of equipment in small firms by setting minimum standards of quality control and subsidizing regional networks of advice on technical and managerial efficiency. The meagre supplies of finance for small producers has been supplemented by state agencies especially for research and development of energy saving equipment. Running alongside this financial support has been an attempt to promote industrial cooperatives where small firms would share distribution facilities or share the production of one brand name.

The problems of small firms have been an increasing focus for the state in most economies following the crisis of the 1970s, and in some ways this is a gesture of concern to those who have been most affected. As elsewhere the impact of this assistance is difficult to assess, but state loans in Japan form approximately 12 per cent of outstanding loans to firms employing less than 300 workers. Certainly small business, through its close connections with the ruling LDP party, has lobbied for a shift in the established policies of support and protection for big business. Financial gestures have been forthcoming, but these were not sufficient to prevent a reduction of 40 per cent in the budget allocation to small and medium-sized firms between 1975 and 1986.

In one other area the state has endeavoured to stabilize the failure rates among small firms by monitoring the variations in credit note maturity dates. From 1956 attempts have been made to regulate subcontracting payments and prevent large companies from making unilateral changes in trading terms. As in some other forms of state intervention in Japan, the policy is backed up not by automatic penalties, but by 'advice and guidance' for offenders from MITI. Even though large firms have continued to vary credit terms to relieve their own liquidity problems, small firms are understandably reluctant to initiate complaints against their trading partners. Small producers appear to see inferior bargaining strength as the price they have to pay for some continuity in orders. MITI argues that their guidance has at least prevented maturity rates from getting much longer than the average of four months. But many small producers fear 'the rectification of unfair subcontracting arrangements is not high on the official list of priorities' (Anthony 1983 p.71).

2.7 Small firms in distribution

As we have seen the confident prediction that the wide disparities in productivity according to firm size would lead to the demise of the small firm sector in manufacturing has been premature. Whether we regard state policies towards small firms as rhetorical gestures or as genuine attempts to protect their existence, there does appear to be renewed interest in preserving a differentiated industrial structure. The rivalry promoted between large companies has its reflection in fierce competition between small suppliers for orders from parent companies. But just as the state appears unwilling to allow the market a totally free reign over the prospects of large companies, state support for small firms seems to recognize their value. In particular the way small firms function as 'a highly elastic shock absorber of underemployed and marginal workers which is extremely important in recessions' (Samuels 1981 p.45). Small firms provide a useful channel for re-allocating labour from large firms without increasing official unemployment rates.

While much of the focus in this chapter has been on manufacturing where the reliance on small producers is relatively unusual among advanced economies, the small firm is dominant in many other sectors. Not only is the proportion of self-employed and unpaid family labour higher in Japan (Figure 2.5), but 75 per cent of all paid employees work in firms with less than 100 workers. In services and distribution especially, very small firms with less than 30 workers account for three-quarters of employment. What is more, in the decade after 1975 employment in these two sectors grew at twice the average rate for all industry.

Japan's dense network of wholesale and retail distribution has been a contentious issue among overseas producers who claim that it acts as a barrier in their attempts to increase sales. Imports of consumer goods they

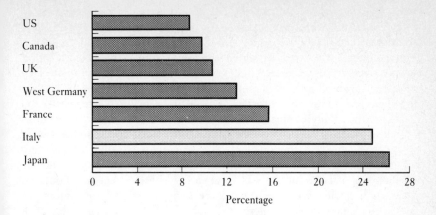

Figure 2.5 Self-employed and family workers as a percentage of the labour
force in the Big Seven OECD economies 1986
Source: *Labour Force Statistics 1966–86*, OECD, 1987

claim, are held back because marketing costs are prohibitive in a country
which has over twice the number of retail stores per head of the population
than in the US or West Germany. Perhaps more significant is the accusation
that domestic producers are able to limit the penetration of overseas goods
by binding Japanese retailers to Japanese products through a range of
restrictive practices. These accusations are frequently dismissed as excuses
for inadequate effort on the part of overseas companies, but even a Prime
Ministerial Advisory Body called in 1986 for 'a stricter watch on unfair
trade practices in distribution' (*JTW* 26/4/86). Leaving aside for the
moment the question of informal import barriers, the restrictive practices
used by larger manufacturers can be used as one explanation of the highly
dispersed structure of distribution.

Small retailers are especially reliant on trade credit, which is often
determined by the acceptance of exclusive dealing in particular brands.
This does have some advantages for small retailers in that they can return
unsold stock, but the retailer loses flexibility where they are required to
maintain the prices recommended by manufacturers. Sales agents acting on
behalf of manufacturers, are vigilant in preventing retailers from selling at
lower prices by threatening to cut future supplies. The retailer may be
cushioned from cut-throat competition from supermarkets but at the cost
of their freedom to sell or price as they wish: like small subcontractors,
being tied to a dominant parent company may be the cost of insuring
against business failure. However it does appear that consumers pay the
final bill as retail prices are over four times the level of wholesale prices,
which is double the equivalent mark-up in the US or Western Europe.

Retailing employment has been a traditional refuge for those workers most exposed to redundancy in other sectors, and as such higher consumer prices 'provides a form of social security for the retired and unemployed' (Hills 1983 p.65).

In contrast, supermarkets which exist by cutting prices on a larger turnover with a lower labour force, have a much smaller share of retail sales in Japan. Partly this reflects the lack of enthusiasm among manufacturers toward any erosion of retail price maintenance. Partly too it reflects the ability of small business to mobilize their LDP connections to oppose planning applications for larger stores. Such opposition is backed by appeals to protect the small retailer as a unique feature of Japanese culture against an alien Western transplant. Few would deny the convenience for shoppers of large numbers of local stores with long opening hours on six and a half days each week, but there is no doubt that consumers pay for the convenience. Nor is there any doubt that the resilience of the small retailing sector has provided a useful form of controlled distribution for larger manfuactures.

2.8 The small firm: a font of entrepreneurship or a haven for skidders?

The inevitable decline in the significance of small firms in advanced capitalist economies has been a theme common to Marxist and neo-classical political economy. For Marxists, petty bourgeois producers seem destined to be replaced by monopoly capital, while the advantages rendered by economies of scale have been sufficiently impressive for neo-classical economists to stress the unreality of atomistic competition. Japan is not alone in experiencing a resurgence in the share of employment taken by small firms or the self-employed in the aftermath of the severe crisis of the 1970s. More emphasis needs to be placed on the continuing role that small firms play in servicing the needs of large corporations. Japan's experience shows how both the state and big business have helped to maintain such a servicing role in response to the immediate problems of recession, and in adjusting to the probability of a lower growth path through the 1980s.

Ideologically, a dynamic small firm sector may be said to reflect the opportunities capitalism offers to those prepared to display individual initiative, self-sacrifice and dedication to hard work. This positive approach to a differentiated industrial structure means for example that 'the Japanese economic and social situation guarantees the right to set up one's own business and the entrepreneurial spirit is alive and well' (Y. Sato 1984 p.21). Social mobility, the prospect of rising incomes and independent control of their working lives are the rewards offered for competitive individualism.

Small entrepreneurs in Japan hold tenaciously to the ideals of self-help and dedication to the work ethic, but it is not at all clear that their presence in the small firm sector is entirely based on free choice. Neither is upward mobility, rising income or independence a necessary consequence of their diligence. In many ways the small firm acts as a 'net that cushions the fall of skidders' (Mayer 1975 p.432). There may be no alternative to working in a small firm for those excluded or transferred from regular employment status in large companies and their primary subcontractors. Access to the status of a regular employee in a large firm is both a highly controlled and selective process which generates two distinct segments in the labour market. When access to one is blocked, the small firm may be all that is left.

We have seen in this chapter how a dual structure of production has been maintained in Japan through the interconnected activities of private business and a state which has supported the simultaneous existence of a limited number of larger companies and a massive network of smaller ones. The question of whether the state merely supported pre-existing market trends or has positively guided the market towards this end is a contentious one which will be addressed in Chapter 4. A more immediate issue concerns the consequences for labour of a structure which gives priority to flexibility yet at the same time promises a lifetime of permanent employment which seems to imply inflexibility. If output and methods of production can be changed so quickly how can the input of labour be varied to accommodate these changes?

3

A Flexible Labour Market

The growth rates of productivity in Japanese manufacturing have consistently outstripped those of its major economic rivals over the past quarter century and output per worker has increased at twice the rate recorded in other OECD states. Although the rate of growth has fallen since the oil crises of the 1970s, Japan's productivity advantage has been magnified by very low rates of increase in unit labour costs. These two trends help to explain how cost and price advantages have resulted in the remarkable increase in exports which has produced such an enormous foreign trade surplus.

One key element in higher productivity is the very high rates of investment in manufacturing industry which has led to both quantitative and qualitative improvements in productive equipment. As we saw in Chapter 2 the expansion of large capital intensive firms has been promoted in a flexible industrial structure which permits them to adjust quickly to changes in demand. In periods of rapid expansion an increase in their own scale of operations has been paralleled by an expansion of output in smaller affiliated companies. In recession large firms concentrate more output within their own plant where economies of scale yield lower average costs compared to labour intensive subcontractors The advantages of a flexible industrial structure was greatly assisted up to the 1970s by a protected home market which gave companies a secure domestic base.

Accusations of unfair trading have been particularly widespread in recessions when Japanese companies have been attacked for dumping products in foreign markets. Foreign firms find it difficult to believe that Japanese costs are really low enough to justify such low prices and there is some evidence that the domestic prices of equivalent goods are higher. However it is equally clear that large Japanese companies do hold a powerful competitive edge because of the ease with which they can alter the balance between their own output and that of their smaller suppliers. Of course all large firms try to gain this sort of flexibility and the fact that they are large indicates that they have succeeded to a greater extent than their smaller rivals. Japanese industry, though, seems to be systematically structured to give large firms that much more flexibility than their international competitors.

Adjusting the output of existing products and rapidly expanding the share of new ones, requires flexibility in the labour market and it is here that the Japanese have even bigger advantages. Regular workers appear to cooperate much more with management over changes in work practices, job allocation, retraining or transfers to related companies. The 10 per cent of employees that are temporary or seasonal workers can be laid off or recruited as required, and altering the proportion of output coming from subcontractors causes them in turn to adjust their labour force. The elastic network of tiny family businesses and the high proportion of self-employed workers give the whole labour market a greater degree of fluidity than other leading capitalist economies.

At first sight this degree of fluidity in the Japanese labour market sits uneasily with the presumption that employment is for life because this would make wages a quasi-fixed cost. When we question the actual extent of lifetime employment it is not surprising to find that a fluid labour market requires that only a quarter of employees can expect such guarantees. Workers in Japan do tend to have fewer employers in the course of their career than in the West even though the comparison is somewhat distorted because of the concentration of lifetime guarantees in the large firm sector. Security of employment is not as uncommon in the West as the stereotypical contrast with Japan implies, but what is more noticeable is the extension of security to blue-collar labour in Japan as well as white-collar employees. In Japan as elsewhere the commitment to employment security is an attempt by firms to reduce the turnover of key employees and so avoid transferring the benefits of training programmes to rival firms. But for those in Japan who do achieve a more secure status it is widely accepted that such benefits are unlikely to be renewed if the individual moves to another company. This then raises the question of how voluntary is the acceptance of cooperation and harmony between labour and management? Given the mobility constraints, is the cooperation of labour not better explained by the fact that employees have little alternative?

Whether or not the analogy of the firm as a cooperative family is a realistic one for the majority of labour, this idea forms a crucial part in the ideology that Japanese industrial relations are different because of a longstanding preference for conformity to group consensus. Promises by management that employment would be for life and the concentration of labour unions within specific firms were in practice a post-war innovation designed to overcome the crisis caused by severe labour unrest following the democratic reforms of the US Occupation. It was during this period that with the cooperation of the US Occupation, parts of the bureaucracy, elected conservative politicians and private employers sought to alter the extent of labour rights in order, it was argued, to maintain internal political stability. But the structure that emerged which judiciously mixes the rigidities of lifetime employment for a minority with flexibility for the remainder, has been maintained ever since. So in addition to considering the advantages the system has for employers, we need also to examine how state policies continue to support a segmented labour market.

The first thing to establish however is the pattern of differences in pay and employment prospects for different segments of the labour force and the implications these have for assessing the extent of lifetime employment.

3.1 Earnings differentials by size of firm

Figure 2.4 in the last chapter illustrated the extent of differences in value-added productivity between large and small firms and these are very clearly reflected in earnings. Figure 3.1 gives support to the view that 'Perhaps the single most distinguishing characteristic of the Japanese wage structure is the effect of firm size on wages' (Hashimoto 1979 p.1098). All the elements that make up total earnings vary according to the size of the firm but the extent of differences in the basic wage is somewhat less pronounced. For instance, if we take the basic wage paid by the largest firms to be 100, firms in the two smallest size bands pay 78 per cent and 52 per cent of these rates. The bonus payment differential though is much larger at only 43 per cent and 22 per cent of the sums paid in large firms.

Bonus payments tend to make up a larger share of earnings in Japan at about one-quarter of the total giving employers more room to adjust wages in line with changes in levels of economic activity. There is some debate about exactly how flexible bonus payments have been and some argue that in recent years bonuses and basic wages have followed similar trends. This may be so if the average for all industries is considered, but in the key areas of manufacturing where demand is more variable, the bonus–earnings ratio experiences greater volatility (Hashimoto 1979 p.1101). But irrespective of these year-to-year changes the size of the bonus is very sensitive to firm size. Employees in large firms throughout the 1970s received a bonus payment equivalent to five or six months basic pay compared to less than three months in small firms.

Overtime pay has accounted for approximately 6 per cent of average earnings since the mid-1970s and this too varies with firm size due to differences in the length of scheduled working hours. Small firms operate a scheduled working week 10 per cent longer than large firms and in manufacturing it is 15 per cent greater. This means that the extra payments received for overtime beyond the scheduled week are earned at an earlier stage in large firms. Once again large firms gain the added flexibility of adjusting actual hours worked to a shorter working week, but where

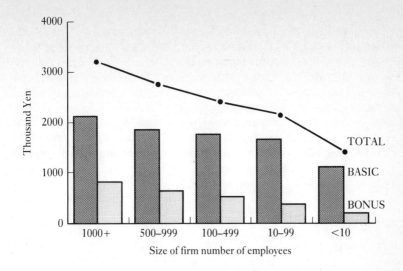

Figure 3.1 Components of average earnings by size of firm in Japan, 1973–85
Source: Shirai, 1983

overtime is used their workers gain more as the extra overtime payment is based on a higher basic rate.

Fringe benefits are also more significant for workers in large companies although their exact size is difficult to estimate because the Welfare Facilities Survey covers only the 50 per cent of labour in firms employing more than 30 workers. The 1983 survey showed that the costs incurred in providing company housing or housing loans, medical, nursery or recreation facilities were at least twice as big in large firms. Even obligatory health insurance and pension payments per employee were one third greater for workers in large firms. A survey of welfare spending by all private firms conducted by the Ministry of Labour in 1975 estimated that such payments yielded benefits equivalent to 10–15 per cent of annual earnings, but did not distinguish very clearly how this differs according to size of firm. Another source suggests that welfare expenditure per employee in 1980 was three times greater in large firms (Steven 1983 p.166) but other estimates indicate that the gap is less than half this figure. Whatever the precise levels are, there seems to be no sense in which the earnings gap is bridged by higher non-monetary rewards in small firms.

By itself this association between earnings and company size is not unique to Japan, but as we saw in the last chapter the number of workers affected is greater. If we take a large firm to be one employing more than 1000 and a small one less than 100, the latter in 1985 employed 15 times as many people in the private sector as a whole and five times as many in manufacturing. Exact international comparisons of wage differentials according to size of firm are difficult to make because wage data is often collected into overlapping or incompatible categories. However it is possible in some cases to obtain a broad indication for 1985 of the contrast between firms with over 1000 and those with less than 100 employees although the data is for manufacturing industry rather than all employees. In 1985 Japanese workers in small manufacturing firms earned 55 per cent of workers in large firms compared to 75 per cent in West Germany, 73 per cent in the UK and 70 per cent in France or Italy and 66 per cent in the US. When we take longer working hours into account the differential widens still further as wages per productive hour in small Japanese firms is only 46 per cent of the sum paid in large firms.

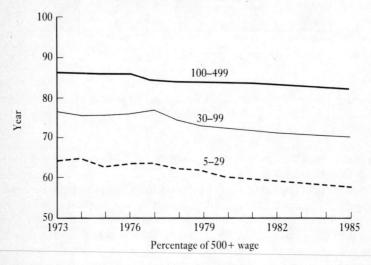

Figure 3.2 Wage differentials by size of firm in Japan (all industries), 1973–85
Source: *White Paper on Small and Medium Enterprises*, MITI 1982, and *Japan Statistical Yearbooks*

The long-term trends in the wage gap between large and small firms are shown in Figure 3.2 and although 'large' is taken to be over 500 employees, the trends are fairly clear. From the mid-1950s to the early 1970s the high levels of economic growth in all sectors increased competition for labour and allowed the gap to close. This trend was then halted or even reversed thereafter as large companies especially in manufacturing transferred their excess labour into smaller subcontractors or satellite companies. A flexible Japanese labour market then has two dimensions: first, the re-allocation of labour to other firms, and secondly, the ability to vary unit labour cost by changing the share of earnings taken by overtime and bonuses.

3.2 How inflexible is permanent employment?

In some ways the movement of labour between firms might be surprising given the tendency to associate the Japanese labour market with notions of lifetime employment and seniority wages. If workers are given jobs for life or if their wages are linked to age and seniority does this not make for a much less flexible labour market? Any answer to this question depends very much on how many workers can realistically expect permanent employment and in what sense pay is related to age. The Japanese Wage Structure Survey is one of the most comprehensive sources of data and allows us to shed more light on the realities of the labour market. While the main focus of the Survey is on basic payments it is nevertheless a crucial benchmark because both bonus and overtime payments are to an extent determined by the basic or standard wage. It is important to stress that temporary, seasonal, part-time (defined as less than 24 hours per week) and those in firms with less than 10 employees are not included. As women make up over 60 per cent of these categories their position in the labour market is not well represented by the wage structure data.

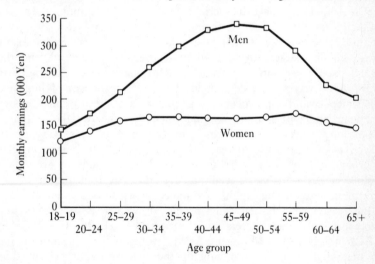

Figure 3.3 Age/wage profiles for men and women in Japan, 1985
Source: *Japan Statistical Yearbook*, 1987

Lifetime employment and seniority wages which are said to be the two defining features of the Japanese labour market, are closely related. Employment for life and pay according to age should produce an earnings curve that rises steadily from recruitment to retirement. The profiles shown in Figure 3.3 do indicate such a curve for men and for women in the early stages of their working careers. This data takes the form of a cross-section in one year to show the average wage in each of the age groups, so 44 year-old men for example earn about twice the wage paid to men aged 20. Proposals that wages should be linked directly to age were put forward by labour unions in the later 1940s as a way of establishing a wage profile that reflected the increasing levels of housing or educational spending, but the slope of the female wage profile shows that the age/wage connection may not be universal.

For employers, the relationship between age and wages may reflect the accumulation of skill that comes with experience in a particular job. Even if labour moves between firms, they carry with them more skill and experience than a new recruit and may therefore expect this to be rewarded. Such a pattern of incremental earnings tends to be common among white-collar workers where general skills and experience are transferable between say schools, universities, hospitals, banks or legal institutions. In industry, although incremental profiles are less explicit mobility between firms may be the route to higher wages on a scale rising with age.

Where skills are more firm-specific, however, they are less marketable and labour cannot necessarily expect to resume their wage profile when they move to another firm. In this case mobility between firms is constrained because labour may have to sacrifice the growth in earnings they could expect if they remained with their current firm. Employers also try to discourage the mobility of their highly skilled labour because they wish to retrieve the investment made in training over the long term, and they certainly would not want competing firms to poach labour that they have trained. One way to reduce mobility is to offer promises of long-term employment, with the prospect of wage increases rising by promotion steps on a long ladder of continuous employment. Another way is to organize no-poaching conventions between firms or to pay only low wages in the early years of a career to increase the amounts that mobile workers have to forfeit. Employers in Japan use all of these methods to prevent the mobility of key workers especially in deferring pay from earlier to later years thereby rewarding highly continuous service to one company.

One reason why the age/wage profile for women is much less steep relates to the way their careers are interrupted between the ages of 25 and 40 by marriage and childbearing. As the average women's tenure is only half that of men, their promotion up the seniority ladder is cut short. There are numerous questions to be raised later about those women who would prefer to continue working, but this example illustrates clearly why it is important to distinguish between age *per se* and continuous tenure when considering wage profiles.

The tendency to reward continuous employment is shown by the much steeper wage profiles for Japanese men in large and small firms in Figure 3.4. After 20 years of continuous service workers record a growth in wages of 150 per cent in small and 180 per cent in large firms compared to 52 per cent and 30 per cent in the US. This data does not mean that absolute

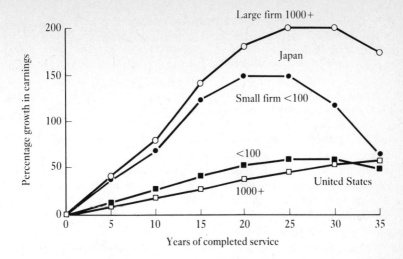

Figure 3.4 Earnings profile for men in Japan and the US by years of completed service, 1979–80
Source: Hashimoto and Raisian, 1985

wages are higher, because in the early years wages in Japan are relatively low. Steeper profiles show that 'the growth rates in earnings attributable to tenure are far greater in Japan than in the US' (Hashimoto and Raisian 1985 p.732). A similar conclusion was reached in a comparison with Britain 'the seniority premium being more than double in Japan' (Collier and Knight 1985 p.25). Comparisons with other Western wage profiles also reveal a contrast particularly for blue-collar workers who in France and West Germany experience a slower growth in wages with a lower peak wage which is maintained from the age of 25 through to retirement (Shirai 1983 p.31).

The offer of longer-term rewards for continuous employment in Japanese firms is common to large and small firms but as Figure 3.4 indicates the profiles begin to diverge after the fifteenth year. Men in small firms experience an earlier and lower peak growth rate which very quickly drops away after the twenty-fifth year of service. In the US however, the rate of growth, the eventual peak and retirement wage levels for both large and small firms are very similar. The distinction between the Japanese profiles highlights the very marked tendency to reward length of continuous employment in large firms and is closely related to their much higher rates of union membership.

The cross-section data used so far gives us little indication about how many workers continue in employment long enough to recoup the wages that were deferred earlier in their career. If lifetime employment is common in Japan we would expect longer periods to be spent with particular firms and less mobility between firms. However the evidence on average tenure and separation rates only partially confirms this expectation. Labour in Japan does tend to work for fewer employers over a typical career and does therefore tend to stay longer in each firm than in the West, but there are very significant variations depending on age, firm size and gender.

Much of the comparative analysis of tenure and mobility has been based on US experience where an average worker aged 55 would, for example have worked for 10 different firms compared to only four in Japan. The average length of employment of all labour in 1982 was correspondingly double in Japan at eight to eleven years for men and six for women. But the averages for Japan mask certain intriguing variations. For example the mobility of labour between firms is especially concentrated in the earlier and later years of working careers. In addition the average length of employment for Japanese men in large firms is 50 per cent longer. What is even more significant for wage profiles is that all of the figures quoted for average tenure are well below the 25–30 years that it takes to reach the peak of the earnings profile. So in small Japanese firms average tenure may be higher but only one in six men have the 20 years or more of tenure that would place them on the higher parts of their wage profile. Even in large firms the proportion is only one in four (Hashimoto and Raisian 1985 p.726). The position for women is even less favourable so although the average length of employment in one firm is greater, few workers are able to recoup the earnings lost in earlier years of their career when wages are lower.

As the overall shape of wage profiles are widely recognized why do workers not stay longer with one firm? Part of the answer is of course that they have little choice if, for example, the firm is made bankrupt. Involuntary discharges through bankruptcy are though much less likely to be significant in larger firms where labour turnover is much more related to age. In the early stages of careers mobility is higher in Japan because part of the workforce is discharged before they reach the higher paid section of the profile to be replaced by younger and cheaper labour. It is also possible at this early stage for workers to transfer to other firms without falling too far down the promotion ladder although such mobility is rarely between large firms. Turnover rates for labour are also higher in older age groups especially among those workers over the age of 45. A larger proportion of labour with continuous tenure means a significant rise in labour costs to firms, and over the past decade Japanese companies have either found ways of flattening the wage profile or have 'encouraged' labour transfers into subsidiaries or satellite firms. Mobility for women who make up 45 per cent of the labour force involves little choice once they reach the 25–30 age group when they are expected to take temporary retirement into marriage.

The differences between the wage profiles of men and women can be

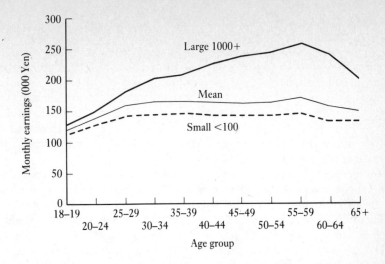

Figure 3.5 Age/wage profiles for women in Japan by size of firm, 1985
Source: *Japan Statistical Yearbook*, 1987

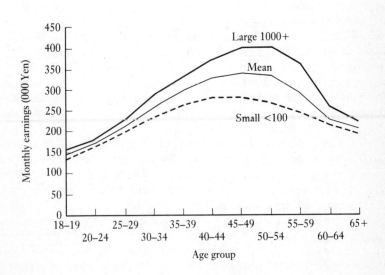

Figure 3.6 Age/wage profiles for men in Japan by size of firm, 1985
Source: *Japan Statistical Yearbook*, 1987

clearly seen in Figures 3.5 and 3.6. Comparing the average profiles brings out the stark contrast in the slopes of the two curves after the age of 30 which is partially explained by career interruption at marriage. But even up to the age of 30 the growth in womens wages is only 35 per cent compared to 90 per cent for men. The slope for women in large firms is much steeper but this has little effect on the average because so few women actually work continuously in large firms. In total women make up less than 20 per cent of the labour force in large private sector firms and the majority are young and unmarried who leave before they have accumulated more than 10 years service. Even if they return to work for the same firm when their children go to school their seniority is lost.

By focusing on wage profiles it is possible to show contrasts between different segments of the labour market. The allocation of labour to these segments is of course partly predetermined by gender, but recruitment to firms of different sizes is based mainly on educational credentials. Rather than recruiting to a specific job or skill, hiring is based on 'intelligence, character and general acceptability as determined by personal history, academic record and company interviews' (Abegglen 1973 p.241). Thereafter an employee is rotated through several sections or jobs making them more of a generalist rather than a specialist in one skill. Given the steeper wage profiles in large firms it is not surprising to find intense competition for employment in these firms and employers are able to select those with the highest qualifications. Thus large firms employ twice as many graduates, but perhaps more importantly they can take their pick of the best graduates from the best universities.

The effect of this recruitment pattern on wage profiles is shown in Figure 3.7 which relates the average wage for each age group to educational background. It is after the first few years in employment that the profiles diverge dramatically and again the male/female contrast is vivid. Although University and College graduates are grouped together in this data, men dominate university places 4:1 and women make up 90 per cent of Junior College students which further accentuates the status of men. In total therefore there are seven times as many graduate men among all employees, so getting on to the wage profiles that grow fastest and last longest is very much a matter of educational credentials. The resulting pressures on children in getting to the better universities and the question of whether access is open will be considered later.

There is then some evidence to show that Japanese workers do indeed work for longer periods with each employer, but only 20 per cent of labour in the private sector stay long enough to get close to the peak of the wages profile. Similar conclusions can be drawn about the number of jobs held in an average career but there remain marked differences according to age, educational background, gender and size of firm. One out of two graduate men aged 40 working in large companies in 1980 are likely never to have changed employers compared to one in twelve men with High School

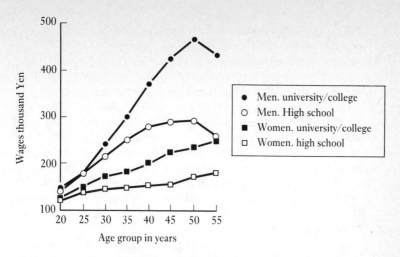

Figure 3.7 Age/wage profiles for men and women in Japan by educational background, 1983
Source: Ministry of Labour, FPC, 1984

background in small firms. By the age of 55 these ratios drop to 1:3 in large firms and 1:36 in small. Women are five times less likely than men to be with the same employer at 40 and eight times less likely at 55 (Aoki 1984 p.82).

If lifetime employment and seniority wages are seen as key distinguishing characteristics of the Japanese labour market then it has to be recognized that they are far from universal features. By focusing so much attention on what is different about the Japanese labour market it can be argued that 'four-fifths of researchers energy has been put into investigating the careers of one fifth of the labour force' (Plath 1983 p.31). As we narrow down the proportion of the labour market that appears to benefit from lifetime employment in Japan, we get closer to the proportion of labour in Western countries employed by large companies who work to seniority wage profiles that offer accumulating reward for experience. In both the UK and the US over 40 per cent of workers are expected to stay with their first employer for over 20 years (Collier and Knight 1985 p.21). If there are tendencies that are different they relate to reduced inter-firm mobility for men between the ages of 25 and 45, and the opportunity for some blue collar workers to experience wage profiles that are in the West generally confined to white collar professions.

3.3 A flexible core of permanent employees

If permanent employment was a universal feature labour would become a quasi-fixed factor in production and the room for adjusting costs would be confined to altering working hours or bonus payments. On the other hand, over-reliance on an open labour market also had disadvantages involving the amount of time taken to recruit extra workers, the need to train new entrants and the possibility that firms may have to bid higher wages to attract labour. Hence Japanese management holds out a promise of permanent employment to a core of selected employees whose numbers are 'limited to a cyclically justifiable minimum' (Taira 1962 p.168). This core can then be supplemented by relying on the open labour market to provide temporary or seasonal workers but also by increasing the share of orders given to subcontractors.

For a selected core, employment guarantees are very much an informal bargain as Japanese labour law forbids work contracts to be extended beyond one year. However even for male university graduates in large firms there is the prospect of retirement at the relatively early age of 55 although there has been pressure from the Ministry of Labour in recent years for this to be raised. There is some indication that the official retirement age is increasing but this may be a mixed blessing for middle-aged labour because of the increasing pressure to take voluntary early retirement! Part of the impetus behind these voluntary decisions also comes coincidentally from the Ministry of Labour who argue that rationalization requires a change in 'the concept of labour cost from being a fixed to a variable one' (Hamada 1980 p.400). As the most expensive section of the labour force, middle-aged workers have faced very severe pressures to terminate their employment. As the President of a leading textile firm put it 'When the ship is about to be wrecked heavier cargoes should be thrown off to sea' (quoted in Tsuda 1980 p.2). One effect of these pressures can be seen in the age structure of male employees in manufacturing where in small firms over one-third of employees are over 50 years, whereas the proportion in large firms is less than a fifth. Thus even for the privileged few the length of time during which they can enjoy their peak earnings is being restricted. Where once lifetime employment was said to be the key factor behind high productivity levels, the need to reduce labour costs now means that 'Lifetime employment is becoming something of a curse to Japanese industries' (*JTW* 12/3/83).

For workers in small firms employment guarantees are very rare, working hours are longer and safety records poor. In the iron and steel industry for example subcontractors not only employ a greater proportion of older workers but the gap between their working hours and those in parent companies lengthened from 2 per cent to 14 per cent between 1960 and 1978. This pattern is common among small firms generally where only one in 25 use a five-day week relative to one in three large companies. Paid holidays are 25 per cent fewer in small firms and only half of this allowance is actually taken. With longer hours at work and less investment in safety devices, the frequency of industrial injuries in small firms is twelve times the rate in large firms. (*Japanese Industrial Relations Series*, 1981 p.9). Indeed 75 per cent of fatalities in the iron and steel industry were reported in subcontracting firms during the 1970s (Shirai 1983 p.74). With less extensive retirement pension or company welfare schemes, those 16 per cent of males who in 1979 had spent in excess of 20 years in one small firm paid a heavy price for their continuity of employment.

The experience of older workers seen in large firms shows how tenuous is the reality of lifetime employment and the working conditions in small firms serves as a reminder of the human costs of long tenure. It seems clear then that 'for the majority of workers lifetime employment is a wishful ideal rather than an established convention' (Aoki 1984 p.6). Nevertheless the ideal is important if labour is encouraged to believe that it is a desirable norm and social surveys show that over 85 per cent of employees express the desire to spend their whole working career with just one firm. In the years before the oil crisis dismissals were frequently justified by arguing that individuals did not merit tenure because they lacked commitment or because of their poor eductional qualifications. Great weight is still given to both of these factors but since the mid-1970s even higher qualifications have not guaranteed continued employment.

In recent years dismissals have been justified much more in terms of the need to rationalize the labour force in the face of external economic problems which are compounded by Japan's ageing population. With the longest life expectancy in the world the Japanese have become obsessed with the burdens this places on private employers, their employees and the state. Dismissals are now explained as an inevitable response to pressures beyond managerial control be they the result of higher taxes to pay for the public finance deficit or the need to introduce even greater levels of mechanization to meet world competition. That business and the state have spent so much effort in explaining why employment has to be more flexible is testament to their previous success in establishing lifetime employment as a longstanding cultural practice. What will be more difficult to sustain is the expectation that labour should show total dedication to work now that lifetime employment is becoming ever more the exception.

3.4 The firm as a surrogate family

The notion that the Japanese are a nation of workaholics who are willing to sacrifice their personal lives for the good of their company has become a popular image. Not only do the Japanese work 10 per cent longer than in the UK, 15 per cent longer than in France or the US and 25 per cent longer than West Germany but absentee levels are less than one-fifth of those recorded in the EEC. Days lost through labour disputes between 1973 and 1983 were also much fewer at one-third UK rates, one-seventh Italian and one-tenth those recorded in the US. After work leisure time appears to be dominated by association with colleagues such that various surveys show that one-half of male employees interviewed ate supper outside their home twice or more each week.

While many of these may be social occasions, work groups especially in large companies may often stay on late to participate in quality control circles or zero defect clubs. There are up to four million quality control circle participants in Japanese industry and in large companies two in five workers are members. Quality consciousness is said to be very high among Japanese workers who endeavour to eliminate components that are rejected as substandard. Each smaller work group attempts to perform better than their rival groups in both quality control and in the number of suggestions they offer to improve productivity. Workplace harmony is enhanced by communal sports clubs, company vacation resorts, one-class cafeterias and the absence of status barriers within the plant. There is an hierarchical structure, but managerial authority is respected as a benign guardian of company interests. Corporate identification with workers knowing their place is in short 'a managers Nirvana' (Galenson 1974 p.697).

Whether or not this picture is a stereotype, it is clearly one which is frequently used to explain why labour productivity in Japanese industry is so high. The association of productivity levels with the extent of company commitment has been a theme among writers who have suggested that elements of the Japanese system should be incorporated into management practices in Western companies. But there is also a tendency in Japan itself to explain economic success by stressing the connections between social attitudes and productivity.

Following the work of social anthropologists on group dependence, company loyalty is said to give the Japanese much greater emotional satisfaction than overt individualism. Loyalty to the company means respecting the authority of management whose position reflects their length and quality of service. Therefore diligence is an 'expression of a uniquely Japanese cultural pattern of strong group solidarity and loyalty to the company on which the employees life depends' (Atsumi 1979 p.63).

In this kind of analysis the firm is often represented as a family in which respect for male elders is expressed by using seniority as the least disruptive and most predictable basis for internal promotion. As one is not supposed to leave a family no matter what the dispute or argument, so a lifetime of commitment to the firm is expected from workers. Seniority promotions and group bonuses act as motivating mechanisms and management displays its concern with the well-being of company employees through the array of company welfare benefits. Cohesion is maintained by building up a structure of consensual decision-making to make every individual feel an important participant. This system of industrial relations 'is consistent with and is based on very fundamental and very longstanding patterns in Japanese society . . . the company is the recipient of the kind of identification and loyalty that is the basis of family organisation' (Abegglen 1973 p.28).

The comparison between workplace and family relations encouraged writers like Abegglen, Khan and Vogel to place this feature at the centre of their explanations of how and why Japan differs from other Western capitalist societies. However their interpretation has been criticized on several counts which show that 'the family-firm analogy is misleading and generally overworked; its character is usually symbolic or ideological rather than descriptive' (Fruin 1980 p.432). This does not mean though that the analogy is unimportant in mobilising habits of deference or in raising individual awareness of the importance that is attached to company loyalty.

Critics of the corporate family model have tended to suggest that it applies more to large firms where promises of permanent employment are more likely to promote corporate identification. While this is to some extent true, it does not mean that workers in small firms are not expected to show family-style loyalties. In fact in many small firms the sense of identification with the family is real indeed because employment may be confined to kin relations. What is missing from small firms is the sense of participation in decision-making as the more intimate working relations between owners and their family result in more authoritarian demands for personal obedience. Even in large firms the reality of consensual decision-making has been dubbed a ceremonial ritual which merely persuades those most affected to feel they are participants. Thus suggestions are initiated from the top which are then presented in detail by lower level employees in order to make acceptance of their consequences a less troublesome process.

It also seems apparent that in overemphasizing harmonious labour relations, the extent of industrial conflict in Japan may be underestimated. Strike statistics by themselves may not reflect the often violent background to the annual Spring wage negotiations. Although strikes tend to be of a shorter duration they are concentrated around this key period when they are accompanied by picketing, working slowly to the rule book and the physical harassment of managers. What is perhaps peculiar to Japan is the way industrial conflict precedes negotiations and takes the form of ceremonial sabre rattling. Industrial disputes are also much more likely to be confined within a single company and although such disputes cast doubt on the image or harmony, they do show the continuing importance of enterprise-specific industrial relations.

Effective participation and industrial peace may not be the rule in all companies but this does not mean that the company loses its central place in the lives of its employees. What remains to be explored is how far labour gives loyalty as a voluntary commitment. If vertical loyalties are so important to the Japanese, why are songs, slogans, badges and other ceremonies needed to raise company consciousness? The presence of aggression rooms where workers can relieve their frustration on plastic effigies of managers might indicate that loyalty is 'perishable and the tremendous fuss about loyalty results not from its spontaneous presence but the need to nurture it' (Woronoff 1983 p.68). In some ways loyalty is perishable because the promises of permanent employment in return for commitment are not kept. Recognizing the possibility that consent and consensus might not be a customary social practice raises the issue of whether Japanese workers are 'passively responding to the ideological insistence of those in positions of authority' (Sugimoto 1982 p.5).

Critics of the firm as a cooperative family have produced a more penetrating assessment of Japanese industrial relations which shows them to be less unique than they at first appear. Management by participation and the delegation of decision-making is a technique commonly used in bureaucratic organizations to reduce feelings of powerlessness or alienation among employees. Similarly large corporations in the West have attempted to reduce undue rates of labour mobility among key workers by offering incremental wage scales or by placing contractual restrictions on their movement to rival firms. Yet despite similar tendencies elsewhere it does appear that conformity to company goals is demanded from Japanese workers to a greater extent. The rewards for those who do conform, and the penalties on those who do not, are justified in terms of a cultural tradition which places the group first and the individual second. Seen in this light the family analogy can still have a powerful influence although all its elements may not be an accurate description of reality. If there are material inducements offered to place the company first they are bound to affect motivation especially as they are backed by sanctions against those who do not display cooperative attitudes.

The work of social anthropologists is important in offering a guide to the ways in which management legitimizes their authority by recourse to tradition. Those who question or reject managerial prerogative can be accused of a selfish rejection of Japanese values in favour of alien Western individualism: 'an obligation of mutual attachment between firm and employee [is] Sanctioned by what is seen as tradition, morally correct and emblematic of Japanese culture' (Clark 1979 p.175).

3.5 Company loyalty: voluntary acceptance or obligatory requirement?

In a society where the uniqueness of Japan's past weighs heavily, employers are able to justify their demands for personal loyalty and sacrifice in terms of longstanding cultural practices. However, 'Like other peoples the Japanese are not averse to inventing traditions' (Karsh and Levine 1973 p.13). Although there are some dissenters, it seems to be accepted that a lifetime of attachment to one company together with seniority promotions and group bonus schemes for all workers did not become a common practice until the 1950s. Traces of all three elements have been found in isolated cases before then so it is perhaps exaggerating to say that an entirely new tradition was invented. It is probably more accurate to say that as a package the new employment system used traditional symbols to make the unfamiliar appear customary. 'In the process of responding to problems people look selectively at their values and historical traditions and select those parts which will reinforce the sort of structure that they think will solve their problems' (Patrick 1975 p.187). What sort of problems provoked the integration of various cultural symbols in to a new package of employment practices?

At the risk of oversimplifying, the new style of labour relations were designed to overcome a high turnover of skilled workers, intense industrial conflict and a lack of motivation and commitment that was said to be the cause of Japan's reputation as a producer of shoddy goods. In other words those very characteristics that are said to be proscribed by the importance the Japanese attach to group loyalty and deference to authority. Manufacturing industry had been particularly affected by very high rates of inter-firm mobility during the inter-war years when average turnover of skilled labour was more than 50 per cent *per annum*. Employers therefore sought to stabilize labour turnover with a package of inducements for key workers in order to insulate their internal labour market from the competition of rival firms. A lifetime of commitment though required not just higher rewards or the promise of permanent employment, but also some limitation on the ease with which labour could move to other employers.

One way of reducing the marketability of labour was to limit a worker's property rights in a particular job or skill. By establishing the practice of job rotation workers become generalists so that their skills and experience are specific to particular firms and therefore less transferable. The promise of security and the expectation that wages would rise with promotion and seniority were offered as the reward for sacrificing the ability to move easily between employers. With positive inducements to continuous employment in one firm and severe constraints on mobility, it is hardly surprising that Japanese rates of labour turnover are now lower than in the West.

The development of the new package was supported by an extension of welfare provision to all regular employees as an indication that management was replacing their old authoritarian image with that of a benevolent or sympathetic parent. This is not to say that workers necessarily believed or accepted the new image of employers especially as during the 1950s memories of the pre-war era were clearly resonant. It may be more pertinent to think of their pragmatic acceptance of the new system. Any attempt to establish how far individuals comply with the ideology of the firm as a family is fraught with difficulty because motives are likely to vary. Some may feel coerced into company-centred behaviour, some may accept for instrumental reasons because there is no alternative while others may see the family analogy as the ideal structure for industrial relations. But because 'the ideological equivalency of firm and family has been transformed into a post-war simile of cultural proclivity' (Fruin 1980 p.447). Japanese workers are encouraged into a greater sense of dependency on their firm and their immediate work groups. It is sometimes argued that the firm has actually replaced the family as the central focus of social existence. Whether this is out of personal preference or a sense of obligatory requirement remains an intriguing and much debated question.

Association with colleagues after working hours could be taken as an indication of the priority given to company matters but it may be reluctantly undertaken. Those who place the company second to private or domestic interests are often accused of possessing little ambition and become an object of contempt. Younger workers living in company dormitories have little opportunity to escape from the affairs of their firm and from an early age their leisure time is dominated by work colleagues. Working, living and playing together in the knowledge that this may continue for many years to come increases the pressure to conform to the wishes of the group.

In a similar fashion a refusal to participate in quality control circles through which management make labour responsible for product quality, is taken as a sign of selfishness. At Toyota at least this added burden meant that QC participation was seen as a ritual necessity 'to keep management off our backs' (Cole 1979 p.163). Exactly how much initiative labour exercises in QC operations does vary but in many cases labour has to meet a target of suggestions on an agenda set by management and coordinated by foremen. Rather than embodying the principle of voluntary participation QCs may 'in practice be semi-compulsory' (Tokunaga 1983 p.324).

The pressure to engage in after-work activities can be intense as it has both social and financial dimensions. Bonus payments in general serve to promote involvement in the company but the share of each individual is determined by their own performance and that of their work group. Any lack of required work effort by an individual will affect the immediate group bonus and so peer pressure can be significant. Free riders may be ostracized because their colleagues can easily detect uncooperative attitudes to the company. Personal evaluations occur bi-annually and are used to assess both changes in the basic wage and individual bonus payments. Seniority as we have seen has less to do with age *per se* than promotion either to a higher position or within a grade. In all aspects of pay and promotion the personal evaluation is critical and it takes account not just of performance at the current job but desirable personality traits such as creativity, emotional maturity and ability to cooperate with others. Evaluations may also be made of the whole work group so that judgements are made of workers' attitudes and performance at both levels.

The role of foremen or front-line supervisors in these evaluations is a central one and it developed during the 1950s as an integral part of efforts to promote QC activities. Foremen are promoted from the ranks of production workers and as pivotal intermediaries they have quasi-managerial status. Although foremen attempt to act as parental elders or trusted friends to the groups within their charge, their evaluation function ensures that all corners of the plant are subject to the gaze of management. Any individual display of selfish or uncooperative attitudes can lead to the allocation of jobs that carry low prestige, smaller annual increments, more limited promotion prospects and which convey a humiliating stigma in the eyes of colleagues. In many cases these changes then result in 'voluntary' withdrawal from the company.

There is then tremendous financial and social pressure on individual workers which can be used to account for high levels of commitment to the company. These same pressures help to explain why vacations are not taken and long hours are accepted as any individual decision to take a holiday or finish work on time places a burden on the rest of the work group. It also seems that the pressures have increased since the 1970s as manufacturing firms especially have reduced their labour force and no worker wants to be nominated for early retirement or transfer. Promotion opportunities have also been restricted and in the competition for higher status positions, personal merit evaluation is now given greater weight in determining pay and position.

Diligence at work then may have more to do with the consequences of non-cooperation than it does with internalizing the primacy of company interest. Dismissal or even voluntary separation from a large company once a worker has reached the age of 30 is unlikely to result in recruitment to a similar position in another large firm. Such mobility may carry the stigma of personal failure or a defective personality that are said to be the result of 'soiling one's *curriculum vitae*' (Nakane 1973 p.111). In any case the financial penalties of moving are sufficient to deter many especially as the inferior wages and working conditions in small firms are widely appreciated.

Company commitment and the willingness to remain with the same firm for long periods may therefore be underpinned by the prospect of heavy sacrifices that accompany the alternatives. Certainly the lower levels of Japanese public welfare make even temporary periods of unemployment appear a bleak proposition. Even those employed in small firms have to accept the limited rewards and the lower level of company welfare benefits if they are to fill the void left by limited state welfare provision. The absence of alternatives to becoming highly dependent on private companies may leave little choice but to accept the parameters set by the ideology of the firm as a family.

3.6 The formation of an enterprise union structure

So far labour has been treated as a passive agency responding to the pressures of market forces and managerial authority but how has labour reacted collectively to the loss of property rights in particular skills? If lifetime employment is so limited, to what extent have labour unions fought to widen its coverage? Unions in Japan have had a major influence on the way the labour market is structured, but this reflects principally the fact that union membership is in large part confined to regular workers in large firms. Therefore unions in representing the interests of their immediate membership have played an important role in supporting the pervasiveness of the company culture.

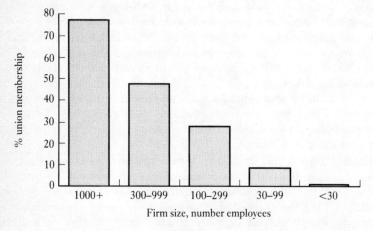

Figure 3.8 Union membership in Japan by firm size, 1979
Source: Steven, 1983, p. 199

Unions in Japan are, with a few exceptions, organized separately by enterprise or where a company has several plants through a federation of plant branches. Although most enterprise unions are affiliated to a number of national labour federations, industrial or trade unions which include workers from many different firms make up only a tiny proportion of Japanese labour unions. All non-managerial personnel belong to the same union, but the privilege of membership is confined to regular workers. Overall union membership at 27.6 per cent in 1988 is comparable with the US but is well below European levels, but what is more significant is its distribution. Figure 3.8 illustrates for 1979 the dominance of large firms in private sector unions. To put this data into perspective, of the 25 million workers in firms employing less than 100 only 5.4 per cent belong to a union. The restriction of membership to regular workers means that less than one in seven private sector union members are women and the bulk of these will cease to be members when they follow the convention of 'retirement' to child raising by the age of 30. With such a concentration of union representation it is not unreasonable to conclude that 'Labour unions are so structured and their membership distributed in such a way as to defend the privileges of the elite' (McGown 1980 p.111).

Any assessment of the impact of labour unions requires us to consider not only their influence on the wages and conditions of their members but also how this affects non-members in the same firm and labour in general. The separation of unions by enterprise may lead them to show an 'excessive identification with the interests of the firm and subordination to the authority of management' (Cole 1971 p.260) or in other words to be unions 'by appointment'. However there is a case for considering the role of unions in upholding and maintaining labour rights more generally. For example, the new constitution bestowed by the US Occupation in 1946 included legal protection for organized labour. This replaced the pre-war notion of duty to the employer and the state, with individual rights to minimum standards of employment and collective bargaining. In a variety of ways these rights were re-interpreted from the later 1940s and this has been taken as an indication that 'duty' remains the norm as 'Japanese business has still not accepted a union's right to speak for its members' (Halliday 1975 p.221). Consequently the regular use of the National Labour Relations Commission by enterprise unions renews the 'certification of their legitimacy by government institutions' (Hanami 1983 p.172). The fact that unions feel it necessary to reassert their inalienable rights to organize labour may be indicative of the threats they perceive. But in the process of renewing their legitimacy they may at the same time uphold general labour rights.

The annual Spring wage offensive fought initially by the larger unions could be said to establish the benchmark for wage increases throughout Japanese industry. Here bargaining on behalf of their own members may have real if indirect effects on non-members. So against the narrow focus of the impact of enterprise unions within their own firms we need to consider how far their achievements are filtered down to small firms where formal labour representation is minimal.

Enterprise unions along with other elements in the association of the firm with the family, developed out of the political turmoil and economic devastation that followed the end of the Pacific War in 1945. In these years of prolonged crisis, the structure of industrial relations was crystallized around separate unions in each enterprise, the partial incorporation of age related wage profiles and a determination to make public sector workers an exception to the constitutional provision for collective bargaining rights.

Aggregate economic indicators give but a partial insight into the extent of devastation after the war because of the shattering emotional impact of Japan's unconditional surrender. The economy had been close to collapse even before Atomic bombs were dropped on Hiroshima and Nagasaki, and the surrender itself coincided with one of the worst rice harvests for decades. Defeat meant the loss of colonial food imports and the allied bomb damage to 75 per cent of urban housing together with the famine saw many Japanese returning to rural areas in a desperate search for food. The general price level consequently rose by 40 per cent per month in the first six months of peace. Even this rate of increase in the official price indices hardly records the real impact as large quantities of food were only available on the black market. Against this background the main concern of Japanese labour was with the basic struggle to live, and to stay alive they needed an income from work.

Production was chaotic partly because equipment had been grossly undermaintained during the war but also because manufacturers were busily hoarding stocks of materials. Fears that the US occupation would wreak vengeance on those who had assisted the war effort, brought about the sabotage of industrial plant and industrial output fell to less than a third of pre-war levels. The fears of retribution were heightened by a directive from Washington not to assume any responsibility for the rehabilitation of Japan nor to assume the obligation to maintain any particular standard of living. Even though this policy was reversed by 1947, the problems of supplying basic necessities remained immense especially with an extra three million mouths to feed when troops and colonial workers returned to Japan. Between the surrender and December 1948 the Tokyo Chamber of Commerce retail price index rose by 4000 per cent and it is estimated that black market prices increased at double this rate. If these post-war years were to be so crucial to the formation of the post-war employment structure, economic dislocation provided an atmosphere in which self-preservation was an understandable objective.

Economic chaos was only one element in the social turmoil that exploded when the new constitution removed the previously draconian constraints on individual rights. The universal franchise and freedom for all political parties saw the development of mass support for socialist and communist parties that had previously been suppressed. With labour rights now guaranteed, union membership rose from 7 per cent to 50 per cent between 1946 and 1948 and organized labour attempted to coordinate the attack on food stockpiling, to use strikes to force management to re-start production and to demonstrate in the streets against those wartime leaders still in power. High levels of public violence eventually forced the US 'occupying forces to take the necessary steps to control and remedy such a deplorable situation' (Yamamoto 1981 p.30).

To the authorities, one of the most disturbing trends was the incidence of production control by workers in companies where management refused to re-open factories. Despite the rhetoric of slogans looking to the socialization of industry, such moves were often based on the basic need to continue working to protect living standards. Without the roots of extensive planning 'these developments did not add up to an articulate challenge to the restoration of bourgeois rule in Japan' (Armstrong, Glynn and Harrison 1984 p.39). What production control did achieve was the combination of blue and white collar labour in ways that reflected the essence of enterprise unions. To an extent these 'mixed' unions of office and production workers built on the wartime associations which had been sponsored by the state to suppress opposition to the war effort. Although these associations were formally banned by the US Occupation, their organizational basis was used to support the development of a collective labour voice in firms.

Two broad alternatives appeared to face labour in these crisis years: either to use united inter-industry unions to maintain a subsistence income or to concentrate activity within particular firms. In some ways the latter offered more short-term gains and also suffered less opposition from the Japanese state and the US Occupation. An agreement in 1946 negotiated by the Electric Power Workers Unions, the *Densan* system, laid the basis for firm-specific bargaining. In order to secure an income that reflected the subsistence needs of families, wages were to be set according to age and family responsibilities. Once the basic wage was agreed, increments would be given each year up to the age of 40 and additional payments made for each family member with a 25 per cent component left for job performance. This agreement offered management some discretion in relating wages to individual ability but it aimed to guarantee labour a basic income that would rise with age and family subsistence needs. The age component was essentially a revival from pre-war wage systems but the 25 per cent merit components soon grew in weight giving management more opportunity to distinguish between individual workers. In the short term though what was crucial for labour was the offer of more secure living standards.

The alternative option, promoted by an intriguing coalition of US Labour Advisors and the Japan Communist Party was to press for a basic minimum wage across all industries with additional earnings to be related to productivity not age. US labour experts warned that age scales would encourage the use of younger workers and would unfairly discriminate against women who would not be given family allowances. Japanese opponents of *Densan* wanted inter-industry bargaining to improve wages for all workers by collective action. A minimum wage was established by the minority Socialist government in 1947 but it suffered from two significant weaknesses compared to *Densan*. First the basic minimum was set at a very low level and was related to pre-war wages thus not reflecting the very steep increase in the prices of basic necessities. Secondly, the minimum was actually interpreted as a maximum, and even then the fact that this was an average wage for each firm left management with control over the way this was distributed among individual employees. *Densan* tended initially to limit managerial discretion much more and thus seemed to offer a better alternative for labour.

In some ways, though, the choice between the two options was constrained by the association of general collective bargaining with the policies of the Communist Party. From 1947 to 1950 there was a contest over the rival merits of enterprise agreements against collective industrial bargaining but the *Densan* precedent had the support of the US occupation, the Japanese state and local employers. With hindsight, therefore, only one outcome was likely although the struggle was often violent and bloody. Many writers have identified the increasing intervention of the US Occupation in labour affairs with the anti-communist spirit in Washington that grew partly in parallel with Mao's growing dominance of China. Certainly the Occupation authorities did take a more interventionist stance, but it is important to remember that US policy directives were the outcome of collaboration with Japanese bureaucrats.

The continuity of unpurged sections of the bureaucracy in economic affairs has been highlighted in the study of MITI (Johnson 1982). Similar continuity of personnel in the Home and Welfare Ministries that administered labour affairs meant continuity in attitudes towards the 'obstruction of trade union organization and activity' (Garon 1984 p.443). About 80 per cent of officials in these ministries survived the US purge and went on to cooperate with the Occupation in containing the labour movement into 'sound' de-politicized unions. Their advice defined political unions as those attempting to follow Community Party policies which sought to replace enterprise-specific agreements with inter-industry collective bargaining in order to widen the class struggle.

Anti-communism thus united the interests of the US Occupation, the Japanese state and private employers especially in the face of a united front of public and private sector workers. The first significant manifestation of joint labour action was halted by General MacArthur in January 1947 when he banned a general strike. In the years that followed labour unity was undermined by further US directives prohibiting national strikes and by revisions to Trade Union laws which sought to isolate those labelled as 'militants'. Effectively this meant sponsoring 'democratic, autonomous and responsible' unions as a bulwark against Communist influence. For bureaucrats this revived pre-war preferences, for the US Occupation this matched their cold war mood and for employers this delivered a labour movement which would be willing to accept enterprise bargaining.

As the main force behind united labour action, the public sector unions felt the full force of US–Japanese reaction when amendments were made to the constitutional guarantees of labour rights. Japanese bureaucrats had long argued against the extension of labour rights to state employees and MacArthur accepted their views in 1948 by depriving civil servants of the right to strike and to bargain collectively. Workers in other public enterprises were also prevented from striking although this did not stop strikes by postal and railway workers. The continuation of labour disputes in both of these sectors heralded a wave of dismissals using anti-communism as a justification. Neither were dismissals confined to the public sector as labour throughout Japan was forced to choose between the labels of militant or moderate according to the degree of support for industrial against enterprise unions.

The political motives for dismissal were in some cases hidden by economic causes after 1949 as a drastic programme of deflationary policies were imposed to rehabilitate the Japanese economy. Senator Dodge from Chicago was given the task of restoring financial stability and he pursued his task in a manner that would have impressed even the most orthodox Friedmanites in his home town. Balanced state budgets, tight controls of the money supply, wage controls and improved tax collection certainly reduced the rate of inflation but at the cost of recession and unemployment. These policies had a profound and lasting effect on the shape of post-war economic policy but in the short term they provided a very useful pretext to extend mass dismissals of labour to over a million workers (Kishimoto 1968 p.28).

Whether dismissals were part of the 'red purge' or the result of deflationary policies, opposition to enterprise-based labour relations was effectively broken and any joint labour reaction was condemned as radical communism. Anti-communist elements were mobilized by the support given to 'moderate' labour federations by the state and the Japanese Federation of Employers which had re-surfaced from US prohibition in 1948. *Sohyo* (The General Council of Trade Unions of Japan) was formed in 1950 as an alternative labour federation but it was hardly a centralized unit rather it was a loose umbrella organization of autonomous enterprise unions. The formation of *Sohyo* did however establish the practice of encouraging second unions to displace what management regarded as unacceptably militant and uncooperative attitudes in existing unions.

3.7 Enterprise unions in a segmented labour market

As enterprise unions began to dominate labour representation in the private sector so also did the wave of mass dismissals allow management to restrict eligibility for union membership. Selective dismissals removed individual recalcitrants and the practice of confining membership to regular employees was confirmed by enterprise unions who were desperate to preserve employment for limited groups of workers. In the years of post-war instability enterprise unions placed job security for the few ahead of fraternal obligations to temporary colleagues or the general labour movement. Promises of permanent employment for a protected minority were the reward for the loss of marketable skills and union cooperation was forged against the ever-present threat of managerial sponsorship of second alternative unions.

It is possible to see historical traces of past employment practices in the use of age/wage scales, corporate family identity and promises of permanent employment. In fact these traces allowed these three elements, in what has become known as the Japanese employment system, to be projected as customary practices. Employers' federations for example guided firms towards internal negotiations and bureaucrats 'joined forces with business to defend the state and social order' (Garon 1984 p.455).

As a seal of approval to the promotion of company identity, the state established the Japan Productivity Centre in 1955 to promote the trend towards more cooperative labour relations. In the process, the role of foremen institutionalized the closer association of shopfloor workers and management. Shimada has called the process 'a monumental achievement from the viewpoint of social engineering' (1984 p.20). While it is possible to argue that this statement exaggerates the degree of deliberate planning involved, the new norms did engineer the effective assimilation of labour into the company domain. Federations that represent enterprise unions have not, as interest groups, had the same access to the state as employers' organizations. But the state has promoted 'corporatism without labour' (Pempel and Tsunekawa 1979) by arguing that labour interests are better represented by employers because they speak for all the members of their company. To what extent do employers' representations of company interest reflect the aspirations of union members and how far have these aspirations been met? What influence have enterprise unions had within their companies?

At first glance unions do seem to have succeeded in improving the wages and working conditions of their members. Differentials in pay between white- and blue-collar workers are narrower than in the West and status distinctions seem less evident. Both the bonus scheme and the provision of welfare benefits have been extended to all regular workers rather than being restricted to management. We have also noted the longer tenure in large firms where union representation is strongest, thus giving members access to higher parts of the earnings profile. Total earnings certainly rose sharply and real wages increased by more than 300 per cent from 1955 to 1975. Although real wages did not rise as fast as real productivity and not all union members benefited from extended periods of continuous employment, the achievements of enterprise unions are not unimpressive.

Great emphasis is often placed on the way these achievements reflect the greater degree of consultation between Japanese unions and management. It is important though to distinguish between consultation and bargaining rights. Originally labour–management councils were promoted by the Japan Productivity Centre to ensure that information was exchanged on proposed changes to production methods in order to smooth the path to improved productivity. But consultation is 'formally, strictly distinguished from collective bargaining. It is the place for . . . information sharing and not for bargaining or making collective agreements' (Shimada 1984 p.9). Consultation was conceded by management in return for acceptance of their prerogative in deciding the agenda. There is no doubt that this system greatly helped the operation of quality control circles, but there is disagreement about whether consultation is really a joint process or simply a ritual structure for disseminating decisions. The agenda of consultation councils has widened in recent years to include general working conditions and fringe benefits. But this extension does of course remove these items from the area of union negotiation or bargaining. Equally important is the trend in some large companies for bargaining to be confined to those matters left unresolved by consultation so restricting the extent of joint bargaining where unions have more control of the agenda.

One key area that has remained as the focus of union bargaining concerns any proposed changes to working hours or employment. The determination to prevent the dismissal of union members has been seen as the bottom line in negotiations with management, although this has not prevented the discharge or transfer of older workers since the mid-1970s. If unions have been able to negotiate changes in the total quantity of labour losses, they appear to have little say in job changes within and between plants in the same company. Job rotation and intra-firm mobility is very common in Japan as labour is not recruited to a specific skill, but the union has little influence on which particular workers are to be transferred. This has been an increasing problem since the 1970s when individuals have been moved by large firms to other areas on a temporary basis, leaving their families behind.

Although enterprise unions do play an important part in negotiating general changes in wages they play a much smaller role in the way these changes are distributed to individual employees. A company bonus may be negotiated collectively but the individual receives a payment which is calculated in proportion to the basic wage according to personal evaluations. The part played by enterprise unions in personal evaluations does vary widely. In some companies the 'actual distribution is left entirely to management's discretion' (Evans 1971 p.132) while at Nissan for example union officials are included in the process of evaluating candidates for promotion. Such differences seem to revolve around the variations in the function of foremen, who in some companies take on a hybrid role of shop steward and representative of management. In such cases promotion 'is influenced by the union officers' own evaluation of each member, that is to say there is the union officers own discriminative control' (Takagi 1981 p.703).

It is exactly here in the middle ground that the distinction between union and management or between foreman and superintendent is so difficult to discern. Foremen have achieved their status by displaying continuous commitment to the company and if they show loyalty to management policies they can expect promotion to superintendent. Hence one survey in 1978 discovered over two-thirds of management personnel had formerly been union officials. As union officials know that their own promotion depends on their ability to mobilise moderate labour attitudes, it has been argued that cooperative labour relations are 'little more than a form for company domination' (Cole 1971 p.259).

There have been numerous instances reported of management interference in union elections where voting against an official candidate is 'tantamount to a declaration of lack of confidence in management as well as union officialdom' (Galenson 1974 p.698). Any failure to produce unanimous resolutions or voting records means that shop foremen are held to account because this reveals a breakdown in the solidarity of their work group, therefore voting often takes place in union offices in full view of officials. At Nissan the 99.95 per cent voting record reflects 'a unanimity of opinion rivalled only by elections in the Soviet Union' (Armstrong, Glynn and Harrison 1984 p.386). Opposition to official union candidates who have the tacit approval of management can, without secret ballots, easily lead to blocked promotion or personal harassment. There is even evidence that employees may be pressed into supporting company candidates in public elections such as those in Kawasaki City in 1983 (*The Guardian* 28/3/83).

These may be untypical incidents but they do reflect the pressures exerted on union members when they are so dependent on a single enterprise. Equally the power of companies to sponsor second unions acts as a warning of the possible consequences of non-cooperation. A series of disputes in the 1950s were generated by the attempts of managers to confine collective bargaining by widening the context of non-negotiable consultative issues. At Hitachi in 1950, Toyota in 1951, Nissan in 1953, Nihon Steel in 1954, Oji Paper in 1958 and in a violent dispute at Mitsui's Miike mine in 1960, management successfully mobilized moderate factions to split from enterprise unions. Even though 'such management involvement constitutes unfair labour practices and is strictly forbidden by Trade Union Law' (Shirai 1983 p.143) these disputes set the limits to negotiating rights. Ever since 1960 protracted strikes in the private sector have been rare and one explanation would surely stress the impact of this experience with second unions.

In the non-unionized sectors collective bargaining is, especially in small firms, said to be unnecessary as the closer working relations with owners means that employers can take a personal interest in working conditions. There are associations of workers in small firms that do attempt to bargain across firms in their area but they are not officially recognized as unions. 'Deterrents to their seeking certification no doubt lie in their ability to obtain improvements without going through the "red tape" of a labor relations commission qualifications examination' (Levine 1982 p.52). Another interpretation though might emphasize the opposition of employers who consider the need for a union to be an affront to their brand of personal paternalism. Consultation agreements are not unknown in small firms but where they exist they act as a replacement for collective negotiations. The relative weakness of small subcontractors who are tied to powerful parent companies, hardly provides a secure base for labour to exert collective effort to improve their lot. Not surprisingly the gap between wages in large and small firms has been widening in the years of slower growth since 1974.

It has been argued that enterprise unions do have an influence on the wages of non-members because their own wage settlement sets the norm for national wage increases. Labour contracts are renewed annually in Spring and this acts as a focus for a Spring Wage Offensive or *shunto*. Joint bargaining over annual wage increases was developed in the 1950s as a way of overcoming the weaknesses inherent in dispersed bargaining by enterprise. The leading labour federations coordinate joint action by supporting the claims of particular unions that lead the Spring Offensive. Their settlement is then taken to be the standard for other workers. For management this system concentrates bargaining into a predictable period during which 60 per cent of days lost through strikes occur. The regularity and predictability of disputes has in fact led some to argue that *shunto* represents a ceremonial ritual in which unions convince themselves that they are actually a powerful independent force.

The ceremonial aspect of *shunto* is stressed because of the way employers and the state coordinate the parameters within which the wage increases are negotiated. During the later 1970s for instance the Japanese state, like many Western states, established the basis for Spring negotiations in terms of the need to match wage increases to the rate of inflation. This strategy was bestowed on unions as the national interest and produced *shunto* settlements which reversed the previous emphasis on matching wages to the rate of increase in economic growth. In both cases it is arguable that the bands within which agreements were to be made were established before the Spring Offensive began, so raising doubts about how much influence unions exerted.

Assessments of how far *shunto* settlements affect wages in general are divided. Levine, for example, has argued that Spring wage changes 'quickly flow into almost all of the unionized sectors and then on into the non-unionized sectors' (1982 p.326). But it has to be remembered that the *shunto* norm acts only as a benchmark against which company performance is compared. Enterprise bargaining can easily alter the rates which are negotiated as the norm of particular companies from which the distribution to individuals is decided according to personal evaluation. Dore also reminds us that *shunto* concentrates on rates of change not wage levels 'thus leaving interfirm differentials much as they were before – as far from the European notion of a negotiated national market rate as ever' (1973 p.326). At best then, *shunto* settlements may standardize the upper limit in negotiations but the limit is very much influenced by the state, and they have done little to correct the inequalities between workers in large and small firms.

Japanese labour federations have consistently proclaimed their concern with representing the interests of all workers, but the results of their activities can give the impression of empty rhetoric. Attempts to secure reasonable retirement pay for all workers or to raise the official retirement age have not been very successful outside the large firms. Various proposals to include temporary or subcontracted employees in enterprise unions have been blocked for fear of diluting the gains to be achieved by regular workers. 'It is safe to say the positive desire to keep temporary workers as a separate unprotected buffer force comes from the employers, and that unions, with some quirks of conscience, see that it is in their members material interests to comply with the employers wishes' (Dore 1973 p.325). Equally the plight of women employees has been part of union rhetoric rather than action. Clark's assessment of one enterprise union is not at all untypical: 'The union rarely concerned itself with the disadvantages of women among the more concrete of which were their low pay and their very early age of compulsory retirement' (Clark 1979 p.195).

It seems therefore that the main efforts of enterprise unions 'has been directed towards improving the already considerable benefits secured by their own members who are overwhelmingly in the large company sector' (Shonfield 1984 p.113). But even within large firms the overwhelming pressures placed on workers to display cooperative and diligent attitudes places severe constraints on the independence of unions. Enterprise unions may view their role in reproducing labour market inequalities as a necessary evil, but they appear none the less to be unable or unwilling to resist the pressures to do just that.

By continuing to focus on the immediate interests of their members, enterprise unions seem to have accepted the parameters of segmented labour market. It is not at all the case that segmentation is peculiar to Japan although elsewhere in the West protected tenure for example, is more often the preserve of white-collar professionals. By extending similar employment guarantees to some blue-collar workers it is clear that the idea of unusually harmonious industrial relations where the firm is portrayed as a united family, holds an important place in ideological statements of why Japanese productivity levels are so high. Equally the association of educational achievement with employment in large companies legitimates employment in higher status categories of the labour market. Such meritocratic ideals persuades parents who cannot achieve lifetime employment status themselves, to press their children into intense study. As we shall see in Chapter 6 this background helps to explain the phenomenal burdens that Japanese children carry in their school days.

In promoting various elements of the so-called Japanese system of industrial relations, the state's role was initially designed to use the enterprise union structure to regulate what was said to be disruptive labour protest and later to disseminate the advantages the structure had for productivity growth. And, as the pattern of *shunto* wage bargaining indicates, enterprise union initiatives can be used to manage national norms for wage increases across the economy. This leads us to the heart of the debate on the economic role of the state and the next chapter will assess the extent to which the state merely supports existing market trends or whether it has led and guided these trends.

4

A Planned Market Economy

4.1 Eulogies for a liberal market economy

Over the past decade there has been a tendency among economists to minimize the role of the state in the contemporary Japanese economy. This trend seems to be closely connected to the general revival of support for the ideology of free market forces with its corollary of rolling back the growth of state interference. The Japanese example of limited state expenditure with consequentially lower tax burdens, has been linked in a causal fashion to its higher rates of economic growth in order to highlight 'this secret of strong growth for a shining future' (President Reagan addressing Japan's National Diet November 1983–quoted in K. Sato 1985 p.105). The publication of *Asia's New Giant* edited by two of the most distinguished US students of Japan most clearly confirmed the greater importance of market forces. 'The Japanese government has never taken the lead in directly encouraging the transfer of resources away from inefficient uses; rather this has occurred through the operations of the market place' (Patrick and Rosovsky 1976 p.46).

In the spirit of other Western studies of Japan at this time, the contributors to the Patrick and Rosovsky volume devoted part of their energies to establishing the lessons that the West can learn from Japan. As we saw in Chapter 1 this theme of learning lessons developed into a popular pastime after Vogel portrayed Japan as the *Number One* society in which the state merely provides a supportive 'framework within which private business can prosper' (1979 p.67). Following the lead given by both of these works, a great deal of recent analysis has sought to divert attention away from industrial policies which smooth the process of change in particular industries toward the impact of freer competition. Gone is the emphasis on growth-promoting trade controls and specially targeted sectors which have had little effect in comparison to the 'actions and efforts of private individuals and enterprises responding to the opportunities provided in quite free markets for commodities and labour' (Patrick 1977 p.239). Instead much greater weight in explaining Japanese economic performance is given to aggressive business attitudes to the importance of high levels of investment and to very high rates of individual saving. In addition more cooperative labour–management relations are founded on an individual work ethic unaffected by the disincentives that are said to follow in the wake of an over-burdening welfare state. Japan's remarkable rates of economic growth are then to be explained not by overt state intervention but by 'the huge 30–35 per cent of GNP that Japan has invested in the past several decades' (Schultze 1983 p.17).

Although the main thrust of the analysis which depicts Japan as the epitome of a liberal free market has come from the US, this interpretation is also popular among Japanese commentators. If there is any difference of emphasis on the role of market forces, it is based not on the current scene, but on the part the state played in the economic recovery of the 1950s. Liberalization starting in the 1960s and continuing at an accelerating rate in the 1970s, thereafter reduced the extent of state licensing controls over imports, foreign exchange, investment programmes and the use of foreign technology. Until the current era of unbridled international economic relations, the state undertook developmental functions to foster speedy recovery, but these functions have since been passed to the free market. In contemporary Japan 'most of the country's industrial activity is developing without the hand of government in a competitive economy . . . under the harsher more entrepreneurial conditions of the market' (Tsuruta 1983 p.48). Thus both in the West and in Japan analysis of the contemporary economy stresses the workings of unfettered free private enterprise.

Acceptable quantitative indicators of the size let alone the extent of state influence over the private markets in capitalist economies are, as we shall see, fraught with difficulty. Ultimately therefore any evaluation of the relative importance of private market forces against public intervention depends as much on normative values as it does on positive measurements. It is clear for instance that the shift in intellectual opinion on the need to diminish the role of the state has gathered support from the economic achievements of East Asian countries like Hong Kong, Japan, Singapore, South Korea and Taiwan where the 'invisible hand' of the market is said to reign supreme. The economic performance of these countries has received 'much admiration and many eulogies' (Sen 1983 p.12) which has then led to suggestions that their market-based systems should provide the guiding path for the West. In particular monetarist and supply-side economists have stressed the way a small state requires small contributions in the form of taxes which places less constraints on individual incentives. This also leaves capital markets free to supply funds for private investment rather than purchasing vast quantities of state bonds.

Equally important in the US context has been the desire to use the

Japanese example to challenge the assumptions of those in Congress and the labour unions who see stringent trade controls and a forceful industrial policy as the way to revitalize manufacturing industry. If it can be shown that Japan's vastly superior exports record is the result not of more state intervention but less, then it is argued that current US problems can only be corrected by restoring the supremacy of the market and reducing the distorting effect of Federal budget deficits. Therefore interpreting Japan as *the* model of successful market capitalism allows the judgement that interventionist policies are unnecessary. At the same time if Japanese experience goes to show what can be achieved with limited state involvement, this justifies the need to cut back interference by public agencies. If Japan could become so efficient without an overburdening state carefully planning industrial change, why should its competitors not do the same?

Within Japan there is, as we saw in Chapter 1, a good deal of self-satisfaction about Western adulation of its society as the model of vigour and private initiative. Particular pleasure is taken from Japanese immunity from the Western disease of a diminishing work ethic and low productivity caused, so it is said, by excessive taxation and an over-protective welfare state. This view has been especially vibrant among business leaders who have been at the centre of LDP policies to reduce even further the number of public employees in a programme of privatizing state enterprises in telecommunications and on Japan National Railways.

State officials have had a particular interest in derogating the extent of their own influence over economic affairs. In the recurrent bouts of Western complaints about the scale of Japanese trade surpluses, LDP ministers insist that the imbalance in trade is essentially due to the inefficiency of Western products and lack of marketing effort by overseas exporters rather than import restrictions. It is of course enormously helpful for the Japanese then to be able to support their case by referring to the analysis of Western commentators who confirm that 'the average level of tariff was lower in Japan than in the US and all members of the EEC' (OECD 1985 p.40). In the absence of tariffs, Japanese trade surpluses are portrayed as the outcome of rational domestic preferences for superior home-produced goods in a competitive market. Equally, those Western writers who have focused on the economic advantages of Japan's small state have provided invaluable evidence to support the case for cutting public expenditure to maintain the vigour of the private sector.

The association of Japan's economic performance with unfettered private enterprise has then provided justification for normative comments on the future role of the state both inside Japan and in the West. What has given these comments added credence has been the intellectual shift in favour of greater market incentives and the debate about how Japan managed to recover more quickly from the 1974 oil crisis. As many in the West have blamed their sluggish recovery on the distorting effects of increased public expenditure, the example of successful market-dominated economies like

Japan holds a crucial position in the general debate on the appropriate balance beween state intervention and free markets. In the rest of this chapter I will attempt to explore in more detail some of the assumptions and implications that follow from the current emphasis on a more limited economic role for the Japanese state.

In particular we need to ask in what sense is the Japanese state less interventionist than in other Western economies? Quantitative measures provide ambiguous evidence because although the Japanese state does indeed *consume* a smaller proportion of GNP in spending on public administration, defence, healthcare or housing, public *investment* is actually higher than other OECD countries. Placing more emphasis on Japan's peculiarly high rates of saving and investment also begs questions about how these high levels are maintained. To what extent are high levels of household savings themselves the result of state policies and how important have public financial institutions been in transferring savings to companies who need to borrow to finance their high investment levels?

Recent attempts to show that Japanese experience illustrates why interventionist policies are not necessary for rapid economic growth has tended to focus the debate fairly narrowly on industrial policy. Nurturing the expansion of new sectors and smoothing the decline of others is only one element of economic policy and the whole array of state management activities ought to be considered. For example one crucial reason why labour costs have been tied more closely to productivity levels in Japan has been the operation of an informal incomes policy where the state coordinates national norms for the annual spring wage offensive – *shunto*. In some ways this informal process has been more influential because it has not been tied to specific public agencies; instead it builds in the expectation that the national interest requires a coordinated approach to wage increases. What matters is the effect this process has had on relative labour costs. Whether the desired result is achieved by informal or indirect state coordination as opposed to formal or direct policy is in the end less significant.

The distinction between formal power and informal influence is crucial, though, to the argument that trade liberalization has eroded the ability of the Japanese state to intervene in the economy. While it is true that important controls have to a large extent been loosened and investment authorization schemes dismantled, this need not imply any lessening of state involvement. Formal power to intervene may have been eroded but informal cooperation and consultation remains pervasive. From a Western perspective the strength of the ideology of liberalism encourages antagonistic reactions from private firms who resent state interference with the rights of free enterprise. Hence more attention tends to be focused on formal powers needed to overcome such resentment. Such an adversarial framework may well be related to the way many Western states are said to have encroached on the rights of free enterprise after the unhindered market system provided the basis for industrialization in the last century. But Japan never experienced a *laissez-faire* stage of economic development and its history since the 1860s has been marked by more cooperative relations between the state and private business. This heritage, supported by specific institutions, has built up different attitudes to the legitimacy of state involvement. Therefore the erosion of formal state powers over Japanese industry since the 1960s has to be balanced by an examination of institutions which maintain the higher degree of collaboration between state officials and business representatives.

First, though, we should look at the sort of supportive environment the Japanese state has maintained to assist economic growth and how it merely 'accelerated trends already put into motion by the private market' (Patrick and Rosovsky 1976 p.47).

4.2 The state as investor rather than consumer

A generally accepted measure for the size of the public sector is difficult to find not least because of differences in the way aggregate economic data is presented. However the OECD has attempted to standardize the national accounts of its 24 members who are the leading capitalist economies. Table 4.1 presents data on the equivalent shares in each country's GDP for the

Table 4.1 Government expenditure as a percentage of GDP in the big seven OECD economies, annual average, 1960–86

	Consumption +	*Investment* +	*Transfers* =	*Total outlay*
United States	18.2	1.9	12.3	32.4
Japan	8.8	7.3	10.3	26.4
West Germany	17.3	3.9	19.2	40.4
France	14.3	3.9	24.4	42.6
United Kingdom	19.2	4.2	18.0	41.4
Italy	16.3	4.2	20.3	40.8
Canada	18.3	3.7	15.3	37.3
Smaller OECD av.	15.2	3.8	18.0	37.0

Source: OECD *Economic Outlook*, December 1982 and 1987

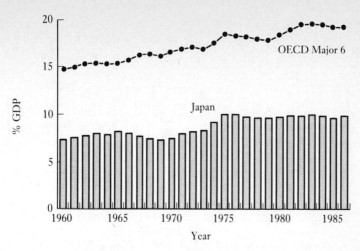

Figure 4.1 Government consumption expenditure as a percentage of GDP in
the Big Seven OECD economies, 1960–86
Source: *Economic Outlook*, OECD, December 1982 and 1987

main categories of government expenditure in the 25 years from 1960–86.
Column 1 covers current spending on goods and services and the contrast
over the whole period between Japan and the average for the other six
largest OECD countries is illustrated in Figure 4.1. The gap on current
spending has remained fairly stable such that the Japanese state has rarely
consumed resources at more than half the level of the other major
economies. In complete contrast Figure 4.2 shows that as a proportion of
gross domestic product government investment in Japan has consistently
exceeded the average of the other six by an equally wide margin. There
are some problems with the US data because part of their public investment
is included under public consumption. Nevertheless Japan's larger share
of state expenditure devoted to public investment rather than consumption
seems to be quite different than the general OECD pattern.

When considering the lower levels of government consumption in Japan
many economists choose to exclude defence spending because of the
unusual constitutional limitations bequeathed by the US occupation. Until
recently Japanese defence expenditure has been restricted to 1 per cent of
GDP in contrast to about 5 per cent in the US and about 3 per cent in
Europe. Therefore allowing for defence does close the gap in government
consumption, but if we assume that some public investment goes on defence
this should in theory widen the gulf between Japan and others who have
no formal limit on defence spending. However we juggle the data, we are
still left with Japan's noticeable 'enthusiasm for investing in the public
sector' (Simon 1986 p.9) in contrast to more limited current purchases of
goods and services.

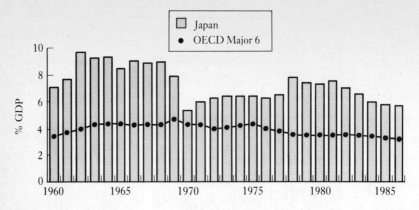

Figure 4.2 Public investment as a percentage of GDP in the Big Seven OECD economies, 1960–86
Source: Economic Outlook, December 1982 and 1987

Thoughout the past 25 years then Japanese public investment has been about twice the level of other Western economies and despite the cuts imposed on public spending in Japan during the mid-1980s the differential remains significant. A large proportion of this investment has been devoted to improving the infrastructure, especially in transport. Construction of roads, railways and new port facilities have been a priority in order to sustain the expansion of industry. Equally important has been public investment in the preparation of sites for private companies who are then able to re-locate their plant into integrated industrial complexes. Even in the service sector public investment has been important in developing real estate utilities around new railway stations to house department stores, hotels and offices.

One feature of rapid industrial expansion in Japan has been the ability of companies to lower average costs and increase productivity by operating within integrated units which house their own production facilities and that of subcontractors. Public investment in necessary utilities such as drainage and roads has sustained this process of integration by providing private companies with the opportunity to earn external economies of scale that follow from concentrating related firms within close spatial proximity. It is difficult to separate industrial from other beneficiaries of infrastructure investment, but the priorities appear to have been weighted towards activities that sustain increases in the private capital stock rather than social overhead investment. One could no doubt argue that individual citizens benefit from better transport facilities, but in general the comfort of passengers has had a lower priority than the needs of industrial users. It is not possible to cram more steel into a given piece of rolling stock but 'it is possible to crowd in three times the passenger capacity into an electric train'! (Economic

Survey of Japan, *EPA* 1963 p.35). Media coverage of rush-hour trains in urban Japan show that this overcrowding is not a thing of the past.

Despite the abrupt shift of concern about environmental pollution in Japan during the 1970s, public spending to correct negative externalities (such as congestion) or to provide more public goods with positive externalities, remains less significant. The lower levels of current spending by the state and the smaller share of public investment in social capital reflect this trend and provision for education, housing and healthcare are left more to the private market than in many Western countries. The public share of fixed investment in housing as a proportion of Japan's GNP has since the 1960s been about one-fifteenth of the total. State spending on education is approximately two-thirds of total spending compared to 90 per cent in the main OECD countries; public outlays on health and social security are but 60 per cent of outlays in the leading Western nations.

The Japanese state still maintains a preference for holding back as far as possible its own current spending and being relieved of the burden of higher defence spending enables the Government's current account to be kept in surplus. Because rising state revenues from taxation have kept pace with the limited expansion in current spending the current account surplus is one source of funds for public investment. Although rates of direct taxation are lower in Japan they are steeply progressive which makes tax liability very sensitive to increases in income. So for example when incomes were rising very quickly up to 1973, so also did state revenues from taxation. Indirect tax revenues are also sensitive to changes in income because they are dependent on sales of more expensive goods. State revenues grew so quickly before the first oil crisis that frequent cuts were made in taxation rates, although tax bands or thresholds were adjusted less frequently meaning that the overall revenue yield continued to grow. The net results of expenditure limitation with rising revenues meant that the state for many years was a contributor to aggregate savings. Part of the background to a cautious fiscal policy can be explained by the legal requirement to balance budgets which was inherited from the US Occupation's anti-inflation programme. In fact cautious spending and healthy revenues meant that the current budget rarely balanced but was in surplus for almost every one of the past 30 years.

The excess of revenue over current spending or consumption provided one source of resources for public investment. But the biggest source has been the accumulated saving of households which since 1975 has been supplemented by substantial issues of government bonds. Household savings in Japan have been approximately 75 per cent higher than in the West over the past 25 years, and the state has occupied a pivotal position in transferring these savings into investment by the public and private sectors. The central mechanisms for this transfer is the Fiscal Investment and Loan Programme (FILP) which lends at lower than market interest rates to a variety of public agencies. These include local governments, public enterprises in transport and communications and public finance institutions who in turn lend funds to private companies. So all Japanese companies have direct or indirect access to FILP from public corporations, to those with mixed public and private ownership to those wholly owned by the private sector.

The size of FILP at 40–50 per cent of the State's current account budget is very significant as may be expected given the resources available from very high household savings. Indeed Eiichi has argued that 'FILP is the key to the economic growth of our country' (quoted in Johnson 1978 p.81). As a programme which is administered separately from the 'official' budget, FILP allocations tend to be freer from the major political wrangles that surround budget decisions. In fact until 1973 FILP accounts were not subject to Diet consent. We will see later how FILP acts as a vital intermediary in the supply of investment funds to private companies, but at this stage we need to recognize the way FILP uses savings to finance the investment activities of a variety of public agencies.

Until 1975 FILP funds and the current budget surplus were sufficient to cover the finance needed for public investment. Since then lower growth rates, smaller increases in incomes have meant a less rapid growth of revenue from taxation which, in the absence of any marked fall in public investment, required high levels of state borrowing. Although the issue of state bonds increased massively even this level of borrowing was more than matched by the continued flow of household savings. In fact with a slower increase in private investment only heavy state borrowing prevented the emergence of excess saving which would have plunged Japan into a serious recession (Y. Sato 1984 p.128).

4.3 Reluctant state intervention on transfer payments

For most of the post-war period high levels of public investment were possible because of cautious attitudes to current state spending especially on the provision of public goods, because taxation revenues rose quickly and because the state had access to household savings. In managing the national accounts the Japanese state in contrast to other leading OECD members chose to minimize its own consumption and give a lower priority to transfer payments. There was a change to the pattern of state finances during the mid-1970s which is frequently associated with the massive increase in public borrowing. As figure 4.3 illustrates, transfer payments began to increase markedly as a proportion of GDP after 1974.

This increase reflected greater state involvement in reshuffling purchasing power from one group of citizens to another – most commonly associated with transfers from the employed to the unemployed, the sick or the aged. Despite the fanfares which Japanese politicians sounded on the arrival of a superior welfare system, there is little doubt that improved public welfare

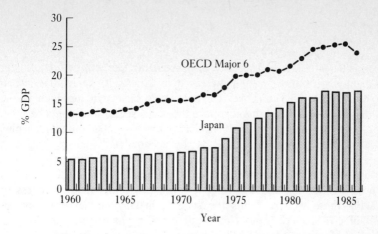

Figure 4.3 Government transfers as a percentage of GDP in the Big Seven OECD economies, 1960–86
Source: *Economic Outlook*, December 1982 and 1987

provision was introduced with reluctance. Business leaders and state officials forecast grave consequences for individual initiative, the work ethic and savings levels once 'the warmth of the Japanese family [was replaced] by the cold and impersonal bureaucratic welfare state' (Campbell 1984 p.57). Warnings were issued that better public welfare would mean bigger public expenditure which would inevitably mean higher taxes and consequently a lower rate of economic growth.

It is evident that from the later 1960s as rapidly rising incomes went some way towards satisfying the demand for private consumer goods, the demand for goods and services of a social or public nature became much more active. In part this reflected general dissatisfaction with the external costs of rapid industrial growth seen especially in environmental pollution. But there was also disenchantment with the underprovision of public services which were seen to have been sacrified in the cause of promoting high rates of industrial investment. A sharp decline in support for the LDP was a catalyst in securing 'improvements in social security provision that led to a large increase in real transfers (OECD 1985 p.91). This judgement about transfers and an improved social security system does though need to be qualified by noting that increases in welfare spending were accommodated by increases in individual contributions and that social security outlays are only one element in total transfer payments.

Social security outlays did rise fivefold between 1974 and 1984 but their share of total transfers actually fell from 75 to 64 per cent and the share of subsidies to local government and public enterprises also fell. The most significant increase came in interest payments to holders of public debt

A Planned Market Economy

which grew twice as fast as the social security component. Thus an important element of the overall increase in transfer payments went not to households who own a tiny amount of public debt, but to financial institutions and corporate enterprises.

Alongside larger social security disbursements has gone an equivalent growth in contributions which increased by nearly 40 per cent between 1980 and 1985. The objective is to minimize the extent to which public subsidies are needed and thereby make the social security accounts balance. In practice the accounts have regularly shown a huge annual surplus equivalent to 3 per cent of GNP as the accumulated pension surpluses from earlier years are invested to produce substantial interest earnings. The excess of income over expenditure is transferred to FILP for loans to public institutions and thence to the private sector. In the process of managing these welfare funds the state is making crucial decisions on behalf of civil society about contribution and payment rates and on the allocation of surplus funds. The priorities expressed in these decisions have stressed individual responsibility for adequate welfare cover, rather than providing resources from the public purse, i.e. from general tax revenues. To reduce still further the chance that social security spending in the future will exceed contributions, changes have been made which not only increase contributions but will limit spending by lowering standards.

An improved state pension scheme in 1973 set the retirement benefit level at 50 per cent of average earnings – although the average pension paid in 1983 was only 40 per cent because the scheme was fairly new and contributions were incomplete. Changes introduced in the early 1980s reduced the retirement pension norm by one-sixth, lengthened the required period of contributions from 32 to 40 years and raised the pensionable age from 60 to 65. As we have seen in Chapter 3 most people 'retire' well before 65 and so the pressure to find other paid work until they reach pensionable age is maintained. Indexation of pensions was a vital part of the 1973 scheme but now this is to be initiated *only* if consumer prices rise by more than 5 per cent *per annum*. Inflation at this level has been rare in recent years, but even price increases of 2 or 3 per cent when accumulated over a number of years significantly erode the real value of payments made.

The other main element in social security is healthcare where again the main objective is to make expenditure and revenue balance. So to match increases in healthcare spending patients have had since 1984 to pay the first 10 per cent of their medical expenses. Not surprisingly spending dropped, especially among the elderly who had previously been accused of 'over-using medical services because they were free' (Campbell 1984 p.57).

As a managing trustee for the social security schemes, the state has established ground rules which will ensure that public welfare is largely self-financing. Prudence dictates that individual responsibility should be the basis of a welfare system that offers what Vogel called 'security without entitlement' (1979 Chapter 9). This system reflects the view that entitlement produces over-reliance on the state which undermines initiative and the propensity of individuals to save. Transferring income from employees to the sick or elderly means moving purchasing power to groups with lower saving propensities thus raising fears that aggregate savings will fall. Equally the saving habits of employees may be changed as the 'guarantee of a state pension is likely to reduce one important motive for household saving' (OECD 1985 p.48).

Concern about the level of personal savings has been heightened because household tax burdens have risen. Although compulsory social security contributions are now bigger than direct tax payments both have risen sharply in the 1980s. Rates of taxation have been reduced on several occasions recently but tax thresholds have not and the minimum taxable income has been frozen since 1977, when to keep pace with inflation it should have fallen by a third. For employees extra tax and social security payments meant a slower growth of disposable incomes between 1980 and 1985 thus the spectre of falling savings levels loomed large. In this scenario the state has sought to confirm the Japanese tradition of self-help as opposed to public entitlement to maintain personal savings and prevent any erosion of FILP resources.

4.4 The Japanese savings rate

At first sight fears that better public welfare provision would depress saving seem to be confirmed as the proportion of disposable income saved by Japanese households fell from 24 per cent in 1974 to 17 per cent in 1984. However it should be noted that the 1974 figure was a record and came in the wake of a record increase in money incomes around that time. It is significant that although the aggregate savings ratio fell markedly in the decade after 1974 the ratio for employee households fell only marginally from 25 to 23 per cent (OECD 1986 p.13). Thus for that half of Japanese households who depend on wage earning rather than income from property and/or who are retired, saving ratios declined only slightly despite a slower growth in gross incomes and despite increased tax and social security contributions.

Even with some decline in the propensity to save, the Japanese still manage to save at levels some 50–60 per cent higher than the OECD average. The debate over why the Japanese apparently prefer to save rather than consume has thrown up numerous explanations which usually highlight unique cultural frugality or peculiar social practices. For example paying a proportion of wages in bi-annual lump-sum bonuses and an underdeveloped consumer credit system are said to encourage saving. It is difficult to see though why lump-sum bonuses, which make an ideal source for purchasing consumer durables, are not used as an alternative to the inadequate consumer credit facilities. Neither is it obvious why the higher paid who receive bigger lump-sum bonuses tend to have a lower marginal propensity to save.

A favoured explanation among monetarist or supply-side economists suggests that the lower direct tax levels in Japan are crucial in generating higher personal savings. But there are several problems with this not least how to account for the relative stability of employee saving ratios despite the increasing direct tax burden in the first half of the 1980s. Over the longer term we also need to explain why those earning higher incomes, whose marginal rate of tax is lower than in the West, actually save a small proportion of their disposable income. At the other end of the scale we find that low income families who have not reached the minium tax threshold and so are not affected by lower direct tax rates, also save large amounts. Therefore saving ratios may actually 'be insensitive to the tax burden' (K. Sato 1985 p.120).

Some have argued that higher personal saving in Japan is really an exaggerated phenomenon because the personal sector includes larger numbers of the self-employed whose saving should really be counted in the corporate sector. As access to external finance for small firms is limited, the self-employed are forced to save more to support their businesses. The self-employed do save at higher rates and there are more self-employed workers in Japan, although the number has fallen in recent years and one would expect this to have a diminishing effect on aggregate saving. Even conceding the role of the self-employed still leaves us to explain why households which depend on outside paid employment save at higher rates.

Socio-cultural theories about unique Japanese practices are common to a whole host of issues as we saw in Chapter 1, and a traditional preference for frugality has been used to highlight the continuity in saving habits since the pre-war era. These theories are more difficult to confront because they tend to be so general and at first sight so appealing. For instance the incidence of typhoons and earthquakes may be common enough to encourage the Japanese to place more emphasis on precautionary motives for saving. But such longstanding habits surely need other supporting processes to maintain cautious attitudes to spending as opposed to saving. Inducements to save whether through tax exemptions, compulsory social security contributions or through the extensive network of state post offices, have to be considered along with apparently longstanding traditional preferences. One can only speculate whether the traditions could have survived without a supportive institutional environment to maintain cautious attitudes to consumption.

The motives of Japanese savers are surveyed regularly and Figure 4.4 compares the main reasons given in 1970 and 1984 according to age group. These particular years may have been untypical but the general features have been confirmed in other surveys using alternative sources. For example the high ranking of precautionary motives to provide for illness or accidents

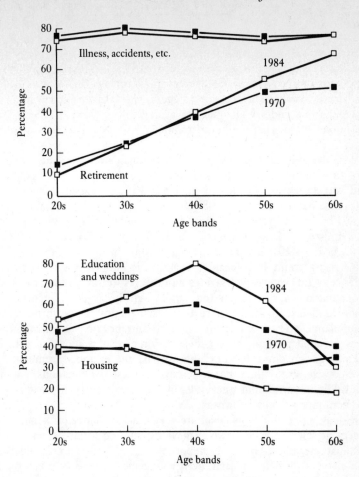

Figure 4.4 (a) and (b) Motives for personal savings in Japan, 1970 and 1984
Source: OECD 1985

which incur medical costs at the same time as earnings fall through temporary absence from employment. This category is the one which 'registers the highest rate of response (60–80 per cent) in all age groups' (1985 Survey on Savings *FPC* p.3).

A noticeable change in saving for retirement is the increase in its ranking for those over 50 which to a large extent reflects the lengthening gap between the earlier age at which many workers leave their tenured jobs and the age when state pensions begin. Older workers may not have sufficient years of contributions to the scheme and so receive a smaller pension; this explains why more elderly people continue to rely on employment than in the West. Growing awareness of the inadequacy of state benefits seems to be reflected in the continuing importance of saving for retirement throughout the age range.

Perhaps the most significant change in responses between 1974 and 1984 concerns the need to provide for children's education and weddings especially for those in the 45–55 age group. Weddings in 1983 according to one survey cost on average a staggering 7 million yen which was equivalent to one and a half times the average wage (*JTW* 4/8/84). This is clearly one place where cultural traditions do play a part in sustaining savings.

In a similar way it could be argued that Japan's meritocratic ideology sustains traditional motives to save for education. Education expenses depend very much on the mix of public and private facilities chosen by parents; one bank survey for 1984 estimates the cost of a mainly state route at 17.5 million yen and a more private one at 25.3 million (*JTW* 6/4/85). Ministry of Labour statistics show that at their peak educational expenses take up 20 per cent of average income in the age range 47–53, and the rising trend in education expense accounts for the increasing importance of this category of savings motives. As we saw in the discussion of labour markets access to tenured employment in larger companies who pay more and offer better welfare benefits, depends on performance in and attendance at prestigious universities. Entrance to such institutions requires parental planning to set their children on the appropriate route from kindergarten onwards to be able to pass the entrance examinations to selected schools. With so much at stake in these examinations, parents pay for additional tuition at weekends, in the evenings and in vacations at private crammer schools known as *juku*.

Individual opportunities in Japan are very much a matter of competition for places at selected schools which have established a good track record of examination passes. Given the importance of educational credentials in the life chances of their children, even younger parents save to be able to meet 20 years of education expenses. These expenses are increased by the relative underprovision of places in state establishments at the extreme ends of the child's educational career: before the age of compulsory schooling at six and in higher education. In both of these sectors the state provides only one-quarter of places yet in both Japan has one of the highest enrolment rates. For example one-third of three-year-olds, 80 per cent of four-year-olds and 95 per cent of five-year-olds attend kindergarten and 36 per cent of the relevant age group go on to higher education. If we add the costs of attendance at *juku* the average parent faces escalating educational costs rising from 6 per cent of disposable income for children under six to 30 per cent for children attending private universities.

A pronounced demand for educational credentials extends across all income brackets and arguably creates more pressure on poorer families because education is seen to be the key to upward mobility. The Japanese state has actively participated in maintaining the ideology of a meritocracy without, as we shall see, paying as much attention to equality of opportunity in the sense of subsidies to low income households. By failing to provide an adequate supply of places in its own institutions especially in the early and later stages of educational careers, the state forces people into the private market. Equally by holding down public spending, parents have to pay higher costs even in state schools. Both tendencies reinforce the need to save to meet expenses which are known to last throughout the educational career of their children.

Saving to buy land or housing has a lower response rate and one which 'has declined sharply in recent years' (1985 Survey on Savings, *FPC* p.2). Two of the main factors causing this decline have been firstly the increased availability of housing loans and secondly the emergence in the 1980s of a switch to rented housing. The state's role in the housing market has been less concerned with the supply of housing itself than with satisfying part of the demand for finance where FILP funds are used through the Housing Loan Corporation (HLC). Apart from a meagre level of tax deductibility for housing loans, the HLC provides finance at a subsidized rate of interest; funds are obtained from FILP at 7.5 per cent and HLC then lends at 5.5 per cent for up to a half of the cost of house purchase. Of the remainder about 20 per cent comes from bank loans and 30 per cent from purchasers deposits. Up to the early 1980s, then, relatively better access to housing loans eased the pressure on individuals to save for house purchase.

Since then there has been a noticeable slackening in the demand for loans to purchase houses. The HLC interest rate subsidy has been cut and as house prices have risen much more quickly than incomes, the maximum proportion borrowable from public or private institutions has fallen. Hence bigger down payments by purchasers are needed. This trend has not increased personal saving for house purchase, rather it has reduced the demand for loans and caused a rise in the demand for and supply of rented housing. This switch reflects other pressures on disposable incomes and the massive increase in house prices. Relative to construction, the cost of land makes up two-thirds of the total price compared to one-quarter elsewhere in the OECD. Given a scarce supply of land available for housing the average price of a house in urban Japan is equivalent to eight years average income or twice the ratio in Europe or the US.

Ostensibly the state has lubricated the housing market mechanism, but it has concentrated more on the demand side. Where action has been more limited is in public construction but particularly in doing little to improve the availability of land. An over-protected agricultural sector not only results in higher food prices for consumers but inhibits the release of poorer quality land for housing. Lubricating just one side of the market has then produced a move towards renting accommodation in order to preserve savings for ill-health, retirement and education.

Higher personal savings may indeed be a matter of Japanese cultural proclivities but we need to consider how such traditions are maintained. Choosing to save appears to be a matter of personal decisions to sacrifice present consumption to pay for future spending whether this is predictable, for expected education expenses, or unpredictable for sickness. However what the state does or does not provide in these areas has crucial implications for individuals. Even with a limited amount of public enterprise employment, the Japanese state has guided individual decisions by moulding the social environment within which these decisions are made. The end result of this guidance has been the accumulation of huge savings over which the state acts the part of managing trustee. In an aggregate sense the personal sector is the major source of savings which have gone to finance the enormous borrowing requirements of private industry. A smooth flow of funds from savers to borrowers could not have been made as effectively without state management because 'there was no market mechanisms to automatically channel private saving into growth-promoting investment' (K. Sato 1985 p.128). Supporting a smooth transfer from net lenders to net borrowers has been the main responsibility of the FILP.

4.5 FILP – a crucial mechanism linking savers and investors

Ever since the programme was reorganized in 1953 the allocation of funds through FILP has been considerable; in the 1980s for example the FILP budget was equivalent to 30 per cent of total investment, or 10 per cent of GNP. As we have seen the excess of revenue over expenditure in the state pension accounts provide funds to FILP and these involuntary household savings contribute about one-third of its resources. Another 45 per cent is collected through the state-run post offices. Therefore not only has the state been instrumental in motivating decisions to save, it has also acted as a collector of savings.

Individual Japanese savers have long favoured low-risk institutions which offer ready access for withdrawals as one might expect given the strength of precautionary motives noted in Figure 4.4. Bank and post office deposits take two-thirds of total savings but in the last decade there has been a marked increase in the share of the postal system which now holds almost a third of all individual saving. This shift has boosted FILP funds but has produced protests from the private sector. 'If this continues the flow of funds will be determined by government agencies and we will have a system of financial socialism' (Employers Association official, quoted in Simonson 1981 p.100).

Has this switch in the share of savings deposits been a response to market forces which has produced a fortuitous increase in FILP funds? In one sense yes, because savers appear to be reacting to better returns. There are less quantifiable advantages which concern the ubiquity of 22,000 post offices which provide easy access in urban and rural areas. But if we probe the reasons for higher post office returns we can see the hand of the state guiding market responses. Interest rates on post office deposits are set through a separate process from ordinary bank deposits. Although both rates have changed in proportion in the years of falling interest rates during the 1980s, the fall in postal interest rates has usually been delayed allowing the postal system to gain the lion's share of new deposits as well as holding on to existing ones. Of more significance has been the introduction of new postal schemes offering flexible mechanized access and withdrawals without loss of interest on long-term deposits which guarantee high earnings for ten years. Private banks have responded with similar terms but always with a delay which makes it very difficult to recover lost deposits.

What have really been significant in the build-up of postal savings were the tax advantages that accrued to these deposits until 1988. Tax exemption has been a longstanding policy to encourage saving and '50–60 per cent of personal savings are tax-exempt' (*JTW* 4/8/84) but postal accounts carried special 'privileges'. All savings up to 3 million yen (£12000 or $20000) were exempt from tax but savers with private institutions had to apply to local tax offices for exemption whereas postal savings were automatically exempt. As checks on the identity of postal account holders were minimal, savers could open a number of separate accounts using different names. This well-known 'opportunity to evade taxes is cherished by the Japanese' (Sakakibara and Feldman 1983 p.21) and has played no small part in raising postal deposits to a level three and a half times greater than those held by the world's biggest private banks.

Thus savers do act rationally to maximize their returns but they are responding to incentives which for example favoured postal deposits and therefore the flow of FILP funds. Approximately one-half of FILP allocations have been earmarked for public financial institutions which provide the vital link from individuals to industry.

Direct loans to industry at low rates of interest and the finance for export market development were particularly significant to the economic recovery of the 1950s when the state provided around 30 per cent of corporate borrowing. As the scale of investment soared the state's share fell, although even in the late 1970s one-sixth of external finance for corporate borrowers came from government (Elston 1981 p.514). The specific designation of loans to projects with great long-term benefits especially in technological research and development remains a priority. It is less a matter of supporting prestige developments with uncertain returns such as the Anglo-French Concorde project, but of socializing the risks involved in lending large sums which will produce high returns only over the very long term. Public finance institutions like the Japan Development Bank support these projects by participating in, and sometimes organizing, syndicates of banks who pool loans. The key issue here is not that the public contribution is in itself very large, but the very presence of public institutions indicates a high level of confidence in the project. In contrast to many Western projects where the presence of state financial institutions is taken as a sign of weakness, in Japan it is a sign of strength. For Japan 'looking only at the level of public intermediation seriously underestimates its significance. Even if only 10 per cent of funds for a project come from public sector intermediaries, private intermediaries feel much more secure in extending their own loans' (Sakakibara and Feldman 1983 pp.21–2).

Obtaining the state's seal of approval for projects with very long-term benefits is all the more important in Japan because the share of public intermediaries in the loans and liabilities of the whole financial sector is large. Public credit agencies in other Western countries may be equally significant, but where Japan differs is in the priority given to industrial plant and equipment. General support for industrial borrowers as we saw in Chapter 2, is given in various ways through for instance generous depreciation allowances and tax remission credits on new investment. In addition the Bank of Japan was frequently called on to support private banks whose liquidity was threatened by lending beyond their means in periods when investment expanded rapidly. So in supporting the motives for which people in Japan save and in mediating the collection and allocation of investment finance, state activities are crucial. The ideology of the free market places great stress on its ability to act as an invisible hand, but in Japan market trends have been guided in various ways. Sometimes by positive action to preserve the role of FILP in transferring household saving into investment. Sometimes by delaying decisions, for example to alter the special advantages that accrued to post office deposits, despite the pleas of the private banks for equal competition in the market for savings.

4.6 The state as manager if not owner

This description of how the Japanese state manages the transfer of savings gives an indication of the sort of supportive environment that has provided the basis for economic expansion. By giving priority to a sustained increase in investment, the objective was to support the expansion of manufacturing industry where productivity gains would yield cost advantages sufficient to increase sales at home and abroad. Maximizing the rate of economic growth would then increase employment and through rising incomes, the benefits of economic growth could be distributed throughout Japanese society.

As the record of the past 30 years shows Japan has, relative to other Western countries, experienced a faster rate of *per capita* income growth which is due in no small way to the very rapid increase in private investment. We have also seen how higher levels of public investment have supported this process both by improving the infrastructure and through financial intermediation. In one sense it could be argued that the state merely supported pre-existing trends of higher investment demand, though this leaves the vexed question of which came first. The flow of domestic savings needed to finance investment was also assisted by incentives in the form of tax exemptions, so again arguably the state simply facilitated market forces. It is difficult though to accept that the 'Japanese government has *never* taken the lead in directly encouraging the transfer of resources' (Patrick and Rosovsky 1976 p.46, my emphasis) once we reflect on the role of the state as collector and distributor of savings through FILP. The motive for supervising the transfer of savings was to ensure that capital was provided in appropriate quantities and on favourable terms to sectors with the greatest long-term potential. This may have merely accelerated what the market would anyway have supplied, but by using the social security surplus and postal savings, FILP led the way. Such activities are common in other East Asian economies like South Korea where 'governmental power was firmly used to guide investment in chosen directions through differential interest rates and credit availabilities' (Sen 1983 p.13).

In managing levels of taxation and expenditure, the state also set a national example by giving public investment priority over consumption. By restricting the share of publicly administered services in education, housing and welfare, the state maintained the need for private saving and at the same time controlled the level of public employment and ownership. Where the state has intervened it tends to be in labour-saving ways by influencing the effective demand for social goods rather than the supply, which would incur greater recurrent salary costs for increased numbers of state employees. Leaving the private market with a significant role in supplying social goods and services has been the dominant objective especially in the past decade, because public provision is associated with higher taxes and state borrowing which are said to lower personal saving and erode incentives.

However as we have seen above it does appear that Japanese saving may be insensitive to tax levels. Equally the evidence that state borrowing distorts the flow of funds to private industry is inconclusive; with smaller state deficits since 1980 domestic savings have increasingly flowed overseas. None the less the ideological imperative of 'small' government has focused attention ever more strongly on reducing the number of public employees by privatizing public enterprises. Japan already has one of the lowest shares of employment in the state sector but further cuts are projected to symbolize the commitment to self-help and individual initiative.

Restricting the share of publicly provided services while maintaining the investment activities of FILP, means continuing the constraints on the state's current spending. It means doing little for example to increase the number of teachers and reduce class size to less than the existing 40:1 ratio. An education reform council in 1985 highlighted the need to reverse the emphasis on examination cramming in Japanese schools, but with such large class numbers alternative methods are difficult to implement.

Increasing the supply of teachers, and therefore state spending, was not a favoured solution in the current mood of public sector austerity. Neither has this mood done much to correct the fact that only 34 per cent of all private residences have sewer connections or that only 51 per cent of the nation's roads are paved. Instead 'grandiose capital investment takes first priority in Japan, while responses to the less spectacular needs of the people are postponed' (Inoguchi 1987 p.126).

Continuing to deny its citizens access to better public services illustrates how the 'state intervenes by omission and by combining omission with commission' (Halliday 1977 p.52). Decisions on the relative shares of public versus private welfare are made on behalf of civil society by claiming support from the Japanese tradition of private welfare from family or employer. But the overwhelming trend is towards the break up of extended families and as company welfare schemes place those in small firms at a disadvantage, many individuals are forced to continue to provide for their own welfare through personal saving. Social insecurity in public schemes may be seen as an instance of the state intervening by omission to maintain the flow of funds for investment.

In some ways the state acts like the management of modern corporations who despite the divorce of ownership from control continue to exercise authority on behalf of the shareholders. Lower levels of public ownership by the Japanese state have similarly done little to diminish its influence over the economy. When we speak then of a 'small' state in Japan we should signify that this means a low-cost operation, 'relatively speaking government in Japan can be described as cheap . . . because the burdens of defence and social welfare are light' (Minami 1986 p.338). We are then able to avoid the implication that 'small' means less influential. Using a wide range of public agencies employing people whose salary is not paid directly out of public funds means that 'the Japanese government spends less but gets more for its money' (Johnson 1978 p.14). With a smaller state sector and apparently diminished formal authority to prescribe responses from the private sector, other less formal but equally effective channels of communication are used. These channels 'rest primarily on an understanding of longer-term mutual interests between government and business made possible by a long history of collaboration' (Boltho 1985 p.192). A history of collaboration when confirmed by contemporary institutions and social practices, gives Japan a much less adversarial context to the oft-disputed boundary between the private market and the public sector.

4.7 A history of regulated competition

One consistent theme that has been used to justify closer collaboration between business and the state is Japan's sense of vulnerability which derives from her very limited supplies of natural resources. Over the past century there have also been numerous spasms of diplomatic isolation which have compounded economic vulnerability into the belief that Japan was an isolated outpost in a hostile world. 'The feeling of loneliness at the international level drives the Japanese into self-defence by building an impregnable industrial garrison in the Japanese islands' (Taira 1986 p.174). Such feelings give the state the ideal means to mobilize collaboration around the exigencies of the national interest.

In the 1860s external economic and political threats to Japanese sovereignty from Western imperial powers precipitated a reaction among the leaders of the new Meiji state designed to safeguard autonomy by fostering a 'rich country and a strong military'. To prevent Western competition from destroying indigenous industry the state 'had to take a direct hand in economic development if Japan was ever to achieve economic independence' (Johnson 1982 p.25). In consequence Japan industralized without any commitment to unregulated market forces. With limited supplies of private entrepreneurship and capital, the state itself opened new ventures in mining, munitions, railroads, shipbuilding and textiles in addition to building a centralized infrastructure for commerce education and finance. The required resources were squeezed from the agricultural sector through heavy land and indirect taxation, but these revenues were by the early 1880s grossly insufficient to finance state expenditure. Increasing rates of inflation led to a dramatic deterioration in the balance of external payments and to avoid the Chinese experience of having to cede territory in lieu of debts, the Meiji state resigned its commitment to public enterprise. Non-military establishments were sold on very favourable terms to the private sector where they were entrusted to a limited number of business combines: the *zaibatsu*.

Some *zaibatsu* had originally been prominent mine owning or merchant families but in the later nineteenth century they combined industrial and financial interests where their prosperity was closely connected to state activities. As the purchasers of state factories, as the vehicle through which the state created centralized banking institutions and as the recipients of state contracts, the *zaibatsu* were used as instruments of state policy which integrated profits with patriotism. The Japanese preference for sponsoring a limited group of capital intensive firms who pioneer technical change can be traced to this era, although today's conglomerates no longer operate as closed family networks, state policy from the 1880s was to develop relations of mutual dependence with the *zaibatsu* in particular to avoid antagonistic confrontation over state regulation of market forces.

In establishing new industries and in coordinating relations with the *zaibatsu* officials in the newly constructed bureaucracy were centrally concerned. These officials operated within a structure modelled on the Prussian system and were servants of the Emperor who was the central focus of state power and authority. Even after the 1890 constitution had established a parliamentary Diet the bureaucracy was charged with serving the national interest as articulated by the Emperor and his close advisors rather than cabinet ministers in the Diet. The bureaucracy was designed to be the professional custodian of state interests to transcend the partisan quabbles of politicians, and individual officials were recruited from the elite students of the Imperial Universities, especially Tokyo law graduates. High educational achievements were necessary to pass the entrance examination for Imperial service and with the prestige that accompanied their meritocratic status went independence from the patronage of politicians.

The symbiotic relationship between the state and the *zaibatsu* which was forged from the 1880s was not entirely unbroken as the *zaibatsu* attempted during the 1920s to exert their independence. In particular they organized cartels to rationalize production among themselves to restrict the entry of other firms and thus increase their monopolization of industrial production. At the same time as the *zaibatsu* sought a greater degree of self-control, the military were forcing through their own solution to economic insecurity through imperialism. Conflict over the allocation of resources between the military and the *zaibatsu* was endemic even in the height of wartime and led to the formation of the military's own *zaibatsu*-style combines in the conquered territories of Asia.

Amidst these protracted disputes the power and influence of the civilian bureaucracy waned into passive resistance to the extension of military rule. In fact it was as a consequence of the policies adopted by the US Occupation authorities that the bureaucracy regained their authority. The US programme of democratization meant disbanding the war-time military state apparatus, which left the relatively unpurged bureaucracy as the only organized group to fill the vacuum. By deciding not to administer Japan through direct military rule, the US Occupation authority had little option but to use existing bureaucrats to implement its policies. In the process, the Occupation's objective of decentralizing national administration and supporting local democracy was undermined by its own actions. At first this reverse course was seen as a temporary expedient as local authorities had neither the qualified personnel nor the finance to replace central control. However after the US withdrawal in 1952, recentralization was made permanent and 'the central government has resumed much of the prewar power over local government' (Park 1978 p.593).

In a similar fashion the US decision to dismantle the *zaibatsu* left economic control to the bureaucracy who began the process of recovery by reorganizing economic institutions. The package of deflationary policies imposed in 1949 did though place severe limits on the resources available for state expenditure, but the creation of a host of public and semi-public corporations allowed the bureaucracy to circumvent the balanced budgets dictated by the US. By 1953 the FILP has been redesigned to allow reformed State financial institutions like the Export–Import Bank and the Industrial Bank to channel capital to selected companies.

The formal end of the occupation did not signal any lessening of reliance on US aid, and as in the nineteenth century, the priority of the state was to promote rapid economic growth in order to reduce such dependence. Despite the boost to Japanese industrial production given by the demand for military supplies in the Korean war, its economic position remained precarious. Labour relations were still precarious, supplies of capital were limited, management structures were distorted by the dissolution of the *zaibatsu* and a chronic balance of payments deficit meant that foreign exchange reserves were exhausted. Long-term reconstruction required not just the replacement of damaged or obsolete plant but a restructuring of the basis of production in which the state was to be intimately involved.

The bureaucracy was at first divided on how best to revitalize industry. More conservative finance officials favoured what appeared to be the rational market imperative of continued reliance on labour-intensive production in which Asian economies had a comparative advantage. Others most notably in MITI, pushed hard for a radical shift in the industrial base towards capital-intensive products to break away from Japan's traditional status as a dependent supplier of cheap low value-added exports to the West. Finance bureaucrats and the Bank of Japan doubted whether the country had either sufficient capital or the technological capacity to compete with other advanced economies. MITI, however, was able to show how even these limited resources might be directed effectively through workable competition between selected companies who would act as technological leaders behind high tariff barriers.

MITI alone could not have sustained such a substantial shift in priorities without the support of other bureaucrats who buried their differences and coordinated a national drive to promote economic independence through rapid industrial growth. By targeting particular firms and sectors, MITI was able to convince Finance officials that limits could be placed on the financial contributions needed from the State. Hence much more use was made of FILP intermediation acting as a catalyst for private bank loans. Establishing workable rather than full competition, required the cooperation of other state officials to alter the effect of anti-monopoly laws enacted by the US occupation. Thus 'the Japanese government has shown relatively little concern for "Anti-trust" [which] has been an empty idea at best, at worst a positive nuisance' (Rotwein 1976 p.75). Equally as we saw in Chapter 3 public corporations like the Japan Productivity Centre have played a vital part in spreading a commitment to best-practice technology and the need to eliminate product defects. Labour officials too vindicated the segmentation of labour market and the formation of enterprise unions which has produced a more conciliatory environment of industrial relations. In all of these dimensions at a time when political leadership was in disarray, the bureaucracy mobilized a consensus around the national interest which demanded that Japan should reduce the length of the technological lead which the West had established.

4.8 *Amakudari* and the boundary between private and public

Despite the gradual removal of controls over imports, foreign exchange and the transfer of technology since the late 1960s, the bureaucracy has maintained its influence. Bureaucrats 'start off with something like a halo of authority' (Dore 1986 p.99) partly because of their previous record of successfully engineering economic recovery. Partly too their elite status invokes respect for their motives in integrating private business plans into their 'forward visions' of the future shape of the economy. But Japanese bureaucrats are not an isolated elite, rather they participate actively in the 'mingling of private and public domains' (van Wolferen 1982, p.126). In a constellation of consultation agencies, through personnel transfers to private or semi-public corporations and into the ranks of the LDP, high level bureaucrats in particular have established a crucial position for channelling state guidance.

Japan's highly competitive merit-conscious society places special weight on educational achievement and access to the bureaucracy is based on an entrance examination in which only one candidate in 40 is successful. The monopoly of Tokyo University in supplying entrants has continued such that 70 per cent of bureaucrats are Tokyo graduates, two-thirds of whom majored in law (Muramatsu and Krauss 1984 p.131). Training in law is not designed to produce specialist lawyers but involves a wider focus on public administration. Indeed very few specialists are recruited as career officials as the preference is for generalists who can accumulate a range of expertise as they are rotated between sections in each ministry. For an economy with such a remarkable record it is intriguing to find that few economics graduates go into public service. This no doubt is a reaction to the strong tradition of Marxist economics in academic life, but it means that in-service training in economics has to be provided. The Finance Ministry for example takes trainees out of routine duties for a full year of courses which stress economic analysis that is 'compatible with the logic and conventional way of thinking commonly accepted within the Ministry' (Komiya and Yamamoto 1981 p.616).

A predictable entry route for elite graduates into the bureaucracy is not at all unusual although the absence of specialist economists is intriguing. One practice that is distinctive in Japan which greatly enhances the degree of cooperation between the state and private business, is the institutionalized outflow of officials who retire early. Movement between the public and private sectors is common elsewhere, but in Japan the direction of the transfer is almost exclusively one-way and is known as *amakudari* – literally translated as 'descent from heaven'! Of the 75 per cent of senior bureaucrats who retire before they reach the age of 55 (Koh and Kim 1982 p.305) the majority are re-employed in private firms or public corporations, some enter the Diet as LDP members and a few are recruited by universities.

Precise data on the extent of re-employment are difficult to determine but it appears that the numbers involved have risen sharply since the early 1960s. We know for instance that the number of public corporation and quasi-public companies doubled between 1965 and 1985, and that nearly 80 per cent of their directors were ex-bureaucrats. Indications of the movement into private firms can be gleaned from the fact that the number of approved exceptions to the rule that two years should elapse between retirement and recruitment to the private sector, rose by 60 per cent between 1963 and 1981 (Blumenthal 1985 p.313).

Analysis of the destinations of retiring bureaucrats shows, as might be expected, not a random pattern but one which reflects the spheres of influence of their previous ministries. When descending from heaven, landing spots appear to be predetermined. Finance officials are thus more likely to move into private financial institutions, the Bank of Japan or into public finance corporations such as the Japan Development Bank. Similarly Transport officials find places in airlines or road construction companies and MITI officials into the more important manufacturing firms. In some public corporations the whole structure of senior management seems to have been developed to allow for shared ministry representation. At the Housing Loan Corporation where six out of 11 executive posts are reserved for *amakudari* officials, the Ministry of Construction controls landing spots for the President and two directors, the Ministry of Finance for the vice-president and one director and the Economic Planning Agency and the Prime Ministers Office for the remainder. The Japan Highways Corporation in a similar fashion has seven out of twelve landing spots reserved for the Ministry of Construction, its financial needs merits two seats for the Ministry of Finance, retiring Transport officials take another and the need to obtain planning approval means that the Home Ministry also has representation. Although the process of relocating ex-bureaucrats is not always smooth as some employees in receiving institutions resent the constraints on their own promotion prospects, *amakudari* is entrenched as at least a channel of communication if not control.

Leaving public employment before the age of 55 necessitates re-employment elsewhere because full pensions are not paid until the official retirement age which is now being raised to 60. But why in that case retire early? By convention each year's entry of bureaucrats is treated as a cohort and promoted according to seniority until it reaches section chief. Thereafter as the number of higher level posts is limited, the colleagues of those promoted to top positions are expected to resign along with any remaining members of earlier cohorts. Eventually this leaves the highest ranking official, the Vice-Minister, with absolute seniority by entry year. Promotion to the most senior posts thus creates a 'chain reaction of retirements' (Koh and Kim 1982 p.305) and if the Vice-Minister remains for several years the succeeding entry cohorts must also resign. Customary resignation to prevent someone with greater seniority having to defer to a junior may seem to be yet another instance of the survival of a uniquely Japanese traditional social practice. In fact the convention was established in the 1950s when the bureaucracy expanded rapidly and some more definite order of promotion was needed. Regular early retirement was one method chosen to offer greater career prospects to younger people and to retain the vigour of the service. At the same time the process allows the total size of the official bureaucracy to appear to be kept under control, although if regular *amakudari* transfers to public corporations were included a different conclusion could be reached.

Placements are handled by the Vice-Minister and the Chief Secretary in each Ministry who seem honour bound to provide retirement posts for colleagues. Finding well-paid landing spots in the private sector depends partly on the contacts the Vice-Minister is able to develop, but also on the experience such companies have had in their dealings with the particular individuals who are to be placed. Decisions about approved exceptions to the two-year period that should elapse before any transfer to firms in the private sector, depend on whether a particular individual has had any close connection with the firm concerned. The National Personnel Authority grants exceptions after taking the advice of the head of the appropriate Ministry, who of course has 'every incentive to deny that any connection exists' (Johnson 1978 p.104). Even if approval is withheld the relevant Ministry usually has the expedient of a temporary landing spot in a public corporation as a stepping stone to a later transfer to the private sector.

It is not difficult to imagine the advantages that private companies assume will follow from employing ex-bureaucrats. At the most basic level this should facilitate the acquisition of licences for new building or transport routes, permission to redevelop land, expand premises or obtain better credit rankings. At a more general level these transfers can cement the process of coordination between the state and business because ex-bureaucrats will be engaged in consultations with people who were previously junior colleagues and 'loyalties between seniors and juniors are not ended by *amakudari*' (Boyd 1985 p.42). As most bureaucrats realize that at some stage they will need re-employment, they can anticipate such a move if they prove their worth to particular firms during their earlier career. Knowing in advance that their Ministry clients can provide a rich source of post-retirement positions clearly creates a framework where adversarial relations with private business are most definitely counterproductive for an individual at the centre of any conflict.

4.9 Administrative guidance, industrial consultation and policy formation

There is no doubt that the practice of *amakudari* brings greater long-term security for individual bureaucrats and maintains important channels of communication with the state for the companies and institutions that offer re-employment. It is also vital to recognize the persistence and increasing prevalence of *amakudari* over the period since the later 1960s when the formal power of the state over economic affairs began to be eroded. With greater liberalization of trade controls and the internationalization of financial markets it is tempting to argue that the Japanese state has withdrawn from its role as a major economic actor. In practice, however, just as *amakudari* continues to structure informal networks of influence, the scale of guidance given by ministry officials has shown no tendency at all to diminish. Administrative guidance about desired output or export levels, research coordination, or product development, carries no legal or constitutional authority. It is none the less proffered in detail to specific industries and firms along a spectrum of emphasis from suggestions or wishes through encouragements or recommendations to warnings or outright directives.

Two particular aspects of administrative guidance stand out, first the depth of detail involved implies that officials have a close working knowledge of the firms and sectors concerned which further assumes continuous contact between middle ranking bureaucrats and company managers. Secondly, despite the absence of formal authority, in the majority of cases administrative guidance seems to be accepted as legitimate, though the spirit of cooperation may be based on resigned reluctance. Although specific policy recommendations may not have statutory authority, the overall administrative remit of each Ministry is very wide. MITI for example was formed to 'assume national administrative responsibility for the promotion and regulation of commerce, the consumption and distribution of industrial goods, to plan and regulate supply and demand, to monitor and improve industrial structure' (K. Sato 1980 p.389). Such an extensive brief gives bureaucrats very flexible guidelines within which they can claim the right to intervene. It should be remembered of course that Japan is not unique in establishing comprehensive statements of intent for Ministries dealing with trade and industry. What does appear to be distinctive about Japanese experience is the scale and extent of contact between state officials and private managers *before* administrative guidance is offered. An array of contact networks are used to incorporate private interests into the process of policy initiation and formulation in order to reduce the tensions usually involved in imposing policies from above.

Almost all of the leading figures in Japanese business have been assimilated into public decision-making processes across the whole spectrum of social and economic policies. Informally this encompasses both personal *amakudari* connections and social networks based on membership of alumni clubs for graduates of the same year in the elite universities. Formal incorporation takes place in trade and industry associations that liaise permanently with officials in appropriate ministries, or through membership of the 150 advisory groups and deliberation councils that offer specific comment on particular issues. This latter style of consultation is not confined to the immediate or direct concerns of business because accepting the right of state officials to offer guidance to the private sector, is reciprocated by offering business the right to assist the formulation public policy in general. In recent years this has involved placing leading businessmen in key positions on Public Advisory Bodies deciding the size and structure of the bureaucracy itself, the content of the curriculum in education, future defence policy and the organization of public welfare payments. If therefore administrative guidance is generally accepted as legitimate, one key reason is that those who receive the guidance and who are expected to act on it, have been involved in the formulation of policies upon which specific guidance is based.

As we will see in Chapter 5 some argue that representatives of large companies have priority in policy formation over the Cabinet, the LDP and especially the Diet. Consultation with private business produces draft proposals which carry the support of a 'core of respected advocates' (Pempel 1982 p.18) when they reach a wider public audience. Then, when bureaucrats prepare advice to their Ministers for Cabinet debate, the proposals have already been subject to prolonged negotiation leaving elected representatives the task of merely ratifying the decision.

Administrative guidance is then a crucial mechanism through which state officials can coordinate the activities of Japanese producers. It would be an exaggeration to say that each and every official notification is accepted entirely without question or that policy implementation is universally smooth. For example during the 1960s MITI took a very defensive line towards Japan's motor vehicle industry by insisting that future prospects could only be assured if production was concentrated into three or four very large integrated companies. This met with fierce resistance from the industry which successfully obstructed MITI's attempts to force through a programme of mergers and the rationalization of component suppliers. This example is a useful caution against claims of infallibility for Japanese industrial policy, but in my view this was an exceptional case which does not prove the rule that state policies have made little difference given the vigour of private enterprise. What the example does show is that effective guidance depends on extensive consultation which in this particular case was replaced with directives imposed from without.

Another widely quoted instance of a large company rejecting guidance occurred in the later 1960s when Sumitomo, one of the eight major steel producers in Japan, refused to cooperate with MITI's plans to coordinate changes in productive capacity. Unlike other disputes over administrative guidance, this disagreement was a very public one involving a protracted row between the Vice-Minister and the Chairman of Sumitomo. Bitter negotiations were conducted through press statements by each of these aggressive personalities although a compromise eventually resulted in a smaller cut in Sumitomo capacity than was originally planned. The process of solving the dispute revealed several interesting features for policy implementation in general. First, the distaste for all but the two main protagonists that the dispute should be conducted in the public gaze when the preferred method was to internalize dissent at the formulation stage. Secondly, the task of mediation was made doubly difficult by the absence of ex-bureaucrats among senior Sumitomo management. In fact once the breach was healed a succeeding Vice-Minister from MITI took *amakudari* as President of Sumitomo making further conflict much less likely. Thirdly, Sumitomo's independent stance isolated the company from other producers who were willing to cooperate in the orderly programme of output adjustment suggested by MITI. This division within the industry was confirmed in 1970 when MITI negotiated the merger of two of Sumitomo's main rivals Fuji and Yawata into the world's biggest producer Nippon Steel. This may indicate how the bureaucracy takes revenge on recalcitrants!

These two cases of confrontation signify that cooperation between the state and large private companies is a process which is not always easy to manage. They do show, however, the significance of attempting to secure approval among as many interested parties as possible before administrative guidance is issued. In the motor vehicles case collective opposition to mergers from within the industry was crucial. In view of Japan's later record the industry was rightly critical of MITI's pessimism about the viability of a larger number of independent producers. With Sumitomo, however, the company stood alone and found it impossible to sustain opposition to MITI and the rest of the industry. So in the first case the failure to prepare the ground in the usual way ensured the defeat of the merger policy, but in the second case even the opposition of a very large and influential company was ineffective against the alliance of rival producers and MITI.

The active participation in state policy formulation of senior management from Japan's larger companies is one consequence of their need to balance unmitigated competition with a degree of collusion. Few would deny the extent of rivalry between major Japanese companies over their relative positions in league tables that rank profits, output or exports. But there is a countervailing recognition of the value of workable not cut-throat competition which has disastrous consequences for firms with huge fixed cost burdens. Equally the necessity for continuous product development with the consequent expenditure on research involves risk and uncertainty for individual companies that can be mitigated by joint research projects. Trade or industry associations have emerged as vehicles for balancing competition with cooperation by allowing major producers to exchange information and organize collective research.

Apart from providing administrators for these associations, larger firms also supply most of the officers in *Keidanren* (the Federation of Economic Organizations) which represents the collective voice of all the separate associations. Membership of *Keidanren* covers the 100 or so Trade and

Industry associations as well as individual representatives of all Japan's largest corporations. Unlike employers groups in other Western countries *Keidanren* excludes medium and small business but its membership is not restricted to the private sector. Senior management from public and quasi-public corporations in banking, transport and communications participate in *Keidanren* adding to its status as a peak association.

Having institutions like these at the centre of inter-industry cooperation gives the state very effective channels to coordinate the collective response of big business. The administrative structure in Ministries facilitates the operation of administrative guidance because it mirrors in part the structure of trade associations by grouping some officials into industry sections. So in Agriculture some bureaucrats have particular responsibility for all aspects of fishing or the food industry, in transport for shipbuilding or aircraft and in MITI there are separate sections for each of the major industries like steel chemicals or aluminium. Regular contact is maintained with the organizing officers in the appropriate association of producers which allows bureaucrats to acquire knowledge of specific firms allowing their guidance to be couched in detail. Such close involvement then produces guidance which has been previously discussed and is set down in realistic terms for the firms involved.

In negotiations with peak associations like *Keidanren* and with particular Industry Associations, the state does play a role akin to an arbiter between competing private firms but this role is not confined to honest brokerage. Where the state provides research funds or public laboratories for the collective use of firms as in advanced computing, this support can be made conditional on administrative guidance being followed. Likewise in industries where capacity needs to be reduced such as aluminium smelting or shipbuilding in the 1980s, bureaucrats have played a direct part in deciding by how much particular firms must cut output.

There are of course a host of issues which affect all industries concerning for example the acquisition of foreign patents, implementing pollution controls, spreading the use of information technology or robotics and generating a coordinated response to wage bargaining. Inter-industry negotiation on these issues is orchestrated by bureaucrats who have lateral or horizontal responsibilities in contrast to those who specialize vertically according to industry or trade. *Keidanren* has parallel sub-committees to coordinate the views of larger firms on these matters, while *Nikkeiren* (Japan Federation of Employers' Associations) has a special brief to oversee approaches to industrial relations and wage bargaining. Together with *Keizai Doyukai* (an employers' Committeee for Economic Development), *Nikkeiren* has also been at the centre of efforts to maximize the use of technological innovations and to raise productivity levels. In addition, members of these key employers' associations have occupied senior positions on various Public Advisory Bodies which, as standing groups, offer advice on particular policy issues. One of the most influential is the Industrial

Structure Council which was established by MITI to advise on the future shape of Japanese industry in the wake of the oil crisis and greater trade liberalization.

The extent to which the representatives of large Japanese companies have been incorporated into the process of policy formulation is so comprehensive that Thayer has argued 'These men do not put pressure on the centre of government; they are the centre of government' (1969 p.67). Thayer had in mind a particular group of businessmen (*Zakai*) who worked very closely with MITI during the reconstruction of the economy in the 1950s. Although most of these individuals have long since departed their role is now performed by others through a variety of channels in trade associations, *Keidanren, Nikkeiren* or through advisory bodies. Consultation with particular individuals now matters less than the preferential access given to the leading employers' representatives. There is a sense in which senior company executives operate as business statesmen, retaining a presidential function with their companies but adding a more general political role in one or more of the key associations. Even though day-to-day company affairs may be left to junior colleagues, senior executives have sufficient knowledge to be able to represent company interests through their membership of appropriate industry associations or *Keidanren*. At the same time they have sufficient status from their past performance as managers to be included as key participants in the deliberations with Ministry officials on a variety of national policy issues.

4.10 The state and private business – allies not adversaries

The practice of *amakudari* and the extensive amount of collaboration in policy formation helps to show why in contemporary Japan the lines of demarcation between the state and private business are less clearly drawn. If to these social practices we add the long tradition of state involvement, there seems to be a different perception of the state's legitimate right to guide the economy. 'The close cooperative relations between Government and business have a quality apt to be missing in countries where individualist versions of "free enterprise" actually constitute an article of faith as well as of rhetoric' (Dore 1986 p.112). In countries where democracy was fought for to protect individual rights against the power of absolute rulers, liberal traditions focus on containing the power of the modern state. Classical economics developed out of such liberal values viewing the market and the state as rivals competing over resource allocation. In Japan, however, liberal democratic traditions are of more recent origin. As the 1947 Constitution was imposed from without by the US occupation there are elements of continuity from the pre-war era which encourage less conflict over the division between the state and civil society. In many ways the 'function of the state is organically incorporated into the market mechanism of individual decisions' (Kitamura 1976 p.115).

It would be wrong to infer from this that the state and business are never at odds, but rather that cooperation is expected to be the norm and collaborative institutions function to maintain these expectations. To be sure there is closer collaboration with big business which creates inequalities of access to the state for representatives of small firms, labour and foreign firms. But for all that, cooperation rather than conflict with the state is built into business expectations. Seen in this light economic debates which polarize market freedom *versus* state intervention or political arguments about the power of business *versus* the bureaucracy, fail to capture the essence of Japanese political economy. The state and private enterprise are not seen as operating in mutually exclusive spheres, which anyway may only be the case in ideal models of perfectly competitive markets. The Japanese state like all other capitalist states recognizes that the market, when left entirely to itself, does not necessarily produce the most politically acceptable way to allocate resources.

In the crisis of the later 1970s all states have sought in one way or another to ameliorate the effects of economic recession. The general objective has been to smooth the process of industrial adjustment to lower levels of demand, avoid damaging price wars and cushion the impact on employment. In Japan, rather than allocating larger subsidies to depressed industries or increasing public spending on unemployment benefits, the state has coordinated the commitment of private firms to reducing their productive capacity. Coordination for industries such as steel, shipbuilding, synthetic fibres, textiles or aluminium smelting uses the relevant trade associations where bureaucrats attempt to secure voluntary agreements to scrap or mothball capacity. If voluntary arrangements are difficult to sustain then producers may need the force of an official cartel which in turn needs exemption from anti-monopoly laws. Adjusting capacity downwards has been more effective in industries where output is concentrated among fewer firms because negotiations are less protracted and the large firms involved can use their conglomerate links to switch more easily to new sectors. Membership of wider groupings also provides access to loans in order to pay levies to those firms who lose a greater share of capacity. In less concentrated industries like textiles on the other hand, cartels are difficult to arrange among so many small firms who are also less able to finance levies to those firms who leave the industry. Closing down plant is not an easy process for firms of any size, but it has been much more painful for small firms who have none of the conglomerate advantages of large companies. Some financial support has been offered by the state but 'total expenditure has not been large: the larger share of state funds for industry has been reserved for growing ducklings rather than for lame old ducks' (Dore 1986 p.112).

Reducing capacity also of course reduces demand for labour. Employment in manufacturing even in large companies fell sharply in the immediate aftermath of the 1974 oil crisis, but redundancies among women were four times as large as among men. As is the case elsewhere in the West fewer women, in common with older men, register as unemployed and together these groups bore the brunt of the redundancies. (Rohlen 1979 p.262). These job losses though were insufficient to meet the reduction in labour costs that the slump in demand required. Rather than allowing a substantial rise in public spending on unemployment, the state offered subsidies to firms in order to slow down the extent of redundancies among male regular workers. The emphasis was on labour re-allocation so the state subsidized retraining costs, the expenses incurred in moving workers to related affiliates, early retirement payments and the financing of temporary lay-offs. Moving labour within companies or their group affiliates is not usually an option open to small firms, but for large ones this went some way towards preserving the image of lifetime employment.

Protecting the employment of regular workers was crucial in securing 'realistic' wage settlements with enterprise unions. Since 1975 the level of *shunto* wage agreements has been kept below the rate of increase in productivity so that unit labour costs in Japan rose more slowly than among its competitors. A second characteristic of *shunto* settlements is the absence of any correlation between wage increases and changes in profits, exports or total sales when these are disaggregated by industrial sector. Market theory though predicts that differences in company performance will produce differential wage increases. In practice *shunto* negotiations distribute to labour 'such amounts as are deemed to be nationally available . . . on the basis of what has come to be socially acceptable rather than on the basis of rewarding efficiency and productivity at the micro level' (Dunn 1986 p.36). It is difficult to see how general agreement on socially acceptable norms could have been secured without national coordination. *Nikkerein* has played a part in organizing a collective approach from employers but the state too has participated in the process of bargaining. In particular by framing socially acceptable norms in terms of the national need to prevent wage-push inflation; in other words 'a *de facto* incomes policy' (Boltho *Times Higher Education Supplement* 7/11/86 p.23).

The unrestrained impact of market forces on output, wages and employment have been cushioned in these ways to reflect social and political as well as economic priorities. What this style of recession adjustment reflects is a determination that the state, or more accurately Japanese taxpayers, should bear a limited burden to preserve the emphasis on public investment not consumption. But there is a sense in which part of the burden of recession is shifted to private consumers. Avoiding potentially ruinous and unplanned price wars may smooth out fluctuations in profitability or male employment, but as a consequence prices do not fall as fast as they would have done with unfettered competition. Notwithstanding arguments about trade barriers, retail prices in Japan have usually risen faster or fallen more slowly than either wholesale or export prices. So what the Japanese save as taxpayers they pay for as consumers. In some ways this may be seen as more 'efficient' as taxpayers have deeper pockets because public subsidies to declining sectors are difficult to terminate and thus exit from the market is delayed. But to arrive at this more 'efficient' outcome the full benefit to consumers of falling prices through market competition has to be withheld. Over a much longer period similar decisions to interfere with the market for agricultural products means that Japanese consumers have to pay higher prices for food in order to protect prosperity of farmers.

Clearly then even with less direct state expenditure on declining sectors there is still a determination to promote a more orderly adjustment than the market would produce if left to itself. Therefore in common with other liberal democracies the Japanese state has to temper the effects of economic competition at the micro level with its national political and social priorities. In ensuring compatibility between market responses and the priority attached to economic growth, the coordinating role of the Japanese bureaucracy has been sustained by its close links with business. As important has been the three decades of unbroken conservative party rule which provided continuity in economic priorities.

5

The Japanese Polity

5.1 Continuous conservatism

The most significant feature of Japanese political life is that in contrast to all the other liberal democracies the Conservatives have exercised unbroken power for over 40 years. Since 1945 in only one short period of less than a year has an alternative party emerged with more Diet seats and even this victory did not produce a majority. Apart from this coalition led by Socialists in 1947–8, the subsequent fifteen post-war national elections have consistently resulted in Conservative majorities. Even after the two main Conservative groups were fused into a Liberal Democratic Party (LDP) in 1955 the prospects for such long-term dominance of national politics was not at all obvious. To this day the LDP has a very limited mass party membership, its structure is riddled with personality factions which appear to retain grievances with each other over long periods and its leadership has had a marked propensity for involvement in corruption scandals. Nevertheless the LDP even in its worst election year polled twice as many votes as the next largest party.

Cynics might suggest that the creation of an Asian bastion of conservatism was as significant to the reforming zealots of the US occupation as their desire to democratize Japan. It is clear that at least in their labour policies the US authorities were keen to support the anti-socialist stance of Japanese governments after 1948, but it is difficult to see how an externally imposed Constitution could have so successfully engineered such a prolonged era of LDP rule. As we have seen in earlier chapters even before the end of the occupation the spirit of the political reforms was already being reversed by the re-centralization of educational administration and the erosion of local government autonomy. Such informal amendments to democratic ideals should not however lead us to underestimate the significance of the changes to established political practices that were encapsulated in the 1947 Constitution.

The most fundamental political change was to shift the focus of sovereign power from the Emperor to a Diet in which both Chambers were to be elected for the first time by all adult men and women. An independent Judiciary was formally charged with the task of safeguarding the Constitution's commitment to 'eternal and inviolable human rights', but there was no formal separation of executive from legislative power as in the US presidential system. Instead executive power was vested in the Cabinet led by a Prime Minister elected from among Diet members. Of the two Diet Chambers the House of Representatives is the more important as its members have the final say in the event of any disagreement with the House of Councillors over the choice of Prime Minister. Democratizing Japanese politics also meant that the US occupation wanted increased popular participation through the tiers of local government, so elected assemblies and chief executives were to operate at regional, city, town and village levels. Hence the Local Autonomy Law of 1947 sought to prevent any return to the high degree of pre-war central government control and make local officials accountable to local electors.

In essence the US reforms were designed to uphold popular sovereignty against the exercise of arbitrary power by non-elected individuals or groups such as the military, the peerage, the bureaucracy or employers. In this vein the Land reform programme aimed to destroy the economic and political influence of landlords replacing the hierarchy of rural society based on tenancy with grassroots democracy based on small independent proprietors. The rights of labour to organize and bargain collectively and to expect equality of opportunity, were included in the Constitution as part of fundamental civil rights in contrast to the pre-war emphasis on duty to employers and thereby the state.

Although no significant changes have been made since 1947 to these formal provisions, we do need to ask how far they have been reflected in political practices. Has the Diet for example remained 'the highest organ of state power and the sole law-making organ of the state' (1947 Constitution Chapter IV Article 41)? As 'political principles differ widely from the conduct of practical affairs' (Baerwald 1986 p.155) to what extent do elected members of the Diet control the legislative process? With such a long period of LDP rule and given the fusion of powers in Cabinets drawn overwhelmingly from LDP Diet members, many writers have argued that the Diet acts merely as a ratifier of legislation handed down by the government. It also is apparent that the majority of policy and legislative proposals are drafted by non-elected officials so is the power of the elected representatives being over-ridden by the entrenched influence of the bureaucracy? We have already seen how the US Occupation chose to administer Japan through the existing civilian administration and the purge of war-time political leaders served initially at least to confirm their dominance of the executive. The short tenure of both Prime Ministers and Cabinet Ministers over the past four decades has served to maintain the influence of bureaucrats whose lengthier years of continuous service in their ministries encourage incoming ministers to rely heavily on their expertise. In addition the fusion of executive and legislative power is sustained by the early retirement of bureaucrats into political life as Diet members, invariably with the LDP.

Just as the focus of the debate on the Japanese economy has tended to polarize the private market versus the state, so also have interpretations of political institutions crystallized around the disputed dominance of the bureaucracy over the elected representatives in the Diet. To an extent even the use of the term 'Diet' rather than 'Parliament' indicates a degree of uncertainty over the reality of the change from the pre-war consultative assembly to a truly independent and sovereign legislature. Equally the independent authority of the Judiciary especially in the Supreme Court has been used so sparingly as to raise doubts about its ability to challenge decisions of the executive. As we shall see this low-key approach has been most manifest in the Supreme Court's failure to oversee alterations to the gross inequalities in the size of electoral districts which has given the LDP a marked advantage in national elections.

Other elements of the political process throw up inconsistencies between the spirit and practice of the 1947 Constitution. Local autonomy was eroded especially in education and control of the police during the 1950s, but the election of non-LDP candidates as mayors and governors in many of the larger urban areas had by the 1970s brought the issue of central government encroachment firmly into the political arena. This tension was in itself part of a general trend which saw the establishment of a wide variety of citizens' groups which reflected a mood of dissatisfaction with the attitude of LDP governments towards environmental pollution and the provision of public goods. Refinements to the labour laws eroded the rights of public sector workers to strike and state support for non-political enterprise unions has had profound effects for the ability of opposition parties to coordinate support from the labour movement.

Against this background of refining or reversing the spirit of the Constitution the first part of this chapter will be concerned with explaining why and how the LDP has managed to retain power for so long. This discussion carries two dimensions; one concerning the attractiveness of the LDP itself and the other concerning the weaknesses and fragmentation of alternative parties who have been condemned to perpetual opposition. Matters of principle enshrined in the Constitution dealing with the supremacy of the Diet and the relative power of the bureaucracy or the Cabinet will be considered through the practices adopted by successive LDP governments. It is also necessary to examine other forms of citizen representation which continue to function between elections, that is interest group activity. In particular we need to ask about the equality of access to the state either through membership of public advisory bodies or through established pressure groups which focus on matters economic or social that cut across political divisions. In other words, to ask how far does the continuity of LDP governments reflect the legitimate outcome of the operation of representative political institutions?

5.2 The roots of conservative majorities

In the mid-1950s the prospect of one party enjoying continuous Diet majorities was hardly anticipated. Once the fusion of the socialist parties into the Japan Socialist Party (JSP) in October 1955 was followed within a month by the amalgamation of the two main Conservative parties into the LDP, alternating governments in a two-party system appeared to be the most realistic prospect. Even though the 1958 election gave the socialists only one-third of the seats in the Diet, the omens were promising for them to secure a majority in the next decade. Rapid urbanization was expected to produce solid support for the socialists among the more progressive groups of younger wage earners. An equivalent decline in the numerical predominance of Japan's rural areas foreshadowed a secular decline in the fortunes of the LDP. On particular issues too the socialist opposition seemed to be closer to public concern with the way the Conservatives had refined the spirit of constitutional safeguards for local control of education and the police, the labour rights of public sector workers and the demilitarization of Japan. Foreign policy was seen to be too closely dependent on the US with widespread demonstrations against the stationing of US forces with nuclear weapons on Japanese soil. Thus the JSP felt optimistic that it better represented the commitment of the Japanese people to neutrality and that by mobilizing a post-war generation of urban voters it could soon become the party of government.

Figure 5.1 indicates clearly that JSP optimism remains unfulfilled and that the expected decline of the LDP was not as dramatic as political forecasters had predicted. Though the JSP remains the largest single opposition party its share of the popular vote and seats won has halved and its 99 per cent dominance of the total opposition seats in 1958 had fallen to less than 40 per cent by 1986. LDP majorities were certainly cut, but even in the later 1970s when the party won only 49 per cent of seats in the House of Representatives, its position as the party of government was never seriously challenged. Technically the Diet votes of conservatively inclined unaffiliated members could usually be relied upon to secure the passage of important legislation, but of equal significance was the inability of the opposition to coordinate its numerical strength. As Figure 5.2 shows the opposition has become fragmented into four competing parties which offer little prospect of a consistently united front against the LDP. The expectation that the JSP could amass the votes of urban labour were

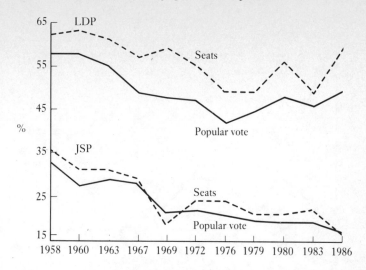

Figure 5.1 Shares of the popular vote and seats won by the JSP and LDP in
House of Representative elections, 1958–86
Source: Japan Statistical Yearbook

undermined initially by the defection of centre-right socialists into the
Democratic Socialist Party (DSP) in 1960 and then by the revival of the
Japan Communist Party (JCP) in the later 1960s. If we add the other party
Komeito, which is a quasi-religious populist organization, the picture of a
fragmented multi-party opposition is confirmed.

Against this fragmentation of opposition parties the LDP itself has been
beset with internal divisions but these have revolved around non-ideological
disputes between rival factions which have not threatened its continuity in
government. Even the defection of a group of conservatives to form the
New Liberal Club (NLC) in 1976 resulted in a loss of only two or three
members who in practice usually voted with the LDP and the new party
was accommodated in a formal coalition from 1983. For the opposition
not only are there real differences in ideology, but the example of the
NLC coalition has encouraged members of the DSP and *Komeito* to see
cooperation with the LDP rather than the JSP as their only route to
government office.

If there was any consolation for the LDP in its decline during the 1970s
it was based on the knowledge that unity among the opposition was very
unlikely. There have been some attempts to operate electoral alliances in
particular districts where the LDP support was thought to be fragile but
there was little evidence that such cooperation would be sustained beyond
the immediate ambition of winning particular seats. The bleak prospects
for an alternative government formed by a coalition among the opposition

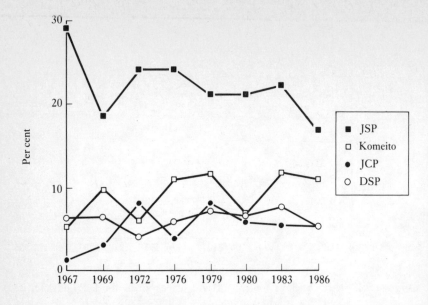

Figure 5.2 A Fragmented Opposition's share of seats won in House of
Representative elections, 1967–86
Source: *Japan Statistical Yearbook*

has to be set against the consistency with which the LDP has won at least
half of the seats in the House of Representatives even when its popular
vote fell as low as 42 per cent in 1976. Figure 5.1 shows that the LDP
has continuously managed to win a higher proportion of seats than its
share of the popular vote would justify. In no small way this trend reflects
the advantage the party derives from the uneven size of electoral districts.

As a much larger number of LDP members are elected from small
districts, a lower proportion of the total votes cast produces more victorious
candidates. Only painfully slow changes have been made to the spatial
apportionment of seats since the organization of electoral districts was
established on the basis of a population census taken immediately after the
Pacific war. In the following four decades though there has been a
significant change in residential patterns from one-third of the population
living in urban areas to three-quarters in 1987; the urban voter is thus
grossly under-represented and in rural areas over-represented. In practical
terms this means that in some rural districts there is one seat for 115,000
electors whereas some urban seats represent 500,000. Inequalities of the
order of 4:1 are not uncommon which means that some candidates can
win with 40,000 votes while others lose despite polling 120,000. The
principal beneficiary of this degree of maldistribution is the LDP whose
main strength lies in the rural districts which regularly yield 60 per cent

of their Diet representation (Ike 1978 ch.5).

The worst cases of inequality in district size do occur at the extremes of population density and sparsity. None the less the overall impact is significant in at least three other senses. First, the turn-out of voters in rural areas tends to be much higher at around 80 per cent making it easier for LDP candidates to gather even the small numbers required to win seats in rural districts. Secondly, even semi-urban areas contain sufficiently high numbers of rural voters to swing results towards the LDP. Finally, eligible urban voters knowing that their vote is grossly under-represented in national elections tend to turn out in smaller numbers. So unequal electoral districts trigger a process which magnifies the advantages of the LDP by encouraging most abstentions where their own support is weakest.

Electoral gerrymandering has, as might be expected, been a longstanding source of dissatisfaction but there is no independent body to impose a redistribution of seats on an unwilling Diet, which means on an uncooperative LDP majority. The Supreme Court has ruled explicitly that three out of the last five elections were unfair and actually labelled the 1983 election as unconstitutional because of the disproportionate allocation of seats. Only one out of fourteen Justices though, was prepared to nullify the result; of the rest only five warned that if no changes were made they *might* nullify the outcome of the next election. Despite the evidence of the 1985 census which shows that the differential value of votes between some urban and rural districts had widened to nearly 5:1, the Supreme Court as on other issues appears reluctant to use its Constitutional right to check the abuse of power by the Diet. Instead 'it prefers to see popular sovereignty as resting on the legislative branch ... and wishes to avoid any repetition of pre-war executive encroachment on legal terrain' (Buckley 1985 p.40). The relatively short tradition of a truly independent judiciary, assisted so the opposition argues by the preferential appointment of conservative judges, makes the Supreme Court more acquiescent than its US counterpart which was the exemplar in the 1947 Constitution.

It would be wrong to suggest that no changes at all have been made to the distribution of seats but re-allocation has been limited to the addition of a few extra seats to urban districts. Even this limited change allows the LDP to claim that it is not impervious to public concern or to the rulings of the Supreme Court. Recent proposals by the Government could certainly be designated as 'limited' as their best offer promises to reduce the inequity in representation to not more than 3:1! The unwillingness of the Supreme Court to become embroiled in a constitutional conflict leaves the opposition little choice but to accept the few conciliatory crumbs offered by the self-styled 'natural' party of government. In itself the hesitancy of the Supreme Court sheds some light on the reality of constitutional checks and balances especially when this involves leaving the LDP with 'a built-in advantage which it will jealously preserve at all costs' (Buckley 1985 p.27).

Election results in the 1980s tend to show that the LDP is not entirely a party representing rural districts and it has gained more support at the expense of socialists in urban Japan. But the rural vote is still strongly conservative enough to tolerate its more tenuous position in densely populated urban areas and makes the LDP reluctant to alter the imbalance in voter representation. How then have conservatives managed to retain such a secure foothold in rural districts?

Despite the fierce suppression of rural socialism under the guise of ultranationalism in the 1930s, the socialist parties did have the opportunity immediately after the war to establish their presence in farmers' unions that opposed the domination of landlords. But by choosing to uphold the principles of dispersed ownership for most small farmers and security of tenure for the remainder, the conservatives effectively undermined the ability of socialist parties to exploit the divisive issues of landownership. Indeed by denying dispossessed landlords the opportunity to recover some of their lost authority in the 1950s, conservative governments thereby made 'Japanese villages safe for conservatism' (Dore 1958 p.88). This pattern has continued and in one sense reflects a distrust of socialist parties that attach priority to propertyless workers rather than owners and proprietors. But other political processes serve to maintain high levels of support for the LDP not least those characteristically conservative policies which protect domestic agriculture as the main prop of the rural economy.

The right of small Japanese farmers to own land was one thing but their ability to earn a reasonable income from their land was quite another. Severe economic difficulties beset the new class of farm-owners because the average size of their holding at two or three hectares was too small to offer much prospect of any substantial reductions in cost through improvements in productivity. As a result if a free market was to rule for rice then imports at a third of Japanese prices, would totally undermine the viability of domestic farming. To safeguard the position of indigenous agriculture and its own rural support base, LDP Governments have restricted food imports and used subsidies to mitigate the full impact of higher Japanese production costs. As the main vehicle through which agricultural producers are represented in national negotiations over the level of state intervention, the agricultural cooperatives exercise political functions as an interest group but they also have crucial economic and political roles at local level. Over 90 per cent of farmers belong to cooperatives which organize the provision of credit, the sharing of capital equipment and joint purchasing schemes for inputs like fertilisers as well as coordinating the sale of output to the government.

Elected officials of the cooperatives inevitably become closely involved with LDP members because of the party's dominance in government and its attachment to agricultural protection. Diet members from rural districts are expected to maintain the level of support programmes, oppose moves to dismantle market controls or the perennial proposals from the Ministry of Finance to reduce the level of public subsidies. For rural areas where the politics of agriculture is paramount, cooperative officials also provide the leadership of elected local or regional assemblies. Where landowning notables previously exercised power and influence, land reform saw this role pass to owners of larger more prosperous farms or to owners of small firms. As elected political leaders and in many cases as key officials of the cooperative, the fusion of political and economic power continues to cement village solidarity through the administration of agricultural support programmes.

Protection for agriculture as a whole is only one link in the chain that connects rural districts to the LDP. The particular needs of local constituencies are expected to be satisfied through the personal intercession of Diet representatives whose own standing is judged, for example, by their ability to secure a share of centrally financed public investment. Most farms are too small to generate an adequate income from farming if this is the only occupation, and this is clearly one reason for the migration of local people to the towns. To slow down the rate of depopulation, public investment in roads and railways is required to foster the growth of non-agricultural employment and so diversify the rural economy. In addition despite their falling population, rural residents demand improvements in the provision of schools and hospitals to prevent further decay to the vitality of their communities. As we saw in Chapter 4 the scale of Japanese public investment is extensive, and higher levels of support for LDP candidates is expected to yield direct tangible rewards through the allocation of resources from central government.

Beneath the general commitment to agriculture that is expected from the LDP, another dimension of a 'patron–client democracy has taken root in agricultural communities, the bastion of LDP strength, under the banner of public investment in rural areas' (T. Sasaki 1987 p.15). Continued loyalty to particular candidates then is based not so much on their party label but to a representative with 'a pipeline to the central sources of government largesse' (Flanagan 1980 p.166). One of the outstanding examples of patron–client practices can be seen in the ability of ex-Prime Minister Tanaka to influence the allocation of public investment to his home district of Niigata, a remote area of western Japan. From 1947 onwards he promised roads, tunnels, railroads, reclamation projects, schools and snow clearing services in return for local votes and throughout his climb through the hierarchy of the LDP he certainly delivered what he promised. Despite his fall from power in 1974 which was precipitated by charges of corrupt dealings with the Lockheed Corporation, and his resignation from official membership of the LDP, Niigata citizens continue to benefit from his patronage. In 1982 for example public investment *per capita* was six times as great as the amount people in Niigata paid in taxes. Tokyo residents in the same year paid twice as much per head in taxes as they received in spending on public works (Johnson 1986 p.8).

Mutual relations of loyalty to Diet members who deliver tangible rewards to their constituency are crucial to the higher rate of voter mobilization which is a feature of rural districts. In addition agricultural cooperatives act as both an administrative vehicle and a political machine to maintain support for the LDP. But the 80–90 per cent support for the LDP recorded in many rural districts also requires careful nurturing between elections. Many small farmers, for instance, produce so little rice beyond their own subsistence needs, that they gain few direct benefits from government subsidies. The importance of the cooperatives is that they give local political leaders the authority to maintain village solidarity to particular candidates by acting as the organizer of a Diet member's support group. Such personal support networks are not simply vehicles for electioneering but they serve to maintain a continuous local presence for elected representatives. The key intermediary – the local political boss – acts as an agent organizing support group meetings, making sure the candidate subscribes to local societies, sending presents on his behalf to local notables or delivering wreaths to the funeral of important residents. As Diet members rely on local politicians to nurse their districts, they provide in return assistance to the political career of their disciples in local assemblies or public institutions. This may mean providing financial assistance in elections to the cooperative and local council or exerting pressure on regional government to make sure that the appropriate villages receive grants that reflect favourably on the work of village leaders. 'By these means Diet members and local officials mutually strengthen each others position' (Dore 1959 p.419). The personal support groups then serve as the mechanism for voter mobilization and also bridge the gap between the members presence at the centre in Tokyo and their constituents in the periphery.

In the initial selection of candidates, area loyalties and personal ties are particularly important in order to portray potential members as people who will know how best to look after 'our' interests because they are 'one of us'. But in maintaining what may be only distant blood or land ties, personal support networks are as vital as affiliation to the LDP. As we shall see, the Japanese electoral system which uses large districts each with between three and five seats, means that members of the same party compete for the single non-transferable vote of each elector. Hence even in rural districts candidates need the security of safe havens in particular villages and towns and it is exactly this solidarity that local support groups can deliver.

It is not at all unusual for conservatives to regard rural areas as their own preserve. But what makes the Japanese political process somewhat different is the way unequal representation magnifies the effect of a solid rural base for the LDP. The intimate connections between agricultural cooperatives, local conservative leaders and sitting members makes it virtually impossible for opposition candidates to break through this web of influence. Having neither a power base in the cooperatives nor any favoured access to central government favours, the opposition can offer little prospect of matching the LDP's 'calculating contractual relations' (Dore 1959 p.419). Political practices which involve the exchange of personal loyalties to particular candidates in return for direct local benefits is not, though, peculiar to rural Japan. Multi-member constituencies mean that individual candidates need support groups to press their personal cause even against candidates from the same party. The ensuing degree of intra-party competition is also one reason why the LDP continues to be organized around competing factions.

5.3 The LDP and factional politics

Once the principle of universal suffrage was enshrined in a reformed structure of political institutions by the US occupation, the choice of electoral system was left to the Japanese themselves. After a brief experiment with a limited version of proportional representation elections to the more influential House of Representatives reverted to the system used before the war: multiple-member constituencies with single votes. By 1986 there were 130 large districts divided nearly equally into three-, four- and five-member constituencies and with 512 seats to be contested, a majority for one party requires the election of on average two candidates per district. Inevitably a degree of rivalry thus prevails among members representing the LDP as well as against opposition candidates because they are all competing for a single non-transferable vote. So in contrast to single member systems the contest can be 'chaotic as candidates (particularly from the ruling party) attack one another regardless of their affiliation' (Steven 1983 p.303).

This type of electoral system was established in the 1890s as a mechanism through which non-elected elites might limit the cohesion of political parties and so retain their power. Until 1945 military personnel and members of the Emperor's circle of advisors shared office with elected politicians in what were usually non-party governments. Since then although Cabinet government through elected representatives is now the rule, political parties have inherited an electoral system which still encourages an unusual amount of intra-party competition. With several seats available, the key problem for the parties is to estimate accurately their likely total vote in order to endorse just the appropriate number of candidates. Too many candidates from the LDP for example may split their total vote to the detriment of them all; too few candidates may produce enough votes to have won extra seats. The delicate act of balancing the number of officially endorsed candidates with estimates of their expected total vote in particular districts is therefore crucial.

In 1986, for example, when the LDP gained a 20 per cent increase in its Lower House majority, Prime Minister Nakasone interpreted the result as 'The voice of god speaking from heaven.' More circumspect political commentators pointed out that this 'landslide' reflected only an 8 per cent increase in the popular vote. One explanation of the discrepancy attributed the extra seats gained to a much more accurate prediction of how many candidates to endorse in contrast to 1983 when too many LDP candidates produced a large number of narrow defeats. What remains a problem for the LDP is the unpredictable impact of the weight electors attach to the performance of their member in delivering local benefits since the last election. Even an official endorsement cannot always counteract the impression that an elected member has neglected local interests either in pursuing their own career in government or following the dictates of national LDP policies.

To increase their chances of election, new LDP candidates need local connections which allow them to establish a support network strong enough for them to be considered worthy of endorsement. In the national allocation of official party candidates, sponsorship from one of the main factions is imperative because the whole process of endorsement is the outcome of informal bargaining between faction leaders. Generally factions aim to secure the endorsement of just one representative per district in order to avoid dissipating their financial resources and to prevent intra-factional rivalry. In return for the initial patronage needed simply to become endorsed, those so selected pledge their commitment to the leadership ambitions of one or sometimes two faction leaders. These reciprocal obligations are then maintained by the efforts of faction leaders to secure party or government posts for their followers in return for providing faction members with the finance needed to continue winning elections.

The ability of faction leaders to provide for the political expenses of their followers is one reason why the Japanese political process continues to function with factions as an integral institution. Although the precise figures are shrouded in mystery, newspaper estimates suggest that the average cost of winning a Diet seat in 1986 was over one billion yen ($7 million or £5 million). A large proportion of this is spent lubricating local constituents with food, drink or presents as well as the more usual expenses of producing leaflets or posters and organizing meetings. To meet these costs the LDP candidate can expect only limited support from central party funds because the party is relatively weak in terms of a mass membership contributing regular subscriptions. Political donations from business are extensive but they are made directly to faction leaders who then distribute the funds to finance the election of their followers. Up to 70 per cent of election expenses are estimated to be met from within the faction's own resources which thus heightens the dependence of faction members on the continued patronage of their leader. Financial backing is also crucial between elections as Diet members need a flow of funds to maintain their local support groups and pay the local election expenses of their district representatives. As a channel of political funds an LDP faction thus extends the network of reciprocal obligations from national to local level and thereby ensures the continuity of its own strength in the Diet.

The existence of sub-groups within political parties which coalesce around the personality of ambitious individuals is a perennial feature in the struggle for power. Where party factions act as a vehicle to challenge entrenched orthodoxies or where they offer alternative policies it could be argued that they offer the electorate the opportunity to influence changes in political goals. Factions rooted in competing ideologies are common among Japanese socialists and have been one reason why parties which claim to represent labour have split into three or four rival parties. Some political scientists have argued that in the absence of any realistic alternative government from among the opposition parties, factions within the LDP serve the function of presenting the electorate with a choice of policies. In other words intra-party competition within an amorphous group of conservatives is a healthy sign that guarantees constructive argument and debate even within a party as dominant as the LDP. Superficially this assessment is appealing yet what appears to be most important in maintaining divisions between the factions are personal disputes between their leaders. These personal differences are usually based on the failure of the faction leader to obtain the senior post they covet or that their followers have not been treated fairly in the allocation of cabinet offices. One such conflict between the Fukuda and Tanaka factions has been a continuous source of division within the LDP ever since 1972 when Tanaka broke the convention that a member of the retiring Prime Minister's faction should not be his successor. Fifteen years later when the two principals had stepped aside as leaders, the acrimonious dispute was still evident among their successors in the battle to replace Nakasone.

It is of course possible to detect that some factions espouse greater or lesser degrees of explicit support for reviving Japan's own defence forces or to see more fervent nationalism in the new right policies of Nakasone. But other factions contain members who would support this platform while at the same time denying the prerogatives of an opposing faction leader. Although factions do have separately organized offices and institutions they tend not to produce distinctively different political manifestos. Hence inter-factional bitterness which may last over lengthy periods is perpetuated by personality conflicts with 'barely a hint of any factor even remotely linked to an issue of public policy' (Baerwald 1986 p.170).

The very origins of the LDP in the fusion of two separate parties which had competed for the limited number of government posts in pre-war Japan, would inevitably have produced competition for the leadership of the newly integrated LDP. But even within these two parties there were divisions. One problem in the 1950s concerned the need to accommodate those politicians who had been purged for their wartime activities and some factions favoured their preferential inclusion. Other factions were dominated by a new generation of Diet members who not only resented the way pre-war leaders had returned to senior positions, but also rejected the right of retiring bureaucrats to take *amakudari* into Cabinet office. Yet other factions developed under the leadership of charismatic figures especially where they were able to deliver their supporters with large amounts of election finance from large Japanese companies. Some factions disintegrated when their leader retired or died without an obvious heir-apparent with reasonably secure prospects for high office. Hence some re-alignment takes place when a faction disappears but otherwise movement between factions is unusual. Faction numbers can be reinforced from the ranks of newly elected Diet members which reinforces the desire of each faction leader to influence the selection of endorsed candidates. 'Small wonder it is then that come election time the Presidential faction gets as a rule the lion's share of newly elected members' (Fukui 1984 p.402).

There is a parallel here between continuity in faction membership and the prospect of lifetime employment offered to certain workers in large Japanese companies. Just as secure tenure is seen as the reward for company loyalty, so also will a faction leader offer to reward personal loyalty from a follower with the prospect of promotions on the ladder of their political career. Just as movements between large companies are effectively precluded by the accompanying loss of seniority, so also are movements between political factions constrained by lost status and rank. 'Soiling one's *curriculum vitae*' for a disloyal faction member means starting again at the bottom of the promotion ladder in their new faction. Factions therefore developed as 'devices by means of which a member of the party in the Diet hoped to acquire either a government post, a party post, political funds or all of these' (Fukui 1970 p.128). As an integral feature of the Japanese political scene, factions are officially registered organizations with offices, procedures and meetings that are separate from the central administration of the LDP. Their focus is primarily based on the preoccupation of the leader or his nominee in securing election to the party presidency – hence in the case of the LDP becoming Prime Minister. The numerical strength of a faction allows the leader to participate in the negotiated distribution of party and government posts which preserves a leader's role as a dispenser of patronage.

When several factions compete over the right to dispense a limited number of appointments there has to be some way of sharing patronage between them. It is unusual for the allocation of senior government and LDP offices to be conducted in public view but the process seems to involve job rotation among the bigger factions. Cabinet appointments apart from the Ministries of Finance, Foreign Affairs or Trade and Industry, appear to be re-shuffled annually to ensure a degree of power sharing between the rival factions. Sato who was Prime Minister from 1964–72 gave Cabinet posts to over 100 LDP members – 'a notable feat in view of the fact that he had only 20 Cabinet-rank jobs at his disposal' (Christopher 1984 p.199). As for the most senior Cabinet offices it is almost a requirement for any party leader to have been Minister of Finance or

Trade and Industry which therefore makes these jobs the subject of the most intense horse-trading. In essence support for a rival faction leader in the election to the LDP Presidency usually results in other faction heads being rewarded with senior Cabinet posts or top party jobs.

The Secretary-Generalship of the LDP is one of the key prizes partly because this position offers the opportunity to influence the endorsement of new candidates and so build up the strength of his faction in the Diet. In addition, since 1978 LDP members outside the Diet have been consulted in the process of choosing a new leader through a party primary election which gives the Secretary-General a power base outside the Diet. Thus a faction that is dissatisfied with the current leadership can mobilize opposition to the Prime Minister within the party at large. Such a dispersal of factional power centres within the LDP has not only led to 'The absurd frequency with which cabinets are made and then re-constructed' (Buckley 1985 p.27) but has also shortened the tenure of Prime Ministers. In the eight years after the fall of Tanaka in 1974 there were five different Prime Ministers whose tenure was fraught with inter-party squabbles over the allocation of senior posts. Faction rivalries continue to make 'considerations of coalition maintenance and personal power maximization often take precedence over those of government performance' (J.W. White 1974 p.424). Not only do these endless struggles undermine public confidence in their elected representatives but they also tend to diminish the power of the Prime Minister.

Elections for the leadership of the LDP are the occasion of quite vitriolic disputes between the factions and the extent of their disagreement has resulted on several occasions in the election of the least offensive candidate from a minority faction. Prime Ministers such as Miki, Ohira or Suzuki presided over their Cabinets in the manner of acting executive chairmen subsequently evoking little respect or loyalty from their ministers. Even a more forceful leader experiences recurring problems as recalcitrant colleagues in Cabinet produce uncertainty which weakens his authority as Prime Minister and encourages rivals to oppose his re-election as party leader. Even though Nakasone lasted as Prime Minister for six years from 1982 his period in office saw a continued process of post rotation as competing factions manoeuvred their followers into positions which would pave the way for a successor.

Frequent changes of ministerial personnel and the apparently endless leadership struggles helps to explain why many writers stress the role of the non-elected officials in governing Japan. In the absence of a settled pattern to cabinet government the bureaucracy participates more extensively in the initiation and formulation of policy as well as overseeing its implementation. Non-elected officials with long tenure and experience in their respective ministries draft legislative proposals and supervise consultation with interest groups outside the Diet even before such proposals are submitted for cabinet approval. Bureaucrats also guide what may be a very inexperienced minister through the Diet Committee hearings by drafting both the questions and answers that LDP Diet members ask. Continuity of service gives bureaucrats a source of expertise which although it does not go completely unchallenged, remains significant so long as factional rivalries diminish the tenure of LDP cabinet appointments.

Highlighting the implications of sharing government posts between competing factions does not necessarily imply that the bureaucracy dominates either the cabinet, the LDP or the legislature. But the rotation of ministers does allow bureaucrats to take more responsibility for policy initiation. Conventional models of decision-making in liberal democracies tend to assign to non-elected officials the role of implementing policies which are formulated by elected representatives. In practice it is not always easy to distinguish the two when limited ministerial tenure makes politicians reliant on the experience and expertise of the bureaucracy. What is even more significant in the Japanese case is that one party has dominated government for so long which serves to institutionalize the close relationship between the LDP and non-elected officials.

In some ways these close connections are the product of a homogeneous social background for elites within the bureaucracy and the leadership of the LDP not least in their common educational careers at Japan's prestigious universities. There is also a tradition of movement by senior bureaucrats into the LDP so that over the past three decades they have made up roughly 30 per cent of Diet members and taken up to 50 per cent of cabinet posts. But in addition to personnel transfers, the general commitment of the LDP to conservative values stressing above all national cohesion and consensus, coincides with the bureaucracy's own brief to preserve social harmony against divisive social forces. Although the LDP likes to make a virtue of not 'having anything so concrete or clear cut as an ideology' (Christopher 1984 p.198) it does claim to be the custodian of the mystical essence of Japanese values for an exposed and vulnerable island race. By tapping the inheritance of the enveloping idea of a total society from the pre-war Emperor system, the LDP portrays the opposition especially those that can be labelled 'socialist', as divisive because they place the protection of class interests before that of the 'nation'.

It is revealing to note how the words 'divisive' and 'class' are associated with representing labour but not in connection with the LDP's own financial backers from business. But whether or not the image of the LDP as a party representing the whole nation is real or imaginary it is clear that each of the opposition parties draws its support from distinct social groups. None of these groups is big enough by itself to produce a majority and it is doubtful if any could do so even with a radical re-apportionment of electoral districts. So in practical terms the bureaucracy can expect to continue working with the same party in government and in such circumstances their relationships with the LDP inevitably become more accommodating.

Secure in the knowledge that disunity among the opposition is endemic the LDP can afford to tolerate the luxury of intra-party strife. The apparent obsession of each faction in taking their turn to provide a Prime Minister, a senior cabinet minister or a high-ranking party official reflects the certainty that their years in government will be prolonged. Factional disputes are certainly intense but they have not thus far been pressed to the point where one large faction deserts the LDP. There are few real differences in ideology to separate the faction leaders and if sooner or later they can expect high office why jeopardize their chances in an alliance with one of the opposition parties? Ultimately what has held the LDP together is not so much a coherent philosophy of conservatism but the unequalled opportunity the party offers for government office.

The public response to the venality and self-seeking opportunism of LDP leaders is reflected in 'astounding levels of political dissatisfaction' (Flannagan, Steiner and Kraus 1980 p.458). As the party in government the reliance of the LDP on election finance from business has seen the fine line between political donations and bribery transgressed by several of its leaders. Their subsequent trial and conviction has in the process fuelled the alienation of large numbers of electors. Yet amidst the public disenchantment with the LDP, the opposition has singularly failed to capitalize on scandals which in most circumstances would have led a disillusioned electorate to throw the party out of office.

5.4 A divided opposition: the eternal outsiders

The most obvious reason why the LDP continues to be the party of government is that no other party endorses sufficient candidates to obtain a majority. Not since 1958 has the JSP contested more than half of the seats available, but since then the staggering costs of national elections has been reflected in a fall of 50 per cent in the number of candidates the party enters. By the 1986 election even the largest opposition party could only hope to win at most one-quarter of the seats, and any alternative government therefore would have had to involve the JSP in a coalition with at least two other parties. This failure to contest enough seats to gain a majority begs questions about inadequate financial resources and the more limited popularity of individual opposition parties. But also why should an anti-conservative coalition be such a remote prospect if it is the only conceivable way to dislodge the LDP?

At the risk of oversimplifying their objectives it is not too unreasonable to say that all of the opposition parties claim allegiance from employee households particularly in urban areas. However by claiming to represent a particular class or section of labour means contesting the ideology of a homogeneous Japanese culture. Various social institutions have, especially since the mid-nineteenth century, reproduced the notion that the Japanese possess uniquely cohesive values in which the collective identity of the nation cuts across class divisions. Those parties therefore that base their organization on shared loyalties among even a loosely defined working class, do so against the background of a less salient consciousness of class in general and a much less distinct working class culture in particular.

Without wishing to underestimate the social change that followed the reforms of the later 1940s, Japan's pre-war history has had a notable impact on her political culture. Despite the total and demanding expectation that individuals should sacrifice themselves to the Emperor and thereby the state, socialists did attempt during the 1920s to mobilize popular support for equal political citizenship and universal labour rights. But such efforts to unify the economic focus of labour unions with the political activities of socialist and Marxist parties were ruthlessly suppressed by the state and more radical labour leaders were imprisoned or forced into exile. From the 1870s compulsory conscription and education were used to inculcate the inviolable notion of duty to the Emperor thus denying the essence of individual rights and making opposing ideologies appear as a challenge to imperial authority. By the 1930s the suffocating environment of ultranationalism heightened the repression of socialism by the police and the military because opposition to any element of the existing system was treated as inherently subversive. As a result, the labour movement was emasculated and less radical unions were assimilated into factory groups pledged to the cause of a Greater Asian Empire. In many European societies the coalescence of socialist political objectives with the activities of trade unions around the struggle for citizenship rights was crucially important in moulding the interests of the working class into a distinctive culture. However in Japan the fusion of political and economic conflict was short-lived primarily because the conception of class interest was overwhelmed by the countervailing pressures for national unity based on loyalty to the Emperor.

The Japanese state was radically reconstructed in 1945 but this did not mean that all pre-war ideas, attitudes and social practices were irrevocably swept away. Conservative politicians, business leaders and bureaucrats continue, for example, to promote the need for a strong sense of national cohesion which they see as a necessary compensation for external vulnerability. This sense of vulnerability derives partly from Japan's dependence on external supplies of raw materials but also from the contradictory consequences of the US alliance. Closer military ties with the US while offering some support for Japan's defence also expose it to the immediate presence of the USSR. Neither has the military alliance prevented Japan from being labelled as economic enemy of the US in the disputes over trade protectionism. Fragile external relations then become a justification, along with claims that the Japanese are racially homogeneous, for retaining the primacy of cohesive values in, for example, school textbooks. The strict regulation of school books by the Ministry of Education is designed to promote a one-nation culture; as a result where opposition parties resist the idea of a classless society they risk being stigmatized as divisive and subversive of true Japanese values.

In a general sense the very term opposition is still associated in Japan with being 'outside' the political process rather than being an essential element of democracy. This association has become stronger as opposition parties remain ever further from power so that their role becomes ritualized in negative or obstructive resistance to the LDP. As the LDP claims its own predominance to be a reflection of the true wishes of the majority, the opposition can be maligned for placing sectional interests above the collective will. All socialist parties are challenged with being divisive when their commitment to class interests confronts the equivalent commitment of conservatives to patriotism. But political opponents of the LDP face this challenge to a much greater degree because conservatism in Japan inherited from the Emperor system a definition of socialism as subversive and therefore superfluous to a nation with such a strong common culture.

Even the post-war political reconstruction was not determined by the collective effort of a mass movement representing those previously excluded from power. The fact that equal citizenship rights were conceded almost immediately by the US occupation meant that one possible source of unity in the labour movement was neutralized. This is not to say that neither the restoration of socialist and communist parties in 1945 nor the massive increase in union membership in 1946 had no effect at all on the programme of reforms. Nor is it to deny that union leaders and opposition parties have forged alliances at various times to protect the Constitution from those conservatives who regard it as incompatible with 'Japan's history, traditions, cultural and natural features' (LDP Representative at the 40th anniversary conference, *JTW* 23 May 1987). All I wish to argue is that the speedy concession of political reform coming so soon after the demise of an authoritarian society meant that the roots of a united labour movement were shallow. Class consciousness was, and some would argue still is, more attenuated in Japan, and the growth of separated enterprise unions weakened the solidarity of labour still further. To an extent the existence of four rival parties each with a particular sphere of influence among those disenchanted with the LDP, reflects the effect of labour market segmentation.

The most crucial division between employees is, as we saw in Chapter 3, based on the higher levels of pay, status, tenure and unionization of regular workers in large firms. Although the extent of lifetime employment is more limited than the stereotyped image of Japanese employment practices would suggest, enterprise unions have maintained distinctly better wages and employment conditions for their members compared to workers in small firms or subcontractors. Enterprise unions have also been instrumental in creating a strong sense of loyalty to the company which serves 'to reinforce a sense of identity with the enterprise and a sense of difference from other workers' (Dore 1973 p.285). This exclusive focus on regular employees means that little if any protection is offered to employees of their own company who are temporary or seasonal nor do enterprise unions concern themselves with workers in associated subcontractors. Operating mainly within the confining environment of their own company encourages loyalty from within but competitive rivalry with other firms and their employees. Both of these aspects of enterprise union exclusivity set workers apart. The first encourages competition within a firm on the basis of status because the employment of regular workers who are union members takes priority. The second weakens inter-union cooperation by placing loyalty to the firm ahead of identification with similar occupational groups in other companies.

Sponsoring the more rapid development of enterprise unions from the late 1940s was the route chosen by employers, the Japanese state and the US occupation authorities to counteract attempts to organize labour unions across a number of firms or industries. The objective was to de-politicize industrial relations in general but in particular to undermine the efforts of the Communist Party to combine industrial with political action to hasten revolutionary change. Although enterprise unions have become the norm this has not resulted in a complete divorce between the economic and political spheres of labour representation. Both the JSP and the DSP are at election times heavily dependent on the financial and organizational capacity of unions. This close association has led to a tendency for employees who are excluded from enterprise unions to become alienated from the socialist parties who are seen to be overcommitted to the interest of regular workers. Hence both *Komeito* and the JCP recruit support from labour whose lowly status denies them union membership. One fissure within the opposition then is based on the extent to which both socialist parties depend on the support of unions whose membership excludes over 70 per cent of all employees.

The divisions between the two socialist parties appear not only in their profoundly different ideologies but also because they draw their main organizational support from separate union federations which in the past decade have themselves become bitterly divided. *Domei*, the main federation for private sector enterprise unions, which take a more appeasing stance with management, favours the centre-right DSP. While *Sohyo* largely representing unions in the public sector who have a record of much more radical industrial action, support the more categorical socialism of the JSP.

These generalizations about the way that divisions in the labour market affects the fragmentation of political parties does not necessarily mean that women for example who are grossly underrepresented in unions never support the JSP. Or for that matter, that public sector workers never vote for *Komeito* or the JCP. But partly because an opposition party is perceived as giving special priority to one section of labour this does tend to produce an adverse reaction from individuals in other sections. For example quite apart from the negative associations of the word communist, the JCP is hardly likely to recruit a large following among unionists as the party regards unions as unrepresentative and in need of strict subordination to its political leaders. In a similar way the JSP dependence on union finance and sponsorship did little to organize support among unattached workers who had recently migrated from rural areas, leaving *Komeito* an important source of members.

The extent to which both socialist parties are financially dependent on the unions is a mixed blessing as far as popular support in elections is concerned. As the proportion of employees belonging to a union fell to 28 per cent by 1986 this, when split two ways, hardly provides a sound basis for electoral support even assuming union households share socialist loyalties. The rivalry between *Domei* and *Sohyo* also means that any attempt by politicians to accommodate their differences in a coalition against the LDP would more than likely result in either or both of the union federations withdrawing their financial backing. Both socialist parties have a very small membership which increases their reliance on union support making both appear to be merely a Diet lobby for competing union federations. In turn this narrow perception of their function limits their appeal to other sections of urban labour who potentially may be anti-conservative. This impasse is one factor that accounts for the stagnation in electoral support for both parties over the past decade.

5.5 Sectionalized support among the LDP's opponents

Over the past thirty years the decline in the fortunes of the JSP reflects in part its inability to reconcile an ideological commitment to the whole of the working class with dependence on unions who represent only a limited proportion of the labour force. While the financial contributions of unions affiliated to *Sohyo* is indispensable to JSP election campaigns, this support is focused on sponsoring particular candidates who are frequently themselves union officials. Political contributions by union members are collected not so much for the party in general but to allow the leadership of particular unions to finance the campaigns of their preferred candidates. As a result by 1986 nearly two-thirds of JSP Diet members were ex-union officials, 80 per cent of whom were from public sector unions. It is therefore not surprising that the party's reputation as merely '*Sohyo's* representative or lobby in the Diet' (Takano 1983 p.3) does little to attract support from the majority of Japanese workers.

The JSP has never had a strong following in the poorest or most deprived households but by the 1980s even organized labour appears to be deserting the party. Both of these features reflect the party's failure to offer a coherent programme of economic and social policies which present voters with a distinctive alternative to the LDP. The JSP has retained a commitment to neutrality and continued to oppose the re-militarization of

Japan. It has also taken a protective role against attempts to erode the provisions of the 1947 Constitution. So in preserving the non-aggression clause, in criticizing the censorship of textbooks or in reclaiming labour rights for public sector workers, the JSP with the cooperation of *Sohyo* has attempted to compensate for the deficiencies of the Supreme Court. But this role has not been widened to any significant extent to include protecting the labour rights of women, minorities or those employed in small firms. On other practical issues such as housing, food prices or social welfare it is difficult to determine how the JSP would change the current structure because its programme is a bewildering mixture of intellectual Marxism and compromise policy statements.

Like many other democratic socialist parties, the JSP has been deeply divided on how to effect working-class power and whether this should be through a non-parliamentary class struggle or through the gradual process of social reform. Amidst the complexity of internal disputes, the dominant theoretical faction in the JSP looks to the inevitability of economic crisis and the immiserization of the working class as the force which will radicalize labour. As active reformist policies will merely delay the decay of capitalism, activists within the party leadership appear to be prepared to let economic alienation take its own course. Hence the JSP hierarchy has been more concerned with factional disputes over socialist theory than with formulating detailed legislative proposals.

In education for example while many Japanese resent the extent of central control, the more immediate problem is how to finance the enormous costs of schooling given the inordinate pressures to pass entrance examinations. Equality of opportunity through public subsidies to poorer families or the revision of gendered curricula in schools has not though been a major priority for the JSP. On high food prices and the need to revise the support and protection of domestic agriculture the 'JSP has been supinely negligent' (Halliday 1975 p.235). Neither has the party offered a clear policy on housing costs which is the other main contributor to the high costs of living especially for poorer families. Other policies usually associated with socialism like income and wealth redistribution or bigger transfer payments have also been constrained by the almost passive acceptance of the inevitability of immiserization. In a similar way the JSP showed a lack of concern in the 1960s with popular protests about the extent of environmental pollution and the limited provision of collective goods and services. The JSP's own post mortem on their 1969 election débâcle accepts that 'we did not face these issues squarely enough or propose sufficiently concrete counter measures' (*Gekkan Shakaito*, June 1970 pp.21–2, quoted in Dore 1973 p.288).

As we shall see in Chapter 7 the majority of citizens' groups which sought to force pollution onto the political agenda were cynical about the motives of opposition parties that attempted to colonize these divisive issues. None the less the failure of the JSP to respond positively to such mass movements was taken to be symptomatic of the party's obsession with socialist theory to the exclusion of current social needs. One reason why the JSP appears slow to respond to popular concerns is that the Party Congress which is supposed to establish political priorities is dominated by theoretical disputes. Diet members are in the minority at these Congress debates but even if they were not, it is doubtful if general social reform would be their main concern. As ex-union officials, JSP Diet members have been preoccupied with the consequences of *Sohyo's* decline as the leading union federation. Once *Domei* became dominant in the private sector, the wider political activities of *Sohyo* were replaced by a narrower concern with protecting the position of its public sector members for example in ensuring that *shunto* wage settlements were extended to public employees. In the 1980s the JSP in the Diet has focused much of its attention on opposing the privatization programme of the LDP because this will greatly undermine the number of public sector unionists. Inside the Diet then the JSP seems engrossed in *Sohyo's* problems, while the party outside appears locked into interminable theoretical debates. Neither activity leaves much opportunity to address the immediate problems facing the majority of Japanese citizens.

Thus the JSP is currently faced with a series of interrelated problems which act simultaneously to accelerate the rate of its decline. The leadership of a party which claims to represent the aspirations of all workers appears to be an isolated intellectual elite uninterested in the immediate concerns of those whose cause it champions. Even with a much slower improvement in their living standards since 1976, it is difficult for most Japanese to relate the outward appearance of material prosperity to the inevitable immiserization and decay of capitalism. *Sohyo's* decline means that less election finance is forthcoming and therefore the JSP contests fewer and fewer Diet seats. Also as *Sohyo* has been unable to prevent the privatization of public corporations and the subsequent redundancies of union members, the JSP has fewer of its traditional supporters to rely upon. As a result the 'JSP appears helpless to halt its long-term decline' (Fukuoka 1985 p.47); a judgement further substantiated in the following year when the party lost 25 per cent of the seats it previously held in the House of Representatives.

The other political party with a socialist label, the DSP, was formed in 1960 by those on the right in the JSP who were disaffected by what they regarded as its unduly dogmatic Marxism and the absence of a pragmatic programme of social reform. Throughout the 1960s the DSP claimed to be the one party commited to a comprehensive welfare state and in view of the contemporaneous growth of citizens' reform movements, the party looked set to become a major force in the centre of Japanese politics. In fact the DSP has never managed to win more than 6 or 7 per cent of seats in the Diet and remains the smallest of the four main opposition parties.

Despite its ambitions to create a party that would appeal to all classes, the DSP has failed to establish a strong mass membership and is forced to rely extensively on the financial and organizational inputs of private sector unions affiliated to *Domei*. But unlike those public sector unions who back the JSP, *Domei* has a much narrower geographical base in those urban districts where industries like electronics, engineering, motor vehicles or textiles are located. Therefore in national elections the DSP concentrates on constituencies where *Domei's* support network is strongest and rarely enters more than 60 or 70 candidates when in excess of 250 are needed for a majority. This more confined regional presence has constrained the development of the DSP especially as many of the party's ideas about social reforms have collided with the immediate concerns of enterprise unions.

Where labour representation is organized as it is in Japan within rather than between firms, employees tend to become insulated by the protective environment of their company. DSP politicians then faced the dilemma of responding to the general demand for public goods and services when the welfare needs of union members were supplied by their own companies. Thus despite the rhetoric of the party leadership, *Domei's* lack of interest in more extensive public welfare provision undermined the credibility of the DSP's reformism. Equally where citizens' groups pressed for state intervention to make private companies accept responsibility for the external costs of pollution, the DSP might proclaim support but enterprise unions were much less accommodating. In local government for example, union-sponsored DSP members were expected to act as lobbyists for their company to oppose stricter production controls because these would raise costs, reduce output and endanger jobs. So the initial commitment of the DSP to reform was deflected by its dependence on enterprise unions whose sectional interests clashed with the wider social needs of non-union households.

By the 1980s the DSP seemed to have abandoned all traces of reformism once *Domei* joined the offensive launched by employers and the LDP to reduce the extent of state intervention and eradicate public finance deficits. For *Domei* excessive public spending was the consequence of the unrealistic and antagonistic attitudes of public sector unions whose 'character must be improved' (Chairman of *Domei* 1981 quoted in Narushima 1984 p.4). This thinly veiled attack on *Sohyo* reflects the extent of the rivalry between these two union federations who have both been forced onto the defensive in the past decade. *Sohyo* has lost membership in larger numbers but private sector unions have also been weakened. The combined effects of adjusting manufacturing output after the oil crises, the increasing use of overseas subsidiaries and the rapid appreciation of the yen has reduced the recruitment of permanent workers to large Japanese companies. It is labour in these export-orientated firms that provides most of *Domei's* strength and it is these firms that have most curtailed their intake of regular male employees. To slow down this decline in membership, *Domei* has joined with employers and the LDP in proclaiming reduced public expenditure to be the panacea for Japan's future prosperity.

Rolling back the involvement of the Japanese state, however, not only means privatizing public corporations but also severe restrictions on public welfare provision. By relying so much on private sector unions, the DSP has had to face the political consequences of *Domei's* pragmatic approach to defending the position of regular employees in large companies. Such a single-minded focus does little to broaden the appeal of the DSP and by supporting the LDP's programme the DSP becomes less and less distinguishable from the ruling Conservative party. Indeed hints that the DSP would consider a coalition with the LDP helps to explain why in the 1986 election more union members than ever anticipated the move and voted for the LDP.

The other two main opposition parties, *Komeito* and the Japan Communist Party (JCP) offer a sharp contrast to the political character and organization of the JSP and DSP. To begin with both *Komeito* and the JCP have made determined efforts to recruit the support of those who have benefited least from Japan's rapid economic growth. They have each established a strong base in local politics which has led to a greater sense of participation and given them a well-organized mass membership. Their more efficient organization produces a flow of individual contributions which allows both to be independent of union finance and thereby to claim the support of labour in general. The close attention that *Komeito* and the JCP paid to continuous local involvement was certainly instrumental in their electoral successes in the first half of the 1970s. However since 1976 as Figure 5.2 shows, their popularity has faded. To some extent their failure to make more progress reflects the fact that neither party has been able to dispel the strongly negative reactions that these two parties provoke among voters in general.

The very name *Komeito* when translated as the 'Clean Government Party' establishes the importance it attached to cleansing Japanese politics of corrupt practices and the undue influence of big business and the unions. At root the party champions the cause of the underprivileged like day labourers, those in tiny enterprises and subcontractors or those providing personal services in roadside kiosks, bars, nightclubs and taxis. In the 1960s when *Komeito* was formed, many of these people were recent migrants from rural areas who relied heavily on the party's local officials to secure accommodation and a first job. As well as satisfying such basic welfare needs the party's association with a populist neo-Buddhist sect offered spiritual consolation for those disorientated in a more anonymous urban environment. Despite the break of the party from its formal religious affiliation in 1970, *Komeito's* enigmatic political platform means that the party is still seen as a source of group support and self-identity for those in the lower echelons of Japanese society.

By using a network of complaints and consultation centres dealing with the practical problems of urban life, *Komeito* built up higher levels of representation in local assemblies which served as a foundation for its candidates in Diet elections. However support for the party is confined to the most densely populated districts and in national elections *Komeito* at best obtains only 10 per cent of the popular vote. The party's image as a quasi-religious organization for the underprivileged has, in Japan's highly status oriented society, severely limited its development. Also as the flow of rural migrants has slowed down the popularity of *Komeito's* religious parent has declined and as a result the party's influence has stagnated.

It took over twenty years for the JCP to recover the share of the popular vote it obtained before the anti-communist purges of 1949 and 1950. But from the later 1960s the fortunes of the JCP revived in the mood of disillusionment with the social costs of economic growth and the inability of the JSP to end the dominance of the LDP. The first breakthrough came in local government where the JCP attempted to rectify the desperate underprovision of urban amenities like sanitation and healthcare. Such an active emphasis on local needs allowed the party to establish a solid core of support as the basis for national election campaigns. The effect of pressing hard for improved community services together with the JCP's rejection of violence as the route to the dictatorship of the proletariat was translated into a surge of new members in areas most affected by the concentration of industrial and residential development. For labour in general the JCP offered an independent stance from what it regards as unrepresentative and self-interested unions but this did bring the party into direct competition with *Komeito* for the votes of urban workers. The rivalry between the two is bitter not least because the JCP sees *Komeito's* religious background as an accommodating ideology which does not seek to change a structure which reproduces inequalities.

A dramatic increase in party membership and lucrative revenues from the JCP's newspaper and magazine sales resulted in the party doubling its share of the popular vote between 1967 and 1972 to 10.5 per cent. Like *Komeito* though it has not been possible for the JCP to maintain this rate of improvement. The JCP has increasingly become more isolated from other Communist Parties in Asia as it attempted to move closer to the position of Euro-Communism. This has involved maintaining a more independent national identity and even appearing complacent over the LDP's plans to revive Japan's military role in Asia. Despite policies that some Japanese Marxists regard as blatant electoral opportunism, public opinion polls continue to show that the JCP is regarded by the majority as a dangerous organization. The party has thus not been able to enjoy the degree of acceptance given to Communist Parties in say France or Italy and the JCP attracts more negative responses than any other party. In part these attitudes reflect the strength of an historical tradition associating communism with revolution which was fostered in the later

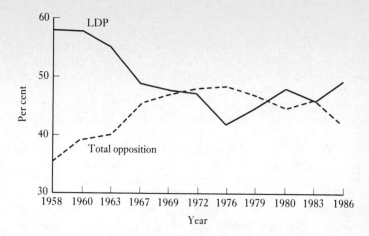

Figure 5.3 The Popular vote for Government and the Opposition in House
of Representative elections, 1958–86
Source: Japan Statistical Yearbook

years of the US Occupation. But the JCP also suffers from national
animosity towards the Soviet Union which has refused to return territory
in Japan's northern islands which it captured in the Pacific War.
Notwithstanding the claims of the JCP that it is completely independent
from the Soviet Communist Party there is a sense in which voting
communist is regarded as supporting one of Japan's perpetual enemies.

Thus both *Komeito* and the JCP used their more effectively organized
local networks to establish a firmer foothold in the Diet when disenchantment
with the LDP was deepest in the mid-1970s. But because they both
provoke such antipathy from voters in general they probably reached the
limits of their popularity when support for the LDP was at its lowest ebb.

5.6 Accommodating a stronger legislature

Each one of Japan's opposition parties has for various reasons had major
difficulties over the past decade in extending their electoral representation.
Collectively they were unable to take full advantage of public reaction
during the 1970s against the way LDP Governments ignored the social
consequences of economic growth (see Figure 5.3). Given the over-
representation of electors and the consequent domination of the Conservatives in rural districts, it is the heavily urbanized areas that offer the best
prospects for ending the era of LDP Governments. There is of course
intense competition between all the opposition parties in urban districts
which does divide the total vote of those hostile to the LDP. It is also

clear that the strength of conservatism among the self-employed and workers in small firms was never seriously undermined even by the populist appeal of *Komeito*. But what was surprising was that when support for the LDP was lowest between 1976 and 1979 the opposition failed to persuade well over 30 per cent of urban electors that it was worth exercising their right to vote.

The much higher rates of abstention in urban districts may well be related to the inequality in the size of electoral districts which encourages apathy. But disenchantment with the electoral system is only one factor involved in the inability of the opposition to recruit more support from urban voters. We have already seen that individual opposition parties produce strongly antipathetic reactions because of their association with unions, communism or the underprivileged. It also seems evident that there is little confidence in the viability of an alternative government to the LDP being formed from a coalition. For example post-election surveys show that a large proportion of those who actually voted for an opposition party had no real desire to drive the LDP out of power though they may despair the corruption and venality of the Conservatives. As 'none of the alternatives on the national political stage are attractive [the electors] find themselves choosing between the lesser of two evils' (Steiner 1980 p.456). For some this means not voting at all while others recorded a protest vote to provoke changes in the policies of LDP Governments.

Alliances of two or more opposition parties have been forged on many occasions, but the joint policy statements that are used to justify their existence make only a tenuous attempt to resolve the ideological differences between the partners. Thus the cooperation arises purely from electoral convenience rather than the desire to form 'durable coalitions . . . to wage effectively coordinated and sustained battles against the ruling LDP between elections' (Fukui 1984 p.389). Temporary electoral alliances hardly provide the basis for a credible alternative government; neither have they been particularly effective in preventing the election of LDP candidates partly because the JCP rarely participate in them. Not only are the other three parties irreconcilably antagonistic to the Communist Party but the JCP itself is pledged to enter candidates in every single district to maintain the right of all Japanese to vote communist. The independent line of the JCP diminishes the effectiveness of tactical withdrawal by JSP candidates in particular because socialist voters are more likely to switch to the JCP rather than *Komeito* or the DSP. Quite apart from the problems of excluding the JCP, as a national strategy to defeat the LDP these electoral pacts are unsuccessful because they simply redistribute rather than increase the overall support for opposition candidates.

By 1979 the LDP was totally uncoordinated in both policy and leadership as it appeared to have lost any sense of direction. Fiscal deficits were accumulating rapidly as demands for higher levels of public spending were conceded at the same time as a second oil crisis slowed economic growth and thereby reduced tax revenues. Yet despite the fall of the Government in May 1980 when some LDP factions refused to vote against an opposition vote of no confidence, the absence of a credible alternative allowed the LDP to win yet another election. The extraordinary recovery of the LDP since 1980 was accompanied by a marked shift towards Conservatism among blue collar labour in particular, eroding still further the strength of the opposition. In these circumstances it was hardly surprising that the opposition was unable to challenge the resurgence of Conservatism founded as it was on a radical realignment of priorities. As elsewhere in the West, the Japanese Government resurrected policies to reduce state intervention, lower taxes and enhance individual initiative. This was linked directly to a vision of economic prosperity and enhanced national status for Japan as a world power embodied in the presidential-style leadership of Prime Minister Nakasone.

Nakasone has been one of the most influential figures in articulating a scenario for Japan's future. This involves maintaining a vigorous economy by curbing public spending and translating the spirit of national self-confidence derived from economic power into a more established role in international affairs. Even before he became leader of the LDP, Nakasone played a significant part in implementing policies to reduce the size of the public sector and his personal popularity with voters was said to be based on his record as a leader who could deliver results not simply make promises. The high personal standing of its leader allowed the LDP to claim that their electoral successes reflected a more responsive and accountable style of government and that positive political leadership had diminished the power of non-elected officials. By leading the movement for reform in public administration, the very centre of bureaucratic power, Nakasone was said to symbolize the shift towards greater influence for elected members of the Diet leading to a greater degree of popular representation.

There are two interrelated elements involved in claims that in recent years the influence of elected representatives has been markedly strengthened. First, the status of the Legislature itself has been enhanced so that it no longer merely ratifies the decisions of the Executive. Secondly that in policy making 'the bureaucracy has lost its position of overwhelming dominance' (T. Sasaki 1987 p.14). While it is clear that political life in the Diet is more accommodating and constructive than it was, it is also apparent that the extent of partisan conflict could hardly have been much worse than it was 25 years ago. Then, the predominance of the LDP was marked by their monopoly of parliamentary committees and the regular use of 'forced votes' to guillotine debate. In reaction, the opposition anticipated the constraints on Diet debate by boycotting proceedings, obstructing normal procedures and on several occasions organizing mass demonstrations outside the Diet. Even physical violence between members on the floor of the Diet was not an uncommon occurrence. Conflict on this scale was hardly compatible with the status of the Diet as the supreme law-making body.

Since the later 1960s parliamentary affairs have become less discordant and various institutional mechanisms have been used to ameliorate the extent of overt conflict. The LDP has used 'forced votes' less frequently, the arbitrating role of the Speaker or House President has been made more effective and the allocation of the Opposition of places on Standing committees of the Diet has been more equitable. As a result the Diet operates in a more peaceful atmosphere where political disputes are conducted within the rules of the parliamentary game.

The motives for such a change in the style of political conflict are still much debated by politicians themselves and by students of Japanese politics. Some argue that the LDP recognized that by monopolizing the deliberations of the Diet they were endangering the legitimacy of the elected legislature especially when this resulted in extra-parliamentary demonstrations organized by the Opposition. Therefore the LDP conceded to the pressure for more effective consultation between the Government and elected members in the Diet. Other commentators place more emphasis on the use of less obstructionist tactics by the Opposition where the JSP was forced to accommodate the more consensual preferences of the DSP and *Komeito*. Certainly a more fragmented Opposition meant that the ruling LDP found it easier to co-opt the support of at least one of the minority parties on contentious issues. A more common explanation of less adversarial Diet proceedings sees this trend as the outcome of the progressive decline in the size of LDP majorities. In other words LDP Governments were forced to become more accommodating in the Diet because they had to respond to wishes of the electorate. While this explanation appears intuitively acceptable, it is clear that more peaceful parliamentary proceedings began well before the very sharp fall in LDP support and continued through the resurgence of the party's fortunes in the 1980s. Has the more effective internal management of Diet proceedings led to a shift in the balance of power from the Executive to the elected Legislature?

There is evidence that during the 1970s bills initiated by the Government faced more resistance in the Diet and that there was also an increase in the number of successful private members' bills. Several caveats are needed though before we can conclude that the Diet had become the powerful institution which the 1947 Constitution envisaged. Although there was more sustained resistance to legislation handed down by LDP Cabinets, the total number of such bills was reduced in preference to using administrative or cabinet orders in order to circumvent the complex process of steering bills through the Diet. This may 'represent a conscious strategy of shunting issues away from the parliamentary process to bureaucratic fiat to avoid conflict or bargaining with the opposition' (Krauss 1984 p.284). It is also clear that once LDP majorities recovered during the 1980s the success rate of bills introduced directly by the Government returned to the 90 per cent level experience in the 1960s. Therefore any judgement about a long-term increase in the power of the Diet as deduced from the extent of resistance to cabinet-initiated legislation, should be treated with caution.

The status of Standing Committees of the Diet has been enhanced by broadening their membership to include the minority parties and by providing more time for their work so that their deliberations are no longer seen as a mere formality. However the degree of independence from the Executive that these Committees enjoy is significantly different from systems based on the US Congressional model. Appointing an Opposition member to chair a Diet Committee may indeed be an indication that an LDP Government thereby recognizes the need to involve members of minority parties more fully in the legislative process. But conceding the chair also has particular advantages for a party whose majority is slim because the chair only casts a vote in the event of a tie. It may be less significant for an LDP member to be in the chair than for the party to have a majority on each committee. Of more importance in judging the extent of opposition involvement in the work of the Standing Committees is the fact that the LDP rarely gives up the chair in the most important committees such as the one on the Budget or on the re-apportionment of electoral districts. This is not to argue that the role of parliamentary committees is purely ornamental, but that their autonomy is limited by the fusion of the executive and legislative branches of government.

The independence of Diet Committees is also constrained because research and administrative support is provided by bureaucrats on temporary secondment from the ministry closest to the area of policy with which a committee is concerned. Therefore the assistance that members receive comes from departmental colleagues of the officials who have drafted the proposals which they are considering. Such close working relationships between elected and non-elected officials in specific areas of administration is also apparent among members of the LDP who attempt to develop expertise in particular subjects. These groups, known as 'policy tribes', have aroused great interest over the past decade because they are seen as an alternative focus of expertise among elected politicians to rival the specialists among non-elected bureaucrats. In a similar fashion the growth of LDP research and study groups has been highlighted as yet another indication that elected politicians have become more influential in policy-making. However most of these specialist groups are structured along lines of ministerial responsibility and are 'typically allied in common functional causes with bureaucrats from their relevant agencies' (Pempel 1987 p.289). In many cases specialist Diet members and ministry officials work interdependently: the former being mobilized to support the position of the relevant ministry in LDP policy deliberations after they have been consulted by bureaucrats during the policy formation stage. While groups such as 'policy tribes' may appear to be rivals for specialist ministry officials, in practice the way their work is structured serves to institutionalize the close links between the bureaucracy and members of the LDP. A more effective set of institutions to formalize the input of elected politicians outside the Government may have limited the dominance of the bureaucracy, but the structure within which they operate makes it difficult to conclude categorically that elected representatives now take precedence.

5.7 Representation through the non-elected

The whole flavour of the debate about the relative importance of elected representatives versus non-elected officials reflects the impact of pluralist theories of policy-making in studies of Japanese politics. In more conventional pluralist accounts, bureaucrats are expected to be politically neutral and to implement policies which have been formulated by elected representatives of the people. Many pluralist writers do recognize that a clear distinction between the proper functions of elected and non-elected officials may be problematic especially in a case like Japan where the LDP has been the party of government for so long. Nevertheless the thrust of recent attempts to minimize the influence of the Japanese bureaucracy seems to be based on the assumption that elected representatives will in a parliamentary democracy, inevitably take precedence.

In addition to the more effective operations of Diet Committees and the emergence of specialist policy groups among LDP members, two other trends have been used to explain the erosion of bureaucratic dominance in Japan. First a decline in the number of ex-bureaucrats who become elected members of the LDP in the Diet, and secondly, the ability of politicians to limit the size and functions of the bureaucracy itself through Administrative Reform and the liberalization of market controls. As a proportion of all members, retired bureaucrats do now take a smaller share relative to career politicians. Having said that, however, if we focus on the leadership of the party or on senior cabinet posts it is still the case that ex-bureaucrats remain very prominent. Career politicans thus 'provide the party with men, and former bureaucrats with officers' (Fukui 1984 p.413).

It also seems possible to detect different attitudes towards the prerogative of elected representatives depending on the level of seniority within the bureaucracy. In a recent survey of both middle and high level bureaucrats in Japan, Muramatsu and Krauss (1984) found decidedly negative views of the role of elected politicians. 'Almost all of the Japanese civil servants believe that political parties often needlessly intensify political conflicts, and a large majority believe that the clash of interest groups seriously endangers the national welfare' (p.132). In some ways it may not be surprising to discover such a reaction from officials who are convinced that they themselves are the more effective judges of the public interest. The same survey though did find that senior bureaucrats were 'more likely to

acknowledge the power of politicians and parliament in policy-making'
(p.141). Among a number of explanations offered for this difference in
attitudes is 'the fact that top bureaucrats have long-range aspirations to
run for the Diet as LDP candidates making them more sensitive to the
desires and aims of LDP politicians' (p.143). So notwithstanding the needs
of senior bureaucrats to prepare their route into the LDP, it seems that
many officials do not share the pluralist assumptions on the prior claims
of elected politicians.

On several occasions before the 1980s LDP politicians attempted to
reform public administration in order to restrict the power of the
bureaucracy. To an extent these efforts were thwarted because the
bureaucracy itself was charged with administering the reforms and could
thus dilute their impact. Nakasone, however, appeared to by-pass the
entrenched resistance of middle-level bureaucrats in particular by using
outside advisory panels to implement the latest round of reforms. Over the
years the Japanese state has made extensive use of Public Advisory Bodies
(PABs) to incorporate the views of independent experts and interest groups
into policy-making, but prior to the 1980s bureaucrats were responsible
for their organization. So the agenda for such consultation, the choice of
appointees, the servicing and drafting of final reports was largely controlled
by officials within the ministries that sponsored the respective PABs. This
degree of control has led many to argue that PABs lacked real autonomy
and merely served to offer an ornamental cloak of legitimacy for the
bureaucracy. Although Harari (1982) has challenged this view of PABs as
dependent puppets, the way Nakasone quite deliberately divorced the
administration of his own advisory panels from bureaucratic control
suggested that he was sceptical about their previous operations.

Certainly the selection of personnel to occupy key positions in Nakasone's
advisory panels and *ad hoc* commissions has not been delegated to ministry
officials. As one of the senior members of the Administrative Reform
Commission admits 'the expert members and councillors who played
leading roles in the commission, as the heads or vice-heads of various
subcommittees or working groups, were mostly Nakasone's inner circle of
friends and former colleagues (Kumon 1984 p.143). This selection
procedure allows the advisory groups to report directly to the Prime
Minister rather than having their views mediated by bureaucrats. What was
also significant in the work of these groups was that the members themselves
took charge of the crucial process of drafting reports and recommendations.
Thus to ensure that this most recent attempt to reform public administration
became effective, Nakasone circumvented the vested interests of ministry
officials by a judicious use of 'independent' outsiders.

In common with other governments in the West who espouse a new-
right approach to policy formation, Nakasone justified his strategy for
reform on the grounds that bureaucrats were not the best people to put
their own house in order. This strategy of imposing controls on a self-

interested and resistant bureaucracy did limit the growth of public expenditure and the privatization of a number of public corporations reduced the number of public employees. As these trends coincided with the remarkable election victory of the LDP in 1986, Nakasone was able to claim popular approval for his commitment to rolling back the extent of state administration. 'For the first time in Japanese history I was able to bypass the Government and party bureaucrats and take my case to the Japanese people' (Nakasone, quoted in *NYT* 16 July 1986). Even allowing for the euphoria of the victor, this sort of comment illustrates how the determination to control the power of non-elected officials can be translated into a move towards more effective democratic representation.

The LDP not surprisingly, saw their electoral successes as an indication of widespread support for their attempt to restore the primacy of individual initiative. In general the most visible objectives of such policies to reduce state borrowing without increasing taxation and ending the notorious deficits of public companies like Japan National Railways, appear to be popular. But these items are but one part of a package of policies designed to establish a whole series of priorities for the rest of the century. This package contains elements that are common to others who share the ideology of the new right, but with the additional emphasis on enhancing Japan's status as a global power. Responding in part to Western pressures especially from the US, Nakasone linked Japan's role in maintaining the international economic order to the need to press ahead with liberalizing domestic markets by reducing the extent of bureaucratic controls. But in parallel goes a renewed emphasis on Japan's responsibility for not only its own defence but a more positive role in Asia as a whole.

To protect the much vaunted Japanese work ethic and to avoid the advanced country disease of lower productivity stemming from an over-protective welfare state, self-reliance and self-help should, according to Nakasone's circle, take precedence over state welfare provision. Then some of the resources thereby released can be transferred into an expansion of Japan's defence and military capability. It is at this point in the logic of the vision of Japan's future that doubts begin to emerge over whether the leadership of the LDP really represented public opinion. While opinion surveys did indicate high levels of support for reductions in public expenditure, defence was the most popular target for economies and social welfare for preservation. If the tactic of circumventing entrenched bureaucratic interests is to be justified by bringing government closer to the people, it is clear that in this case Nakasone's policy preferences were the reverse of the popular consensus.

In re-defining Japan's national priorities Nakasone and the LDP had the great advantage that the opposition parties had 'paltry policy agendas and virtually no capability to press for radically different alternatives on new policy issues' (Pempel 1987 p.295). The absence of an effective alternative government certainly gave Nakasone the freedom to shape the political debate and in the process to attempt to circumscribe the power of the bureaucracy. But it is vital to recognize that this did not necessarily lead to any significant increase in the influence of elected members of the Diet even among the ranks of the LDP. Instead policy formation relied increasingly on outside advisory groups made up of selected individuals whose presence was justified by their status as independent experts. Business leaders in particular were allocated a major role. This trend was most noticeable in the work of the Administrative Reform Council from 1981 where Doko, the President of the Employers Federation took the chair, and five out of seven sub-groups were chaired by representatives of business. What these individuals had in common was the belief that the private sector had proved its efficiency by successfully weathering the oil shocks of the 1970s whereas the size of the public sector deficit indicated inefficient uncontrolled profligacy.

The language used in the Council's report and in the consequent public discussions conveys in vivid terms the underlying assumptions that 'state-run health services or education systems or TV channels are necessarily less efficient or less capable of producing a desirable end product than systems without government involvement' (Stockwin 1984 p.265). So public sector deficits became 'failures' and spending on health or pensions were '*drains* on the National Treasury' (Kumon 1984 p.163, emphasis added.) In essence the course of the public debate that accompanied the work of the Reform Council was dominated by the rules of private business where a deficit is the hallmark of inefficiency. The very fact that the debate was constructed along these lines by business leaders whose high status as self-made heroes of the economic miracle added legitimacy to the statements of the political leadership in the LDP. Doko for example was one such charismatic figure whose record in saving Toshiba from bankruptcy was crucial in establishing the 'expert' status of the Reform Council.

The functioning of the Administrative Reform Council was not an isolated example but is typical of a more centralized style of policy-making designed to transcend entrenched interests in·the bureaucracy and among their political allies in the LDP. In constructing the agenda for educational reform, initiating proposals for greater defence spending or promoting a more open economy, Nakasone backed up his own pronouncements with the establishment of a range of *ad hoc* advisory groups. Those selected to serve on such advisory panels appeared to offer representation to unions or included leading academic and media figures, but the particular individuals invited were chosen largely because their views were known to be close to senior business leaders. Even in the consultations over educational reform where the Japan Teachers' Union and the Ministry of Education had to be involved, their well-known resistance to de-regulation was accommodated by allocating their representatives to less important sub-groups. Behind the rhetoric of strategies designed to overcome sectional interests and enhance the channels of direct democracy, lay the reality of policy-making by selected outsiders.

Alongside the increased use of advisory panels went administrative changes to strengthen the Prime Minister's own cabinet office in order to centralize control over the bureaucracy as a whole. There was also a greater tendency to use parliamentary vice-ministers to integrate the reports of advisory panels into the deliberations of LDP policy groups and within those ministries affected by their proposals. In itself the enhanced status of vice-ministers appointed by the Prime Minister from elected LDP members is significant because senior bureaucrats as administrative vice-ministers previously took on such collaborative functions. However although bureaucrats may have resented institutional changes which apparently limited their control of policy formation, it would not be accurate to imply that the bureaucracy *in toto* was implacably opposed to the spirit of Nakasone's commitment to the new right.

Given the attachment to fiscal reform and stricter control on public spending, officials in the Ministry of Finance, for example, certainly favoured the privatization of deficit-ridden public corporations. Similarly, as limitations on public expenditure constrain the financial independence of local and regional government, Home Ministry officials are unlikely to oppose changes which increase the power of central government. When the Japan National Railways was privatized in 1987, not only did the Ministry of Transport officials lose a major source of embarrassment but in the process they helped to emasculate the power of public sector unions affiliated to *Sohyo*. Health and Welfare bureaucrats likewise were not unequivocally opposed to cuts in state welfare progammes partly because their spending ceases to be the target of criticism by the Ministry of Finance, but also because of their close association with the private healthcare industry. Neither is it surprising to find that Defence and Military officials appear to be strong supporters of policies which will increase Japan's commitment to its own defence.

So there is a real sense in which sections within the bureaucracy share the objectives espoused by the Nakasone leadership. Indeed it could be argued that Nakasone needed to recruit powerful allies from among bureaucrats in those ministries which were central to his vision of Japan's future. There certainly seems to have been a shift since the 1970s in the ministerial background of bureaucrats who 'retire' into active politics with the LDP. Where previously economic ministries dominated this flow, the balance has swung towards 'Home Ministry officials with a background in police or education or in defence and military fields,' (McCormack 1986 p.59).

5.8 Japanese-style pluralism

There is little doubt that in his six years as Prime Minister, Nakasone made a sustained effort to introduce more central control over Japan's political process. The very fact that his tenure in office was much longer than his immediate predecessors certainly marked a clear break from the uncertainties of earlier years. Nakasone sought to build his personal charisma into what he himself described as 'presidential-style politics' (*Nihon keizai shinbun* 11 April 1986) in order to subordinate sectional interests in the bureaucracy and the LDP. His personal style was marked by frequent appeals to the Japanese public over the heads of other politicians to dissolve the image of the LDP as simply the mouthpiece of particular constituency interests. For some this style of leadership signifies taking 'big steps towards making Japan a country governed by elected representatives instead of mandarins,' (*Economist* 22 August 1987). Such a sweeping testament to the enhanced influence of the elected legislature does, though, minimize the increasing significance of advisory panels personally selected by the Prime Minister. Equally we need to emphasize the success Nakasone had in colonizing those parts of the bureaucracy that actively supported his visions of Japan's future. So what may appear to be a secular increase in the power of elected legislators may be more apparent than real.

In assessing the long-term impact of Nakasone's attempt to strengthen the executive role of the Prime Minister it is important to remember that Japan does not have a presidential constitution. In particular. the practice of limiting the term of office of LDP President and therefore the Prime Minister, places real constraints on their personal power. The fact that Nakasone managed to serve three terms as party leader partly reflected the extent of factional rivalries within the LDP which precluded the emergence of an alternative leader in 1984 and 1986. Nakasone, through the adept manner in which he allocated ministerial offices was able to take advantage of divisions within his own party, but his record in imposing changes on the LDP, or for that matter the bureaucracy, was equivocal.

For example, despite the overwhelming support of domestic consumers and industrial leaders for lower food prices, Nakasone never managed to overcome the alliance of rural LDP politicians and Ministry of Agriculture officials which protects the 'world's most heavily subsidized farmers' (Johnson 1986 p.24). Despite the vociferous support of big business for a reform of the tax structure and a move away from direct to sales or value-added taxes, Nakasone in 1987 was forced to withdraw his proposals in the face of the particular opposition from traditional supporters of the LDP in Japan's army of smaller retailers. Western pressure to reduce Japan's huge trade surplus produced in 1986 the report of an advisory panel recommending that domestic consumption be expanded by reducing incentives to save. A major feature of this report was the elimination of tax-free savings deposits in Post Office accounts, but the Ministry of Posts delayed such a move. In foreign policies too, Nakasone had to modify his ambitions to increase spending on defence to accommodate the deep-seated pacifist inclinations of the Japanese. The LDP itself has been critical of yet closer military links with the US, and Nakasone was accused of too readily conceding Japan's role as a tributary American state. Even the leaders of big business suggest that Nakasone went too far during negotiations with Western leaders by accepting that Japan is 'guilty' of distorting international trade patterns because it exports too much. Many in Japan argue that the real reason for trade surpluses is the inefficiency and ineptitude of its trading partners.

So although Nakasone's leadership style was based on exerting more central control there are continuities in the Japanese political process which limited his influence. While the Opposition in the Diet may have been ignored, the same cannot be said for rank and file LDP members whose re-election depends on protecting the interests of farmers or small retailers. While Nakasone captured sections of the bureaucracy, this did not curtail the resistance for example of the Ministries of Agriculture and Posts to more extensive de-regulation. Neither are leaders of business totally committed to economic policies which involve reducing the length of the working week or reforming the structure of distribution to reduce the prices paid by domestic consumers. Like all Japanese Prime Ministers, Nakasone had to govern by managing the often conflicting demands of the bureaucracy, the LDP and the representatives of big business.

In describing the operation of political institutions in Japan, the existence of several centres of power suggests that policies are the outcome of competition between a plurality of rival interests. But even those political scientists who would accept the label pluralist, qualify their characterization of Japanese politics in a variety of ways to account for the deviation of observed practices from the assumptions of pluralist theories. The clear separation of influence between a neutral civil service and elected politicians is surely an inadequate assumption in Japan where the bureaucracy has such a long tradition of involvement in policy making. Accepting this difference meant using the label 'bureaucracy-led mass inclusionary pluralism' to highlight the way the bureaucracy took the lead in organizing interest group representation. More recently the growing role of LDP politicians meant using a different qualifying phrase: 'pluralism guided by the integrated party-bureaucratic apparatus'. Yet another variation is 'patterned or compartmentalized pluralism' to reflect the integrated approach of LDP policy tribes and bureaucrats but also to recognize the preferential access to the state accorded to business leaders.

The basic problem which each of these qualifying epithets is designed to confront, is that many of the key aspects in Japanese politics undermine some of the central assumptions of pluralist theory. Bureaucrats, elected politicians and representatives of big business do not occupy separated and clearly-defined spheres of influence not least because the LDP whose election campaigns are financed by business, has enjoyed such a long period in government in which ex-bureaucrats still take senior posts. Neither can ordinary citizens easily secure that their voices be heard through voluntary association in interest groups, because labour, the consumers lobby or environmental groups are seen as outsiders. Even the ultimate constraint on elected governments of losing office to an alternative party seems to be a remote possibility so long as the LDP controls the distribution of electoral districts and opposition parties remain so divided.

6

Social Division in Japan

A recurring theme in the analysis of Japan's social structure is the notion that it is 'a society almost totally composed of people of the same class' (Christopher 1984 p.127). Several interrelated factors help to explain why this image of Japan as a classless society is a common one in both Japanese and Western publications. Perhaps the most immediate reason is that for over 25 years opinion surveys conducted annually by the EPA and the Prime Minister's Office, show that between 80 and 90 per cent of respondents consider themselves to be middle class. These self-ascribed testimonials to the extent of social equality are then related to estimates of a more even distribution of incomes to produce a picture of an unusual capitalist society where class conflict is absent.

It is clear that the policies of the US occupation which dismantled the *zaibatsu* and reformed the system of landownership did remove some important sources of inequality. By undermining the dominance of *zaibatsu* families and the position of larger landlords, the post-war reforms swept away two of the institutions which structured the reproduction of differentials in income and wealth. Land reform for instance was certainly one significant reason why income differentials between urban and rural Japan narrowed dramatically after 1950. Equally the ownership of industrial and financial capital became more diffused once the holdings of the *zaibatsu* were replaced with public companies in which management shareholdings were in the minority.

Going alongside these changes went, as we saw in Chapter 3, the development of the idea of the firm as a cooperative family in which wage differentials between white- and blue-collar workers appeared much less pronounced. The absence of distinctions based on dress, working hours or canteen facilities and the rotation of labour across a variety of jobs also contributes to the relative absence of differentials based on occupational status.

Two decades of very rapid economic growth after 1955 sustained a remarkable improvement in living standards compared to pre-war levels, and despite much lower rates of growth since 1975 GNP *per capita* has continued to rise faster than in many Western economies. Thus in terms of consumer durables like colour TV sets or motor cars, Japanese households have probably the highest ownership rates in the world. Larger incomes and better living standards have played no small part in raising life expectancy rates so that Japanese women now live on average for 80 years, which is the longest in the world.

As dramatic as the general improvement in living standards has been the increase in educational provision. Literacy rates were always very high in Japan, but the post-war education reforms vastly increased the number of places available up to and beyond the years of compulsory schooling. Now, something like 95 per cent of Japanese children stay in school until the age of 18 compared to 43 per cent in 1950; and 36 per cent graduate from higher education institutes compared to 6 per cent in 1950.

It is the massive increase in Higher Education provision that underpins the belief that by guaranteeing equality of opportunity the Constitutional reforms of 1947 laid the foundation for a truly egalitarian society. Notwithstanding the widely publicized surveys which highlight feelings of equality in living standards, there are recognizable status differentials according, for example, to the corporate standing of employing companies or to the position of individuals in a firm's hierarchy. But what is crucial to the notion of a Japanese meritocracy is that access to these higher status positions should be open to all through equality of opportunity in education. Thus although graduates from Higher Education institutions can expect greater lifetime earnings, these additional rewards are seen as 'the results of individual merits. What people do at work and what they receive in return seem to be shaped by what they are or have made themselves through their education' (Steven 1983 p.291).

As we have seen in other chapters the lower levels of mobility between large firms does mean that once recruitment to the large firm has been missed immediately after graduation, it is highly unlikely that individuals can gain employment as regular workers in such firms later in their career. But the limited prospect of intra-generational social mobility is seen as the result of an individuals under-achievement at school or college which does not impinge on the prospects of the next generation from that family. Instead unlimited prospects for inter-generational social mobility is said to encourage parents to make their children work harder to avoid their own mistakes. In no small way does this meritocratic ideology explain the pressures of 'examination hell' for the majority of Japanese children.

The image of Japan as a uniquely harmonious collective is crucially supported by the idea that the significance of class or other social divisions is undermined by an egalitarian social structure where individual life chances are not dependent upon the inherited income status or wealth of their parents. Instead the post-war reforms meant that social background has had 'a decreasing influence on individual status achievement' (Cummings 1980 p.276). Thus divisions within Japanese society are assumed to be based not on social institutions or practices which reproduce inequalities between generations, but result from personal merits and failings as revealed by success or failure in education. For the predictability of social status based on differential access to income and wealth is substituted a classless, egalitarian society with individuals differentiated by ability.

In the rest of this chapter we will examine some of the major types of social division in Japan against this assumed background of social equality and egalitarianism.

6.1 Social equality: the distribution of income and wealth

One element in the belief that in Japan there are less significant social or class divisions derives from the assumption that the distribution of incomes is more equitable. Estimating trends in income distribution is fraught with difficulty because accurate and consistent data is scarce especially in a country like Japan where the very large numbers of self-employed can lead to serious under-recording of incomes. However up to the early 1970s there appeared to be general agreement that the distribution of incomes in Japan was as, if not more, equal than in other capitalist societies. Even with caveats about the data available it certainly seems, for example, that Gini coefficients measuring the cumulative shares of total incomes among households were lower in Japan. There was less agreement about the distribution of wealth where controversy over appropriate definitions let alone measurement, is much more intense. The distinction between income and wealth is crucial as state policies to reduce inequalities of income can be counteracted by failure to correct an unequal distribution of wealth which adds a greater flow of income from wealth creating assets to more prosperous households.

What is undeniable is that the post-war reforms deconstructed the concentration of wealth held by absentee landlords and the *zaibatsu*. Such abrupt institutional changes were then followed by over two decades of rapidly rising incomes which encouraged 'many to believe that poverty was a thing of the past' (Mouer and Sugimoto 1986 p.76). This impression was reinforced by the tendency of wage differentials by region, size of firm and to a lesser extent gender, to narrow. In addition steeply progressive rates of income taxation suggested that the Japanese state was committed to the maintenance of a more equal society. It would, however, be misleading to infer from this that marked differences in life chances and incomes had disappeared even though absolute poverty by pre-war standards had been ameliorated.

For example, over two-thirds of Japanese households have consistently

earned less than the national average and one-fifth received less than half
the average income. Equally the gap between the top and bottom 20 per
cent of households has remained fairly constant and the poorest 20 per
cent of households have continuously accounted for only 8 per cent of all
incomes. Even at the height of the post-war economic boom, poverty was
intense among casual labourers existing on daily contracts who lived in the
'flophouse' districts of Japan's larger cities (Caldora 1969, Nee 1974).
These urban ghettoes still exist and are populated in part by members of
an outcast group, the *burakumin*. Estimates of the total number of residents
in these districts vary widely, but even the conservative estimates quoted
by the Japanese state mention over one million people living in grossly
inadequate housing, earning very low incomes and experiencing very high
rates of unemployment (Ministry of Foreign Affairs, Dowa Problem 1984).

It is also worth recalling from Chapter 3 how the input of labour in
terms of hours worked varies inversely with the size of employing firm. So
it may have been possible for employees in small firms to close the wage
gap but only by working much longer hours, in less safe surroundings and
with much more uncertain contracts. Even then actual money incomes
would not reflect differences in non-monetary perquisites such as housing
and welfare benefits. Workers in firms employing over 1000 for example
receive 40 per cent more in non-monetary benefits than do those in firms
employing less than 100 (*Japan Statistical Yearbook* 1985 p.109). We also
need to remember that as late as 1975 one-quarter of women in the labour
force were *unpaid* family workers. Generally though the impression of
greater equality was reinforced by rising real incomes and narrowing wage
differentials which were brought about by a sharp increase in the demand
for labour generated by the economic boom.

Even in the early 1970s some writers argued that these trends masked
deeper underlying tendencies in the widening of differentials between
incomes from employment and those from property. The reforms of the
US Occupation may have dismantled the pre-war structure of wealth
inequality but it was not a once and for all change. Much more attention
has been focused on the issue of wealth distribution since 1975 because
the rate of growth of incomes has fallen and 'wage differentials by industry,
size of firm, profession and sex ... began to grow again' (Kusaka 1985
p.50). As these differentials in the annual flow of incomes from employment
began to widen, disparities in unearned incomes from property have become
clearer.

One cause of inequalities in wealth obviously lies in the existence of
differentials in employment incomes which leave higher income groups
with a greater opportunity to accumulate wealth in land or financial assets.
But it also appears that the preferential tax treatment of incomes from
property in Japan has served to erode the progressive stance of fiscal policy.
As corporate tax credits and exemptions were used to stimulate private
investment so similar techniques were used to maintain the equivalent flow

of private savings. One consequence of preferential tax rates on property incomes has been that in Japan as in the US this 'tends to destroy the equity of the existing tax system' (Ishi 1979 p.303) because it benefits higher income households who have larger earnings from property.

In theory income tax rates in Japan are steeply progressive but in practice their equalising effects on incomes have been eroded in several ways. To begin with there are a host of exemptions and deductions to be allowed from employment income before the taxable base is reached. Pechman and Kaizuka estimated for instance that 'the tax base amounted to only 33 per cent of total income in Japan as compared to 59 per cent in the US' (1976 p.340). Then certain categories of income are either excluded from taxation or taxed separately at reduced rates. Capital gains on the sale of securities and shares are not subject to tax while income from interest and dividends is taxed separately at a flat rate. In fact a proportion of dividend income is regarded as a tax credit allowable against income tax. Maximum rate of tax on land sales were introduced to increase the supply but this has meant the sacrifice of equity objectives. It is true that the exemption of post office savings from taxation benefits all households, but 'because property income accounts for the major fraction of total incomes in the highest income classes the tax burden in these classes may well be less than half in Japan as in the US' (Pechman and Kaizuka 1976 p.342).

The range and extent of exemptions or exclusions appear to be widespread enough to make direct taxation in Japan at best only mildly progressive. If one then takes into account the regressive effects of indirect taxation especially on households below the direct tax threshold and the failure to raise such thresholds in the first half of the 1980s, the overall effect on income distribution may be neutralized. One source estimates that a household earning 20 per cent below the national average would pay 500 per cent more in taxes in 1984 than the equivalent household in 1977; whereas a household earning three times the national average would pay only 45 per cent more (Steven 1983 p.273). Doubts about the redistributive effects of direct taxation are confirmed by the knowledge that property incomes are self-assessed and undoubtedly under-recorded while income from employment is deducted at source.

In common with other capitalist economies gift and inheritance taxes in Japan are largely ineffective. 'If stress is placed on their small yield relative to total taxes, taxes on property transfers are likely to be ineffective (as they are in most countries) and, to do little to prevent an increasing concentration of wealth and economic powers as the nation grows' (Ishi 1980 p.45). Thus 'because taxes on property incomes or the accumulation of wealth have been light it is virtually certain that inequality in the distribution of wealth also has been increasing' (Pechman and Kaizuka 1976 p.370).

There is evidence that since 1975 the distribution of incomes by household has grown more unequal. One reason concerns the increase in the number of households made up entirely of elderly people and an increase in single person households. Indeed if income distribution is measured among households rather than individuals, it may well be that the overall impression of greater equality was largely a function of Japan's extended family network. As this now appears to be breaking down, more household units especially of single people and the elderly makes Japan's demographic structure more typical of an industrial society. In such circumstances the greater dispersion of household incomes around the national mean which has become more apparent in recent years in Japan, may reflect the outcome of changes in family structure.

But in addition to these changes in the organization of households, the effects of lighter taxation on property may be as significant because property incomes make up a larger share of total incomes in Japan. The mid-1980s has seen the publication of several studies which highlight the impact of growing disparities in the ownership of assets and incomes from such assets. 'As things are the poor stay poorer while people who manage to become rich automatically continue to be rich' (Kusaka 1985 p.50). By itself this tendency appears to violate the egalitarian ethos that surrounds discussions of Japan's social structure as it implies that differences in income and wealth may be transmitted between generations. Is there any evidence that a meritocratic education system counteracts such a tendency?

6.2 Education and open access to a meritocracy

The programme of educational reform begun by the US occupation in 1947 produced a remarkable increase in the provision of schooling at all levels. Not only was the length of compulsory education lengthened from six to nine years but the numbers attending Senior High Schools beyond the compulsory period rose from 7 per cent in 1940 to 50 per cent in 1955 to 95 per cent in 1986. This rate of attendance is matched only in the US and both rates are twice the level of countries like West Germany or the UK. Expansion of numbers in Higher Education has been equally dramatic with in 1986 36 per cent of the appropriate age cohort attending College or University; again twice the level of most countries in Western Europe.

As in all societies the length of educational career has significant effects on income differentials, and the overall impact of educational background on wages was a feature of the Japanese labour market stressed in Chapter 3 (see Figure 3.7). We saw there that competition for recruitment to large firms is intense because of the advantages this has for both higher wages and secure tenure of employment, and entrance to these firms is often based on educational achievement. Of course higher lifetime earnings are only partially determined by educational status at the age of recruitment, but one other source of income differentials, promotion within the corporate hierarchy, is also linked to education. While level of education is not by itself a sufficient reason for advancement, it may be a necessary requirement. The *Wage Structure Survey* in 1976 showed that in manufacturing only one in 20 men recruited with just the compulsory years of schooling rose to the supervisory position of section head which involves managing the smallest unit in a firm. This is compared to one in seven recruits from Senior High School and one in three graduates from Higher Education (Tachibanaki 1982 p.458). Education is thus one key determinant not just of access to large companies but of future promotion prospects within them.

Having established that level of education is important in differentiating incomes how open is access? One group that are under-represented in post-compulsory education are members of the *burakumin* and Korean minorities. Members of both minorities stand only half the chance of an average Japanese in gaining entrance to university (De Vos and Wetherall 1983). Of more significance in quantitative terms is the under-representation of women university students who account for less than a quarter of all undergraduates. While it is true that only slightly fewer women than men enter Higher Education institutions in total, women make up over 90 per cent of numbers at 2 year Junior Colleges but only 22.6 per cent on 4 year university courses (Ministry of Education Survey on Schools 1983). One question that needs to be considered later is why only 17 per cent of women even apply to enter university when the equivalent proportion for men is 60 per cent (*JEJ* 1986 p.12).

The financial burdens on parents of financing the education of their children has already been mentioned in Chapter 4, and it is not therefore surprising to find that children in the top 20 per cent of households by income are at least five times as likely to attend university as children from the bottom 20 per cent (Glazer 1976 p.839). We do need to disaggregate university education in total because Japan has over 460 universities with about 25 per cent of student places in national universities where tuition fees are only one quarter of those charged by private universities (Pempel 1982 p.217). At national universities children from the bottom quintile of income earners are better represented, but the gap between the top and bottom quintiles has widened dramatically over the past twenty years. As the share of undergraduates from the richest households has risen from 27 to 40 per cent, the share of the poorest has fallen from 20 to 12 per cent.

The main reason for this change in shares lies in the fact that the public sector contains the more prestigious institutes where competition for entry is at its most ferocious. With such a vast increase in university places there has been an indisputable decline in the quality of education offered by the majority of private universities. Hence as demand for Higher Education rose it became as important to consider not just the length of education but the reputation of the particular university that students attend. In order to pass the rigorous entrance examinations to the best universities, it became necessary to incur substantial expenses on extracurricula tuition in order to gain entrance to the better secondary schools and then to stay in the highest tracks or grades within those schools. From the age of 15 examinations sort out children into five or six grades at High School. At 18 'pupils from the top 2 or 3 grades are again sorted out according to performance in university entrance examinations among a spectrum of universities ranked in a well-charted hierarchy of prestige' (Dore 1987 p.212). Even for the 65 per cent of young adults who do not go on to Higher Education, securing employment in large companies requires attendance at the better schools as this can be used as criterion for the recruitment of manual or blue-collar labour.

In one sense it is the very character of the method chosen to ration out the scarce supply of places at the best educational institutions that discriminates against poorer households. Selection is based almost entirely on multiple choice objective tests of memorized facts which lend themselves to long hours of practice both at school and outside: 'even if public schools are available to all regardless of ability to pay, the edge gained through extra, private tuition in *juku* or through work with a home tutor makes an expensive difference in later educational opportunities' (M.I. White 1986 p.159). With approximately 36,000 *juku* recording a turnover of 50 billion yen the level of parental income has become a major determinant not just of the length of education but, more importantly, of entrance to particular schools and universities.

Yet it is not simply incomes that affect access to university education; gender is an equally important barrier. For women students preparation for entrance into junior colleges is expensive as are the tuition fees, yet so few women compete for places in national universities where fees are so much lower. As we shall see this phenomenon has much to do with the strength of opposition in the home to attempts by women to enter the race for entry into the best universities.

Despite the dominance of an egalitarian ideology in Japan there are at least three variables, in addition to ability, that guide access to equality of opportunity through education: racial or minority status, gender and household income. In some cases the effects of one may counteract another; a wealthier family is able to pay for a daughter's university education but in most cases chooses not to do so. Poorer families, which include the vast majority of *burakumin* and Koreans, face much more constrained choices for both daughters and sons. Quantifying the significance of differentiated access to education on social mobility is problematic because surveys frequently use different measures of status or ignore one half of the population by comparing only fathers and sons. But in general differential access to the attainment of crucial educational credentials would lend weight to the conclusion that although 'the Japanese . . . feel that their

intergenerational mobility must be very high . . . it is in fact rather low'
(Morishima 1982 p.174).

6.3 Uniform patterns of consumption but predictable social differentials

The widespread publicity given to the role of the firm as a corporate family
in which antagonism between management and workers is less pronounced
is a further reason why many suggest that class divisions are less significant
in Japan. In return for an informal pledge to maintain security of employment
and progressive wage increases based partly on length of service,
management is said to earn the loyalty of their workers and common
membership of enterprise unions cement closer in-house working relationships. Such a system, it is argued, tends to extend to all the conditions of
employment usually associated with white-collar labour allowing everyone
to enjoy a sense of mutual belonging. Thus Japan appears unusual because
customary divisions between capital and labour are cross cut by countervailing
loyalties to, and identity with, one's corporate family.

This deep-seated connection between Japanese industrial relations and
the notion of a classless society is predicated on the disputable assumption
that permanent employment is widely available. So we do need to consider
what criteria are used to exclude some people from the privileged sector
of the labour market. First, though, we should explore briefly whether the
distribution of income, power and authority is really so equal and alienation
so rare among employees in Japan's larger companies.

There is little doubt that the rotation of labour across a variety of tasks
in Japanese factories undermines strong occupational identification and that
wage differentials between blue- and white-collar labour are narrower than
in the West. White-collar workers in manufacturing on average earn 25
per cent more than manual labour compared to around 45 per cent more
in the UK. One reason for this incidentally is because white collar
employees are expected to spend as long at work as other workers but
unlike production workers they 'are not paid overtime for extra hours
worked' (Tachibanaki 1982 p.455). Even though money wage differentials
may be less dramatic, there are status and authority rankings 'associated
with blue-collar versus white-collar rather than specific occupations' (Cole
and Tominaga 1976 p.87). As we have already seen educational achievement
seems to be a necessary if not sufficient determinant of access to supervisory
positions where extra rewards are not always visible in monetary terms.
More substantial housing subsidies and lavish expense accounts are the
most common of such additional benefits. It was possible up to 1965 to
estimate the scale of such perquisites because specific data on total business
consumption expenditure were identified in national income accounts.
Although the data is no longer as readily available, it is very unlikely that

expense accounts are currently any less than they were in 1965 when they were the equivalent to over 4 per cent of the whole nation's consumer spending (Boltho 1975 p.165). Taking both types of reward together it seems that differentials between white- and blue-collar employees 'are largest in the large firm where the rhetoric of groupism and team work as the major component of Japanese society is most vigorously disseminated' (Mouer and Sugimoto 1986 p.120).

Going with income differentials according to hierarchical position are clear differences in power. The selection of personnel for transfer to subsidiaries, for retraining or early retirement are jealously guarded prerogatives of management. Acceptance of such decisions by individuals and enterprise unions may well be seen as instances of the wholehearted desire to sacrifice personal interest for the good of the company. It could equally be a matter of resigned submission on the part of the powerless. A similar debate rages over whether the motives of employees engaging in unpaid overtime, unpaid quality circles or other after-work activities reflect the depth of loyalty to the firm. Kamata's (1984) experience of working on the Toyota production line is but one example of the contrasting view which stresses the significance of alienation, indifference and apathetic compliance in explaining the relative absence of conflict between management and labour in Japan.

Just how real is the sense of loyalty to a Japanese company is an impossibly difficult question to resolve depending as it does on subjective attitudes and feelings. What is less problematic is that permanent employment status cannot be accorded to all workers because such status 'inevitably raises labour costs [so] employers may be expected to complement long-term labour with a pool of highly "disposable" labour' (Giddens 1973 p.220). At most only 30 per cent of the labour force in Japan can expect security of tenure and we then need to ask about the criteria which disqualify people from membership of the privileged sector. I would suggest that three groups have been consistently excluded on grounds of gender, cultural minority status and age.

Women are employed in Japan's larger companies where permanent status is most common, but they tend to be recruited for short periods before they marry. Thus one-quarter of women employees work for large companies with over 1000 workers but 70 per cent are below the age of 25. As we shall see later in this chapter the pressures on women to interrupt their careers in full-time paid work outside the home are enormous and this thereby structures the prospects of the minority that attempt to pursue a permanent career. Because it is taken for granted that women will be mobile, they cannot pledge a lifetime's continuous service and so are excluded from the reciprocal rewards of secure tenure and higher wages.

Members of the *burakumin* and minorities like the Koreans make up a smaller proportion of the total population in Japan than ethnic minorities in Western Europe or North America, but they are similarly treated. In general, access to high status positions in Japanese society is more difficult for them because their educational credentials are poorer in quality. More important for recruitment to large companies is that fact that even well-qualified candidates find it difficult to counter discrimination based on their family background. Until very recently official family registers detailing social background were freely available and even now 'Most major companies spend considerable sums to hire private detective agencies to investigate short-listed applicants' (Sugimoto 1986 p.72).

Disqualification by age has been an integral feature of exclusion from permanent employment because once a young man has failed to be recruited to a large firm there is little prospect of entry thereafter. But since 1975 it has become evident that even those recruited immediately after graduation cannot expect permanent employment and escalating wages until old age. It was always the case that retirement at about 55 years was common and that this reduced the length of time during which a worker received maximum earnings (see Figure 3.3). Since the oil crises of the 1970s, however, it appears that even before the designated retirement age there is great pressure to transfer to subsidiary companies which involves lower earnings, or to leave employment completely.

The reasons for such pressures are largely a function of labour costs because of the practice of partially relating wage to age. Slacker demand for labour in general has resulted in particular pressures on middle-aged men to retire early. Between 1978 and 1984 'the peak of the wage curve for male workers has shifted from the age group 50–54 to 45–49 . . . [and] . . . the rise in male unemployment rates is largely due to the increase in the unemployment rate among older male workers over 50' (OECD 1986 p.77). As life expectancy has soared in the past two decades the supply of older workers has increased so much that the prospects for the elderly look bleak.

Stereotypical images of the Japanese system of industrial relations appear to show only imperceptible differentials within the corporate famiy but it is not at all certain whether this makes for a less-developed consciousness of the distinction between white- and blue-collar workers. Even if differentials within large companies are less apparent than in the West, the clear lines of demarcation between employees in large and small firms creates a 'segmentation of the labour market . . .[which]. . . is no more than a class problem in another guise' (Morishima 1982 p.174).

The pattern of social divisions based on position in the labour market stands in stark contrast to the predominance of middle-class consciousness revealed in opinion surveys. In the mid-1970s several studies of Japanese society attempted to address this issue by identifying the 'emergence of a new middle class . . . an enormous intermediate stratum of society whose members are highly homogeneous in style of life and attitudes' (Murakami 1978 p.1). A great deal of weight was placed in such studies on homogeneous patterns of consumption as the ownership of durable items diffused rapidly among Japanese households. In the 1970s for example ownership of a car, cooler and colour television set, the three 'sacred treasures', was said to symbolize the arrival of a mass consumer society. It is not clear why particular consumer durables were chosen to show increasingly homogeneous lifestyles, but the enormous penetration of the mass media in a country with some of the highest viewing and readership figures in the world, certainly reinforced, if it did not induce, beliefs about the uniformity of tastes.

As in other societies there has been a lively debate over whether uniform patterns of consumption are simply 'surface phenomenon . . .[while] . . . the underlying "structural principle" of a class society remains unchanged' (Tominaga 1978 p.10). In other words whether mass ownership of certain consumer goods simply conceals the real effects of inequality. Certainly if one were to disaggregate consumer goods by quality a rather different conclusion on uniformity emerges. The consumer goods which have been most in demand in recent years are very expensive, clearly identifiable and frequently foreign *brands*. Some have argued that this reflects the translation of 'widening asset differentials and income differentials' . . . [into] . . . 'the age of stratified consumption' (M. Ozawa 1985 p.53).

Even if we accept that rising real incomes have extended the ownership of consumer goods more widely, this has not necessarily diminished other differences in spending patterns. The National Consumption Survey does show that the richest and poorest 10 per cent of households each spend very similar proportions of their incomes (about 4 per cent) on consumer appliances. But the same survey showed marked differences in other categories. For example the richest households spend only 25 per cent on food compared to nearly 40 per cent in the poorest. The gap in spending on housing was even wider with the poorest 10 per cent spending four times the proportion of their income on living quarters than the richest 10 per cent.

Housing tenure itself appears to be differentiated according to income, especially since the price of land has risen so steeply. Although Japan ranks highly in owner occupation at nearly two-thirds of all dwellings, there are marked differences between urban and rural areas. In the latter owner occupation often accounts for 80–90 per cent compared to less than 50 per cent in metropolitan Japan. There are also clear variations within urban Japan according to income group. One survey for 1978 showed that 79 per cent of the richest quintile of households owned their own homes compared to 27 per cent in the poorest quintile (Steven 1983 p.281). Such differentials show the profound impact of land scarcity in densely populated cities where the share of private sector rented accommodation is almost the same as owner occupied.

The growth of densely inhabited districts reflects the decline in rural population from 70 per cent of the total in 1950 to 25 per cent today and the parallel decline in the agricultural workforce from nearly one half to less than a tenth. Household incomes in rural areas, however, have risen dramatically since 1950 in absolute terms and relative to the national and urban average. There are problems in comparing urban and rural households because commuting distances are considerable and households are classified by residential address rather than place of employment. Nevertheless the gap between farm and non-farm incomes which was very large before 1940 had closed by 1960, and since then agricultural households have on average earned 10–15 per cent more than the national mean. Despite a drop in the number of agricultural households, this reversal in fortunes is one factor explaining the more equal distribution of household incomes compared to pre-war Japan.

It is tempting to argue that state policies of agricultural price supports and deficiency payments 'has been an effective means of income redistribution from consumers and taxpayers to farmers' (Patrick and Rosovsky 1976 p.40). But at least two points of caution need to be added. First to note that farm holdings are very small with 71 per cent of farmers owning less than one hectare. So as output per farm is consequently low, the impact of price support schemes is limited. Equally it is estimated that output from a quarter of these small farms is only sufficient to meet subsistence needs and is not marketed making agricultural protection less significant. Larger farmers benefit most, especially agricultural companies that account for 36 per cent of total sales.

A second point of caution about the impact of farm protection policies emerges from the fact that *non*-agricultural sources provide over 80 per cent of the incomes in agricultural households. Only one farm household in eight relies solely on income from agriculture and such households earn 11 per cent *less* than the national average. It is the remaining seven-eighths of agricultural households that earn more than urban households because of the size of their earnings from other sources. Some members of agricultural households depend on regular or seasonal employment in local industry or the service sector, but for others non-farm work involves travelling away from their home villages.

Two key features of households that rely solely on farming are their dependence on women who make up two-thirds of economically active members, and the growth in the proportion of elderly households. As younger people migrate to the towns it is the elderly who remain, so that Japan has three or four times the proportion of people over 65 in agriculture compared to Western Europe. In addition to the impact of migration, the ageing of farming households has since the late 1970s been influenced by an increase in people over the age of 50 returning to agriculture as a result of compulsory retirement pressures in non-agricultural sectors (Ministry of Agriculture White Paper 1983 p.13). This same source also noted that the reduction in demand for industrial labour after 1979 resulted in fewer part-time job opportunities for agricultural households, and in certain regions this has led to rural incomes falling behind urban levels.

It may be that the reduction in non-farm employment opportunities for agricultural households is a short-term trend. But even if it is, the significance of *non*-agricultural earnings in the reduction of regional inequalities in incomes should not be underestimated. 'If non-farm income had been excluded from farm household income, the rural–urban income differential would have continued to widen for the entire post-war period' (Ono and Watanabe 1976 p.383). So once again it is worth emphasizing that the process of closing income differentials involved much greater labour input for particular groups. In the case of agriculture dual occupations had been the norm before the war, but thereafter incomes from non-farm employment grew as the overall economy boomed, For many in rural households work on the family farm is done in the evenings and at weekends after a day's work elsewhere. If we were able to quantify total income per hour we would get a clearer idea of the extra effort needed to ensure that 'washing machines, vacuum cleaners, colour television sets and other appliances have made their way into almost all farming households' (Hasumi 1985 p.4).

6.4 Class affiliations from social surveys

Despite the mosaic of differences in income and status across a variety of groups in Japanese society, the appearance of shared affluence continues to be reflected in common feelings of being middle-class. It is easy to criticize survey data on class affiliation because respondents may choose categories which they know will be the majority view or give answers which will preserve themselves from humiliation. There is an uncanny uniformity in the reluctance of people at either end of the income spectrum to volunteer affiliation to either the upper or lower class. The EPA survey for 1985 separated respondents by income group and showed that even in the poorest households earning less than a third of the average income, 67 per cent of men and 82 per cent of women claimed to be middle-class. Similarly 'One newspaper recently surveyed several dozen presidents of major companies, all of whom identified themselves as middle class' (Kusaka 1985 p.41). Even though the shortcomings of such surveys are well known, their results are quoted extensively because they confirm that social and class divisions are not significant in Japan. The survey results are just one small part of a system of ideas which suggest that Japanese society is unusually cohesive. If clearer social divisions were recognized then group conflict would be inevitable; but as Japan is frequently depicted as a harmonious nation how can there be social or class divisions?

People may be reluctant to be identified as upper class because this is associated with living a life of leisure on inherited wealth not determined by individual ability or effort. In a society where the spirit of egalitarianism and the work ethic are so strong it is anathema to be seen as someone living solely on unearned income. Lower classes were easily recognized in pre-war Japan with widespread poverty, high numbers of landless peasants, massive income differentials and small numbers educated beyond the elementary level. The post-war economic boom was a period in which incomes rose rapidly, farmers became owner occupiers and lengthier education was made available to all, so few people in the 1980s want to be stigmatized as lower class. As the backbone of Japan is said to be its middling groups, not the parasitic rich nor the subordinate poor, the majority choose to label themselves among the safe, secure and normal middle class.

One consequence of portraying Japan as a national family under the pre-war Emperor system was, as we saw in Chapter 5, to suffocate distinctive elements in working-class culture. As this period was followed by the imposition of democratic reforms rather than a long struggle which may have cemented unity among the deprived, there appear to be few positive or distinctive associations in being working class. Instead, to be working class is to be lower class is to be inferior. Given the belief that Japan is an egalitarian society the failure to take advantage of an open education system makes 'working class life a punishment for laziness and a lack of ability' (Steven 1983 p.291). Thus it is small wonder that limited numbers wish to publicly acknowledge what are said to be personal failings.

Notwithstanding these subjective and understandable responses to social surveys, it is acknowledged even by one of the foremost theorists of social harmony in Japan, that there are 'cruelly heavy handicaps facing the powerless and socially inferior' (Nakane 1973 p.155). And from our earlier discussion of differential access to education or to protected positions in the labour market, it appears that there are certain social groups whose handicaps are predictable. In other words Japanese society is structured in dimensions which are reproduced over time according to gender, level of income, minority status, size of employing firm, industrial sector and age. Data on the more equal distribution of income does indicate that some among the disadvantaged groups have been able to earn higher incomes, but at the cost of much greater input of effort and under much more insecure circumstances. So agricultural households could raise their income levels but by continuing to have dual occupations; poorer households have been able to join the mass consumer society but by working much longer hours and relying extensively on women's part-time earnings from paid employment. Likewise the plight of the elderly is relieved by continuing in employment well beyond retirement age such that participation rates in 1986 for those over 65 in Japan were four or five times higher than in the US or Western Europe.

Up to the 1980s the ability to work longer hours, continue in employment well after official retirement age or to take advantage of part-time job opportunities concealed the real effects of differentials between households.

Even if such social inequalities are becoming more visible, they are readily justified by prevailing ideologies. Securing the acceptance by women of their unequal role in paid employment has usually involved stressing the primacy of their role as 'good wives and wise mothers'. Hence inferior public status is said to be compensated by their dominant and essential role in the private family. The aged should continue in employment to show commitment to the work ethic and rely on their family for any additional support, not the state. Discrimination against Korean minorities may be justified in the eyes of the majority by insisting on their racial inferiority as outsiders in an otherwise homogeneous nation.

This is not to argue that individuals in Japan unthinkingly accept such justifications imposed from above nor that dominant ideologies are undisputed. Indeed there are clear contradictions within and between components of such ruling ideas. For example the dominant view that a woman's place should be in the home means suspending egalitarian ideals for the 12 per cent of women who graduate from university. Equally the traditional Confucian belief of honour and respect for elders does not sit easily with the poor treatment accorded to elderly workers by private employers or the state, especially as so many now live alone in nuclear households. Discrimination against Korean 'outsiders' does not explain why other minorities like the *burakumin* who are part of the homogeneous 'insider' culture, face severe social handicaps.

In the remainder of this chapter we will explore more fully the social divisions based on gender, minority status and age. Gender divisions because they affect every single Japanese household. The minorities because their smaller number is often taken to imply that social divisions based on ethnic or cultural diversity is not a problem in Japan. The position of the aged because after ignoring differentiation by age for so long, the very recent extension of life expectancy rates has in a privatized welfare society forced their position onto the political agenda.

6.5 Women in the labour market

One of the major problems with traditional measures of income distribution based on household units is that they obscure income differences between members of the same household. Looking at Figure 6.1 it is like concentrating on what appears to be a remarkably even distribution of yearly incomes for *all* employees and ignoring the underlying bi-modal distribution based on gender. This data shows that on average a full-time woman employee in the private sector earns about one half of the sum earned by a man. If we were to include everyone in the labour force, the whole of the distribution for women would shift to the left because more women than men are employed part-time, act as unpaid family workers and are self-employed piece workers. In contrast, the men's distribution

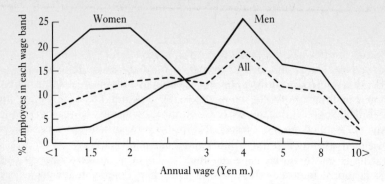

Figure 6.1 Frequency distributions of the national wage structure in Japan, 1982

Source: Japan 1984: An International Comparison, p. 73

would shift to the right as two-thirds of the relatively well-paid public sector workers are men and the bulk of self-employed men are also employers. While it is correct to say that women are employed for fewer hours than men, Figure 6.2 shows that the differential in hourly earnings even for full-time women employees has been fairly stable at about 55 per cent of men's for most of the 1980s halting the gradual trend towards narrower differentials of the previous 20 years. Both the level and the trend of wage differentials between men and women in Japan is

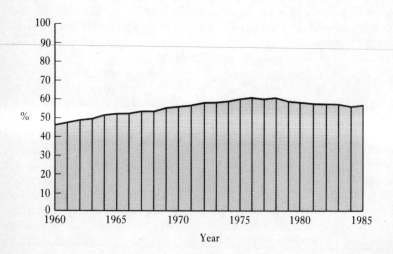

Figure 6.2 Women's cash earnings per hour as a percentage of men's, 1960–85

Source: Japan Statistical Yearbook

unrepresentative of other advanced economies where the trend for full-time employees has been towards reduced differentials to an average level of about 75 per cent. We saw in Chapter 3 that the total package of rewards to employees in Japan is determined by factors such as education, age, tenure, status and size of firm. For wage differentials between men and women, the size of the employing firm seems to make little difference; women in firms employing more than 1000 earning 53.5 per cent of the average for men and those in firms with less than five workers 52.5 per cent (*JTW* 1 February 1986). Educational achievement is generally associated with higher wages but the association for women employees is less direct and at times contradictory. For example women graduates in very large companies experience wider differentials with men in the same firm than in smaller companies. The reasons for this anomaly will be explained later but the key factor appears to be that women are much less likely to be promoted in larger firms. Turning now to age it was evident from Figure 3.3 that the wage profile for women is much flatter than for men so that the average woman employee at 50 earns only 17 per cent more than a 25-year-old in contrast to a 104 per cent gap for men between these ages. Figure 6.3 shows the effect that this has on differentials among full-time employees across the age range and although the differential narrows after the age of 50 this is due to the faster rate of decline in men's earnings.

Linking wage to age *per se* is misleading because what really matters is the length of continuous service with one employer. It is in length of

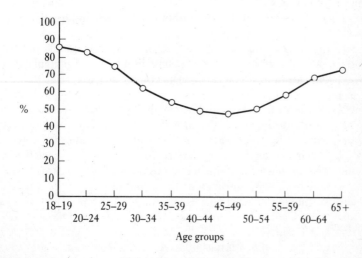

Figure 6.3 Earnings differentials between men and women by age group in private sector firms employing more than ten workers, 1983
Source: *Japan Statistical Yearbook*, 1986

service that there emerges a marked gap between men and women. Over the past 30 years the average length of service has increased for both men and women and although this has been slightly faster for women, their average tenure has increased only from 51–57 per cent of men's. So the gap in average years of continuous service to one employer remains conspicuous. Another significant feature of data on relative tenure is the extraordinary lack of variation around the average for women both by size of employer and industrial classification. In 1984 for example women on average stayed in large firms for 6.6 years, in medium-sized firms for 6.2 years and in small for 6.7 years, whereas for men the averages were 14.8, 11.2 and 9.1 (OECD 1986 p.69). Disaggregating firms into 37 industrial classes also shows a remarkably low standard deviation in the average length of women's employment compared to the men in the same sectors (*Japan Statistical Yearbook* 1985 pp.96–7). Such similarities in women's tenure does tend to focus attention on the importance of social customs particularly those concerning the customary exit of women from the labour force when they marry.

Although continuous tenure with one employer is rewarded highly in Japan, women's shorter length of service is not the only factor explaining higher pay for men. Even the tiny proportion of women who at 45 have worked for one employer for over 20 years only earn 75 per cent of a man with the same service. A similar pattern in manufacturing industry was revealed when age, occupation, firm size and education were held constant: a woman would only earn 63 per cent of a man of equivalent background showing 'there has been considerable discrimination against women in the determination of wages in Japan' (Tachibanaki 1975 p.571). Repeating this exercise a few years later the same author found such differentials were even more pronounced (1982 p.445).

Some of the reasons for the persistence of wage differentials between men and women arise from peculiar elements in the Japanese employment system. Making bi-annual bonuses proportionate to basic wage rates or paying to men as the head of the household family, education and housing allowances only serve to maintain differentials. Other legal restrictions on women's hours of overtime work also provides men with built-in advantages for larger earnings. In other ways the limitations on women's wages are affected by labour market features that are common in other societies. In Japan only one in thirteen of higher status jobs in administration and management are occupied by women and most of these are in the 'women's professions' of nursing or teaching. As elsewhere over one half of clerical or service workers are women and the routine work in retailing, hotels, restaurants and business offices is allocated to women. There are more women in Japanese manufacturing industry than is common in the West, but these are mainly women under 30 working as assembly operatives in electrical equipment or in poorly paid work in clothing and textiles where small firms are predominant. Women employees are either concentrated

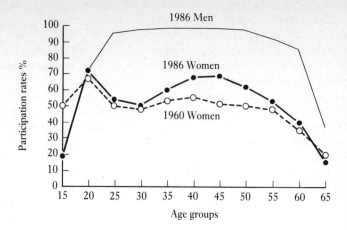

Figure 6.4 Labour force participations ratios, 1960 and 1986
Source: Japan Statistical Yearbook, 1987

in sectors where average earnings are in any case low or are unable to occupy anything other than menial positions in other sectors

In Japan as in almost all other societies the '"interruption" of women's careers by the birth and bringing up of children, for example, is – both materially and ideologically – a major factor confining women to underprivileged sectors of segmented labour markets' (Giddens and Mackenzie 1982 p.6). The full force of the dominant idea that a women's place in the home should take priority is thus used to explain and justify why in paid work outside the home, men should take precedence. This separation of priorities between domestic duties and outside paid employment has its greatest impact on recently married women in the 25–35 age group which produces a sharp drop in the number of women of this age that remain in the labour force. Figure 6.4 shows vividly the effect of this change in the pronounced 'M'-shape that characterizes women's participation ratios. Comparing 1960 with 1986 we can see a marked reduction in the number of women under 19 in the labour force because so many now remain longer in education. The other significant change is that many more women over the age of 35 re-join the labour market. What has not changed is the very sharp decline in women's employment ratios beween 25 and 35 which in 1960 fell by 29 per cent and in 1985 by 32 per cent. It is precisely within this age band that over three-quarters of Japanese women marry for the first time which suggests that it is unacceptable for large numbers of women to continue to work for the same firm upon marriage.

Women's participation ratios in other countries do show a decline around the age of 30, but only in the UK is the rate of exit from and subsequent re-entry into the labour force as steep as in Japan. In the US and Sweden by contrast women's participation ratios are becoming more like men's with no appreciable difference between 25 and 50, although these are exceptional. Where Japan differs from other countries is in the strength of the conviction that women should marry and then give their domestic world absolute priority. Such attitudes are reflected in the fall in participation ratios after 25 but the expectation that most women will follow this pattern informs employment practices for all women whether married or not. In other words the dominant view is that women should be seen as transient members of the labour force. By itself this expectation disqualifies almost all women from that privileged sector of employees whose lengthy and continuous service is rewarded with informal promises of lifetime employment.

6.6 A woman's 'proper place'

The pressures on women to terminate their service to a company when they marry, become pregnant or reach the age of 30 are in some cases very direct, but for the most part involve accepting informal rules. There are companies that formally insist on such resignations sometimes with the added incentive of payments akin to dowries. In such cases it is open to women to seek legal redress, but the litigation process is so lengthy that even if judgement is in their favour they would have already lost precious years of service. Legal actions are therefore not common and favourable judgements rarely result in re-instatement but financial compensation. Maternity leave has been a guaranteed right since 1972 although the burden of financing it is borne not by the state but by employers who rarely replace the absent employee. This then imposes extra burdens on the woman's work group that leaves a residue of ill-will to be faced by those women who take leave of absence. Thereafter those who do return are regarded as passengers who will always place the company second to family life so that applying for extended maternity leave 'would be professional suicide. Such an act is interpreted as a lack of commitment to the career and the company' (Osako 1979 p.21). Accepting informal rules on resignation may well then be influenced by the atmosphere in the workplace that women face if they insist on their legal rights.

Unmarried women who decide to work on in the same company after they reach their early 30s face many personal and material pressures. In a society where for women marriage and motherhood is identified as life's purpose, those who deviate have to cope with the pity or scorn of colleagues at work that is often embedded in labels such as 'old maid' or 'old aunt'. Single women are rarely eligible for company housing allowances, face a severe scarcity of public apartments and have poor access to housing loans. Within her own family she has to live with the prospect of being considered a 'failure' in the bridal market who will remain a burden on her parents. At work both unmarried women and those who return after maternity leave have little chance of promotion into management as they are 'generally speaking not welcome. Most employees would prefer to see them replaced by fresh young women just graduated from Junior College' (McLendon 1983 p.176). Such widely recognized attitudes towards those women seeking permanent careers, and the prospect of monotonous unchallenging jobs, merely increases the incentives to terminate their career.

It is argued by management and many trade unions that resignation at marriage or pregnancy is merely a reflection of social customs, but these customary practices themselves help to convey dominant ideas about women's 'proper' place especially as they determine the employment conditions of all young women. This is particularly noticeable for the 60 per cent of young women who are white-collar employees. Here women are assigned the role of men's assistant to sharpen pencils, take messages or to photocopy and distribute memos. These women are colloquially known as 'Office Ladies' and their dependent status is ritualized in the pouring or tea for male colleagues; followed of course by the ceremony of cleaning the teacups before the next session. Tea preparation is not part of their assigned duties but attempts by women to reject this role can produce serious conflict (Pharr 1984). Young women in white-collar work are valued as flowers in the office whose ornamental use ends when they wilt in their late 20s to be replaced by fresher blooms.

This picture of women office workers in Japan is often portrayed as an eccentric oriental practice quite different from Western experiences. However I would argue that what is really different about Japan is not the basic inequality between men and women, but rather the open admission that this is the way things should be. In many Western societies the increasing publicity given to token women in senior positions and the lip-service that is paid to gender equality merely serves to mask the underlying continuity in unequal gender relations.

The open admission of inequalities at work in Japan was most noticeable during the debates about Equal Opportunities Legislation in the mid-1980s. The state finally introduced legislation which, after pressure from employer's organizations was advisory not mandatory, and this was quickly followed by open admissions from companies that their attitudes to women would on the whole remain unchanged. The main justification given is that it is not worth incurring substantial training costs for women employees when they will leave the company before the costs can be recouped in the form of improved productivity. Hence women will continue to be allocated to menial auxiliary tasks which require less training and they will not be given the opportunity to move between sections as are men who will remain longer with the company. A typical explanation by management is 'The company cannot distinguish those girls who want to pursue a career from those who do not. And after all the primary corporate purpose is to increase profits not to help women establish themselves' (Takeuchi 1982, p.321). So management engages in risk minimization by reducing training costs for all women on the assumption that they will not remain with the company for very long.

These attitudes tend to be more pronounced for women graduates from Higher Education who enter employment at an older age but who are expected to resign at the same time as other women. As their expected length of service is shorter, there is even less time to recover training costs. We therefore find that women graduates in Japan are less likely to pursue a permanent career, or even enter employment at all, compared to women who leave education at an earlier age.

There is some debate whether this decision to remain outside the labour force is a voluntary or an involuntary one because it is argued that the specialist subjects studied by women graduates are ones that prepare them for their domestic role not paid employment. In practice there seems to be a series of barriers that reduce the attraction of women graduates into permanent careers. Numerous surveys conducted in the past decade by various institutions have highlighted differing recruitment patterns for men and women graduates. The Ministry of Labour for example found 'Of the firms that advertised for university graduates, two thirds advertised for male graduates only' (FPC 1985 p.5). Of the third that advertised for men and women, 60 per cent said there were some jobs that would in any case not be given to women. Promotion opportunities into supervisory positions were available to women in only 56 per cent of companies and even there specific ceilings were set at lower management levels. As a result, the earnings of women graduates are likely to fall further behind men who enter companies in the same year. Women university graduates therefore aged between 40 and 44 are scheduled to earn only 65 per cent of a man with the same educational background and years of service. In contrast a woman with a Junior High School education would earn 74 per cent and Senior High women 71 per cent of an equivalent man (Takeuchi 1982 p.321).

If anything employment prospects for women graduates have worsened as the economy has moved onto a slower growth path which means that the supply of graduate men is more than sufficient to meet demand. Of the 60 per cent of women graduates who do become employees, the majority enter the service sector whereas those women who leave education earlier are concentrated more in manufacturing. Both groups are considered as guestworkers and 'lower salaries for female employees, enforced retirement on marriage or pregnancy, and restriction of women to non-career positions all act to persuade women that there is little alternative to the domestic role' (Buckley and Mackie 1986 p.183).

6.7 Preparing women for domestic dominance

Access to the highest incomes in Japan is crucially determined by continuous service and commitment to the company but as motherhood is deemed to be a woman's sacred mission, they are thereby severely handicapped in the race for high status well-paid positions. Women are the only sex that can physically bear children but to attribute to them a consequentially segregated role in society involves several socially constructed assumptions, for instance that all women will bear children, that family care and housework will then be women's personal responsibility and therefore that women are not suited to permanent careers in paid employment outside the home. Although we have so far focused mainly on the attitudes and behaviour of employers towards women, what happens to women in paid work is but one part of a social process which goes far wider than the labour market. 'Persistent sexual inequality and sexual segregation are rooted in the very nature of the current Japanese social system' (Osako 1979 p.22).

In a number of ways social relations within families and education actively prepare women for motherhood. Although co-education for instance was introduced during the US occupation, like other reforms the original intentions have been eroded. Many of the private institutions that have proliferated in education do not enrol both boys and girls and such private schools recruit nearly 30 per cent of High School students. In the public sector home economics was made compulsory only for girls 'to recognize the special qualities of womanhood, helping them to become good future wives and mothers and to play that role gladly and with competence' (Ministry of Education 1969, quoted in Fujii 1982 p.305). It is not surprising then that in Higher Education women students are grossly over-represented in home economics and to a lesser extent in the humanities or teacher training; but under-represented in science, technology or law. Although Educational Reform has been a major issue in Japanese politics since 1982 the reform of a gendered curriculum is not even on the agenda for change.

In choice of subject and institution within Higher Education, the state plays a much less direct role relative to parents and the women students themselves. There are now only slightly more men students in Higher Education as a whole, but women make up only a quarter of those in four-year universities. In contrast 92 per cent of the students in two-year Junior Colleges are women, and most of these are privately run women-only institutions specializing in 'women's subjects'. At the highest ranking National Universities only 7 or 8 per cent of students are women not because they fail to pass the entrance examination but because they apply in much smaller numbers. Choice of institution does involve financial factors because a university education means two extra years of fees and the additional expenses of pre-university *juku*. But Junior Colleges are by no means inexpensive which suggests that the purpose of higher education for women is seen to be different from men. The limited employment prospects for women university graduates, or the view that in any case education is less important for daughters, or the belief that the content of education in Junior Colleges is more suited to apprentice 'home makers' are factors which influence decisions. For those parents who hope their daughters will marry graduates from the best universities there is the additional danger of them appearing over-qualified because 'Most men prefer to be slightly superior to their wives in academic achievement, which is the man's sphere by definition' (S.H. Vogel 1978 p.20).

Many of the ideas about a dependent role and position for women in the public sphere of Japanese society are transmitted as underlying assumptions in social communications: 'it is the covert expression of these . . . [patriarchal] . . . power structures in language, education and the media that are more difficult to identify and challenge because of their perceived neutrality' (Buckley and Mackie 1986 p.179). Much more visible is the way in which the state has supported dominant ideas about separate gender roles through in a gendered curriculum. Equally, Labour Standards Laws restricting women's hours of work or providing for leave of absence during menstruation, highlights the notion that women need special protection. Such initiatives were designed to preserve women's domestic role and in the case of menstrual leave safeguard their reproductive capacity. There is little evidence that fertility is affected by continuing in employment during menstruation; even if there was, the right to take leave from companies would be undermined if there were no equivalent provision for leave from housework.

Trade unions do defend the general rights of women to work but they also favour a continuation of rules protecting motherhood. So by supporting the right to menstrual leave, even though they know that very few women are able to take it, the trade unions reinforce the view that women as mothers need special protection. But at the same time they deny women as work colleagues the right 'to ask for "special privileges" such as equality in pay' (Molony 1985 p.555). Neither have trade unions been particularly helpful in translating the principle of maternity leave into a realistic proposition for women. In fact it appears that by their concern with the need for special treatment for women in employment, trade unions share with the education system, the media and the state the same dominant view of women's prior duty as homemakers.

It appears that because special privileges are offered to women in employment, little needs to be done to relieve women of some of their domestic tasks. The provision of day care for children in Japan is particularly poor reflecting in part the ethos of a welfare system based firmly on the private family, and trade unions have done little to encourage private employers to supplement public facilities. What seems to be influential here is the belief that the demand for child care is limited because of

Japan's extended family network. Those people that cannot, or choose not, to use the services of their extended family but turn to specialist childminders do of course have to face accusations of shameful neglect. But it is wives not husbands who are said to let 'latch key' children into juvenile delinquency because they are not fulfilling one key part of their proper role. The other aspect of this role involves household chores, but because Japanese men spend long hours in employment and endure lengthy absences from their homes, their ability to share childcare or housework is diminished even if they were willing to contribute.

There are therefore numerous interlocking pressures which delineate the domestic sphere as a woman's province and their freedom to choose beween alternative roles is constrained by the way social attitudes are reinforced by social practices. Although there is little dispute that gender roles tend to be more sharply segregated in Japan, there is debate about whether women wish it were otherwise. So a common response would be to say, yes there is a clearer separation of roles between men and women but it is an agreed separation into equally important positions. In exchange for an inferior position in the public sphere women in Japan enjoy domestic dominance.

The development of separated realms for men and women has been clearly affected by the decline in households that operate as family units and centres of production because the share of total output from agriculture and very small family businesses has fallen. Those Japanese men who now spend much less time with their families and much more in after-hours company activities, do so to the exclusion of wives. Men may not have much option, but putting the company first means men and women have 'mutually exclusive and . . . separated networks of personal relationships' (Atsumi 1979 p.67). Although company business may press less heavily on blue-collar workers, men in these occupations seem to hold very firmly to the view that as women's natural talents lie in homemaking and their own in the world outside, a division of labour along these lines is ideal. But in what sense are women dominant in the private sphere and is a mainly domestic role really equal to a mainly public one?

It is said to be common practice for men in Japan to hand over 'their' salary as family income and for women then to take control of spending decisions thus earning power and financial management are coordinated equally. Secondly, women are reputed to have independence in the care or disciplining of children and in the supervision of their education which is so crucial to their future. Thus a 'good' husband is said to be one who is 'healthy and absent'; healthy to maintain the flow of income and absent to confirm his commitment to his company while not interfering too much at home. In short 'the typical Japanese household is a disguised matriarchy – and a rather thinly disguised one at that' (Christopher 1984 p.58).

The question of whether women's status as homemaker is equally important to men's pre-eminence in public is problematic partly because this depends so much on their personal relationship. But there is little doubt about the low esteem bestowed on the basic tasks of housework. Where men, after their arduous routine in the workplace, do 'help' in housework this 'has the function of relaxation' (Herold 1979 p.19). Despite the fact that their 'help' is limited, their experience seems sufficient to prove how much the spread of electrical appliances has reduced the burden of housework which certainly does not necessitate menstrual leave! So as housework is taken to be the woman's burden and as it cannot compare to men's perception of their burdens in outside employment, this aspect of domestic life is devalued.

There are aspects of family relations where women cannot be dominant given, for example, the prevailing methods used in Japan to control their rate of reproduction. Prescription of the contraceptive 'pill' is illegal and as the most common method of birth control is the condom, this leaves men with the prime responsibility for family planning. But even if we do accept that women have more control over other areas of domestic life, it is vital to recognize that their power has been delegated to them by men.'The brutal fact is that should a husband decide to withdraw financial support, the carefully crafted and vaunted domestic authority of the professional housewife will fall in ruins. The autonomy of the married woman is wholly contingent' (Smith 1987 p.19). Neither is it just married women without paid work whose domestic power is conditional, because women in general have little chance of earning sufficient income to be financially independent of men.

Just how much of a woman's power and control is contingent upon men may be seen in the position of divorced women. In Japan not only are men more likely to be given custody of any children than in the West but alimony awards are very meagre. In fact according to Health and Welfare Ministry Statistics for 1984 only one divorced woman in ten gets financial support for the children from their fathers (*JTW* 11 January 1986). The financial settlement after divorce usually favours men because the personal property system makes the husband's income and savings his alone. Yet public welfare benefits for divorced women are still proportionate to the income of the former husband until he remarries when he is usually able to cease paying alimony. The divorce rate in Japan has increased over the past 30 years so that it now approaches its pre-war level, but it is still less than half the rate in Europe or the US and the economic problems of divorced women is surely one factor in this difference.

It is common to attribute the lower Japanese divorce rate to the general satisfaction of people with the *status quo* and to use this to support the proposition that inequality for women outside the household is compensated by domestic supremacy. But should we not also ask whether women, being fully aware of the alternatives to remaining married, have much choice? Becoming financially equal from paid employment is almost impossible and the prospects for divorced women are hardly attractive. As the socialization of women is said to stress especially qualities such as endurance and forebearance, perhaps they become resigned to the lesser of two evils.

There is little evidence in opinion surveys to suggest that large numbers of women are willing to record publicly much dissatisfaction with their current position in Japanese society. What has changed is the level of agreement with the statement 'men work and women stay at home' in the regular surveys on women's issues undertaken by the Prime Minister's Office. Over 80 per cent of women respondents agreed with the statement in the early 1970s compared to less than half that figure in the mid-1980s. In many ways this change reflects what actually happens: although segregated gender roles are explained and justified by assuming women will become homemakers more than 70 per cent of women in paid employment are or have been married. Thus the division of responsibilities means that many women combine unpaid domestic work with outside paid employment. In other words these married women, unlike married men, are engaged in a 'double shift'.

6.8 Role harmonization and a double shift for married women

The proportion of women over the age of 15 who are recorded as members of the labour force in Japan currently stands at 49 per cent which is among the highest ratios for advanced capitalist societies. But in contrast to the West where women's participation rates have been steadily increasing for over 20 years, the Japanese rate fell from 56 per cent in 1955 to 46 per cent in 1975 only to rise again thereafter. Two factors in particular caused the rate to drop. First, as is illustrated in Figure 6.4 there was a spectacular reduction in the numbers of young women under 20 who were in the labour force as their years in full-time education lengthened. Secondly, the labour force in agriculture fell from a third of the total to a tenth, and as women made up over a half of workers in agriculture in 1960, this pulled down their overall share of the labour force. Both of these influences outweighed, until the mid-1970s, the increase in non-agricultural employment.

A related consequence of falling agricultural employment was that the number of women classified as unpaid family workers has fallen from one-half to one-fifth in 1986. This fifth incidentally represents 82 per cent of all persons working without pay in enterprises owned by a related person in the same household. As the decline in the household as a unit of production began before higher rates of economic growth became established as the norm, the relatively sluggish demand for women employees coincided with changes in attitudes to women in the labour force. In the late 1950s the label 'professional housewife' began to be applied to women in all classes, and the co-educational stance of the post-war reforms began to be eroded. In other words, dominant ideas about women began to be more clearly constructed around the primacy of their career as homemakers. It should be noted though that even at the time when the mutually exclusive character of gender roles was articulated most forcibly, there were never less than 40 per cent of women of any age group in the labour force.

By the mid-1960s with the economic miracle in full swing, Japan was then faced with a growing shortage of labour especially as the number of young men and women in Higher Education began to rise which delayed their entry into the labour force still further. Against this background prevailing ideas about women being exclusively 'professional housewives' were also being adapted as some married women were urged to 'harmonize' their domestic role with another one in paid employment. Despite being thought of as a new and progressive approach, it was something that at least 40 per cent of them had always done. From 1965 there were more married than unmarried women in the labour force and advising them to 'harmonize roles' marked a compromise between patriarchal values and the economic need to increase the supply of labour. What was not altered was the basic belief that their prime responsibility lay with their family. As men did not relieve women of the burden of domestic work, and as the state did not increase the provision of public care facilities this new era meant 'harmonizing' a double burden for married women. By 1985 this double burden has increased as the proportion of unmarried women in the labour force has fallen to less than 30 per cent, and well over two-thirds of women between 30 and 50 were in paid employment.

Despite the movement of the Japanese economy onto a slower growth path since 1974, 'role harmonization' with domestic primacy, remain the watchwords for women. To maintain their guestworkers status in the labour market, women now occupy more of the positions in the labour market that carry least security of tenure and they now comprise over two-thirds of all casual and day labourers. As significant has been the increase in women part-time employees, a trend common elsewhere in the West. This 'innovative compromise between capitalism and patriarchy' (Ueno 1983 p.8) has resulted in an increase of 75 per cent in the number of part-time employees since the first oil crisis in 1973, and 85 per cent of these employees have been women. Indeed the degree of flexibility provided by women in the labour market has been highlighted as crucial to the ability of the Japanese economy to absorb the impact of the second oil crisis in 1979 and cope with the phenomenal 50 per cent increase in the value of the yen between 1986 and 1988.

As flexibility in the labour market has increasingly meant more women in various categories of insecure employment, management can vary labour input and justify such adjustment by arguing that they are not the main breadwinners. In manufacturing, *kanban* methods of inventory control requires daily or hourly changes in the supply of components which also means daily or hourly changes in labour input among subcontractors. Thus in firms of all sizes women part-timers are convenient for management, but especially so in subcontracting firms and 62 per cent of women who are part-timers in manufacturing are employed by firms with less than 100 employees. Apart from being able to vary the numbers of hours worked the 'great merit of such housewives is the lack of any need to pay them high wages' (Takeuchi 1982 p.322). Having previous work experience married women incur less training costs, they require less pension insurance or retirement allowances and take less paid leave which makes their establishment cost much lower than full-time workers.

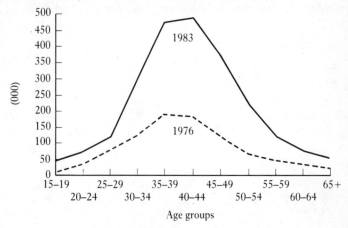

Figure 6.5 Women part-time employees by age group 1976 and 1983
Source: OECD, 1986, p. 76

From the demand side the incentives for employers are obvious while from the supply side there is undoubted interest in part-time employment. During the 1980s the rate of increase in the real income of Japanese men has slowed down while housing and education expenses have not, which helps explain why the supply curve of part-time workers has shifted to the right. The outcome of demand and supply side factors can be seen vividly in Figure 6.5 which compares the age distribution of part-time employees in 1983 with that in 1976, showing especially the threefold increase in the age range 35–50. Japanese women in this age group have on average two young children which suggests that 'married women can conveniently combine part-time work with their family responsibilities' (OECD 1986 p.76). But 'convenient' for whom?

Clearly convenient for management because this provides an elastic supply of low-cost labour which perpetuates the tendency to end women's first experience in employment at marriage. These women can be replaced with part-timers and cheaper entrants from school or college. Convenient for taxpayers and the state because women can continue to function at the heart of a mainly privatized welfare system sited on the family. Convenient too for households as units of consumption because this provides some compensation for the earlier peak in men's earnings which now occurs while education expenses are still rising. Consequently the age distribution shown in Figure 6.6 shows marked differences between women who are in full-time employment and those in part-time or piecework jobs. The latter are clearly substituted for the former after women marry. It should, however, be borne in mind that even with both spouses in employment the average contribution of married women to the total earnings of a household is only 20 per cent which leads us to the question of whether these employment patterns are convenient for women themselves.

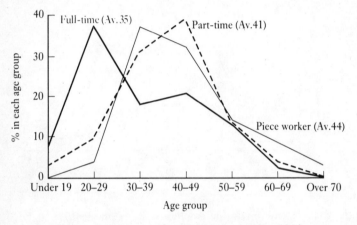

Figure 6.6 Age profile of women workers 1983
Source: Kawashima 1987, p.607

Quite apart from totally inadequate pension or insurance provision, poor pay and insecure tenure, we need to consider the effort required from women to earn their 20 per cent of household income both in employment and when they return home. The Japanese define part-time employees as those scheduled to work less than 35 hours per week, which by Western standards is high, but then all working hours are longer in Japan. It is more revealing to compare women's employment hours with men in full-time employment so that women part-timers in 1986 averaged 75 per cent of the hours of men full-timers. Women pieceworkers were employed for two-thirds of the men's average while the 60 per cent of women between 30 and 45 in full-time employment averaged nine-tenths. In total, married women employees average something like 80 per cent of the hours men spend in full-time employment.

When we consider what the Ministry of Labour calls the 'domestic routine', we discover that employed housewives still manage to contribute two-thirds of the time spent on household affairs and/or the raising of children that is spent by housewives without paid employment. What is sacrificed by married women employees from their 24-hour day, is time spent sleeping or eating but principally less time on 'leisure amusement and recreation' (FPC 1983 p.23). Men's contribution to household affairs is notoriously low with only one half of husbands admitting to any at all. The average for those that do contribute is actually shorter where women are in outside employment: but only by one minute at 6 minutes compared to 7! (Higuchi 1982 p.315).

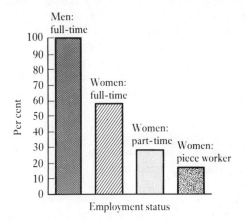

Figure 6.7 Women's hourly earnings as a percentage of men's, by employment status, 1986
Source: *Japan Statistical Yearbook*, 1987

Wages for women in outside employment lag far behind men's as is illustrated in Figure 6.7 and because women are employed for fewer hours the gap in annual earnings is even wider. Taking men's average annual earnings in 1986 as 100, women full-timers take away 46 per cent of this figure, women part-timers 23 per cent and women pieceworkers 12 per cent. In absolute and proportionate terms the numbers of women pieceworkers has declined to one-tenth of women employees but on average they spend as long with the same employer as women full-timers. For the one million homeworkers, tenure as such is not rewarded nor do they receive bonus payments. Part-time women employees are eligible for bonuses but these average only a quarter of women full-timers and one-tenth of men in full-time employment.

'Role harmonization' for married women does boost household incomes, but at a tremendous cost for scant reward. The state, employers and trade unions in various ways help to maintain women's position as supplementary and therefore marginalized employees. Equal opportunities were enshrined in new legislation passed in 1986 but not only are there grossly ineffective sanctions against offending employers, other state policies undermine its impact. Rolling back the influence of the state in welfare merely confirms women's prior role in the family. Labour policies to protect workers who are laid-off temporarily or provide re-training subsidies exclude most women who are actually among 'the first to feel the adverse effects of technological innovation' (Fujita 1987 p.595). Nowhere can this be seen more clearly than in the rapid pace of automation in offices where women are in the majority. In the absence of state pressure to improve the terms and conditions of part-time women employees, employers continue to use them as the essential flexible complement to a relatively fixed number of full-time regular workers. By supporting special protective legislation for women, the trade unions help to convey the ideology of women as homemakers. They have also been preoccupied in the 1980s with preventing redundancies among their members most of whom are men in large companies; so women, and men in smaller companies, are left to the mercy of market forces.

Given the power of dominant ideas about women's employment and the prevalence of social practices that confirm these ideas, women themselves appear to accept their status as temporary guests in the labour force. Thus they are much less likely to declare themselves as unemployed if their jobs are terminated. In the immediate aftermath of the oil crisis in 1973, three-quarters of the 1.7 million jobs lost were women's but only a quarter of these women declared themselves as unemployed while the rest disappeared into the ranks of the non-employed. Because women's employment status is regarded as transitory, the official unemployment statistics grossly underestimate the number of women who would take employment if it were available. By applying equivalent measures to the US, which are themselves not as rigorous as the EEC, one source estimates that after the second oil crisis in 1979 the official unemployment figures of 2.4 per cent for women would be increased to 8.9 per cent. For men the re-calculation increased the official figure from 2.5 per cent to 3.3 per cent (Taira 1983 p.8).

6.9 Patriarchy in the public arena

The primary focus of the relegation of Japanese women into the private, domestic sphere has thus far been illustrated through an analysis of the labour market, but there are other theatres of public life in which women play subordinate parts. In politics, in professions other than teaching or nursing or in the media women are even more conspicuous by their absence than in the West.

Among elected politicians at the highest level there has only been one woman cabinet member since 1960, rarely are more than 3 per cent of Diet members women and even fewer are elected to local or provincial assemblies. Among appointed public officials it is in health and welfare administration that women appear most, making up for instance over one-third of mediation commissioners in the family courts. The general level of participation by Japanese women in political activity is low but there are two interesting exceptions.

First, apart from the national election in 1946 which was the first time women had been allowed to vote, the turnout of women has consistently exceeded that of men. But they are then expected to entrust political affairs to the men that are elected and wait until the next election to re-assert their symbolic claim to political citizenship. When women heed this advice they are castigated for lacking interest although it is widely known that men too show little inclination to participate in politics. 'That a major government study on women should conclude, without qualification or amplification, that the voting rate of women bears no relation to genuine political interest is somewhat remarkable' (Jones 1977 p.233). Remarkable possibly, but as consistent as ever.

The other main exception to what appears to be low levels of political participation by women, arose out of the part played by them in the various citizen movements that mushroomed from the later 1960s. Women in particular were the driving force behind the attempts to assign to private firms the responsibility for the social costs of pollution. In the campaign for compensation to the sufferers of mercury poisoning or *Minamata* disease, local public officials and the trade unions were reticent whereas women were brave enough to challenge the companies through the courts. Eventually this led to positive state action in the whole field of environmental pollution. In a similar way women have consistently been prime movers among consumer groups protesting that goods produced in Japan cost more to domestic consumers than they do to overseas purchasers. Women too lead the protest when a rising exchange rate is not reflected in falling prices of imported goods, and they have also been prominent in the 20-year campaign opposing the confiscation of land to build a new Tokyo airport at Narita.

Women do then have a clear presence in all of these movements, but in the process they face abuse and ridicule for interfering in affairs about which they are said to know little. This was especially evident in the early stages of the *Minamata* protest when they were accused by the companies of exaggerating the effects of pollution because they did not understand medical science. In some of the protest movements once women have forced the issue on to the public agenda, it is men that then colonize the issue as they did in the case of environmental pollution when all the political parties appeared to take credit for the tougher legislation. In other cases the more significant role played by women seems to offer a good excuse not to respond at all as happens in protests about higher domestic prices. Public ridicule is certainly the response of the media and politicians to Japanese feminists after the same fashion as Western attitudes to the women's peace movement.

A particularly virulent form of contempt and abuse has been heaped on an aspect of a woman's role which straddles the boundary between their private family role and a more public one. The label 'education momma' is used with contempt for those women who are seen transporting their children from home to school to *juku* and back home again, who are earnest PTA members and who themselves attend *jukus* to learn how best to supervise their children's education. From 1985 the Education Reform Council has constantly criticized the education system for producing dull, regimented automatons among the young who then respond with more violence in school, more delinquent behaviour and higher rates of juvenile suicide. Yet, while 'education mommas' provide handy scapegoats, both parents are involved in accepting the rules of the educational credentials game for which the prize is permanent employment. In playing the game created by society to its limit, 'education mommas' are stigmatized for using their children to maximize their own personal prestige.

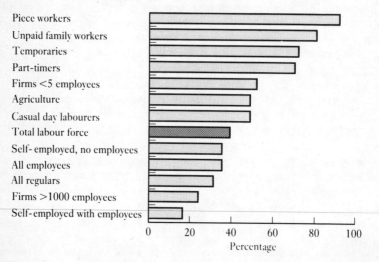

Figure 6.8 A summary picture of women's representation in the Japanese labour force, 1986
Source: Japan Statistical Yearbook, 1987

The pattern of social inequality based on gender in Japan has many similarities with other societies whether capitalist or not. What does seem apparent, however, is that in Japan women's domestic priorities are so firmly grounded in attitudes and social practices at all levels, that women's lives are even more constrained and their freedom to choose between alternatives more limited. There have to be sure been changes in the past 30 years, most notably the reduction to 20 per cent in the numbers of women who work unpaid both inside and outside the home. But not all change has been for the better as the ranks of marginal or peripheral workers have been increasingly feminized. Adding together temporary workers, casual day labourers, part-timers, pieceworkers and unpaid family workers as the periphery, we find that since 1970 the share of women has increased from 60 to 75 per cent. Figure 6.8 displays the current position of over-representation of women in the least well-paid categories and under-representation in the better paid.

In exchange for a bigger share of low-paid employment, married women have been encouraged to work a double shift and harmonize domestic work with paid employment. This double burden appears to benefit the whole household in a material sense and it certainly benefits Japanese men. 'Above all it is men themselves who can enjoy a middle-class standard of life with the financial support of their wives without threatening their male dominance' (Ueno 1983 p.10). Women's answers in Japanese social surveys on class affiliation suggest that the vast majority wish to be associated with a middle-class standard of life. Even in the poorest fifth of households earning less than a third of the national average income, 82 per cent of women categorize themselves as middle-class. Rather than accusing Japanese women of false consciousness in a patronizing or arrogant manner, I would prefer to speculate that in responding to social surveys Japanese women display how fully they have been incorporated as components into the household unit. There has been a substantial growth in incomes and women are materially better off than their mothers, but as individuals women's inferior position in Japanese society reminds us that 'the patriarchal value system has not disappeared' (Kawashima 1987 p.611).

6.10 Japan's segregated minorities

In contrast to the abundant information available on the position of women, there is considerably less data available about the living conditions of minority groups in Japan. The majority in Japan prefer to shun physical contact with minorities who reside in separated districts and descriptions of life in these areas are rooted in stereotypical beliefs. Thus poorer educational performance is alleged to show the intellectual deficiency of minorities who are also scape-goated for criminal tendencies, for aggression, disorderliness and personal uncleanliness. Such districts are to be avoided as their inhabitants are labelled as different and inferior because they apparently reject the common values and rules of behaviour of the majority.

Prejudice against minorities in Japan does appear to have socio-biological strands that underpin discrimination. Just as women's biological capacity for child-bearing is used to justify socially constructed expectations of their place in society, so also can discrimination against minorities be explained away in terms of biological or racial differences. People born in Japan to families of Korean origin are classified as 'aliens' and are subject to abuse deriving from the notions of racial superiority that marked the colonization of Korea earlier this century. Ideas about the racial purity of the Japanese may have little scientific or historical credibility, but two centuries of self-imposed isolation from the seventeenth century fomented myths about common bloodlines. For those minorities who have full Japanese nationality like the *burakumin*, a number of folk tales are used to explain their inferiority among which are some which relate their origins to the transportation of Korean prisoners or slaves to Japan. Indeed one survey in 1965 showed that 70 per cent of those interviewed thought that *burakumin* were of a different race (Hane 1982 p.139). A common thread therefore that runs through attitudes to minority groups relates their current social status to spurious ideas about different racial origins and fixed biological traits.

Racism in Japan does not for the most part take the overt political form noticeable among organizations in Europe and the US which strive to give biological explanations of minority status scientific credence. The Japanese majority prefer to ignore the existence of minorities and appear fetishistic about their degree of social homogeneity. It was not uncommon then to hear Prime Minister Nakasone in 1986 contrast the presence of 'blacks, Puerto Ricans and Hispanics' in the US with the absence of minorities in Japan (*JTW* 8 November 1986). There are clear inconsistencies and contradictions here not least because his own Ministry of Foreign Affairs had only two years earlier agreed that there were segments of Japanese society whose 'fundamental human rights are grossly violated even in present day society' (MOF *Dowa Problem* 1984 p.3). Such inconsistencies become clearer when we see estimates of the numbers of *burakumin* vary from one to five million. As individual *burakumin* know full well how much they have to lose by declaring their ancestry and as the majority prefer to ignore their presence, under-recording the numbers affected by discrimination is common. Most independent sources suggest that the size of the *burakumin* community is between two and three million.

In addition there are another 1.5 million Japanese nationals who are subject to discrimination. Inhabitants of the scattered islands to the south of Japan centred on Okinawa were only incorporated in 1872 and remained in the periphery until they were placed under US military administration from 1945 to 1972. Okinawans are regarded as backward as are Ainu people in the north of Japan who are said to be the 'primitive' original inhabitants of the Japanese islands and like the original peoples of the US or Australia, Ainu citizens are treated with condescension. There are also resident minorities who are not Japanese nationals and the largest group are those with Korean ancestors who number 0.7 million.

Poverty and deprivation for Okinawans or the Ainu is influenced by their location in peripheral areas and migration from these areas is limited by the discrimination they would face elsewhere in Japan. Other minorities occupy separated residential areas which are all too easily labelled ghettoes. The very name *buraku* implies segregated or separate communities in major urban areas or on the outskirts of villages in rural districts. Living conditions remain inferior for all minorities despite the demolition of some shanty towns and their replacement with high-rise housing. Relative deprivation is still apparent especially because of much poorer sewage systems and inadequate water supplies. Although it is difficult to quantify differences in income levels, it is clear that segregated districts contain large numbers of low-income households and one survey of major urban areas found only one *burakumin* household in ten with an income at or above the average of the Japanese majority (Sabouret 1983 p.30).

Low incomes in themselves reflect the dependence of minorities on transient day labouring jobs. Most sources suggest that only one in four members of the minorities are employees at all, with the rest either in self-employed work in shops, restaurants and taxi driving or permanently unemployed apart from occasional jobs on public works schemes. Over 25 per cent of *burakumin* work in agriculture, for the most part farming tiny plots of the poorest land which is either ill-drained or in mountainous terrain. Eighty per cent of those employed in agriculture in 1945 worked plots of less than one acre and so were ineligible for purchase under the Land Reform programme even if they could have afforded to purchase their land. All the segregated districts have high concentrations of unemployment, ill-health and below average educational qualifications which for the majority confirms that these districts and their residents are to be avoided at all cost.

6.11 Prejudice, the state and social action

The influence of ideas from the past on current attitudes is not peculiar to Japan, but for *burakumin* as the connections between their origins and the present day are readily identifiable history plays an important part in explaining the persistence of discrimination. Today's *burakumin* are descended from outcast groups who until 1871 were allocated sub-human status at the very bottom of the feudal hierarchy. By being associated with animal trades such as butchery or leatherwork, outcasts were despised as sacrilegious and for fear of contamination were condemned to live outside the main community. In practice many were not involved in 'polluting' occupations but the assumption that they were meat-eaters 'gave a religious rationalization for the persistence of discrimination against them' (Neary 1979 p.54). Outcast numbers were swollen by including among their ranks itinerants, criminals and other rebels or mis-fits, and by the early nineteenth century outcasts took on key social control functions as executioners, prison guards and suppressors of peasant unrest. 'By having the outcasts perform the most despised tasks of ruling . . . the feudal rulers were able to direct the anger of commoners away from themselves and onto the despised outcasts' (Ruyle 1979 p.60).

Residents of Japan with Korean ancestry face discrimination which is transferred from attitudes towards the inferiority of colonial subjects. The record of civilian unrest against Japanese rule, tales about sexual promiscuity and the idleness of Korean workers, confirmed for the majority in Japan the picture of an inferior race. As the current minority are directly descended in many cases from colonial subjects brought to Japan in the 1930s, they inherit from their predecessors the status of inferior aliens.

There are a number of reasons why the passage of time has not seriously diminished the influence of historical antecedents for the *burakumin*. The legal status of outcast was revoked in 1871 yet it is still possible for potential employers or marriage partners to trace an individual's origins back to the outcast status of their ancestors. As these checks are still made over a century after the abolition of feudalism, *burakumin* rights and freedoms are violated. Japanese residents with Korean origins are required to register and be fingerprinted as aliens maintaining in a very public way their position as 'outsiders'. All minorities have to live with the knowledge that the majority will assume they are more likely to continue a tradition of behaving in ways thought to be untypical of 'ordinary' Japanese.

In a society where educational achievement is a major preoccupation, higher than average rates of truancy or incidents of violence at school are the subject of particular notice. If examples of these forms of indiscipline appear to be more common in areas thought to be inhabited by minorities, then it is said to show a failure to accept essential elements of the social system. In turn associating minority districts with poor education records, allows the majority to justify the preponderance of low incomes from poorly-paid jobs. Equally, observing that minorities are over-represented among recipients of public welfare, encourages the belief that all members of minority groups show 'dependent opportunism towards welfare programmes initiated by the majority culture' (Wagatsuma 1979 p.52). Again this stands in stark contrast to the notion that being Japanese means being self-reliant and labels minorities as deviant as also does the association of higher rates of recorded crime with particular districts.

Associating minority districts with various kinds of rule-breaking serves for the majority to confirm stereotypical beliefs about individual members of these communities. Minorities as a whole are labelled as fundamentally different in ways which echo the historical origins of discrimination. Thus for four or five million permanent residents of Japan there exist a formidable set of barriers to their participation in an apparently egalitarian society because they are shunned as deviants. Each individual in a minority has if they wish to 'pass' as a member of the majority to disguise their family background.

Numerous obstacles stand in the way of individuals who seek to 'pass'. Some of these obstacles are common to other societies where among other things, 'passing' produces a personal trauma of severing links with one's own community and appearing to accept the prejudices of the majority. Other obstacles are more peculiar to Japan where detailed records are kept by the state on each individual's family and residential history. Copies of such records are generally required with job applications or on enrolment in school which means that 'passing' demands thorough preparation. Every effort must be made to erase previous addresses in segregated districts and this involves changing residence frequently until the original address disappears from the municipal records. By itself this necessitates detailed planning and expense but it also involves disassociation from one's family as even an occasional visit can be dangerous.

Family records unlike residential registration are extremely difficult to disguise as these detail the official record of births, marriages, deaths, occupations and criminal convictions which can be compared across generations. Not only may *burakumin* origins be traced through place of residence or occupation, but also by examining the 1871 status of families where outcasts were classified as 'new commoners'. Since 1969 family records are no longer open for public inspection, but circulated in their place are 'book length compilations of the names, locations and main occupations of the thousands of *Buraku* ghettoes throughout Japan' (Yoshino 1983 p.45). In most cases resort to such lists is not needed because if an individual is reluctant to provide a copy of their family record, it is assumed that they have something to hide.

Japanese residents whose family were of Korean origin face exactly the same problems in 'passing' with the additional proviso that they become a naturalized Japanese. This is in itself not an easy process as the qualifying 'good behaviour' clauses may be applied to an applicant's whole family and naturalization is sought only by small numbers. In an important way this reflects the irrevocability of denying one's Korean ethnicity which is intrinsic to 'passing'. Naturalized Japanese are also unlikely to be accepted fully by the majority while at the same time being castigated as ethnic deserters by their kin.

Burakumin who attempt to 'pass' experience similar crises of personal guilt in face of the continued inequality bestowed on other *burakumin* and live in mortal fear of their origins being discovered. A particularly crucial time comes when they contemplate marriage as family investigations are a common practice. If a non-*burakumin* family discovers a minority identity then it is almost certain that the couple will be forced to cancel the marriage or suffer the consequences of being ostracized. As a result of these impediments, 'Passing is seen more and more as a socially impractical if not personally impossible solution' (de Vos and Weatherall 1983 p.8). Most members of minority groups resign themselves to living within their own communities which appears to be their only realistic option.

A range of organizations exist to represent minority communities in their struggle to end discrimination, but their impact has been diluted by internal differences over the basic causes of inequality and strategies to remove social prejudices. All these interest groups have in addition to contend with feelings of resignation within their communities in that prejudice is so pervasive better not 'disturb sleeping children'.

Buraku representation has been divided in several ways but the major split has been about whether to press for assimilation or liberation. Those stressing gradual assimilation emphasize following the 'Japanese way' of self-help and personal effort provided that some assistance is given by the state for economic and environmental improvement in separated communities. This strategy places more weight on negotiating with state agencies to increase housing or infrastructure spending and draws these groups closer to the LDP. Equally financial support is pledged to individual *burakumin* who challenge particular cases of discrimination and seek personal recompense. In contrast, those groups seeking liberation for all *buraku*, stress the need for a united minority voice through a stronger sense of *buraku* ethnicity. They are wary of what they regard as piecemeal state assistance which, without fundamental changes in social attitudes and practices, merely encourages dependence on the state. The liberation movement in short calls on all Japanese to accept their culpability for centuries of discrimination.

Political action to defend the rights of those born in Japan to families with Korean origins has also been dissipated by organizational and ideological fissures especially in rivalry determined by competing affiliation to the People's Republic of Korea or the Republic of Korea. With roughly equal halves of this minority associating itself with one or the other state it often appears that the main focus of their anger and frustration is directed at the rival organization.

In articulating their demands, minority organizations have received vacillating degrees of practical support from anti-conservative political groups. As we have seen repeatedly the trade unions are in effect representatives of the privileged sector of the labour force, and as 'foreigners': 'Koreans are generally regarded as competitors rather than people in need of assistance' (De Vos and Lee 1981 p.378). Neither do those *buraku* organizations that support trade union activities receive reciprocal help in improving access for *burakumin* into primary sections of the labour market. The support of political parties on the left has continually stumbled over ideological questions about whether minorities are a special case of oppression or should be integrated into the wider class stuggle. At one time the JSP appears to place the *buraku* cause first then later to reverse their position, while the JCP seems to alternate their priorities with the JSP. The key moment in assessing the real extent of support for the *buraku* cause by those on the left, comes when liberation groups require all Japanese including the left itself to share responsibility for discrimination. It is at these moments that priorities are not infrequently reordered. Other differences concern the extent to which *buraku* organizations should cooperate with LDP policies to ameliorate conditions in the separated districts.

The response of the state and the LDP to the demands of minorities for real equality has been contradictory in basic principles and divisive in policy implementation. On the one hand, there are continual restatements of equal and fundamental human rights for all, while at the same time the Japanese state limits citizenship rights for the 75 per cent of people with Korean descent who were born and wish to remain in Japan. As 'foreigners', whether they have permanent resident status or not, they are required to carry alien registration cards which because they are finger-printed carry criminal associations. Those who take permanent resident status do so according to the Ministry of Justice simply because they wish to be eligible for insurance and education benefits. Those who become naturalized are told by the Prime Minister that 'persons of unclear nationality cannot be respected' (*JTW* 17 January 1987), thus confirming from the highest level their ambiguous status.

The first effective attempt to address *buraku* problems came in 1969 when after denying that *burakumin* were racially different from other Japanese, economic assistance was pledged to the more deprived urban districts: the *Dowa*. These districts did include many *burakumin* but as they did not cover those in rural areas part of the principle of helping all *burakumin* was lost from the start. The very name of the policy meaning integration or assimilation established a connection with organizations pressing for change through self-improvement. It seems that the impetus behind the new approach was to 'mollify *Buraku* radicalism and to weaken the link between the *Buraku Liberation League* and other opposition organizations' (Neary 1986 p.563).

If this was the objective it succeeded as *buraku* groups split into those wishing to administer at least some relief to their members and those opposing token aid without attacking the fundamental roots of social prejudice. In practice the whole programme has been poorly coordinated and has always been high on the list of budgets to be cut in times of fiscal stringency. Much of the programme has been administered at a local level where before aid was allocated, some authorities required proof of *burakumin* descent which some withheld because this would provide yet another source of information about their background. The JCP too opposed the targeting of aid to special minorities as this would do little to relieve other victims of capitalism living in the same district. Not surprisingly the JCP and the main *buraku* organizations were again in dispute over whether the working class as a whole or a minority within it should take priority.

Dowa legislation has been renewed several times but in 1982 even the word *Dowa* was removed in favour of Special Measures for Regional Improvement which distanced the policy still further from the *burakumin*. Of much more importance is that despite highlighting the need to correct deepseated social attitudes, little change has been initiated by the state. The 1969 legislation followed a report which called for both economic aid and measures to eradicate social prejudice. However the latter 'has always been the least vigorously implemented aspect of the report and it seems that official efforts in this direction have become still weaker' (Neary 1986 p.572). The underlying problem is that the state has never fully accepted that prejudice is anything other than a feudal remnant whose demise will be hastened simply by additional public spending. This is reflected in the refusal to accept that discrimination is the responsibility of all Japanese but instead to insist that *burakumin* should focus on particular cases of discrimination.

Taking examples of state action and inaction together, the whole approach resembles ritualized cleansing gestures which leave it open to charges of only token concern. Family registers for example, could easily have been closed by administrative order without the full fanfare of formal legislation claiming that this was a second emancipation. But when this official closure of family records led to a proliferation of unofficial investigations by private detective agencies (*koshinjo*), the state took no action. 'No rigorous governmental measures have been adopted to curtail or regulate the activities of *koshinjo* in so far as they are detrimental to the effective implementation of the spirit of the 1969 law' (Hah and Lapp 1978 p.504). As long as minority organizations accept that they should follow traditional Japanese preferences for individual restitution, the state and the Japanese majority can continue to maintain that discrimination is merely a local problem. In consequence general legislation outlawing discrimination which prescribes penalties for offenders and which contains provision for affirmative action for positive discrimination will remain but a distant dream. Otherwise members of minority groups, like women, remain trapped in marginalized sections of Japanese society.

6.12 The consequences of an ageing society

Whereas the extent of discrimination against minorities has been a subordinated public issue, the past decade has seen an enormous amount of attention paid to the implications of the speed at which Japanese society is ageing. Since 1970 as birth rates have fallen by a third and life expectancy lengthened by 10 per cent, the 'dependency' ratio of the proportion of elderly people to those between 15 and 65 has increased by over 50 per cent. Although this ratio is now about the same as in other industrial societies, if the speed of increase is maintained, the ratio will double again in the next 20 years. The main thrust in the public debate about an ageing society has centred on the question of who in Japanese society is to bear the burden of higher numbers of 'unproductive' citizens. As in other Western societies the Japanese state has continuously reminded society of the impact these demographic changes will have on public pension and healthcare schemes. At the same time there is concern for the Japanese 'tradition' of privatized family care of the elderly because 'young people

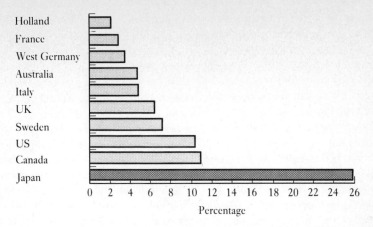

Figure 6.9 Labour force participation rates of the elderly: an international comparison, 1984
Source: Management and Coordination Agency, FPC, 1986

are being influenced by newer western ways' (Yoshino 1983 p.5).

The notion of the elderly being unproductive burdens is based on the assumption that very few of them will continue in employment beyond 65 but as Figure 6.9 shows this is not necessarily so in Japan. Well over 50 per cent of men and 25 per cent of women continue in employment through their 60s and, compared to the US, Japanese men are 10 times and women three times more likely to remain in the labour force beyond 70 years of age. Two-thirds of the elderly are self-employed or unpaid family workers, but the proportion of the elderly who are paid employees has risen as the number of elderly in agriculture has fallen. In one sense the family care is reciprocated by the elderly themselves as they continue to work in small family businesses such as shops or restaurants. There are, however, more who now have to seek employment outside their family network.

The average income of an elderly household is currently about half of the average for other households and pensions provide roughly 40 per cent of this income. The two main pension schemes each cover something like 26 million people, but of the two the Employees Pension Insurance (EPI) which pays substantially higher benefits is the younger and so over two-thirds of current beneficiaries qualify for National Pensions (NP). Benefits here are equivalent to less than 10 per cent of average cash earnings and are meant to provide a level of benefit close to the minimum standard of living in rural areas. It is true that the savings of the elderly are higher but this still only represents three years of average income from all sources, and as interest rates to depositors are low the income from savings provides less than 5 per cent of total income. Though the elderly spend less on consumer goods and food, as 85 per cent are owner-occupiers of aged housing stock their repair and maintenance costs are higher than average. Financial insecurity then encourages the elderly to look for employment and the share of those over 65 among all people seeking work for example rose by a third between 1971 and 1982 (Prime Minister's Office, FPC 1983).

Neither are the economic consequences of ageing confined to those above the official age of retirement because since the oil crisis in 1973 the working conditions of middle-aged workers have deteriorated. Although women bore the brunt of the initial adjustment, because middle-aged men are the most highly-paid cohort their share of labour costs has been reduced in various ways. For some this meant establishing promotion ceilings and lower annual wage increments which explains why peak earnings now occur at an earlier age. For others, wage reductions followed transfers to 'inferior industries, firms and occupations as compared to former occupations and careers' (Taira 1986 p.79). Even though firms were under pressure to raise their scheduled retirement age beyond 60, they at the same time increased selective early retirement in a range of voluntary schemes. This was especially noticeable where technological change through the increased use of robotics and microelectronics was thought to make older workers as obsolete as older equipment.

Of course not all in the upper age range were given transfer options nor did they thereafter find it easy to obtain other paid employment and the 'middle-age bulge in unemployment rates is widely regarded as extraordinary by international standards' (Taira 1983 p.9). This bulge means that the share of those over 55 is twice the level in the US or UK, and of all separated employees between 1970 and 1983 the share of those over 55 rose by 150 per cent while the share of those between 45 and 55 increased by 60 per cent. Nor has the position changed since 1983 because in the initial reaction to the spectacular rise in the value of the yen, one half of those who lost their jobs were over 40 (*JTW* 13 June 1987).

For those middle-aged workers affected by the processes of adjustment to economic crisis, their main pre-occupation is how they can maintain their incomes through lower wage increases, job transfers or voluntary early retirement. Then when they reach pensionable age they face the prospect of finding ways to bridge the gap between their pension and an income which would provide a reasonable standard of living.

6.13 A super welfare state for loved and respected elders

During the early 1970s the underprovision of social security by the state became a much more significant political issue especially as the Socialist Governor of Tokyo embarrassed the LDP Government by initiating a local scheme providing free medical care for the elderly. Political support for the LDP was then at its lowest ebb and inadequate social security together with the scandalous levels of environmental pollution, seemed to symbolize a lack of state concern with the social costs of economic growth. By 1974 the electoral problems of the LDP forced the state to concede not only free medical care for all those over 70 but also improved pensions which were to be index-linked to the rate of inflation. LDP politicians and state officials were unenthusiastic about the changes and the new programme was accompanied by warnings that public welfare would be a debilitating disincentive for individuals to work hard to save and be self-reliant. The Labour Minister was heard berating residents of homes for the elderly as a 'stagnant pool of self-seekers' (Pempel 1982 p.160); the Ministry of Finance were totally opposed to such profligacy with public funds and Health Ministry officials reacted to the changes with consternation (J.C. Campbell 1984 p.55). Compared to the Japanese tradition of family welfare, the new schemes were said to provide conditions in which the Western disease of dependency would thrive and Japan was in danger of losing its national vigour. Yet at the same time the LDP was not averse to proclaiming the new 'super welfare state' as its own political triumph.

The new programme was clearly an improvement but the pension benefits for the elderly were in practice not nearly as generous as they were in principle. To begin with as pension schemes were relatively young, many who retired in the 1970s had insufficient years of contributions to gain the full rate of benefits. Furthermore, benefits were related not to cash earnings but to contractual wages taking no account of overtime bonuses or special allowances which make up at least a third of average earnings. Although international comparisons of pension benefits are difficult, comparing countries with roughly the same ratio of beneficiaries to contributors for 1984 shows that total pension benefits relative to GNP in Japan was 50 per cent less than the US and UK (Social Security Research Institute FPC 1986 p.11). But it is not this relative gap that is the focus of state concern but the growth rate of absolute expenditure which quadrupled between 1974 and 1980. As demographic projections implied that such massive increases would continue, finance officials by the later 1970s led moves to reconsider the extent of public welfare. 'Reconsideration' meant re-emphasizing the responsibilities of private families in order to justify lower rates of growth in public welfare spending and thereby ensure that public sector finance deficits were reduced. Clearly the emphasis was on what Japan could not afford to pay in the future because as we saw in Chapter 4 the social security accounts remain in surplus as the number of contributors exceeds beneficiaries. But in the meantime free medical care was ended and social security contributions increased in order to stress a tripartite responsibility for social security based on private companies, the family and then the state.

The role of the company in contributing to and administering a compulsory element in workers savings is very significant especially in larger firms, but this does have serious consequences for those whose acccss to such companies is blocked. Better pensions for EPI subscribers is partly a function of their higher earnings as benefits are linked to wages. But for the 26 million NP members among the self-employed and those working for very small firms, their lower pensions magnify the differentiation of rewards according to position in the labour market. Minorities and women in particular suffer the consequences in lower pension contributions of more limited representation in large firms, shorter tenure and more part-time employment. For women this has become yet more significant as 80 per cent of people over 65 living alone are women. In short 'such a privatized system excluded numerous needy individuals and groups' (Pempel 1982 p.145) and extends into old-age the consequences of social divisions based on employment status.

Neither is the other element of privatized welfare through the family an unproblematic strategy. Since 1970 as the number of households with elderly persons has increased by a fifth the number of elderly people living apart from their families has doubled. Currently nearly 20 per cent of elderly households consist only of an elderly couple and one in eight contain a single elderly person most of whom are women living longer and alone. Even in extended families the tensions of sharing cramped living space and family budgets are compounded by the likelihood of a deterioration in health which with poor public care facilities creates added pressures on women to continue as carers. Making the family the key site of welfare throws into sharp relief the contradictions of state policies on equal opportunities because for women caring for a parent follows on from caring for children and makes outside employment of secondary importance. Even where geriatric hospitals do exist such a designation from 1983 carried 'lower staffing requirements and lower government reimbursement' (J.C. Campbell 1984 p.64). The position of the state as guarantor of 'appropriate public welfare according to priorities' (EPA, Seven Year Plan 1979 p.12) has not been interpreted in ways which have increased the supply of public care facilities despite the extensive publicity given to longer life expectancy. Rather the state has been more concerned to show how free medical care for the elderly creates excess demand and the aged are accused of overusing public medical services. 'Over use' is measured by contrasting how 7 per cent of the population over 70 are responsible for 24 per cent of total medical expenses. Curbing the tendency to 'over use' free public services was then a justification for restoring an element of patient contribution in 1984.

Respect for elders in Japan has been celebrated with a national holiday for centuries and this tradition was even in 1963 enshrined as a National Law requiring 'elders to be loved and respected as those who have for many years contributed towards the development of society'. Yet the essence of this statement is hardly reflected in the way the elderly are labelled as burdens nor by revoking the automatic adjustment of pensions to the rate of inflation which has eroded their real value in the 1980s. Delegating care of the elderly to the family also ignores the increasing tendency for them to live alone and the social tensions that exist where they reside in extended families. One reflection of this tension is that suicide rates among the elderly, particularly those living with their families, have returned to their pre-war levels and for elderly women they are four times the level in Western Europe (Fuse 1984 p.9). Equally little love and respect is shown in highlighting the burdens of medical spending by the elderly when it is hardly their fault if they need more treatment than younger people. Neither do current pension provisions reflect their previous contribution to Japanese society. Rather they reflect the 'shameful treatment of older workers who were responsible by their sacrifices for the economic miracle' (Woronoff 1983 p.85).

6.14 Legitimating inequality

Beneath the superficial façade of Japan's classless society it seems that there are clear divisions which result in some groups consistently receiving disproportionate rewards. Yet such social divisions contrast sharply with strongly held feelings that Japanese society is a highly cohesive collective where the vast majority consider themselves to be middle class. Neither is this belief confined to the Japanese themselves as many Western writers echo this perception: 'the racial homogeneity of the population and the country's social structure may well have prevented the emergence of those groups that form the bulk of the poor in Western countries – racial minorities, immigrants and the old' (Boltho 1975 p.168).

Feeling part of a prosperous classless society certainly reflects the collective memory of pre-war society where class divisions were so obvious and poverty so ubiquitous. There is also a sense in which the standard of living for the majority in Japan contrasts with contemporary poverty in neighbouring Asian societies. But though absolute poverty for the majority may be a thing of the past social inequality and relative deprivation are still present in Japanese society. It may well be that the wealthiest third in society can rest easy in their occupation of high-status positions in larger firms or the bureaucracy knowing that privileged access to Higher Education allows them to pass on their prosperity to the next generation. But others who identify themselves as middle class cling tenuously to their position by working longer hours in smaller firms and rely on women working in various types of temporary employment to maintain household incomes. There is always uncertainty for this group that economic crisis will require labour adjustment which will be targeted disproportionately on women and older men. 'Thus middle class means in effect the class that fears falling into the lower class' (Hidaka 1986 p.232).

Whether the majority rest easy or remain uneasy, the ideology of an egalitarian cohesive nation consisting principally of 'insiders' is a powerful one whose 'stark simplicity is also a source of appeal' (Befu 1980 p.139). Such an ideology is used to legitimate inequalities whenever their existence is addressed. So cohesion requires that women should function as homemakers, egalitarianism implies that income inequalities are a matter of individual failings and minorities suffer discrimination because they are not truly 'insiders'. The notion that Japan has a uniquely collective social identity may be a folk model, but as it is so widely disseminated within Japan and without, it provides a useful vehicle for explaining away or ignoring social divisions.

7

Continuity and Change in the Japanese Social Process

Each chapter in this book has contained examples of the debates that surround key aspects of contemporary Japanese society and reveal the extent of disagreement about the formal or substantive character of social processes. Do Japanese workers display greater loyalty to their companies through voluntary commitment to the firm as a surrogate family or because they have little alternative? Are loosely affiliated *keiretsu* not in essence the reincarnation of pre-war *zaibatsu*? Does the Diet actually function as the highest organ of state power or is policy formulated in substance by the bureaucracy? Is the economy the epitome of a liberal free market or is it in practice carefully orchestrated by the state?

Students of Japanese political economy have struggled to relate contemporary social processes to the ideal assumptions of economic and political models and often produce hybrid concepts which appear to reconcile the irreconcilable. So pluralism is 'patterned' or 'compartmentalized' and is variously led or guided by the bureaucracy while the economy can be 'sponsored' capitalism, market 'oriented not dominated' or even at times a 'planned' market. The complexities of fitting actual practices into value laden models is by no means confined to Japanese studies, as for example can be seen in the difficulties of reconciling new Right ideas about rolling back the economic role of the state with continued intervention in a host of social policies. Or for that matter in debates about whether capitalism and socialism are converging as a consequence of inserting market transactions into the economies of Eastern Europe or China. At the heart of these debates lies the problem of evaluating the extent to which the fundamental character or structure of society has changed and in distinguishing surface phenomena from underlying processes.

The distinction between form and substance or principle and practice is not only a problem for social scientists. Discrepancies between the normative ideals of a society and social practices crucially affect all social actors and may threaten the legitimacy of the state itself where high ideals such as democracy or equality of opportunity are concerned. Various Japanese expressions are used to reflect the difference between form and substance among which are *omote* (in plain view) and *ura* (hidden from view) or *tatemae* (principle, form) and *honne* (reality, essence). In their various nuances an appreciation of the difference between say *honne* and *tatemae*, can guide attitudes and behaviour as they do in all societies where what people say and do reflects the interpenetration of ideals and customary social practices. An acute difficulty facing social scientists looking at the way social economic and political institutions function lies in assessing whether ideals and practices do diverge, and if so how do individuals and the state reconcile this divergence.

In the first part of this chapter I will look at the responses to several controversial issues such as equal opportunity legislation, educational reform and the extent of environmental pollution to show how the divergence between ideals and social practices has been managed. My objective here is to use these examples to draw together the conclusions of other chapters in order to shed light on how the legitimacy of Japan's social order has been maintained. Then the second part of the chapter will consider how deeper involvement in the international economic system has especially since 1985 involved major adjustments in Japan's domestic economy. The process of responding to external pressures for change will then be used to form some general conclusions about the characteristics of state society relations in Japan.

7.1 Equal opportunity legislation: superficial or profound social change?

The example of the 1986 legislation to guarantee equal pay for equal work and equal promotion opportunities for women has prompted competing reactions to its form and substance. 'Most observers agree that bureaucratic measures against early retirement and similarly discriminatory practices are, though belated, effective and in good faith' (Upham 1987 p. 215). Mackie in contrast argues that the legislation 'is a travesty which is virtually free of punitive provisions and promises little change' (1988 p. 65). The legislation was undoubtedly a belated re-affirmation of constitutional guarantees, but state officials argue this was because social attitudes had changed only slowly. It has taken time for instance for employers to recognize that as more women graduated from colleges and universities so more would seek permanent careers. The current generation of women are only now benefiting from the higher qualifications of their mothers whose socializing patterns have changed because they 'are apt to hold more liberal views towards sex roles and less traditional aspirations for their daughters' (Fujimura 1985 p. 488).

Contrasting views on the belated timing of the legislation focuses more on the embarrassment of the Japanese Government at being one of the last nations to ratify the UN Treaty on Discrimination against Women. Only at the very last moment before the end of the UN's International Women's Decade did the Government concede whereupon it was obliged to implement internal legislation. Of equal importance in this view were a number of successful legal actions by individual women against forced retirement on marriage and discriminatory promotion practices. Though legal judgements like these do not carry the same force of precedent in Japan, the very fact that litigants were successful in upholding their constitutional rights galvanized the state into an unequivocal prohibition of discrimination in employment.

The state defends itself against charges that the legislation lacks sanctions by pointing to the establishment of mediation offices in all the main regional centres, which, it argues, reflects the Japanese preference for conciliation instead of confrontation with employers. But as most of the debate on the proposed legislation centred on the question of sanctions rather than equality *per se* – which could hardly be denied given the Constitution – it is easy to see why the absence of sanctions is portrayed as conceding to the opposition of employers to punitive provisions.

Mediation as the 'preferred' Japanese alternative to legal confirmation of an individual's rights is also open to a rival interpretation as a tradition which keeps the pace of social change under the control of the bureaucracy. Indeed some argue that formal mediation agencies are a useful way of preventing judicial interference as individual litigation is hindered and disputes are in effect colonized by the bureaucracy at the pre-trial stage (Upham 1987 p. 17). In articulating the need for gradual incremental change, the state, employers and enterprise unions make much use of the way public opportunities for women are changing without the need for sanctions. 1986 saw the election of the first woman leader of a political party, the JSP; 1987 saw the selection of the first woman High Court Judge, the first woman captain of a coastguard vessel and the first woman controller of international operations at the Bank of Tokyo. Numerous other 'firsts' came to light in the aftermath of the legislation together with prominent publicity given to the increasing presence of women executives in department stores, fashion houses and firms producing consumer goods.

Such an array of 'firsts' immediately raises the question of how representative are these examples of progress; are these individual women the *omote* and are women in general, who are hidden from view, not still typically subject to discrimination? There has certainly been an increase in the number of JSP election candidates who are women, but for the Prime Minister and leader of the LDP change will be slow because 'campaigning is too physically tough for women' (quoted in *The Economist* 14/5/88 p. 21). For the vast majority of Japanese women there has been little dramatic change and wage differentials have actually widened because, according to the Ministry of Labour, of the large increase in part-time employment for women. It could also be argued that equal pay for equal work is inhibited by vertical segregation in the labour market especially in service and tertiary sectors where women take up the vast majority of low-paid clerical jobs. If the demarcation between clerical and management tracks is maintained, there will be only limited promotion prospects for women and as these tracks are gendered there is no comparable wage for men against which to argue the case for equality.

Critics of the equal opportunity legislation argue that it is weak because it is making only a token attempt to change the surface phenomena of employment practices while ignoring other institutions and practices which underpin gender inequalities. The gendered curriculum and higher education institutions guide women towards low-status jobs as clerical assistants or 'office ladies' which will reproduce vertical segregation in the labour market unless changes are made in schools. Equally the stress on women as homemakers and carers will, without more public care facilities, maintain their temporary employee status. Also more part-time employment for women denies them direct access to labour–management negotiations on pay and working conditions which is the preserve of full-time regular employees. In addition restrictions on women's working hours limits their ability to engage in overtime activities which are the *sine qua non* for progression up the corporate hierarchy. So the *omote* of change which is in plain view is undermined by the failure to alter the structural foundations of inequality which is the *ura* and is invisible in the equal opportunity legislation.

7.2 Reconciling individual rights to collective social values

The disputed effects of the equal opportunity legislation centres on the divergence which some argue separates actual and continuing experience from ideals of equality and disagreement is deepened by the difficulty of distinguishing one from the other. Being hidden from view, being less visible, means that the reproduction of inequality may be obscured by the prominence given to a notable first High Court Judge or political leader. Concealing the divergence between principles and practices may involve refining some basic principles; the notion of universal individual rights, for example, is often said to be an alien one which was imported from the West. Similar instances occur when the ambivalent application of anti-monopoly laws is justified by arguing that they are based on US ideals of the virtues of competition and do not reflect the Japanese tradition of coordinating the activities of producers especially in economic recessions. Such attitudes attempt to redefine formal principles in order to bring them closer to actual practices and obscure any divergence between them. A recent example of this can be seen in the first report of the *Ad Hoc* Council

on Education which was formed by Prime Minister Nakasone in 1984.
Here the current malaise in the education system was linked to the
inclination of post-war schooling to put 'a disproportionated emphasis on
rights in comparison with duties' (abridged translation *Japan Times*,
22 September 1985). Individual rights according to the report need not be
emphasized as much as they do in the West because the Japanese tradition
encourages mutual moral obligations between benevolent authority and
dutiful citizens.

This approach to the need for less explicit concentration on civil rights
is then rationalized by pointing to the lower levels of civil litigation in Japan
because the alternative preference for mediation based on mutual sincerity
and good faith shows what is in plain view actually reflects normative ideals.
Overemphasizing legalistic practices would undermine the smooth operation
of consensus formation because litigation is more likely to produce outright
victors and losers which sows the seeds of future dissensus. Social order
is thus assumed to be the norm and if civil litigation has any role it is to
deal with isolated disputes which will be limited in extent and do not need
to be accorded universal applicability.

There is of course an alternative view which sees the ideals and practices
of dispute resolution as clearly separated and which explains the lower
rates of litigation not because of deficient demand for lawyers services, but
to an inadequate supply. So with less than half the number of legal
professionals per 1000 people than in the West, it is not a 'preference' for
settling disputes through non-legal channels that matters but the difficulties
of using civil litigation. With such a shortage of lawyers litigation takes
many years to produce a final verdict. In the dispute between women
workers and Nissan over compulsory retirement on marriage, the verdict
in 1982 came 14 years after the litigation began and in some of the
pollution cases the verdicts took even longer as we shall see later. Not only
must litigants show great patience and determination, they also face heavy
financial burdens as 'Japan has only a very primitive system of Legal Aid
for civil matters' (Rokumoto 1982 p. 9). Litigation rates are apparently
lower in Japan, but whether this reflects the practical difficulties involved
or the ideals of non-legal resolution of conflict is disputed.

The decision of the *Buraku* Liberation League not to use the legal
process as an avenue for resolving conflict over discrimination may well
have been justified by the argument that the judiciary was, like the rest of
Japanese society, tainted with guilt. But foregoing civil litigation as an
avenue for public recognition of their cause certainly seems to have allowed
the bureaucracy to play a greater mediating role and thereby control the
direction of measures to ameliorate the position of the *buraku*. So the
emphasis was able to be directed more towards defining the problems of
minorities in terms of 'Dowa' projects for deprived urban areas than in
directly addressing the universality of discriminatory attitudes and practices.
Although there are differing views about the form and substance of judicial

independence, the decision not to assert *buraku* rights through the courts proved useful to the majority because it kept minority discrimination out of public view. As a result, discrimination continues to be viewed as a matter of conscience for those individuals denounced by the *Buraku* Liberation League as being guilty of particular acts of discrimination. The offenders are then meant to purge their guilt by accepting their moral obligations and duties towards fellow citizens. Such strategies however, by focusing on individual cases, fail to reveal the extent of prejudice because many *buraku* are reluctant to engage in denunciation as this exposes their identity. By deciding not to contest the divergence between ideals of equality for all Japanese people and the reality of widespread discrimination through civil litigation, the plight of the *buraku* has not been shifted fully into the public arena.

We have seen in other chapters many examples of the ways in which the Japanese state has attempted to obscure the difference between form and substance. Is the Self-Defence Force really just a vehicle for emergency earthquake relief with responsibilities which do not infringe the constitutional commitment to non-aggression? Here again several initiatives have been launched by factions in the LDP to refine this high ideal by arguing that it was forced on Japan by the Allied victors in 1945 and should be altered to bring it closer to the reality of Japan's role as a bulwark against communism in Asia. The divergence between non-aggression ideals and practices came into sharper focus when the Nakasone Government in 1986 eventually succeeded in pushing defence expenditure over the customary limit of 1 per cent of GNP despite the wishes of the majority of Japanese to preserve the limit.

Similarly the state has assisted employers in obscuring the difference between the form and substance in lifetime or permanent employment. This is not simply through public statements which remind the world that recessions in Japan can be managed to avoid redundancies nor in the very restricted definitions of labour markets which are reflected in low official rates of unemployment. In very practical ways the state administers schemes which subsidize the retention of surplus labour, smooths job transfers and assists with the finance of retraining programmes. What is less well publicized and obscured from view, is that the burden of avoiding redundancies among 'regular' employees is borne by non-regular workers among which women, the minorities and those over 45 figure highly. In this case a half-truth is portrayed as the norm which serves to blur the distinction between normative ideals and actual practices.

Private companies too, need to obscure the distinction between *tatemae* and *honne* not just in the extent of permanent employment but also as it is experienced in authority relations within their firms. This 'has led management to indulge in the lavish use of slogans and company insignia, and to make unremitting efforts through ritual and ceremony to promote a sense of common purpose' (Smith 1983 p. 117). Senior management especially in large firms, need to be able to present themselves as truly representative of employees and affiliated subcontractors because their privileged access to state policy formation is at face value inimical to the ideals of equal access in a liberal democracy. We have noted similar questions of representation raised in the selection of personnel to serve on Public Advisory Bodies and *Ad Hoc* Reform Commissions. Are the individuals chosen as publicly respected representatives or because their views are known to coincide with policy initiators in the LDP or the bureaucracy?

Where high ideals of equality, democracy and open access are concerned, the state cannot allow principles and practices to be seen to diverge radically because of the inherent dangers this carries for social conflict and disorder. But it would be a mistake to imagine that the Japanese state is so responsive and far-sighted as to be able to anticipate and accommodate all those social issues in which form appears to differ from substance. Neither is it always the case that the state wishes to reconcile the two, preferring at times to explain away the divergence in terms of people's individual responsibility. So the plight of the elderly in Japan may differ from the ideals of honour and respect for elders, but this is explained away by suggesting that they should have worked harder and saved more in their earlier years they would not be so reliant on state pensions.

Nor should we assume that individuals and outsider groups fail to recognize that they are being encouraged to interpret social practices in terms of ideals which have been refined to bring the two closer together. In fact some argue that the Japanese are particularly adept at living with differences between the ideal and lived experience because their 'socialization produces a value structure which . . . smoothly accommodates discrepancies between *tatemae* and *honne*' (Koschman 1974 p. 102). Whether this view of especially accommodating values in Japan is valid is difficult to evaluate because the resolution of similar discrepancies seems to be an essential part of socialization in all societies. There are also dangers in assuming that the process of accommodation is 'smooth' and certainly the increasing levels of violence in Japanese schools signifies that for young people accommodating the ideal of equal opportunity with the ferocious competition for places in the better universities can be traumatic.

Another danger in suggesting that social values in Japan are particularly conducive to accommodating *tatemae* and *honne* is that it leads all too quickly into generalizations about Japanese people being especially pliable. This characteristic is ascribed by those who are convinced that there is a clear cultural preference for conformity which constrains individuals to sacrifice their own interests to preserve social harmony. As common is the alternative tendency to replace the all-embracing power of Japanese culture with the dominating force of monopoly capitalism which encompasses crude notions of false consciousness. Both of these approaches to social order whether through cultural conformity or oppressive social control, treat individuals as though they were marionettes to be 'manipulated, more or less visibly, by forces extrinsic to the content of their performance for they are themselves completely powerless' (Smith 1985 p. 43). There may be limitations on their degree of freedom but it is none the less important to consider the ways in which individuals choose to resolve and live with the contradictions between form and substance.

7.3 Accommodating the divergence of ideals from social practices

The remarkable growth of institutions supplying after-school tuition, illustrates how Japanese families have recognized and responded to the conflict between ideals of equality in education and the reality of fierce competition for the limited number of places in the most prestigious universities and colleges. For parents, expenditure on *juku* or other forms of private tuition represent an acutely pragmatic approach to education as the route to privileged sectors in the labour market. For their children, additional hours spent studying after school as well as a longer than average school week, means learning that accommodating practices involve sacrificing leisure to give educational achievement top priority. Wealthier households do spend more on private tuition which may cast doubt on the substance of equal opportunities, but parents in all income groups show a propensity to forego current consumption to finance extra tuition.

Just how acutely aware Japanese parents are of the need to act according to the reality of fiercely competitive entrance examinations, can be seen in the way *juku* themselves are ranked according to examination results. Just as higher education institutions are arranged in a hierarchy so also going in parallel are *juku*. The ultimate objective for parents is entrance to universities with the highest status which is partly measured by their reputation for placing their graduates into employment with large corporations or the bureaucracy. Thus 'ranking amongst *juku* is now intense and elaborate' (Rohlen 1980 p. 239) according to their effectiveness in securing entrance to universities with better graduate recruitment records.

The expansion of what has been called the *juku* industry, shows how parents in Japan have accommodated ideals of group harmony among children of the same class or year in ordinary schooling, to the reality of intense competition in university entrance examinations. In the process institutions like the *juku* facilitate this accommodation even though the wider social consequences are not necessarily acceptable to the state. The *Ad Hoc* Council on Education sharply criticized 'overheated competition in entrance examinations' for fomenting a conspicuous and grave increase in violence or bullying in schools and more juvenile delinquency. Incidentally this scenario contrasts vividly with those Western studies which eulogize the Japanese dedication to education and praise the value of competitive examinations (for example, Lynn 1988).

What the Japanese education system lacks according to the Reform Council is creativity and individuality which have been lost in the intense pressure to memorize objective facts to score high marks in examinations. Creativity is vital, the Council argues, not least because the rapid pace of technological change requires individuals to be more flexible in their thought processes in contrast to the dull uniformity produced by the current system. As may be expected, the Council's first report is replete with calls for more emphasis on traditional values of harmony and cooperation which implicitly it seems to think have been diluted by importing notions of individualism from the West. But herein lie a number of contradictions which reflect the difference between form and substance in the links between individuality and group consensus. The 'top priority' given to 'respect for individuality' has to be qualified by stressing not individual rights but dutiful respect for the value of group harmony in work or in society writ large. But how can individuality be reconciled with rigid labour market practices which penalize those who attempt to transfer their creative skills between firms? Equally individuality does not sit easily with the host of other socializing pressures which encourage compliance. Thus the Council's views on the desirable ideals of individuality in education contrasts with the apparently traditional norms of conformity which children will face outside school.

Educational reform is one example of the way the Japanese state, in this case through carefully chosen personnel leading the Council, struggles to cope with social change that has developed because individual families have found their own ways of accommodating democratic ideals and meritocratic practices. A similar example was noted in the last chapter when the ideal of 'professional housewives' was challenged by the reality of growing numbers of married women in paid employment. Here the state led an accommodation by refining the ideal into role 'harmonization' but the primacy of women's private role in the family had to be supported with notions of their domestic dominance to take account of their inferior position in public. Just as individuals have to accommodate changes in practices which diverge from ideals, so also has the state.

In the development of a 'super welfare-state' the Japanese state appeared in the mid-1970s to concede new practices which collided with ideals about the primacy of self-help and privatized welfare. The financial implications of improved public welfare schemes especially for the elderly, were magnified by demographic trends which the state then used to highlight the need to re-order welfare priorities. So in addition to dire warnings about fiscal crises, the dilution of public schemes was accommodated with the justification that this would merely restore practices to the ideal normative network of families, firms and then the state as provider of last resort.

These examples illustrate that social change makes the separation of form and substance 'fluid and relativistic. Today's *tatemae* may be tomorrow's *honne* and vice versa' (Koschman 1974 p. 100). It may well be that the Japanese state supported by the perennial re-election of LDP Governments, is particularly adept in accommodating social change which threatens the established order. Pempel (1982) used the phrase 'creative conservatism' to epitomize the skills of the state in responding to any serious divergence between formal principles and substantive practices. It is at the same time necessary to recognize that social control is not always extensive enough to make the resolution of social conflict and the subsequent reconstruction of consensus an easy or smooth process. Perhaps the best example of the difficulties the state faces in smoothly accommodating social pressures that emanate from civil society, can be seen in its reaction to the spectacular growth of environmental protest in the later 1960s.

7.4   A fragile consensus: the state and environmental protest

By 1970 up to 3000 local citizens groups existed to protest over the extent to which industrial pollution was wounding their lives. The methods of protest used and the widespread public support they received throughout Japan represented for some 'not only a new form of political action and participation but also the emergence of a new political culture' (Tsurutani 1972 p. 442). Deferential political spectatorship was being transformed into mass democratic action which according to an official of the new Environment Agency (EA) was 'a cultural revolution of Japan'.

The immediate cause of protest was the ruination of the health of the nation by very rapid industrialization which was concentrated among densely inhabited districts. Then, as the immediate cause was either ignored or denied by the state and industrialists, the activities of citizens' movements generated more fundamental questions about democratic representation which seemed to challenge the legitimacy of the established political order.

It was not simply the pace of industrial expansion that mattered but its spatial concentration. By 1970 the industrial heartland of Japan ran along a narrow coastal belt in which one-third of the entire nation lived on less than one twenty-fifth of available land producing 75 per cent of the economy's industrial output. As one key factor in industrial growth was the ability of firms to capture both internal and external economies of scale, heavy industry like metal processing or petrochemical plants were constructed in integrated industrial parks. The external costs of rapid industrialization were therefore imposed on local residential districts and by 1970 pollution in Japan was four or five times the level in similar industrial areas of Europe.

Uncontrolled industrial development meant indiscriminate disposal of industrial waste into the atmosphere and water supply which affected entire districts. The citizens' movements at this time were particularly noted for their heterogeneous membership covering the whole range of income and social groups which was one reason why their challenge was perceived to be so serious. All residents were affected by atmospheric pollution in particular, because smog and air poison are indivisible externalities and even the rich cannot exclude themselves from consuming these collective 'bads'. Quite apart from general public health hazards, several specific diseases were identified as being caused by specific firms dumping specific types of waste. As early as 1953 mercury poisoning was transferred to humans through the consumption of fish caught in polluted waters. Then when cadmium-contaminated effluents poisoned rice paddies, both the twin pillars of the Japanese diet were affected. Specific lung ailments, asthma and pulmonary diseases were causally related to various kinds of atmospheric emissions and the whole of western Japan was regularly blanketed by industrial smog.

Citizens protested at first through traditional methods: organizing mass demonstrations, marches to the factory gates of offending firms and then direct confrontation with management inside plants. What gave the protests their most dramatic public face were victims' movements with the victims themselves in the lead, exposing in full the consequences of pollution in chronic illnesses which led inevitably to slow lingering deaths. Victims' movements pressed firms to end indiscriminate waste disposal, demanded compensation and public apologies to symbolize their moral neglect. Other groups in other areas concentrated on prevention, fearing that their own districts would be afflicted without more open planning procedures. Media coverage was profoundly important because it created links between geographically separated protests and the plight of individual victims captured the national imagination by highlighting that Japan had become the world's number one economy for pollution.

For over a decade the specific firms involved rejected the attribution of particular diseases to their operations by using their own experts to question the validity of the medical evidence and insisting that the spatial correlation of victims to their plants was not causal. Victims themselves were labelled as bizarre hypochondriacs and middle-aged women who were particularly susceptible to cadmium poisoning 'were told that they had no right to complain since it was a woman's nature to suffer' (B. Smith 1986 p. 161). Protesters were harrassed and intimidated by company security guards and on occasion by the riot police, which only served to maximize the interest of the media as the violence was transmitted into every Japanese household. Alongside physical opposition, the companies argued that the effect of reducing external costs would be to raise internal costs of production and therefore prices which would reduce sales and increase local unemployment. Prevention groups were classed as egoists who were unwilling to sacrifice personal interest to the national goals of economic growth or who were divisive elements wishing industry to be located anywhere but not near them.

If these kinds of argument did little to appease citizens' groups it did give company employees a basis for rationalizing their own ambivalent position. Although citizens' movements were representative of a range of local interests, organized labour was not, to put it mildly, very visible in its support whether by choice or through the intimidation of employers. In some areas too, local government was ambivalent to the movements not least because 'corporate power governs city politics' (Miyamoto 1983 p. 3) as well as the local economy.

Despite the resistance of local industry and despite the uncoordinated organization of their protest, pollution as a source of social conflict was forced onto the political agenda by the later 1960s. This was no mean feat as 'one would be hard pressed to find such a clear and so long successful example of issue suppression in any other country' (Reed 1981 p. 263). In some ways the extent of suppression drew even more attention to the plight of individual victims especially after 1967 when they took their cases into the public arena of the legal process. The court hearings were surrounded by massive publicity with daily reports of dramatic instances of personal suffering and the total intransigence of those in authority.

Resorting to litigation marked the exhaustion of other avenues of mediation and reflected widespread disillusionment with both companies and the state for failing in their obligations to protect the Japanese public. Although legal actions were directed at specific firms, the state became tainted with guilt by revelations that bureaucrats had collaborated with companies and had 'suppressed scientific studies that established connections between particular industrial wastes and diseases or death' (Pempel 1982 p. 222). To the evidently slow and half-hearted response of the state was now added evidence of positive actions to deny the existence of specific pollution-related diseases. For neglecting its overarching responsibility to the public good, legal judgements in the pollution cases specifically mentioned not just errors of omission but the executives own part in aggravating environmental damage especially in encouraging economic growth at any cost.

While citizens' groups were radical in action, for the most part they were conservative by inclination which made their disillusionment with the state so much more intense. The state had reneged its formal role as arbiter of social harmony by taking a very partial role in defending private business interests. The first major revision to national legislation on pollution, in 1967, attempted to resolve the divergence between the competing ideals of economic growth versus environmental protection in a framework of hybrid principles. Internal production costs had to be kept down to maintain economic growth but, industry was charged with the duty to recognize that this should be done 'in harmony with' and 'taking heed of' external costs to society. As with Equal Opportunity legislation 20 years later, penalties sanctions and formal standards were avoided. Yet within the bureaucracy the Ministry of Health and Welfare had proposed much stricter controls and general compensation schemes but these were lost in the process of consensus formation where the alliance of MITI and the leading Employers' Federations was insuperable.

Then within three years in the famous Pollution Diet of 1970, the whole picture was transformed and fourteen separate bills were passed making Japan's industrial environment one of the most strictly controlled in the world. Waste disposal and atmospheric emissions by industry were tightly regulated, a new bureaucratic agency, the EA, was formed and within a few years a state-administered compensation scheme was established together with initiatives to encourage public participation in planning processes. The prime mover in this *volte face* appears to have been the third arm of the establishment, the LDP. Their interest in environmental issues was presented as a positive response to the views of public as epitomised by citizens' movements which included many of its own grass-roots supporters. Thus the party claimed to have led the formation of a new national consensus on the need to replace the economic ideal of industrialization at any price with the social ideal of a safe environment and better provision of collective goods. At national level the party 'largely hi-jacked environmentalism for itself' (*The Economist* 19/3/88) and paraded its legislation as the model for other societies to follow.

A more cynical view would be that the LDP really had few options as the extent of pollution was horrendous, its national electoral position had weakened throughout the 1960s and increasing numbers of Japan's major cities had returned opposition administrations. These local and regional assemblies had seized the initiative in environmental regulation and in the provision of public goods. They had also enshrined citizen rights to a safe and clean environment and imposed penalties on companies who ignored these rights. Once it became clear that a shift in basic principles could be sustained by the local state, any failure by the national LDP Government to accept the validity of such populist initiatives would carry the danger of translating opposition strength at local level into the national Diet. Whatever their motives the LDP did force industry and economic bureaucrats to accept substantive change and with legal victories for individuals in the major pollution cases, the citizens' movements did seem to have mobilized a new mass participatory political culture.

7.5 Pollution control and a responsive state

By the appalling standards of 1970 a major improvement in Japan's industrial environment was evident by the end of the decade. Much less cadmium, mercury or cyanide was discharged into rivers, lakes or the sea and levels of nitrogen oxide, sulphur dioxide and carbon monoxide in the atmosphere fell significantly. The petrochemical smogs which had obscured Mount Fuji from residents on the Western coast have all but disappeared and traffic police are no longer forced to wear protective masks. Spending by local and national governments on pollution control tripled between 1970 and 1975 and private firms spent even larger sums. Private investment on pollution research and adapted technical processes amounted to one-fifth of capital investment between 1973 and 1976.

Separating private from public is in some ways misleading because a proportion of industrial investment was provided through state subsidies. Loans, grants, preferential tax credits, massive depreciation allowances and tax remissions ensured that the taxpayers paid their fair share of the increase in internal costs that resulted from stricter environmental controls. Industry did object that standards were technologically impossible but with their own investment, financial assistance and state-coordinated research programmes pollution control actually became a new growth sector. In controlling the emission of exhaust fumes from motor vehicles Japanese manufacturers gained a leading edge over Western competitors that became even more significant when stricter standards were imposed in Europe and North America. Together with major improvements in fuel economy, the ability of Japanese manufacturers to reduce exhaust pollution ensured that motor vehicle exports especially to the US increased enormously.

In fact the objections of Japanese industry to pollution control on the grounds that it would raise costs and lose sales seemed by 1980 to be groundless. Japan became the world's leading exporter of whole plants in a range of industries from petrochemical processing to aluminium smelting, ore refining or basic metal production. Whole operations were exported *en bloc* to the Middle East, Latin America and South East Asia which reveals another alternative to adapting existing plant in Japan. Relocation of operations which are more likely to endanger the environment, became even more important after the oil crisis in 1974 when Japanese producers sought to ensure a continuous flow of energy and raw materials by investing in more down-stream production at source.

Relocation also proceeded within Japan which helped reduce the concentration of national output in central Japan from 75 per cent in 1968 to 50 per cent in 1988. Relocating plant overseas or in more peripheral areas of Japan, indicates that stricter pollution controls *per se* were not the only reason for the reduction in environmental damage to Japan's industrial heartland. New plant built elsewhere did incorporate control technology, but at the same time relocation allowed some of the most dangerous processes to be removed from areas that had been so badly affected. It is also apparent that choosing to construct, say, a Nuclear Power station in Okinawa is likely to produce much more isolated citizen protest than it would if the project were located closer to Tokyo. What makes judgements about the effectiveness of environmental controls more difficult, is that since 1974 the overall rate of industrial expansion has slowed markedly and heavy industry in particular has become a sector to be discarded. Falling levels of industrial pollution in central Japan was surely the result of stricter controls, but in addition we do need to recognize the impact of relocating plant and the deceleration in growth rates of heavy industry.

As the new agency in plain view, the EA took much of the credit for administering the shift away from purely economic priorities and accommodating the opposition of MITI and private producers. Not all of the strict controls were maintained and in any case MITI coordinated relief in those sectors where internal costs increased most. Where the EA appears weak relative to other state agencies, however, is not just in its formal authority but in its substantive power especially in periods of recession when other ministries take precedence. As an 'orphan' and a newcomer, the EA is not powerful enough to resist greater than average reductions in planned budgets when the Ministry of Finance negotiates expenditure restraint. Then whenever public investment needs to be increased in the recession's second stage, Construction or Transport Ministries take precedence; in 1978 for instance the EA was unable to resist a lowering of 50 per cent in nitrogen dioxide standards. This partly reflected industry's claim that standards were too stringent but more importantly that 'highways the government had planned as recession measures could not be constructed under the existing strict NO_2 standard' (Miyamoto 1983 p. 3).

The other main weakness of the EA is that it delegates to local government the tasks of setting and monitoring of specific standards. As an agency with a formal role of national coordinator, the EA is therefore dependent on the tenacity of local officials who were until the later 1970s more demanding than the central EA. But since then the enthusiasm of local or regional government for environmental issues has waned. This reflects in part constraints on spending by the local state through smaller fund allocations from central government and tighter controls on the issue of deficit bonds. In addition many of the local authorities that were controlled by the opposition parties and who were especially vigilant in pollution control, have now been recovered by conservative administrations. These local administrations and for that matter even those under opposition executives, have had to forego environmental issues in favour of regional initiatives to protect employment. While environmental ideals may remain in spirit, recent experience has in practice forced local government to placate private business to slow the pace of outward movement of firms from their districts. In turn this weakens the base from which the EA exercises influence.

Public interest in environmental issues generally has become more muted, although whether this reflects the 'victories' of the early 1970s or that adapting to slower rates of growth in incomes switches the emphasis to job security, is arguable. Media attention in the 1980s is more sporadic as almost all of the victims that sued companies have been successful even though the legal process was lengthy and some residual actions are still pending 20 years after they were begun. For other victims the state-administered scheme financed principally by the private companies involved, provided compensation to those who could supply certificated evidence that their illnesses were caused by specific pollutants. As the number of claimants had fallen to a trickle by 1988, the state presuming that the episode was over with all victims compensated announced that no new claims will be registered. This presumption though may not necessarily be valid.

State mediation between the victims and companies was justified as a faster and cheaper route to compensation than individual civil litigation, but the barriers to relief through mediation are greater in practice than they appear in principle. Claimants have to prove specific causation of their illnesses and while the time taken in approving claims is no doubt shorter than through the legal process, it still takes an average of five years extending to 14 years in some cases. Fewer victims have come forward since 1984 but 'The unwillingness of some people to be recognized or designated as suffering from pollution problems may have contributed to the decline' (Lincoln 1988 p. 49). Reluctance to become labelled as diseased is compounded in some of the first areas to be contaminated by mercury poisoning – Minamata disease after the name of the local town – by the belief that the disease is either hereditary or contagious. For some of the younger victims the widespread support of the moral majority has now become a stigma which ruins marriage prospects and limits employment opportunities as businesses are reluctant to move into the town.

Closing the compensation register, together with the knowledge that no new pollution diseases have been recognized for over a decade and suggestions that reference to Minamata poisoning should be removed from school textbooks, encourages the impression that the state has closed the file on industrial pollution. It is almost as though intervention in the early 1970s was a terminal gesture to purge the moral guilt of the state just as public apologies by company presidents purged their neglect. This impression has become stronger as the ideals of environmental rights have not been transferred to concern with the quality of life in general. Doubts about the extent to which the focus of economic policies had really changed were evident in 1977 when the OECD Environmental Committee, after praising the first wave of controls, added the rider that the Japanese state 'has not won the war for environmental quality' (p. 83). Has there indeed been a fundamental change in priorities or were environmental controls merely a convenient way of accommodating in the short term the destabilizing impact of mass protest?

7.6   Internal dissent and non-political protest

The ability to identify directly culpable companies was enormously important to the victims' movements but for those groups concerned with the general quality of life the absence of specific targets is a major source of weakness.

There are groups who complain bitterly about excessive noise and vibration in larger cities but the immediate causes of this type of pollution are multifarious and more difficult to confront. With five times the number of vehicles per square kilometre of space than Europe, with the extension of 'bullet' trains across Japan and ever increasing air traffic, cities in particular are becoming desperately polluted from non-industrial sources. Congestion, the enormously high cost of living and unacceptably high levels of population density have even prompted serious proposals to relocate Japan's capital city outside the metropolitan district of Tokyo. Although the discharge of industrial effluent has declined little has been done to control the disposal of sewage and less than one-third of dwellings are served by sewage treatment systems. Domestic effluent is discharged into inland lakes, rivers and coastal bays and in one 'nation-wide sample of inland waters 23 per cent of rivers and an alarming 58 per cent of lakes did not comply with desired standards' (MacDonald 1985 p. 2).

The failure to transfer earlier enthusiasm for environmental protection to noise abatement or sewage treatment casts doubt on the substantive effect of environmental priorities. In comparison to the very visible costs of industrial poisoning, the social benefits of industrial expansion in terms of increasing employment opportunities were hardly overwhelming. Building airports or expanding road and rail networks, however, has clearer social benefits for some which divides protest groups just as the non-excludability of individuals from air pollution united their predecessors. It is also becoming clearer that widening income differentials can make noise pollution divisible between citizens. In the most badly affected cities, wealthier households can either move away and commute adding to the noise problems of those left in the city, or afford better insulation should they choose to remain. Being spatially and economically segregated means that the newer environmental groups cannot display the same levels of community solidarity that was a key characteristic of the earlier citizens movements.

Ecological disputes over infected rivers or lakes appear less pressing and social costs more difficult to quantify than in the attribution of pollution diseases. Even the target standards set and administered by local government are only guidelines, and in the Japanese way of mediation not confrontation, they carry no legal standing which again illustrates the relative weakness of the EA. In planning, the EA has never managed to translate the principle of binding environmental impact plans into legislative reality which is not to argue that voluntary consultation is always disingenuous. But the onus is on environmental groups to develop wholesale alternatives to proposed projects which they have neither the finance nor expertise to supply. Objectors do have hearing rights, but only for those who are local residents which restricts the appearance of outside experts and therefore prevents any national coordination of the environmental lobby as an effective interest group. Opposition to schemes initiated by the state in transport or nuclear energy is even more difficult as local citizens have to confront the full authority of the bureaucracy with little help from local government whose influence in many cases prompted the choice of the current site.

In principle the EA should provide coordinating functions for local actions but where large public projects are concerned the agency finds it difficult to sustain environmental arguments against more powerful voices in the Ministries of Construction or Transport. With such projects, the EA also has to overcome pressures from LDP party members in the Diet who see public investment in infrastructure as a way to reward the loyalty of their regional support networks. Constructing new tunnels, widening major highways, or building new airports bring more visible and immediate economic effects than projects to improve sewage systems. In essence the EA seems unable to assert a long-term perspective in the choice of public projects against the immediate political priorities of the LDP or the belief in other ministries that investment in public health projects has less impressive multiplier effects on the economy.

There is little doubt that although industrial pollution has been reduced, the general quality of life has not been a dominant preoccupation in the Japanese polity during the 1980s. After the formal confirmation of rights to a safe environment in the 1970s the numbers of citizens' groups declined as 'members of the movements reached their goal and the legitimacy of the movements existence thereby diminished' (Jost 1979 p. 47). Citizens groups have not by any means disappeared: in addition to environmental issues such groups press for action among other things on consumer prices, on educational reform, and on women's rights. Unlike the early pollution protest the state does at least address these issues even if its response appeared piecemeal and superficial in the case of equal opportunities, or contradictory in educational reform.

The media no longer exercises the same coordinating influence as it did with pollution diseases and the effect of media coverage is at best ambivalent and at worst counterproductive. In the 20-year struggle to oppose the construction of a new airport for Tokyo at Narita for instance, much less attention is paid to the basic cause of the dispute which is the attempt by small farmers to resist the compulsory confiscation of their land. Instead, the Narita protest is labelled as 'political' given the intermittent appearance of radical students or 'Red Army' factions whose presence is said to indicate that the whole dispute is a subversive class struggle unlike the 'non-political' protests over industrial pollution.

By claiming that their movements were 'non-political' or 'non-ideological' the victims' movements were able to legitimize their protest when such mass action was said to be unnecessary in a representative democracy. The visible suffering of victims undoubtedly enhanced in the public's view, the right of pollution movements to engage in extra-parliamentary protest. What was also crucial was the heterogeneous character of their membership with socially respectable leaders eschewing what they saw as the dogmatic

Marxism of national opposition parties. Being such broadly based groups meant that the citizens movements were distinguishable from other forms of mass protest which were more narrowly based on either the peasantry or factory workers led by labour unionists or opposition politicians. Victims movements could not so easily be dismissed as subversive, in fact as they had a core of members who had traditionally been LDP activists, their threat to the political establishment was profound. When it became clear that the judiciary was likely to favour the claims of individual victims, disillusionment among LDP supporters threatened its position as the party of national government. Even if this did not happen the alternative would be open confrontation in a dual polity between a conservative national government and local or regional government dominated by the opposition.

With hindsight there does not appear to have been any real danger that disillusioned conservatives would switch to opposition parties in national elections; abstention was much the more common preference. Citizens movements were apparently alienated especially from the JSP and JCP who sought to widen the pollution debate into a structural critique of the whole capitalist system, whereas victims' movements preferred to confine their criticisms to very specific agents (McKean 1981 p. 215). In their need to maintain a broadly based local consensus among their members, victims' movements set limits to their protests which were aimed at the unacceptable behaviour of individual producers, bureaucrats or LDP leaders.

Concessions on pollution control were followed by incorporating the local government initiatives in welfare and the provision of other collective goods into national programmes, and the electoral performance of the LDP improved accordingly. To an extent the LDP was favoured by the sense of national crisis that accompanied the first oil shock in 1974 which, as the economy was so much more dependent on imported energy, served to re-integrate disillusioned conservatives. The state did have real difficulties in handling the mass dissent over pollution because it came from outside the usual channels. Once a change in priorities was signalled though, new institutions and consultation processes were established to incorporate environmental issues into the established network for consensus formation. Individual litigation on environmental damage did not cease once state mediation schemes were organized, but their focus shifted towards challenging the effects of public projects where the cases were much less successful. Compensation through mediation and consultative planning procedures, effectively limited any further radicalization of victims or preventative citizens' movements.

Several areas of general debate emerge from the mass protest over pollution which reflect disagreements over the form and substance in the operation of liberal democratic institutions in Japan. It could be argued that the *volte-face* by the state over the need to regulate the independent actions of producers, confirms that democratic institutions were functioning well. Or that the 'victories' of groups with restricted access to established

channels of policy-making, show the responsiveness of a political system
that makes ideas about pervasive social control much exaggerated notions.
But should we not also 'be discouraged because a country with all the
trappings of democracy failed to respond quickly to an obvious problem
and clear public demand' (Reed 1981 p. 267)? It could equally well be
argued that the 'victories' of the citizens' movements were hollow, which
in substance had '"safety-valve" functions forcing the bureaucracy to alter
priorities just enough to calm the protesters' (Johnson 1982 p. 316). The
formal confirmation of citizen rights to a safe environment through judicial
decisions in individual litigation, has been portrayed as an indication that
individual rights were firmly ensconced as the *ura* replacing yesterday's
ideal of citizen duties. Rights were indeed confirmed in the pollution cases
and this did legitimate the initiatives taken earlier by several local authorities,
but were these not collective rights of residents *en masse* to expect that
industry would not damage their health? Certainly if the spirit of the
Education Reform Commission's first report is any guide, there is little to
indicate that respect for individual rights is an unquestioned principle.

Another debate focuses on whether citizens' movements make advances
in constraining the authoritarian involvement of the state in civil society
by legitimating mass opposition and critically examining state–citizen
relationships. Given their limited focus and their reluctance to widen
discussion beyond the immediate causes of pollution diseases, state–citizen
relations were raised almost incidentally. It was not the right of the state
to intervene that was questioned but whether, by consistently favouring
private industry, the authority of the state was being exercised in the
traditionally benevolent manner. On the whole the citizens' movements
were seeking not less, but more state intervention. Stricter control of
industry's disposal of waste has also been viewed as a significant defeat for
business interests, and that the switch away from economic growth priorities
by national LDP politicians shows that the party is not nearly so dominated
by big business as is often suggested. If we focus on the immediate costs
of compensation, yes industry was forced to pay, but in the longer term
industry, with public assistance, quickly turned disadvantage into advantage.
Even more questionable is the substantive long-term effects of the LDP's
commitment to social as opposed to economic priorities.

Does the spectre of internal differences within the bureaucracy over
pollution controls make it unlikely that non-elected officials are really as
dominant and powerful as they are often claimed to be? While there were
and still are clear differences between say MITI and the Ministry of Health
and Welfare or between the EA and the Ministry of Transport, every effort
is made to avoid transferring the negotiation of conflict on major social
issues to other sites. Continuity in this collective approach is clearly seen
in the emphasis on mediation through state agencies in preference to legal
confrontation, which in effect confines the extent of judicial intervention.
Informal resolution of disputes may be the Japanese tradition, but it is a

tradition which restrains the opportunities of the judiciary to review the administrative activities of the executive.

The reaction of the Japanese state to unanticipated mass dissent on the social costs of economic growth illustrates that accommodating social conflict is not always a smooth and untroublesome process. In the example of citizens' movements the pressure for change came from within, but a notable feature of the recent past has been external pressures to change the way Japan's domestic markets have been insulated from international competition. At first the state was able to control the rate of internationalization but the dramatic re-alignment of foreign exchange rates after 1985 forced the pace of change in economic relations.

7.7 Accommodating external shocks: the high yen crisis after 1985

In the eight months after October 1985 the foreign exchange value of the yen appreciated to 150 to $1 from around 250 where it had hovered since early 1983. The yen then continued to appreciate at a slower pace and by mid-1988 it appeared to have stabilized at about 125. Although the trade weighted exchange rate had not risen quite as fast, the dollar exchange rate was especially significant as over one-half of Japanese exports were destined for the US or countries like South Korea or Taiwan whose exchange rates follow the US dollar. Reducing the value of the dollar was a major objective of international exchange agreements so that the US trade deficit could be cut, and forcing a substantial increase in Japanese export prices was essential because approximately one-third of US imports originated from Japan. At a rate of 250 a typical motor vehicle imported from Japan priced at $20,000 in June 1985 would a year later be the yen equivalent of $33,000 and by June 1988 be $40,000. Demand, it was hoped, would fall accordingly.

With hindsight a substantial re-alignment of currencies was inevitable since the Japanese trade surplus had tripled between 1982 and 1985, and there was general agreement that the yen had been undervalued for years. But the immediate effect of what was seen as a catastrophically rapid adjustment, produced a sense of paralysis among those companies whose performance dominated the public view of Japanese business as a whole. The yen crisis was said to be more significant even than the oil crises of the 1970s because this time competing economies were not equally affected. What deepened the sense of crisis was the knowledge that domestic demand had expanded only slowly throughout the 1980s when foreign demand had been growing twice as fast. Although exports in total accounted for just 15 per cent of GDP, this aggregate obscures significant differences between sectors. By 1985 something like 85 per cent of consumer electronics output was exported, 80 per cent of cameras and photocopying equipment and

232   *Continuity and Change in the Social Process*

60 per cent of motor cycles and cars. With domestic demand patently inadequate to fill the gap created by falling exports, a deep recession for manufacturing seemed inevitable.

When steel and shipbuilding companies announced a 30 per cent fall in exports by mid-1986 few were really surprised because both sectors were known to be structurally depressed. A fall of 85 per cent in iron and steel profits and 250 per cent in shipbuilding merely confirmed their structural weaknesses. Much more significant were the financial results of companies that had been developing new technologies and increasing productivity by an annual rate exceeding 10 per cent since the early 1980s. Electrical, precision and general machinery producers as a group recorded a reduction in profits of over 50 per cent and motor vehicle producers by 33 per cent. Above all it was the results of companies that had previously topped the league table of profitability that caught the attention. Companies like Toyota, Nissan, Sony, Cannon and Toshiba all recorded either very substantial reductions in profits or absolute losses.

Neither were the shock waves confined to leading exporters as a sense of national crisis was transmitted in a series of predictions about the way the economy and society had to be transformed. To ameliorate diplomatic pressure from the US and the EC, the Japanese were called on to spend more on imported manufactured goods which had traditionally been a very small proportion of total imports. The Japanese were urged to break the habits of a lifetime and save less; in form to consume more imports, but in substance also to provide compensation to domestic producers for lost export markets. In the longer term the economy would have to be 'hollowed-out' – a euphemism for de-industrialization – which reflected the effects of relocating more manufacturing operations in overseas economies while developing high-technology labour-saving industries at home. Future growth in employment would have to be in services especially those connected with leisure which would of course require an increase in time available for leisure. So the length of time spent in employment would have to fall to give people the ability to consume the output of leisure industries and allow extra time to purchase consumer goods in general. More dramatic still was the prediction that norms about a lifetime's commitment to one company had to change. If knowledge-intensive industries were to be the new growth sector, then individual employees had to accept more flexibility in those firms operating at the frontier of information technology and mobility was to be the new norm.

Particular items on this list of projected change had surfaced well before 1985. The yen crisis however crystallized the whole package as the EPA or MITI through their 'forward visions', Employers' Federations and the LDP sought long-term solutions to the inevitable consequences for employment of 'hollowing-out' the domestic economy. Radical change was being planned in normative prescriptions for the future basis of Japanese society, but in what sense was the crisis reflected in national economic performance as opposed to the more visible fortunes of leading companies?

The rate at which GNP was growing did decline in the year from October 1985, but only by a marginal amount and by 1987 the growth rate was back to and probably even higher than in the two years before the yen appreciated. Industrial production did fall though only by 0.2 per cent for 1986 while 1987 saw output recover quickly so that by mid-1988 production was a full 12 per cent greater than 1985. In many ways this marginal deceleration in aggregate economic performance was not surprising since the sectors most affected by the rising exchange rate contributed only one half of value-added by manufacturing industry which is itself only equivalent to 30 per cent of GDP. Some industries were very dependent on exports but it must be remembered that the overall contribution of overseas demand is less than half the level in Western Europe.

Profits in 1986 did cease to grow as fast in the export sectors but this has to be set against very high profits in the preceding years and neither were the export sectors representative of other industries. Electric power companies increased profits in 1986 by 30 per cent, in pulp and paper the increase was 50 per cent, in petrochemicals profits were 60 per cent greater and in food, chemical and pharmaceuticals the increase was over 10 per cent. The whole of the finance sector was equally prosperous as banks, life insurance and securities companies increased their intermediating functions for Japan's huge surplus of domestic savings. The wave of speculation in land and property that accompanied the expansion of trading in financial assets also generated increased profits for real estate companies. In fact a longer term analysis should perhaps concentrate more on why the rate of economic growth fell at all, especially as a currency appreciation should have increased domestic demand because the costs of imported primary products had fallen substantially.

The extent to which Japan depends on imported food and raw materials should, according to the OECD, have yielded a net gain for the economy as a whole because lost export revenues were estimated to be less than the advantage gained by cheaper imports. This net advantage was only marginal but as the yen was appreciating at the same time as world oil prices were also falling, the net gain to the Japanese economy from changing terms of trade was estimated to be worth 2 per cent of GNP by the end of 1986 (OECD 1986 p. 56). Such a projected advantage reflects the fact that imported oil, raw and partially processed materials accounted for nearly two-thirds of all imports. The wholesale price index for imports fell by over 40 per cent from 1985 to 1988 and imports did increase by over 25 per cent in value, but exports despite their higher prices rose by 10 per cent partly because input costs had fallen. If we also recognise that the enormous outflow of capital after 1980 was producing a sharp increase in invisible receipts from interest profits and dividends, the overall current account surplus was only marginally smaller by 1988.

When assessing the impact of higher exchange rates it is important to remember that the interlocking structure of many Japanese companies in affiliated *keiretsu* gives the groups as a whole representation in many sectors. So declining profits in some export-oriented companies was matched by increased profits for other affiliates in raw material processing, finance or real estate. The other advantage for individual companies affiliated in *keiretsu* is that the benefits of lower input prices for materials are relayed more quickly through intra-group trading connections. This advantage is not as apparent for many of the producers of electrical goods or motor vehicles who, as relatively independent companies engage in more open trading of materials. But they too found ways to mitigate the impact of currency appreciation.

In particular they accelerated their money management operations and became even more involved with dealing in financial assets. With a surplus of domestic savings and with domestic interest rates three or four times lower than in the US or Europe, *zaitech* fund management produced far more profits than did manufacturing operations. Toyota in 1987 produced and exported 10 per cent less than in 1986 yet recorded profits of 180 billion yen of which no less than 160 billion came from trading in financial assets. Nissan converted a substantial operating loss into a small overall profit because of their *zaitech* profits. For the top 10 exporters of electrical goods in 1987, the average contribution of money management profits to their total profits was a staggering 49 per cent (*J Ec J* 23/1/88 p. 3).

Zaitech fund management involved forward exchange dealing, long dated currency contracts, trading in currency options, switching into dollar-denominated lending borrowing and payments for transport and fuel. Sony for instance accelerated the reorganization of its financial structure around a subsidiary in Switzerland which handles all the foreign exchange transactions of its European plants. Manufacturing subsidiaries are left to concentrate on production while financial settlements denominated in Deutschmarks are arranged by the specialist financiers. It is not just the leading exporters who hedged against changes in exchange rates: shipping and mining companies too, for example, renegotiated contracts for periods of up to three years at fixed rates of exchange. None of these financial operations is unique to Japanese multinationals, neither did any emerge simply in response to the yen appreciation from 1985. But they have been particularly crucial in allowing Japanese exporters to continue to earn profits even with a higher yen and have to an extent insulated them from the full impact of higher export prices.

7.8   Domestic consumers and a flexible labour market as shock absorbers

A further source of insulation was provided by not adjusting the prices of exports or imports to reflect the total extent of the yen's appreciation. In other words overseas prices for Japanese exports have not increased in line with the higher exchange rate neither have domestic prices fallen *pro rata*. Exporters had earned substantial profits in the period immediately preceding 1985 and this allowed them to bear some of the burden of the appreciating yen. Productivity had also been rising much faster than among their Western competitors and by maintaining their higher levels of efficiency while at the same time tightly controlling any rise in labour costs, they could afford not to increase export prices by the full amount. By early 1987 therefore only 50 per cent of the increase in export prices required by a higher yen was passed on to overseas consumers.

Some industries did increase prices by substantial margins but the effect on sales was not inversely proportionate. This may well have been because of the non-price advantages Japanese products possess in terms of quality, reliability or technical superiority. It could also have reflected the dominance of Japanese companies in Western markets for colour television sets, video cassette recorders, cameras or microwave ovens. Indeed in some products Japanese companies had already agreed to voluntary export restraint even before 1985 which had created a shortage and allowed exporters to ration scarce supply through higher prices. In these cases passing on the full effect of appreciation merely continued the existing trend.

As far as the prices of imports were concerned it was noticeable 'that industries and distributive outlets are extremely slow to share the gain of increased terms of trade with users and consumers' (Yamamura 1987 p. 453). Whereas the wholesale import price index fell by 40 per cent between 1985 and mid-1988, consumers' prices *rose* by 2 per cent in the same period. The labyrinth of intermediate distributors is often blamed for higher consumer prices in Japan but in passing on the gains from improving terms of trade, it was not just smaller companies that took advantage of the new exchange rate. A 60 per cent fall in oil prices resulted in a cut of just 15 per cent in petrol prices and a 10 per cent reduction in the price of electricity for which oil is the major energy source. There may have been technical reasons why consumers were slow to benefit because at first the levels of oil stocks were replenished and current prices reflect the average cost of the whole stockpile. But in the meantime windfall profits were earned by large corporations. With food imports it is the state trading corporations that benefited as a 30 per cent fall in the price of imported beef or a 60 per cent fall in wheat prices was reflected hardly at all in the prices paid by consumers. Equally, administered prices for transport services failed to reflect the substantial fall in the basic cost of fuel.

There was a clear tendency then for producers to absorb the benefits of changing terms of trade at the expense of consumers. For particular items like cameras, domestic prices were so much higher that some retailers in Japan were able to re-import them from the wholesale market in the US and still make a profit. Other more essential items of the household budget remain very expensive and the effect of the yen crisis was to accelerate still further the shift in the distribution of income from labour to capital that had been clear in the first half of the 1980s (OECD 1986 p. 18). The Ministry of Labour itself highlighted the consequences of this trend by noting that although labour costs were higher in Japan after the 1985 appreciation, 'taking the purchasing power of Japan as 100 that for the US is 184 and for West Germany 152' (analysis of Japan's Labour Economy 1986, FPC p. 14). The effect of using domestic consumers as shock absorbers of the yen crisis did protect profits in the short term, but it was counterproductive for those manufacturers that needed to increase domestic sales as a substitute for overseas orders. It therefore became even more urgent for consumers to be encouraged to save less in order to consume more.

Ever since the later 1970s when the flow of household saving clearly exceeded domestic demand for investment funds, private households have been exhorted to spend more of their incomes on consumption. As living costs continued to rise and as manufacturers sought to keep the increase in labour costs below the increase in productivity, the state was forced to use alternative methods to increase domestic consumption at the expense of saving. So from April 1988 the tax exemptions on most post office savings accounts were abolished which in form was said to be a matter of placing the taxation of unearned incomes on a more equitable basis. In substance the move appeared to be an attempt to make saving much less attractive for employee households. Increasing domestic consumption by allowing higher wage settlements would have been particularly damaging to the export sector, because after the yen appreciated the differential in labour costs relative to Japan's Asian competitors were even wider. In newly industrializing countries (NICs) like Hong Kong, South Korea or Taiwan the effect of lower labour costs was compounded by increases in productivity in electrical goods that more than matched those in Japan.

Although those export sectors most affected by the yen's appreciation and by competition from Asian NICs account for only 10 per cent of employees in Japan, changes in the pattern of wage offensives mean that all wage settlements are more closely related to the problems faced by exporters. *Shunto* offensives are now led more directly by the enterprise union federation representing labour in the electrical and engineering industries, which ensures that wage settlements in general are guided by the norms negotiated in this particular sector. Company performance is related to changes in earnings but this is largely through bi-annual bonuses, whereas the basic wage rate which accounts for 75 per cent of earnings is adjusted in the light of *shunto* norms. In this way wage settlements across the economy reflected the sense of crisis communicated by management and unions in the export oriented sectors.

Therefore despite the very marked variations in profitability between companies in different sectors, in the 1987 'spring offensive wage negotiations, unions nationwide won a nominal 3.5 per cent hike on average, the lowest since the Ministry of Labour began collecting and publishing relevant data in 1956' (Fukui 1988 p. 24). The growth in earnings for many employees in 1987 was less than this norm because of a sharp reduction in overtime payments which tends to be the first response of manufacturers to an approaching recession. Unlike other countries Japanese 'manufacturing employment does not simultaneously respond to changes in manufacturing production but responds to them with a time lag of one half to one year' (Seike 1985 p. 28). Seike's analysis was based on responses to the oil crises of the 1970s but the process he identified was apparent after 1985. At an ideological level the preference for maintaining permanent employment even in recession is said to be a unique feature of Japanese industrial relations. In practice employers do have much more flexibility than is apparent if we concentrate only on the employment of regular employees. Casual and part-time employment is adjusted quickly and other regulars are encouraged to transfer to subordinate companies and to accept voluntary early retirement. It is also clear that the hours spent working overtime beyond the weekly schedule provides great potential for varying the input of labour.

The employment index for regular manufacturing employees only began to fall in later 1987 some two years after the yen began to rise quickly and this pattern was similar to the economic reaction to the oil crises. What did decline almost immediately was the index of overtime hours which gave employers time to organize job transfers. Labour adjustment subsidies organized by the state increased fourfold between 1984 and 1986 to provide financial support for the retention of labour that was regarded as surplus to current requirements. Transferring workers does limit the initial quota of redundancies but this frequently involves reduced earnings which, with less overtime payments, erodes the increase in real purchasing power of the *shunto* wage settlements. Each affiliated company or subcontractor that receives additional employees then finds its own labour force in surplus and in turn has to press its own subordinates to accept labour transfers. In time such transfers create a ripple effect until the smallest firms have no option but to cut employment. Transferred employees are also more vulnerable to redundancies as they tend not to transfer seniority when they move.

This adjustment process does take time and it was not until August 1987 that the index of regular employment in manufacturing fell below its 1985 level, but then in the next six months it fell by 250,000. Once manufacturing output began to recover, those who remained in employment were faced with a return to overtime working and in the first quarter of 1988 overtime hours were 80 per cent higher than in the equivalent quarter of 1987. In short a return to 'long hours and a readiness to work overtime have been the price paid by Japan's shrinking army of industrial workers for job security' (FEER 14/4/88 p. 62). 1987 also saw an increase of 25 per cent in the numbers working part-time most of whom were in non-manufacturing jobs, but even part-time work in other sectors is sufficient to prevent any substantial increase in the rigorously measured unemployment statistics.

What appears as a smooth labour adjustment process does have serious consequences for the purchasing power of those involved not to mention the personal trauma of being classified as surplus. If we add to these employment effects the rapid increase in housing and social security expenses and the consequences of unadjusted income tax bands which make even a small increase in incomes the subject of higher marginal rates of tax, it is easy to see why real disposable incomes rose by little more than 1 per cent from 1986 to 1987. Even this aggregate figure is misleading because it includes unearned incomes from financial and property assets. Overall the yen crisis made it clearer that a 'class division seems to be forming between those who have assets on which they can reap capital gains and those who do not' (*J Ec J* 15/8/87 p. 6).

Despite the apparent contradiction between holding down labour costs and at the same time looking to the home market for a larger share of sales, production, profitability and exports rose significantly from the middle of 1987. In the year to June 1988 GNP grew by 5.3 per cent, industrial production by 12.4 per cent and exports by over 15 per cent. Corporate profits, boosted by financial dealings, rose by an average of 19 per cent and by just under 25 per cent in manufacturing. Productivity was growing even faster than output partly because increased production was accompanied by a fall in the index of regular employment. In addition economic recovery was enhanced by improvements in productivity which became popularized as 'cost-down' measures designed to supplement the short-term strategy of exporters to absorb part of the increase in export prices required by a higher yen.

7.9 'Hollowing-out' or Japanese-style de-industrialization

For the five leading electronics firms the effect of 'cost-down' measures was to increase profits in 1987–8 by 30 per cent from a much smaller increase in total sales of 4 per cent and a 12 per cent fall in exports. At Toshiba its 'total productivity drive' reduced costs at an annual rate equivalent to 10 per cent of sale revenue, it sold only 4 per cent more but reduced production workers by 20 per cent to record an increase in pre-tax profits of 20 per cent. As with many other firms, part of the burden of reducing costs was transferred to subcontractors who were required to supply components at a lower cost to more strictly regulated delivery schedules so that in the single year 1987 Toshiba reduced its inventory ratio by 50 per cent. Other companies like Matshushita concentrated on reducing sales and marketing costs and began to diversify into high-speed computers as well as trading in raw materials. Sony and Cannon moved towards new products at the more expensive end of the market where competition from NICs was less intense. Cannon thanks partly to its network of specialist dealers marketing highly priced superior products managed to increase profits by 60 per cent. The general trend in electronics was for Japanese manufacturers to plan for shorter product life-cycles in higher value-added consumer goods where their competitive position was better insulated from Asian producers. Increased imports were noticeable in the supply of components which added to the pressures on domestic subcontractors.

In motor vehicles although productivity also rose, profits were less buoyant but a less severe reduction in exports due to existing voluntary export restraint compensated for a very small growth in domestic sales. The productivity drive in motor vehicles was however no less intense. Toyota, easily the largest domestic producer, even managed to shift weekend holidays into the middle of the week to take advantage of lower energy costs and in the first two months of the scheme reduced costs by over 1.5 billion yen. In adjusting the schedule of the working week Toyota moved a step ahead of official proposals to reduce working hours from 48 to 40 per week. The new schedule was in form an attempt to increase leisure time but in substance served to deregulate standard working hours. The 40-hour week was to be taken as an average over three months which allows employers to extend daily hours from 8 to 12 in some periods thus reducing eligibility for overtime payments. Such a proposal could then allow Toyota to maximize production at the weekend when power costs are much lower. The ambivalence of enterprise unions towards a shorter working week is therefore clearly reflected in their reluctance to sacrifice overtime wages, while a further decline in union membership to 27.6 per cent of all employees undermines their collective ability to oppose the proposal to deregulate working hours.

The two major exceptions to the recovery of profits after 1986 were the steel and shipbuilding industries where losses continued and the productive workforce was cut by 25 and 40 per cent respectively. From shipbuilding many employees have been transferred into shipbreaking, and construction subsidiaries took on infrastructure projects or marinas that epitomized the new age of leisure. Steel companies have diversified into completely new products as well as replacing subcontracted cleaning, printing, catering or transport suppliers with in-house subsidiaries. Both of the two largest steelmakers Nippon Steel and Kobe, have diversified into the production of electronic information and communication systems in which they had previous experience only as end-users. They now market transputers, laser scanners or robots and have pioneered automated methods of inspection to replace visual quality control.

But the scale of planned reductions in capacity and therefore employment in both industries has created serious regional problems. The closure of integrated industrial complexes especially in peripheral areas has undermined the economic base of local economies in a similar way to the de-industrialization of Northern Britain or in some of the states in the north of the US. It is not simply redundancies among those directly employed by the big companies that damages the regional economy but the cut in orders for numerous small firms who produced components or supplied services to the major producers. Whole towns in peripheral areas to the north in Hokkaido or to the south in Kyushu 'are highly dependent on a single industry, and so those who are dismissed from this industry find it hard to obtain another job in the same locality' (analysis of Japan's Labour Economy, Ministry of Labour, FPC 1986 p. 11).

Geographical mobility is constrained by much higher living costs in Japan's central heartland and very limited demand in these areas for blue-collar workers between 35 and 55 who were the majority of those made redundant. It was exactly this cohort who benefited least from diversification into knowledge-intensive sectors like computing because their manual skills was said to make them unsuited to such a dramatic change in occupation. A depressed local economy offers few attractions for inward investment either in manufacturing or services and as a result towns which were once highly dependent on steel or shipbuilding have been labelled 'ghost towns' with unemployment three or four times the national average.

In metropolitan Japan household incomes in the aftermath of the yen crisis became more differentiated according to the level of unearned incomes, but differences in the industrial and regional impact of economic change have in turn widened differentials 'between metropolitan areas and other parts of the nation' (Long Term Credit Bank of Japan, reported in *JTW* 8/8/87 p. 12). Economic adjustment to the higher yen exchange rate therefore accelerated some of the trends in income distribution identified in earlier chapters.

Even outside the more peripheral areas, sectors in which small firms made a significant contribution were also seriously damaged. In ceramics, textiles, glassware or in the production of toys, many firms were too small to be able to absorb any of the change in export prices demanded by the new exchange rate. It is from these small firms located in larger cities, often employing members of minority groups, that labour moves out into the ranks of self-employed retailers whose underemployment is hidden in official statistics of unemployment. Smaller subcontractors were either replaced by in-house subsidiaries of larger firms or lost orders to Asian suppliers or at best were faced with sharp reductions in the prices they received for components. Official bankruptcy figures appeared to indicate that fewer firms went out of business entirely than in the aftermath of the oil crises of the 1970s, and in part this was the result of easier bank lending. With a huge surplus of saving and with larger firms now able to finance their own investment from undistributed profits, the small firm sector was just about the only one willing to borrow from the banks. The boom in land prices also assisted some small firms because their property could be used as collateral or be partially developed in Land Trust schemes which realized part of the increase in value without selling land, and was therefore not subject to capital gains tax.

It is worth emphasizing that many of the smallest firms are too small to be counted as companies and their demise would not be recorded in official statistics. These very small firms were unable to cooperate with parent companies in their move towards more higher quality products because they were unable to undertake the major technological changes required in their own plant. 'The exchange rate of 125 yen against the dollar is severe enough for major makers to forget their traditional feeling of responsibility towards subcontractors, and small parts makers without technology attractive to big makers are being wiped out' (Small and Medium Enterprise Agency Official, quoted in *J Ec J* 16/1/88 p. 3). Being aware of the particular problems of small suppliers did not mean that any sustained effort was made to resolve these problems. In fact the central budget allocation to Small Enterprise Assistance fell by 12 per cent in 1987 when the total was one-fifth less than it had been in the early 1980s. Various programmes were established to encourage small firms into the service sector by organizing Technology Exchange Plazas where arranged marriages between firms from different sectors were facilitated. But the initial budget for this scheme and other loans and subsidies to small firms was hardly immense being equivalent to the energy costs saved in one year by Toyota's shift to midweek holidays.

Ministry officials concentrated on mitigating the high exit costs for large firms in declining sectors through the main trade associations. In the traditional fashion, the state tended to delegate to larger companies the responsibility for distributing the consequences of reducing capacity among their suppliers. But in a continuing fashion this is usually 'achieved primarily by the exit of small firms' (Peck, Levin and Goto 1987 p. 121). For shipbuilding the Ministry of Transport's rationalization programme did manage to reduce capacity by 40 per cent through mergers and informal collaboration and the number of firms in the industry fell by 25 per cent. What was also noticeable was that subcontracted employees from small firms suffered a more than proportionate share of redundancies.

Neither was it only in declining sectors that the state assisted the process of collaboration. Two decades after MITI's plan to reduce the number of motor vehicle producers was rejected by the industry, the yen crisis saw a revival of interest in such a proposal. Toyota was encouraged to establish joint ventures with either Daihatsu or Suzuki in order to complement its range of larger vehicles. Not uncoincidentally this would assist the two smaller producers to withstand the growing competition in compact cars from Hyundai in South Korea, whose own development had earlier been organized by another Japanese firm Mitsubishi. Even more pressing were the problems of Mazda whose small share of the domestic market seemed to expose it to any attempt by Ford to increase the 24 per cent of Mazda that it already owned. The danger for MITI was that Mazda might become Ford (Pacific) and a major Japanese company would become part of a foreign corporation. One suggestion was for Nissan to join with Mazda in order to compete more effectively with Toyota which currently produces over 50 per cent of vehicles sold in Japan. Whether or not this happens, MITI's interest in Mazda was sufficient to facilitate *amakudari* for one of its retiring officials to become President of Mazda.

The reaction of MITI to the possibility of a foreign takeover contrasts with the general attitude of the Japanese state to the expansion of overseas production by Japanese companies. Indeed it is difficult to imagine how Japanese producers could have accommodated a dramatic appreciation in the yen without their overseas production operations. Companies that attempted to revive the growth of profits by increasing sales at home, recognized that this could only be a short-term strategy because of the intense competition in a home market that was growing only slowly. In addition, the new yen exchange rate had pushed labour costs in Japan to a higher level than equivalent costs in the US or Western Europe. From an hourly labour cost which was 30 per cent below the US in 1985, the new exchange rate meant that in 1988 Japanese hourly rates were almost 30 per cent higher. Compared to South Korea the change was from 70 per cent higher to 90 per cent higher. The contradiction here was that 'Japanese wages are now too high and too low: too high from the point of view of employers costs and too low to constitute an effective demand for consumer goods' (Steven 1988 p. 116). The immediate response of some exporters to a higher yen was to delay the increase in export prices and absorb some of the resulting losses. In the medium term they raised productivity and kept unit labour costs down to compensate for the change in relative prices. But for the longer term, Japanese manufacturing is to be 'hollowed out' as a greater share of production is to come from overseas plants.

7.10   Becoming the largest exporter of capital in the world

A massive increase in Japan's current account surplus after 1981 implied a similarly spectacular increase in the outflow of long-term capital which as Figure 7.1 shows increased by over 500 per cent by 1988. Despite the high profile given to Japanese companies abroad, direct investment has taken only a small share of the total outflow. Direct investment in overseas production did rise sharply after 1985 but even then over two-thirds of capital exports flowed into securities especially US Government bonds. To a very large extent it was Japan's savings surplus that financed the huge public deficits of the US especially after 1980 when the outflow of funds into foreign assets was liberalized. Insurance companies, trust banks and

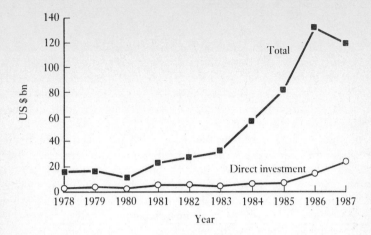

Figure 7.1 External capital outflow from Japan, 1978–87
Source: Ministry of Finance, FPC, 1987

other financial institutions attracted by higher interest rates in secure assets, avoided industrial securities and invested in US government stock where risk was minimized and yields were predictable. The annual increase in Japanese external assets was so enormous that after 1984 it became the world's largest capital exporter exceeding even Saudi Arabia, even though on an accumulated basis it lay a distant third behind the US and UK.

Direct foreign investment is much smaller but has made a peculiarly positive contribution to Japan's long-term economic performance. 'In general Japanese firms' foreign direct investment is strictly subordinated to Japan's foreign trade policy, which in turn is an instrument of industrial policy' (Taira 1986 p. 158). For some time subordination did mean state direction but more important since the 1960s were coordinated programmes of financial incentives and risk-sharing through which the state, and therefore taxpayers, facilitated overseas investment by private Japanese companies. Where Japan differed from other Western economies until the 1980s was that foreign investment complemented and enhanced overseas trade and was to a much smaller extent a substitute for domestic production. However the critical difference highlighted by the yen crisis was that 'hollowing-out' the domestic economy meant more and more direct investment abroad to replace production from Japan.

Treating foreign investment as an integral instrument of trade and industrial policies involved from as early as the 1950s establishing companies overseas to lubricate the acquisition of raw materials and the marketing of exports. Being desperately short of natural resources meant that Japan was enormously dependent on imported food and materials whose import bill required an equivalent level of exports. While it is true that Japan's foreign trade has always been a lower proportion of GDP than in Europe for example, it had by 1987 a 40 per cent share in the total world trade in iron ore, 30 per cent in coal and copper, 25 per cent in aluminium and 20 per cent in zinc and lumber. Being 90 per cent dependent on imported energy (including 99.8 per cent for oil) and well over 90 per cent dependent on other raw materials meant that it was imperative to secure stable supplies at predictable prices. Equally, marketing its exports to pay for imports and then to stimulate economic growth required that foreign trade as a whole be planned and coordinated.

We have already seen how the state managed a system of financial incentives especially in export development, but in its general trade policies it is doubtful whether effective coordination by the state would have been possible without the *sogo shosha*. These trading companies dominated overseas transactions particularly down to the 1970s, but even in 1988 they control the flow of two-thirds of all imports and one-half of exports. As a proportion of total direct investment overseas the trading companies account for only a small share, but this belies the inestimable value of services they supply to Japanese companies either as traders or overseas producers. Through their bases in almost every country the trading companies organize local market research, wholesaling, shipping and finance by acting as surrogate marketing divisions for Japanese companies. In other words they act as crucial intermediaries and provide a local presence through which Japanese companies and the state incorporate foreign activities. Their pivotal position in overseas transactions may not be as crucial to those larger exporting companies who in the past decade have established their own subsidiaries to lubricate trade and investment. But the close links between trade and investment flows symbolized by the trading companies, is clearly reflected in the large share of direct investment in commerce, finance, insurance and transportation services. It is not manufacturing ventures that dominate direct investment but trade related companies, who by the end of 1987 had been responsible for 60 per cent of the total invested abroad since 1951.

Direct investment by the trading companies themselves underestimates their role, because on the whole they limit themselves to minority shareholding in joint ventures as well as establishing relatively small overseas offices. But acting as quasi-bankers to local firms and intermediating finance for Japanese companies means that both can be very dependent on the trading companies. Their other crucial function has been in the words of a trading company director to act as 'expeditionary forces of the government in its overseas assistance programmes' (quoted in Woronoff 1984 p. 55). Where this function had its most spectacular effects was in organizing colossal projects to develop and process raw materials in places as far apart as Brazil, Zambia, the Persian Gulf, Indonesia and Australia. The *sogo shosha* joined with the state and private companies in risk-sharing consortia not simply to secure the flow of materials but to organize infrastructure investment in local roads, ports and power supplies. Part of the cost was financed by private direct investment, part by Overseas Department grants and part by loans from the Japanese state and private companies. The state also granted export credits, allowed 100 per cent tax remissions to Japanese companies investing in National resource projects and organized insurance schemes against unforeseen events like changes in local political regimes.

Alongside the large share of trade-related investment therefore went a high proportion of resource projects which in the years after the 1973 oil crisis accounted for over 70 per cent of foreign investment. Resource projects secured a supply of materials at relatively stable prices, and processing operations which were potentially dangerous to the environment were completed overseas. Such processing saved transport costs on bulky items, but more importantly allowed Japanese companies to break the monopsonistic control previously exercised by major companies from the US and Europe. The Fair Trading Commission in Japan did argue that monopsonistic controls by Japanese companies was no less of an evil, but through their own participation in resource development other Ministries were able to respond by insisting that an orderly monopsony by Japanese companies was essential to the national interest. Hence overseas investment in this case into resource development was integrated into industrial policy.

In a similar fashion a proportion of manufacturing investment abroad during the 1970s was promoted to permit declining sectors to fade gradually from prominence. Seventy per cent of direct investment by manufacturing firms at this time went to Asia and Latin America in response to the shift in the domestic economy to products with a higher proportion of value added in manufacture. Relatively obsolete industries producing cheaper textiles, footwear, plastics or furniture were encouraged to relocate abroad. This programme was extended to the production of electrical appliances, transistor radios, or black and white television sets where simple soldering and assembly work could be transferred to countries whose lower labour costs would have the greatest advantage for labour-intensive final processing. This type of investment was to an extent in simple finishing tasks with two-thirds of intermediate inputs being supplied from Japan, but with less than a quarter of final output being shipped back to Japan. In this way the effects of rising labour costs in Japan could be mitigated, firms in obsolete sectors could survive longer without generating excessive competition, and the threat to domestic employment could be minimized. Industrial structure was re-aligned towards higher quality output while at the same time component suppliers continued to profit by selling intermediate inputs to foreign plants.

The companies in Japan that were the least likely to be able to finance investment in higher value-added production were small and medium-sized firms. It was these smaller firms that therefore took a leading role in direct foreign investment contributing up to one half of the total for manufacturing during the 1970s. Ninety per cent of their projects were in

Asia particularly in NICs such as Singapore, Taiwan and South Korea where labour was not just cheaper but well disciplined by political controls on the collective organization of labour. The mean size of company that invested in Asia was, at less than 200 employees (Taira 1980), too small to have relocated overseas without financial incentives from the state nor without the assistance of trading companies. Through their local agents the *sogo shosha* found sites, local partners and finance, organized the import of components from Japan and arranged local and international distribution of their output. In short the trading companies replaced the affiliated networks that smaller firms had been part of in Japan.

It has been argued that this whole process involved a 'systematic shifting of structured dualism to the developing countries' (Park 1979 p. 177) and in a sense this was true. But this did not mean that dualism in Japan was ended even though at the time it appeared to many that the days of the small firm were over. What the transfer achieved was the removal of some firms in obsolete sectors or those using simple processing methods, leaving other subcontractors to move into the supply of parts for colour televisions or VCRs for example. Moving overseas those smaller firms that could not finance the change to higher quality products, facilitated both industrial adjustment and technological change.

Upgrading Japan's technological base has along with export promotion, security of raw material supplies and smooth industrial change been a fourth objective of industrial policy. Here the Japanese state and MITI in particular faced a real dilemma because technology is often transferred through inward direct investment. Foreign domination of domestic industry had been unacceptable since the nineteenth century and in the post-war period it was felt to be a major disturbance to the delicate process of coordinating industrial change so inward direct investment has been discouraged. Instead best-practice technology was imported under licence or where this was not possible, foreign firms operating in Japan were required to take Japanese partners so that only 19 per cent of foreign affiliated firms in manufacturing are wholly owned by foreigners. Joint ventures and licensed imports were crucial to industrial policy because they restricted the emergence of foreign enclaves and encouraged domestic producers into adaptive technological change and improvement engineering. This meant that 'foreign ownership advantages have successfully been translated into home based ownership advantages' (T. Ozawa 1985 p. 175). Incidentally this aspect of industrial policy was a lesson that some NICs themselves learned and it was used to control Japanese investment in their own economies from the later 1970s.

Whether the lower levels of inward investment were caused by the reluctance of foreign firms to share ownership or whether foreign companies lacked interest is debatable. What is not in dispute is the effect on the relative proportions of inward and outward investment. Inward direct investment particularly into basic processes such as petrochemicals, did average 20 per cent of outward flows in the 1970s but has since fallen to less than 10 per cent. Payments for imported technology remain larger than receipts from technological exports, but from the later 1970s receipts increased and they now approach one-third of payments. Interestingly most of Japan's technological exports are incorporated into direct foreign investment or embodied in the exports of whole plants so that ownership advantages in exports of technology are not eroded as quickly as they are with imports.

The overall importance of trade complementarity which integrates direct foreign investment into industrial policy shows through in the aggregate distribution of overseas investment by sector and region. Between 1951 and 1986 the cumulated share of non-manufacturing direct foreign investment was 73 per cent of which three-quarters was by companies in commerce, finance, insurance and transport services. It is in these tertiary sectors that direct investment has grown fastest even in the 1980s when

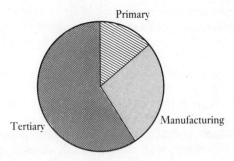

Figure 7.2 Proportions of direct overseas investment by sector: Japan 1951–86
Source: Ministry of Finance, FPC, 1987

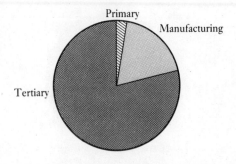

Figure 7.3 Proportions of direct overseas investment by sector: Japan's cumulative total, 1982–6
Source: Ministry of Finance, FPC, 1987

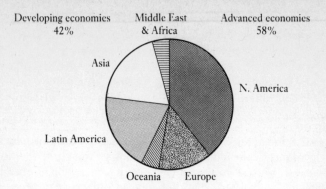

Developing economies 42% Middle East & Africa Advanced economies 58%

Figure 7.4 All direct overseas investment from Japan by region, 1980–6
Source: Ministry of Finance, FPC, 1987

manufacturing overseas became the object of attention especially in the West. If we focus on the years since 1980 the share of investment by tertiary companies leapt from 60 to 80 per cent with two-thirds of this flowing into the US and Western Europe. This trend reflects the growing importance of these areas as export markets for, in the past decade, their share of total Japanese exports rose from 30 to 50 per cent. Much of the increase in foreign investment by finance and insurance companies is associated with outflows of portfolio investment and shows again the way direct investment complements the prevailing pattern of commercial transactions whether through trade in goods or finance.

Primary processing foreign investment was bound to take a smaller share once the output of many of the colossal projects reached full capacity and

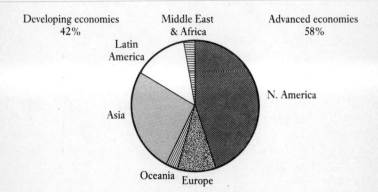

Developing economies 42% Middle East & Africa Advanced economies 58%

Figure 7.5 Direct overseas manufacturing investment from Japan by region, 1980–6
Source: Ministry of Finance, FPC, 1987

even though foreign investment in this sector increased by 75 per cent in the 1980s its overall share fell to less than 10 per cent. There was an increase in manufacturing investment abroad but at a rate only one-fifth as large as in the tertiary sector. By region foreign manufacturing investment increased most rapidly in the US and Europe where 76 per cent of the value of new plant was located largely in response to the threat of tighter controls on imports from Japan. Within manufacturing it was in electronics, electrical machinery and transport (especially vehicles) that grew fastest while textiles in particular declined in share. However it is important to stress that by 1986 overseas manufacturing was still tiny relative to domestic production with just 9 per cent of manufacturing output generated by overseas plants.

Seen in this wider perspective, overseas production down to 1985 was not at all as significant in quantitative terms as the public focus in the Western media would suggest. It is overstretching the point to say that Japanese manufacturers were reluctant foreign investors, but there were a number of reasons why overseas production was less attractive. Until 1985 an undervalued yen more than compensated for any tariff barriers that their exports faced. Where quotas were agreed, Japanese manufacturers frequently resolved this supply constraint in higher prices which increased profits on their exports. In any case Japanese manufacturers benefited directly and indirectly from existing overseas investments in the primary and tertiary sectors. Assembly-style processing in Asia generated demand for intermediate inputs and one MITI survey for 1979 showed that over 70 per cent of inputs into electrical and transport machinery plants were imported from Japan (T. Ozawa 1985 p. 116). Compared to profitable exports and supplying inputs to overseas plants, the prospect of increasing investment in new foreign ventures was for many of Japan's larger manufacturers not necessarily compelling.

Overseas production had also brought very mixed returns throughout the 1970s both financially and politically. Large material processing operations did secure a flow of imports but at no small cost to investing companies. Politicians in host countries and from Japan frequently pushed the scale of development faster than was financially prudent, and actual costs in some of the bigger projects in Brazil or Indonesia escalated way beyond initial projections. Neither had various collaborative ventures in electronics and motor vehicles, especially those in the West, produced impressive results. In addition Japanese personnel working abroad faced a range of problems from racist abuse in the West to accusations of imperialist domination in Asia.

The most serious difficulties for Japanese manufacturers abroad centred around the problems of exporting their particular style of management and production methods. In the development of electronics factories in Wales during the 1970s for example, complaints were made that local suppliers did not appreciate the value of dependency relationships with parent companies (Blunden 1982 p. 87). This reaction was typical of many overseas operations because outside the Japanese context smaller subcontractors realized the dangers of relying too heavily on orders from a dominating purchaser. They continued with their traditional preferences for diversified supply contracts and even played one ordering firm off against another. Such behaviour was totally alien to large Japanese companies, and the problems of quality control and delivery timing among subcontractors were legion. In some parts of Asia life became even more difficult when host states began to impose stringent controls on local content ratios for inputs. Taking their lead from Japan's own practices meant imposing limits on the extent of foreign equity participation and insisting on the use of indigenous personnel in management. Neither in Asia nor in the West did local suppliers easily accommodate to the role of shock-absorber that is the special function of subcontractors in Japan.

Labour management in overseas plants brought similar problems because of the difficulties of operating outside the peculiar structure of the Japanese labour market. High rates of labour turnover, almost the antithesis of expected behaviour in large companies, were the norm in the US where job mobility is regarded as a sign of individual ambition whereas for Japanese managers it indicates a lack of individual commitment. In South East Asia where labour was in general more pliable, the pressure of work was so intense in Japanese factories that labour resisted not by collective action but by quitting. Electronics factories in Singapore experienced labour turnover rates of 10 per cent per month which resulted in an unacceptably high proportion of defective products as inexperienced recruits dominated the labour force (Lin 1984). In Thailand the authoritarian style of management in Japanese plants, where wages were similar to those offered in the slightly less oppressive regimes of other foreign companies, encouraged workers to move 'out of Japanese firms as soon as marketable experience is obtained' (Taira 1980 p. 392). Japanese managers attempted to instill the ideology of a lifetime's employment bargain but without institutional constraints on mobility in the labour market, exhortation by itself had little effect. In the financial sector of the City of London, Japanese management expressed great dissatisfaction with British white-collar employees for behaving as though their skills and expertise were their own personal possessions to be freely transferred to other firms as they wished (White and Trevor 1983 p. 108). Such 'selfishness' was difficult to reconcile with the Japanese principle that expertise should be the joint possession of the individual and the company.

With blue-collar employees the major difficulties, especially in collaborative ventures, lay in relations with organized labour. When a Japanese preference for job rotation in multi-skilled work processes through simplified wage payment systems met with strict craft identification, clear demarcation procedures and a highly complex structure of wage differentials, the notion of operating in an alien environment was real indeed. Where unions were strong the idea of unpaid participation in quality control circles or undertaking voluntary overtime was simply inconceivable. Dissent about the overwhelming presence of Japanese nationals in supervisory positions was widespread. In Asia, host states imposed quantitative limits on the proportion of Japanese managers, while in the US several highly publicized law-suits were brought alleging racial discrimination in the preferential allocation of promotion opportunities to Japanese personnel (Sethi, Namiki and Swanson 1984 ch. 4). The whole idea of considering women white-collar employees for supervisory positions was so alien that in the US and Britain women were singled out as the least satisfactory of employees because they failed to suffer in silence as their sisters in Japan would have done.

Profitability in overseas subsidiaries is difficult to measure because of the problems of disentangling the contribution made by foreign plants to the overall profits of parent companies in Japan. Poor overseas returns could be due to parent companies overcharging for intermediate inputs or the valuation of investment in overseas subsidiaries may be exaggerated making a percentage return on capital invested seem low. But superficially at least profits were poorer than domestic rates, productivity lower and the ratio of defective products higher. Ohmae (1983) for instance concluded that all but a handful of Japanese manufacturing plants in the US were marginal to disastrous in their economic performance. Hitachi electronics factories in the UK were also reported to have been unprofitable (*FT* 25/3/86 p. 24). Whether or not these reports were accurate, the problems of exporting Japanese methods of production and peculiar expectations about labour relations were sufficiently acknowledged among larger Japanese companies to make overseas production a risk-laden proposition. This did not mean that manufacturing investment overseas ceased to grow. Rather that the difficulties of adapting Japanese practices to foreign principles meant that decisions were delicately balanced despite the undoubted advantages of circumventing export restrictions and incurring lower labour costs.

What really tilted the balance in favour of expanding overseas production were long-term changes in the way Japanese firms integrated themselves into alien economies and the short-term effects of the very rapid appreciation in the foreign exchange value of the yen.

7.11 Japanese investment overseas: towards a preference for the First World

By the early 1980s it had become clear to the management of larger Japanese companies that a permanent manufacturing presence in the US and Europe in particular, would require changes in their traditional practices. Adapting some aspects of their management style was complemented by foregoing collaborative projects so that some elements of the Japanese house-style could be introduced into overseas factories. While in no sense were Japanese manufacturers totally enthusiastic, they were acutely aware that as fast as their exports rose so also did political pressures for import controls especially in electrical goods and motor vehicles. Not a few apprehensive company executives were overwhelmed by the way they were fêted with invitations and financial incentives to establish subsidiaries in the West. This was much more apparent than in Asia where host states were a good deal more circumspect about the effects of Japanese investment on the long-term development of the indigenous economy. In the US by contrast it proved 'difficult to curb the enthusiasm of state governments; the problem of overbidding for increased investment already exists' (Turner 1987 p. 107). Nissan were allocated public subsidies equivalent to £32,000 per employee to entice them to open their first wholly-owned plant in Europe on a site in north east England. Their welcome as missionaries who could lead the revitalization of British industry being symbolized in the conspicuous presence of the Prime Minister in the official opening ceremonies.

A new wave of expansion into Asian sites was obviously desirable from the Japanese perspective because NICs like Taiwan and South Korea had dramatically improved the quality of their products and upgraded their technological standards. With higher rates of productivity growth than in Japan, close proximity to the Japanese market and an increase in their labour cost advantage after the 1985 yen appreciation, their competition could not be ignored. Although the share of manufacturing investment in Asia as a whole continued to decline as the Western portion increased, the share of NICs in the total for Asia increased from 50 to over 70 per cent. To a significant degree the expansion of operations in Asia had for the first time defensive implications and unlike earlier direct investment included plans to export more output from these plants back to Japan.

Intentions and plans to produce more abroad were clearly under consideration before 1985, but the rise in the yen fairly galvanized manufacturers into action. In the single fiscal year 1986–7 direct foreign investment doubled and had risen by another 50 per cent by June 1988. The manufacturing sector invested more overseas in the first half of 1987 than in the whole of the preceding year and by 1992 the share of output produced abroad is expected to rise from 9 to 22 per cent. The state has incorporated this change into its forward visions and predicts that the expected 14 per cent annual increase in investment abroad will mean the loss of 0.7 million jobs in Japan. This is clearly a different scenario from previous periods when foreign investment complemented trade and relocated less important industries and processes overseas.

'Hollowing-out' domestic production for Honda has meant increasing the output of its plant in Ohio to a level which approaches 50 per cent of its current exports to the US. What is more significant is that the company plans by 1990 to be exporting back to Japan twice as many vehicles as the whole of the US motor industry is expected to export. Nissan too is scheduled to replace exports to Europe from its domestic plants with production from its factory in England and then begin exporting back to Japan. Toyota was for many years noted for its reluctance to produce overseas preferring to use its market leadership in Japan as a safer base for exporting, but since the yen crisis the company has accelerated the development of factories in Kentucky and Canada. The effect of this expansion of motor vehicle production in the US will by 1990 mean that in that country alone, the capacity of Japanese plants will be equal to one-quarter of domestic output. As domestic demand in Japan is hardly likely to increase by a quarter, job losses are inevitable.

In electronics, Matsushita is to increase its foreign production from 10 to 25 per cent as its export ratio is projected to fall from 37 to 27 per cent. NEC increased overseas production by a half in the two years after 1985 and plans to raise the proportion to 40 per cent by 1990 when its network of inter-company trading will integrate processes in Mexico, the US, Australia, South East Asia and the UK. Fujitsu in doubling its overseas production share, seems to have replaced Japanese sources of components for its US plants with supplies from Singapore. Similarly Canon now produces 80 per cent of its calculators in Taiwan and Hong Kong, and is doubling the capacity of plants in Virginia and France. It seemed as though every issue of the Japanese economic press in 1987 and 1988 carried corresponding reports for other companies; what they had in common was that many of them were in what are known as 'sunrise' industries in contrast to earlier foreign investment by 'sunset' industries.

Clearly the higher yen did propel many hesitant companies into increasing their shares of overseas production. But as this immediate cause had such a prompt response it seems to indicate that manufacturers had already begun to resolve some of their problems in operating in an alien environment. In the West there has been a significant loss of interest in joint, collaborative ventures in preference to wholly-owned subsidiaries on greenfield sites. Collaborating with indigenous firms meant operating within host countries traditional institutions and practices because their local partners were less able to withdraw from longstanding agreements with component suppliers or labour unions. On greenfield sites, completely new plants can be constructed in areas with more limited experience in the particular industry concerned.

As larger Japanese companies expand overseas there has been an increase in the tendency for some of their dependent subcontractors to accompany them. 'We ask subcontractors to come along but don't provide any financial assistance' (General Manager of Matshushita, quoted in *J Ec J* 16/1/88). The costs of relocation are heavy so smaller subcontractors are less likely to move, but those that do are used to lead the organization of indigenous component suppliers. This then allows Japanese practices to be exported using Japanese subcontractors as the model for expectations about *kanban* deliveries or the total commitment to quality control. In some cases mergers or arranged marriages are promoted between Japanese suppliers and local firms so the Honda plant in Ohio over a third of components are supplied by firms with direct or indirect Japanese origins.

At the same time as suppliers are integrated the 'local' content of inputs is raised. Just how much value is added from indigenous sources is one of the most delicate political issues and it raises questions about which inputs should be included and what indigenous means. But by moving into wholly-owned foreign subsidiaries, Japanese manufacturers were able to control more effectively the base on which local content is measured. So 'local' for Japanese producers in the UK is anywhere inside the EC which allows other Japanese plants in Europe to be included. Equally the notion of value-added in production can be widened to include the cost of local services such as catering, cleaning, local rates or taxes and transport. What seems to be apparent is that states in the West are much less attentive to local content standards than those in Asia, in most cases because Japanese investment is so actively pursued.

Part of the attraction for Western states is surely economic especially in revitalizing depressed areas, but there are other advantages in the demonstration effect of changes in production methods or labour relations. The ideological value to the new right for instance of the Japanese model of industrial relations, has been important either in arguing that a benevolent management renders obsolete the need for collective labour representation or that single union plants with no strike agreements should be the norm. Manufacturing on greenfield sites permits Japanese companies to choose areas where organized labour has been traditionally weak and some have avoided union representation completely in a number of southern states in the US. Alternatively particular groups of workers with low rates of unionization can be recruited; in electronics factories from Wales to Taiwan this usually meant recruiting a high proportion of young women. Where unionization cannot be avoided, only one union is recognized and this is frequently one with little previous experience in the industry. Incorporating no-strike agreements has been more a matter of substance than form because industrial action as such is not prohibited; it is just that no space is allowed for collective action in arbitration arrangements. With automatic external conciliation or binding arbitration clauses 'No official industrial action is provided for under the agreement' (Garrahan 1986 p. 11).

With wholly-owned subsidiaries, personnel can be carefully selected to avoid the recruitment of active union members. A clear preference for Honda's Vice-President in Ohio was to recruit 'very fresh people like blotting paper' (quoted in Sethi, Namiki and Swanson 1984 p. 195). Younger recruits are particularly valued as they can be taught Japanese ways without challenging expectations based on previous work or industrial experience. Very careful screening of potential employees is crucial where job rotation is required and where low rates of absenteeism are demanded (Sayer 1986 p. 67). Without having the total package of family and residential records that are used in Japan, foreign subsidiaries adapt their recruitment procedures to achieve similar objectives.

Most Japanese factories abroad attempt to recreate the networks of smaller work groups that are so vital in encouraging intra-company competition to meet production targets and in delegating responsibility for quality control. Within such smaller groups career patterns and to an extent payment systems are individualized to counteract the emergence of collective wage grievances. What has changed in the recent past is the tendency for supervisory or managerial positions to be totally dominated by Japanese nationals. Work group supervisors in particular are used as a key mediating link between employees and management and, unlike companies in the service sector, are positively encouraged to join training courses with parent companies in Japan. Rather than imposing new practices from above, local supervisory staff can proselytize management's expectations among their fellow workers.

It would be misleading to imagine that all Japanese companies overseas follow the same pattern in labour relations. Some persist in allocating a majority of management positions to Japanese nationals who exist in an enclave which is clearly differentiated from indigenous employees. Such enclaves are common in manufacturing plants in Asia and among financial companies in the West. At the other end of the spectrum are companies in high-technology sectors where high turnover rates are universal and in these companies the use of peculiarly Japanese practices is minimized. Even here however some adjustments are made by, for instance, attempting to reduce the mobility of highly skilled specialist technicians through promises of job security and longer contracts in industries where today's technological frontier is tomorrow's technological history.

After their troubled learning experience in collaborative ventures, management in Japanese factories abroad have applied their domestic principles in a wide range of adaptations according to the circumstances of the area or the industry. Wholly-owned plants are easier to control and some Japanese practices have spread to other local companies. Some problems in labour management are bound to continue because Japanese companies cannot insulate their internal labour market as effectively as they can in Japan, and labour turnover remains higher in overseas plants. When compared to their local competitors, foreign subsidiaries do have better productivity records and lower defect rates, but in neither does overseas performance match that of the parent companies in Japan. Given these limitations, it is not surprising to find that industry in Japan continued to press the state to find ways of increasing the rate of growth of consumer demand in Japan. 'Hollowing-out' was never intended to replace domestic production entirely but to give producers maximum flexibility. Through their various interest groups, employers were particularly keen to free some of the domestic purchasing power constrained by an antiquated distribution system, by the administrative control of food prices and imports or by high levels of direct taxation. In pressing for liberalization of food supplies, structural changes in distribution and the introduction of value-added indirect taxation, we can see examples of the continuing interplay between the LDP, the bureaucracy and private business.

7.12   The yen crisis and the domestic politics of compartmentalized pluralism

Private consumer spending for most of the 1980s was limited partly because the percentage of income taken from employee households in direct taxation, social security contributions, insurance and housing payments grew twice as fast as gross incomes. Several attempts were made to reduce the effect of one of these constraints by shifting the balance of taxation towards indirect sales or value-added taxes. With only one-quarter of revenue collected through indirect taxes compared to one half in Europe, Finance officials pressed for a new tax which could be collected cheaply, have a more predictable yield and offer fewer opportunities for avoidance. In addition to revenue raising objectives the new tax was justified as a shift towards greater individual choice which would increase disposable incomes and raise consumption. Lower levels of direct taxation which might accompany the sales tax was an important element in accommodating the arguments of Japanese Employers' Federations that high direct taxes were overburdening manufacturing companies compared to the self-employed and farmers who paid less than half the effective tax rates on industry. This argument became more significant after the yen crisis though it is worth recalling from Chapter 5 that the actual yield from company taxation is greatly eroded through the impact of numerous allowances and exemptions.

It was not until 1985 that legislation to introduce a sales tax was tabled, and alongside the proposal were to go direct tax concessions and the abolition of tax exemption anomalies on post office savings accounts. Despite being personally presented by Prime Minister Nakasone as a key component in his vision of Japan's future economic direction, his proposal met with tremendous opposition from a section of his own party, from all sides in the distribution industry and from opposition parties in the Diet. Large chain store groups and smaller retailers opposed in particular the implementation of a tax that included the compulsory inspection of their accounts. Organized representatives of retailers and wholesalers used their leverage within the LDP to gather the support of over one third of the ruling party's members and the opposition in the Diet was for once united in attacking the new tax. Opinion polls showed that 80 per cent of those surveyed were opposed to the sales tax, not least because the accompanying direct tax concessions were aimed principally at those individuals and companies earning the largest incomes. Nakasone was forced to withdraw his proposal early in 1987.

Less than one year later the succeeding Prime Minister Takeshita, operating in the more traditional manner of pragmatic consensus-builder revived the spirit of the tax but this time within a package designed to divide opposition to a sales tax. Revenue collection objectives were hidden from sight, there were to be reductions in direct taxes for all income groups and the distribution sector was pacified by replacing compulsory inspection with nominal assessment. Takeshita even appeared to divide firms in distribution with promises to the Chain Stores' Association that intermediate layers in distribution would be rationalized and restrictive practices challenged. Small retailers were therefore to lose some of their privileges but the increase in competition that was forecast would, it was argued, lower overall profit margins and reduce consumer prices. Such predictions had enough appeal for LDP members to outweigh the political disquiet among smaller retailers and wholesalers especially as very high living costs had become a general source of disaffection. Food was to be exempt from the new tax which, with the promise to reduce all direct tax rates, enticed the support of organized labour. The JSP were left almost alone in the Diet in insisting that capital gains tax should be increased to compensate for the loss in equity that went with the shift to indirect taxation.

Takeshita's plans have not, as of late 1988, been implemented, but in the extensive round of public negotiations that has accompanied the new package several clues have been offered to the extent of change and continuity in Japan's political economy. First the package of measures has been presented as more equitable because it promises more direct tax reductions. Yet this still cannot hide the clear shift towards a kind of tax that will take the same amount from rich and poor alike. Nothing was proposed to reduce the erosion of the redistributive substance of taxes on incomes from property or on companies, and no promises were made to reverse the delay in adjusting income tax thresholds which continuously erodes the disposable incomes of employees. An increase in domestic spending was one objective, but it is inevitable that a sales tax will increase prices and could well do little for consumption. Even the taxation of post office savings accounts has not produced any marked change in consumption but has merely seen the transfer of some of these assets to life insurance and securities companies.

That Takeshita's package could be presented as more equitable in form than Nakasone's even though there was not a great deal of difference in substance, is testament to the new Prime Minister's style as a skilful political manager. For all the comment that Nakasone epitomized the shift to a new style of political leadership, his record was not at all impressive. This may be another case of confusing *tatemae* with *honne* among those political analysts who predicted more forceful presidential leadership to relegate the bureaucracy and the mass of LDP membership into second place. While Nakasone was long on rhetoric and short on delivering concrete changes, Takeshita's less forceful role produced much less opposition to his own version of a sales tax. Similarly the Ministry of Finance may have lost a number of battles on the new tax but it looks likely that it will succeed in the end. MITI may have been pushed out of its dominating position but its voice in Cabinet is now heard through a powerful Minister who is one of the Prime Minister's closest faction colleagues and the yen crisis has increased the importance of MITI's role as coordinator of economic adjustment. Being closely connected to Employers' Federations, MITI is ideally placed to push forward their views on other measures to raise consumer demand by liberalizing the supply and price of foodstuffs.

The costs of extending special protection to agriculture involves higher retail prices and public subsidies equivalent to 12 per cent of the value of agricultural output. With much higher expenditure on housing, the high price of basic foodstuffs helps to explain why with a *per capita* GNP 5 per cent greater than in the US, the average Japanese has 28 per cent *less* in equivalent purchasing power. Similarly an income level 25 per cent above Western Europe is eroded to 8 per cent when it is calculated what this nominal income can actually buy. Although 60 per cent of calorie intake is derived from imported food, domestic consumers have to pay five times more for their rice and twice as much for their beef than they would if these foodstuffs were freely imported. Import quotas have restricted imported rice to less than 1 per cent of domestic consumption and price controls have forced the price of imported wheat, sugar or beef way above world price levels.

State trading corporations control the flow of foodstuffs. They buy cheaply on world markets but sell at high prices in the domestic market in order to transfer the surplus to producers whose costs are far in excess of farmers overseas. Apart from providing a secure domestic market for Japanese farmers, the controls are frequently justified by arguing that imported foodstuffs do not match the quality or varieties desired by domestic consumers. This argument seems particularly flimsy as even with quotas and higher prices the consumption of imported beef for instance has risen to over 30 per cent of domestic sales. But as a result of protecting agriculture 'the Japanese consumer pays far more than the average American for the same quantity of food which means that the Japanese family spends a larger proportion of its income on food than consumers in other developed countries' (Kain 1988 p. 18). Liberalizing trade in agriculture would according to one estimate reduce household spending on food by a sixth (Mitsubishi Bank Bulletin reported in *JTW* 30/5/87).

Quite apart from conceding to the demands of GATT and the US that food imports be deregulated, the need to release domestic purchasing power has been a powerful argument voiced by Japanese manufacturers to help them to compensate for reduced profitability in exports. *Keidanren* and *Nikkeiren* have long pressed for an end to what they regard as a profligate use of public funds and their case has added force as consumers have benefited little from the falling exchange cost of food. Public disquiet has been sufficient for the 55 per cent of LDP Diet members that are not directly elected from rural areas to join the calls for freer trade in agriculture. Finance bureaucrats have for years sought to reduce subsidies, and officials in MITI or the Ministry of Foreign Affairs are looking to deregulation to pacify the US protectionist lobby. Even the 1987 White Paper from the Ministry of Agriculture seemed to be more concerned with the pace of de-control and had resigned itself to the inevitable.

Whether deregulation will be complete or will result in much lower consumer prices is very uncertain. Less than a half of LDP members are now elected from rural districts, but 45 per cent is still a large enough share to make the choice between losing safe rural support in exchange for volatile urban voters a delicate one. More likely is the continued use of symbolic price reductions like the first post-war reduction in rice prices by 6 per cent in 1986. At the same time the Union of Agricultural Cooperatives which is one of Japan's most redoubtable interest groups is engaged in a campaign to replace import quotas with surcharges and additional support payments to farmers following the model of EC schemes. Granting limited concessions of symbolic value may also include sacrificing domestic producers of specialist foodstuffs in peripheral areas. The latest suggestion of this form would be to make concessions in fruit imports, which in the case of pineapples would mainly affect farmers in the Okinawan islands but leave the bulk of rice and dairy producers relatively untouched. There has even been a revival of propaganda about impure food imports in films financed by the Agricultural Cooperatives linking imported wheat to deformities in newly-born children (*Guardian* 4/6/88 p. 7).

Lowering direct taxation and consumer prices were proclaimed as national priorities throughout the first half of the 1980s especially in international negotiations over trade imbalances. The yen crisis gave both of these objectives added urgency in domestic politics, but attempts to give Japanese consumers the ability to purchase more and persuade them to save less have revealed various contradictions. In many senses it is not that consumers prefer to save, but that they have little choice given the central importance of educational expectations, high housing costs and the priorities attached to privatized welfare. An antiquated distribution system makes it likely that a fair proportion of any reduction in import prices will disappear before it reaches consumers. But dismantling such a system would at the same time remove the safety-net of surrogate welfare provision for many of the elderly or less privileged sections of the labour force. With this uncertainty, savings become even more important and liberalizing the outflow of capital gives savers access to higher interest rates elsewhere. If internal interest rates are deregulated it might even make saving more attractive. Some in the LDP may be willing to risk the loss of rural voters but the overall maldistribution of constituency representation still exists. Even if the LDP were to concede more equitable electoral districts, it is doubtful whether their majority would survive the alienation of agricultural interests *and* large numbers of small traders in urban areas.

The current dilemmas facing the Japanese state are the outcome of social processes that were designed to achieve the fastest rates of economic growth in the shortest possible time. Changing some of the fundamental features of post-war society is made more difficult because other features remain unchanged. Enabling policies which are designed to increase consumption, will inevitably lose part of their impact if the underlying reasons for saving continue to be reproduced in the race for educational credentials or in precautionary provision for ill-health or old age. In the economy, the pace and direction of change is more obvious as 'hollowing-out' affects industries that could by no means be classified as declining sectors. Continuity in the process of economic adjustment to external shocks like the yen appreciation, however, can be seen in the way profits are protected while labour is urged to make sacrifices in the national interest.

Organized labour is currently in the midst of a major change in its representative institutions. *Domei* was disbanded in 1987 to join forces with *Rengo* the Private Sector Trade Union Confederation and *Sohyo* is due to do the same by 1990 leaving a single federation to represent 10 million workers. This change has been heralded as a prelude to 'significant structural change in Japanese politics' (Fukui 1988 p. 31), because it will remove vital bases of support from the DSP and JSP who are heavily dependent on *Domei* and *Sohyo*. The new federation may then lead to a realignment of parties that claim to represent labour and unify opposition to the LDP which has dominated government for so long. It could equally well be argued though, that *Rengo's* much more confined focus on wage bargaining as opposed to wider political objectives, may well reduce the strength of the opposition and allow the LDP to continue as the 'natural' party of government.

For the remaining 30 million employees not directly affiliated to *Rengo*, the previous record of this organization in ignoring less privileged and more marginalized sections of the labour market offers little promise of significant changes to their uncertain prospects. Part-time employment for men and women has continued to increase and those over 45 continue to bear more than their fair share of transfers, secondments or early retirements. Most of these people will gain little benefit in terms of employment security because *Rengo's* main purpose in recent years has been to limit the damage of 'hollowing-out' on the permanent employment prospects of its regular core of members.

Despite the apparent shift in national power centres under Nakasone, the atmosphere of crisis after 1985 highlighted the substantial role the state plays in controlling the way change and adjustment are negotiated. There were shifting alliances within and between the LDP, the bureaucracy and institutions that represent private business so that the existence of one dominant power centre is diffused. The bureaucracy may have lost much of its statutory authority but its informal controls of the process of negotiating change remain continuing features of the Japanese polity. This role was clearly evident in reconciling the conflicting objectives of employers and those pressing for equal opportunity legislation. Nakasone did attempt to increase the power of the Prime Minister in alliance with favoured parts of the bureaucracy and respected leaders of private business. But as his abortive attempt to impose his own version of the sales tax indicates, he could not ignore for too long the traditional supporters of the LDP. Takeshita's style, though far less domineering in form, seems to have been more effective in negotiating substantive change through pragmatic accommodation.

7.13 A concluding comment

The examples I have used in this chapter were intended to show that the Japanese state remains as the central site where conflict over social change is negotiated. There does seem to be a notable degree of continuity in the presence of key actors from the bureaucracy, the LDP and leaders of private business in this process of negotiation. But as the examples show, it would be misleading to imply high levels of unity among these key groups. The bureaucracy has been divided in deciding how best to accommodate external pressures to accelerate the pace of liberalization in domestic markets. The tax reform issue even for a time separated the leadership of the LDP from its own supporters inside and outside the Diet. In a similar way business interests were divided between footloose multinational companies and those tied more closely to the domestic market; between agriculture and industry; between large and small retailers.

Thus even with Prime Ministerial leadership of powerful finance bureaucrats and the support of the leading Employers' Federation, the proposed move towards greater indirect taxation was postponed. Given the continuation of divisions within the establishment especially within business I remain, as I indicated in Chapter 1, sceptical of Marxist views which see the capitalist state as merely the managing agent for the affairs of the Japanese bourgeoisie. But what light do pluralist models of a liberal democratic state throw on the management of social change?

One key aspect of a pluralist model is that the state appears as an autonomous and neutral arbiter of the national interest amidst a variety of competing sectional interests, but as we have seen throughout this book the Japanese state is surely an active participant rather than a passive umpire. The notion of the state's autonomy has also been questioned by showing the interpenetration of economic and political elites which casts doubt on the principles of separated loci of power that were enshrined in the Constitution. Refining the principles of the US Occupation reforms ensured that 'the bureaucracy remains the pivot of the policy-making process' (Krauss and Muramatsu 1988 p. 208). This pivotal role centralizes consultation networks with politicians and business not least through the flow of ex-bureaucrats into Japan's leading corporations and into the ruling LDP. Thus the boundaries between the private and public sectors are blurred in contrast to pluralist assumptions of a clear boundary between the two. The history of Japan since industrialization began in the 1860s was one in which clearly defined constraints on the state were never fully established within a secure framework of civil rights and freedoms. Even though citizenship rights were extended after 1947 the validity of the clear distinction between the state and civil society remains dubious as we have seen in a number of chapters.

Interest group participation is intense and there are numerous points of access into policy-making processes in Japan but there are also clearly unequal levels of influence especially for leaders of business who have their preferential access institutionalized. The bureaucracy, notwithstanding the innovations introduced by Nakasone, continue to exercise power in setting agendas and selecting the membership of advisory bodies. This chapter has demonstrated how divisive issues such as pollution control or equal opportunities could be kept from the political agenda for long periods. Then even when some reformist concessions were made in the area of public welfare spending in the 1970s, this initiative was prepared for reversal through the agendas of administrative reform in the 1980s. What emerges from a consideration of interest group activity is that although consultation is widespread it is channelled 'within relatively predictable parameters' (Stockwin 1988 p. 12). These parameters ensure continuous access for conservative interest groups rather than an open-ended process of balancing multifarious inputs from all sectors of Japanese society.

Pluralist models inadequately account for the continuity of elite power centres in Japan within a system characterized by the dominance of one party in government, by the continuing role of a powerful bureaucracy and by sectionalized consultation networks. At the same time we should not ignore the other main pillar of pluralist theories which concerns electoral accountability in a mass participatory democracy. So what maintains the legitimacy of this stable pattern of centralized power in the eyes of the electorate?

It is tempting to explain the continuity of conservative power centres in the Japanese state in terms of a stronger national inclination towards deference and conformity to authority especially as this characteristic has since 1947 been protected by the institutions of representative democracy. But as I have tried to show in other chapters, there are problems in distinguishing voluntary cooperation from manufactured compliance and if explanations rely only on cultural preference for cooperation they ignore other processes through which consent has been secured. While the notion of a stronger sense of collective identity is an important strand in the ideology of Japan's uniqueness, there are a number of other factors that in my view explain the continuity of the social order in Japan. Among other things we need to recognize that this social order has resulted in a substantial increase in material welfare since the 1950s, that the state has been tireless in justifying the existing system and has in the process created barriers to the mobilization of an effective opposition to the current social order.

As we saw in Chapter 6 despite the continued existence of social inequalities, it has remained possible for even the most disadvantaged groups to increase their standard of living albeit with unequal inputs of personal effort. Legitimacy through delivering material goods has been supplemented by the barrage of publicity about Japan being the world's number one economy, which has given the state and employers the opportunity to justify labour's sacrifice in terms of the national interest as well as their own material comfort. Similarly the widespread penetration of a meritocratic ideology has allowed elite status to be justified as the reward for personal effort and individual merit rather than inherited position.

However even these sources of legitimacy would not have secured the stability of the existing order without a sustained effort to divide alternative centres of power. It was this ability to disarm, divide and immobilize the opposition especially of organized labour, that in my view has been paramount in explaining the continuity of the social order in Japan. Perhaps the most crucial moment in this process came during the late 1940s when, after a muted history of pre-war activism, labour appeared more united and powerful. As we saw in Chapter 3, the combined response of the state and employers in Japan with the support of the US occupation very effectively diffused this unity with a combination of coercion and material incentives for enterprise union members. Within the system of employment that resulted, the concessions given to one section of labour were large enough to undermine the unity of the labour movement as an alternative political force.

For individuals within the enterprise union sector, the constraints on inter-firm mobility place real financial penalties on non-compliance with management. So protecting their members' long-term interests became the overwhelming concern for enterprise unions to the exclusion of other workers. At a political level, enterprise unions have increasingly recognized that being tied to political parties which oppose the establishment with varying degrees of intransigence means being excluded from any political influence. So the demise of *Sohyo* the radical labour federation, was hastened by the privatization of its public sector base which its political allies could do nothing to halt. In contrast, the reorganized private sector federation *Rengo* actively cooperates with employers in the state's consultation networks. This cooperation as we saw with the 'cost-down' productivity drives that followed the appreciation of the yen in 1985, is now even more crucial if *Rengo* is to mitigate the impact of greater overseas production on the employment of enterprise union members.

If pro-labour political parties can no longer rely on the support of union members, their chances of replacing this backing from the ranks of non-union employees seems remote because for so many years they have ignored the plight of women, minority groups and employees in small firms. With this section of potential opposition to the conservative *status quo*, it is the long years of neglect by pro-labour parties themselves as much as the positive actions of the state and private employers that has been crucial.

Okimoto has argued that it is not surprising for both society and the state in Japan to 'assume a strongly pro-business posture' (1988 p. 215). Not surprising at all in view of the intense efforts made to convince the Japanese people that there is no alternative to the existing social order, at the same time as a disunited and fragmented labour movement provides such an incoherent alternative to conservative social values.

Bibliography

Official publications from Japan

Economic Planning Agency *Economic Survey of Japan* (1963).
Economic Planning Agency *Seven Year Plan* (1979).
Foreign Press Centre (*FPC*) Summary Translations:
  Summary of the Actual Labour Market for Women Ministry of Labour (1983)
    S-83-3.
  Survey on Schools Ministry of Education (1983) S-83-11.
  Public Opinion Survey on the Life of the Nation Prime Minister's Office (1983)
    S-83-13.
  1983 Basic Wage Structure Ministry of Labour (1984) S-84-10.
  Survey on Savings Central Commission for the Promotion of Savings (1985)
    S-85-7.
  Summary of the Actual Labour Market for Women Ministry of Labour (1985)
    W-85-8.
  Expenses for Social Security Benefits Social Security Research Institute (1986)
    R-86-5.
  Statistical Analysis of the Elderly Population of Japan Management and
    Coordination Agency (1986) R-86-6.
  Direct Overseas Investment Recorded in 1986 Ministry of Finance (1987)
    R-87-2.
  Analysis of Japan's Labour Economy Ministry of Labour (1987) W-87-9.
Keizai Koho Center *Japan 1984: An International Comparison*.
Ministry of Agriculture *Annual White Paper* (1983).
Ministry of Foreign Affairs *Dowa Problem: Present Situation and Government
  Measures* (1984).
Ministry of International Trade and Industry *Fifth Basic Survey of the State of
  Industry* (1979).
Ministry of Labour *Wage Structure Survey* (1976).
Statistics Bureau, Management and Coordination Agency *Japan Statistical
  Yearbook* (annual publication).

Newspapers and periodicals

Economist, The Economist Newspapers, London.
FEER Far Eastern Economic Review, Hong Kong.
FT, Financial Times, London.
Guardian, The Guardian Newspapers, London.
J.Ec.J. Japan Economic Journal, Tokyo.
JTW, The Japan Times Weekly Overseas Edition, Tokyo.
NYT, New York Times, New York USA.

Books and journal articles

Abegglen, James C. (1973) *Management and Worker: The Japanese Solution*, Tokyo, Sophia University Press.
Alessandrini, Pietro (1979) 'Lagged Development and Structural Imbalances' *Banca Nazionale del Lavoro*, 129.
Allen, G.C. (1965) *Japan's Economic Expansion*, London, Oxford University Press.
Allen, G.C. (1981) *The Japanese Economy*, London, Weidenfeld & Nicolson.
Anthony, D. (1983) Chapter 3 'Japan' in *The Small Firm: An International Survey* D.J. Storey (ed.) London, Croom-Helm.
Aoki, Masahiko (1984) *The Economic Analysis of the Japanese Firm*, Amsterdam and New York, North-Holland.
Armstrong, Philip, Glyn, Andrew and Harrison, John (1984), *Capitalism Since World War II*, London, Fontana.
Atsumi, Reiko (1979) '*Tsukiai* – Obligatory Personal Relationships of Japanese White-Collar Company Employees', *Human Organisation*, 38, 1.
Baerwald, Hans M. (1986) *Party Politics in Japan*, London, Allen & Unwin.
Befu, Harumi (1977) 'Power in the Great White Tower' in *The Anthropology of Power* R.D. Fogelson and R.M. Adams (eds), New York, Academic Press.
Befu, Harumi (1980) 'A Critique of the Group Model of Japanese Society', *Social Analysis*, 5/6.
Benedict, Ruth (1946) *The Chrysanthemum and the Sword*, Boston, Mass., Houghton Mifflin.
Blumenthal, Tuvia (1985) 'The Practice of *Amakudari* within the Japanese Employment System', *Asian Survey*, XXV, 3.
Blunden, Margaret (1982) *Industrial Social Systems*, Module 3 of T241 Systems Behaviour, Milton Keynes, The Open University Press.
Boltho, Andrea (1975) *Japan: An Economic Survey 1953–1973*, London, Oxford University Press.
Boltho, Andrea (1981) 'Italian and Japanese Postwar Growth: Some Similarities and Differences', *Revista Internazionale di Scienze Economiche E Commerciali* XXXVIII, 7–8.
Boltho, Andrea (1985) 'Was Japan's Industrial Policy Successful?' *Cambridge Journal of Economics*, 9, 2.
Boyd, Richmond A. (1985) *Government and Industry Relations in Japan*, Economic and Social Research Council, London, unpublished.
Buckley, Roger (1985) *Japan Today*, Cambridge, Cambridge University Press.
Buckley, Sandra and Mackie, Vera (1986) 'Women in the New Japanese State' in *Democracy in Contemporary Japan* G. McCormack and Y. Sugimoto (eds), London and New York, M.E. Sharpe Inc.

Caldora, Carlo (1969) '*Doya-Gai* – The Japanese Skid Row', *Pacific Affairs*, 41, 4.

Campbell, John Creighton (1984) 'Problems, Solutions, Non-Solutions and Free Medical Care for the Elderly in Japan', *Pacific Affairs*, 57, 1.

Christopher, Robert C. (1984) *The Japanese Mind*, London, Pan Books.

Clark, Rodney (1979) *The Japanese Company*, New Haven and London, York University Press.

Cole, Robert E. (1971) *Japanese Blue Collar: The Changing Tradition*, Berkeley, University of California Press.

Cole, Robert E. (1979) *Work, Mobility and Participation: A Comparative Study of American and Japanese Industry*, Berkeley, University of California Press.

Cole, Robert E. (1980) 'Learning from Japan: Prospect and Pitfalls', *Management Review*, September.

Cole, Robert E. and Tominaga, Ken'ichi (1976) 'Japan's Changing Occupational Structure and Its Significance' in *Japanese Industrialisation and Its Social Consequences* Hugh Patrick (ed.), Berkeley, University of California Press.

Collier, P. and Knight, J.B. (1985) 'Seniority Payments, Quit Rates and Internal Labour Markets in Britain and Japan', *Oxford Bulletin of Economics and Statistics*, 47, 1.

Cummings, William K. (1980) *Education and Equality in Japan*, Princeton, Princeton University Press.

De Vos, George A. and Lee, Changsoo (1981) *Koreans in Japan*, Berkeley, University of California Press.

De Vos, George A. and Wetherall, William O. (1983) *Japan's Minorities*, London, Minority Rights Group.

Dore, Ronald P. (1958) 'The Japanese Land Reform in Retrospect', *Far Eastern Survey*, XXVII, 12.

Dore, Ronald P. (1959) *Land Reform in Japan*, London, Oxford University Press.

Dore, Ronald P. (1973) *British Factory–Japanese Factory*, London, Allen & Unwin.

Dore, Ronald P. (1986) *Structural Adjustment in Japan 1970–82* Geneva, International Labour Office.

Dore, Ronald P. (1987) 'Citizenship and Employment in an Age of High Technology', *British Journal of Industrial Relations*, 25, 2.

Dower, John W. (1975) (ed.) *Origins of the Modern Japanese State: Selected Writings of E.H. Norman*, New York, Pantheon Books.

Dunn, Neil (1986) 'The Japanese "Shunto": Are there Lessons for the UK?' *Royal Bank of Scotland Review*, 151.

Elston, C.D. (1981) 'The Financing of Japanese Industry' *Bank of England Quarterly Bulletin*, 21, 4.

Evans, Robert J. (1971) *The Labour Economies of Japan and the United States*, New York, Praeger.

Flanagan, Scott C.L. (1980) 'National and Local Voting Trends: Cross-Level Linkages and Correlates of Change' in *Political Opposition and Local Politics in Japan* K. Steiner, E.S. Krauss and S.C. Flanagan (eds), Princeton, Princeton University Press.

Flanagan, Scott C., Steiner, Kurt and Krauss, Ellis C. (1980) 'The Partisan Politicization of Local Government' in *Political Opposition and Local Politics in Japan* K. Steiner, E.S. Krauss and S.C. Flanagan (eds), Princeton, Princeton University Press.

Fruin, Mark W. (1980) 'The Family as a Firm and the Firm as a Family in Japan', *Journal of Family History*, 5, 4.

Fujii, Harue (1982) 'Education for Women', *Japan Quarterly*, 29, 3.

Fujimura, Kumiko (1985) 'Women's Participation in Higher Education in Japan', *Comparative Education Review*, 29, 4.

Fujita, Kuniko (1987) 'Gender, State and Industrial Policy in Japan', *Women's Studies International Forum*, 10, 6.

Fukui, Haruhiro (1970) *Party in Power: The Liberal Democrats and Policy Making*, Berkeley, University of California Press.

Fukui, Haruhiro (1981) 'The Liberal Democratic Party Revisited', *Journal of Japanese Studies*, 10, 2.

Fukui, Haruhiro (1984) Book Review of *Japan's Electoral Process* in *Journal of Japanese Studies*, 11, 2.

Fukui, Haruhiro (1988) 'Japan in 1987', *Asian Survey*, XXVIII, 1.

Fukuoka, Masayuki, 'The Ailing Opposition', *Japan Echo* vol. xi, 1.

Fuse, Akiko (1984) 'The Japanese Family in Transition', *Japan Foundation Newsletter*, XII, 3.

Galenson, Walter (1974) 'The Japanese Worker', *Science*, 10 May.

Ganguly, Pom (1982) 'Small Firms Survey: The International Scene', *British Business*, 19 November.

Garon, Sheldon M. (1984) 'The Imperial Bureaucracy and Labour Policy in Postwar Japan', *Journal of Asian Studies*, XLIII, 3.

Garrahan, Philip L. (1986) 'Nissan in North East England', *Capital and Class*, 27, Winter.

Giddens, Anthony (1973) *The Class Structure of Advanced Societies*, London, Hutchinson.

Giddens, Anthony and Mackenzie, Gavin (1982) *Social Class and the Division of Labour*, Cambridge, Cambridge University Press.

Glazer, Nathan (1976) 'Social and Cultural Factors in Japanese Economic Growth', in *Asia's New Giant*, H.T. Patrick and H. Rosovsky (eds), Washington DC, Brookings Institution.

Hah, Chong-do and Lapp, Christopher (1978) 'Japanese Politics of Equality in Transition: the Case of the Burakumin', *Asian Survey*, XVIII, 5.

Halliday, Jon (1975) *A Political History of Japanese Capitalism*, New York and London, Monthly Review Press.

Halliday, Jon (1977) 'The Japanese State and Socio-Economic Change in the 1970s' in *Proceedings of the British Association for Japanese Studies*, vol. 2, part II, D.W. Anthony (ed.), Sheffield.

Hamada, T. (1980) 'Winds of Change: Economic Realism in Japanese Labour Management', *Asian Survey*, XX, 4.

Hanami, Tadashi (1983) 'Japanese Labour Law' in *Contemporary Industrial Relations in Japan*, T. Shirai (ed.), Madison, University of Wisconsin Press.

Hane, Mikiso (1982) *The Japanese: Peasants, Rebels and Outcasts*, New York, Pantheon Books.

Harari, E. (1982) 'Public Advisory Bodies in Japan', *Journal of Asian and African Studies*, XVII, 3–4.

Hashimoto, Masanori L. (1979) 'Bonus Payments, On-the-job Training and Lifetime Payments in Japan', *Journal of Political Economy*, 87, 5.

Hashimoto, Masanori and Raisian, John (1985) 'Employment Tenure and Earnings Profiles in Japan and the United States', *American Economic Review*, 75, 4.

Hasumi, Otohiko (1985) 'Rural Society in Post-War Japan', *Japan Foundation Newsletter* XII, 5.

Hayes, Robert (1981) 'Why Japanese Factories Work', *Harvard Business Review*, July–August.
Hein, Laura A. (1984) 'The Dark Valley Illuminated: Recent Trends in the Study of Japan's Post-War Economy', *Bulletin of Concerned Asian Scholars*, 16, June.
Herold, Renate (1979) 'Problems of Women in the Labour Market with Special Reference to Japan', *Proceedings of the Tokyo Symposium on Women*, Tokyo.
Hidaka, Rokuro (1986) 'The Crisis of Post-War Democracy' in *Democracy in Contemporary Japan*, G. McCormack and Y. Sugimoto (eds), New York and London, M.E. Sharpe Inc.
Higuchi, Keiko (1982) 'Japanese Women in Transition', *Japan Quarterly*, 29, 3.
Hills, Jill (1983) 'Industrial Policy in Japan', *Journal of Public Policy*, 3, 1.
Iida, Kane (1970) 'The Origins of the Enterprise Union in Post-War Japan', *Keio Economic Studies*, VII, 1.
Ike, Nobutaka (1978) *A Theory of Japanese Democracy*, Colorado, Westview Press.
Inoguchi, Kuniko (1987) 'Prosperity Without Amenities', *Journal of Japanese Studies*, 13, 1.
Ishi, Hiromitsu (1979) 'Individual Income Tax Erosion: By Income Class in Japan', *Public Finance Quarterly*, 7, 3.
Ishi, Hiromitsu (1980) 'Effects of Taxation on the Distribution of Income and Wealth in Japan' *Hitotsubashi Journal of Economics*, 21, June.
Japan Industrial Relation Series (1981) Series 9 'Industrial Safety and Health', The Japan Institute of Labour, Tokyo.
Johnson, Chalmers (1978) *Japan's Public Policy Companies*, Washington DC, American Enterprise Institute.
Johnson, Chalmers (1982) *MITI and the Japanese Miracle*, Stanford, Stanford University Press.
Johnson, Chalmers (1986) 'Tanaka Kakuei, Structural Corruption and the Advent of Machine Politics in Japan', *Journal of Japanese Studies*, 12, 1.
Jones, H.J.L. (1977) 'Japanese Women and Party Politics', *Pacific Affairs*, 49, 2.
Jost, Gesine (1979) 'Some Reconsiderations Concerning the Political Function of Anti-Pollution Movements in Japan', in *European Studies on Japan*, C. Dunn and I. Nish (eds), Kent, Paul Norbury.
Kain, Michael (1988) 'Recent Trends in World Agricultural Trade', *National Westminster Bank Quarterly Review*, May.
Kamata, Satoshi (1984) *Japan in the Passing Lane*, London, Unwin Paperbacks.
Karsh, Bernard and Levine, Solomon B. (1973) 'The Concept of a National Industrial Relations System' in *Workers and Employers in Japan*, K. Okochi, B. Karsh and S.B. Levine (eds), Princeton and Tokyo, Princeton and Tokyo University Presses.
Kawamura, Nozomu (1980) 'The Historical Background of Arguments Emphasising the Uniqueness of Japanese Society', *Social Analysis*, 5/6, December.
Kawashima, Yoko (1987) 'The Place and Role of Female Workers in the Japanese Labour Market', *Women's Studies International Forum*, 10, 6.
Khan, Herman (1973) *The Emerging Japanese Superstate*, Harmondsworth, Penguin Books.
Kishimoto, Eitaro (1968) 'Labour Management Relations and the Trade

Unions in Post-War Japan', *The Kyoto University Economic Review*, XXXVIII, 1.

Kitamura, Hiroshi (1976) *Choices for the Japanese Economy*, London, Royal Institute for International Affairs.

Koh, B.C. and Kim, Jae-On (1982) 'Paths to Advancement in Japanese Bureaucracy', *Comparative Political Studies*, 15, 3.

Komiya, Ryutaro and Yamamoto, Kozo (1981) 'Japan: the Officer in Charge of Economic Affairs' *History of Political Economy*, 13, 3.

Koschman, J. Victor (1974) 'The Idioms of Contemporary Japan VIII: *Tatemae to Honne*', *Japan Interpreter*, 9, 2.

Krauss, Ellis S. (1984) 'Conflict in the Diet: Toward Conflict Management in Parliamentary Politics' in *Conflict in Japan*, E.S. Krauss, T.P. Rohlen and P.G. Steinhoff (eds), Honolulu, University of Hawaii Press.

Krauss, Ellis S. and Muramatsu, Michio (1988) 'Japanese Political Economy Today: The Patterned Pluralist Model' in *Inside the Japanese System*, D.I. Okimoto and T.P. Rohlen (eds), Stanford, Stanford University Press.

Kumon, Shumpei (1984) 'Japan Faces Its Future: The Political-Economics of Administrative Reform', *Journal of Japanese Studies*, 10, 1.

Kusaka, Kimindo (1985) 'What is the Japanese Middle Class?' *Japan Echo*, 13, 3.

Lee, Sang M. and Schwendiman, Gary (1982) *Management by Japanese Systems*, New York, Praeger.

Levine, Solomon B. (1982) 'Japanese Industrial Relations: An External View', *Papers of the Japanese Studies Centre*, No. 4. Melbourne, Monash University.

Lin, Vivian (1984) 'Productivity First: Japanese Management Methods in Singapore', *Bulletin of Concerned Asian Scholars*, 16, 4.

Lincoln, Edward J. (1988) *Japan: Facing Economic Maturity*, Washington DC, The Brookings Institution.

Lockwood, William W. (1965) *The State and Economic Enterprise in Japan*, Princeton, Princeton University Press.

Lynn, Richard (1988) *Educational Achievement in Japan*, London, Macmillan for The Social Affairs Unit.

Macdonald, Donald (1985) 'The Environment in Japan: Twenty Years On', *Japan Education Journal*, 25.

Mackie, Vera (1988) 'Feminist Politics in Japan', *New Left Review*, 167, Jan/Feb.

Mayer, A.J. (1975) 'The Lower Middle Class as a Historical Problem', *Journal of Modern History*, 473.

McCormack, Gavin (1986) 'Beyond Economism: Japan in a State of Transition' in *Democracy in Contemporary Japan*', G. McCormack and Y. Sugimoto (eds), New York and London, M.E. Sharpe Inc.

McGown, Valerie (1980) 'Paternalism: A Definition', *Social Analysis*, 5/6, December.

McKean, Margaret A. (1981) *Environmental Protest and Citizen Politics in Japan*, Berkeley, University of California Press.

McLendon, James (1983) 'The Office: Way Station or Blind Alley?' in *Work and Life Course in Japan*, D.W. Plath (ed.), Albany, State of New York University Press.

Mesatoshi, Yorimitsu (1980) 'A Note on the Working Conditions of Subcontracting Establishments in the Iron and Steel Industry', *Hitotsubashi Journal of Social Studies*, November.

Minami, Ryoshin (1986) *The Economic Development of Japan*, London, Macmillan.
Miyamoto, Ken'ichi (1983) 'Environmental Problems and Citizens' Movements in Japan', *Japan Foundation Newsletter*, XI, 4.
Molony, Barbara (1985) Review of R. Herold, *Japan's Working Women* in *Journal of Asian Studies*, XLIII, 3.
Moore, Ray A. (1979) 'Reflections in the Occupation of Japan', *Journal of Asian Studies*, XXXVIII, 4.
Morishima, Michio (1982) *Why Has Japan 'Succeeded'?* Cambridge, Cambridge University Press.
Mouer, Ross and Sugimoto, Yoshio (1986) *Images of Japanese Society*, London, Routledge & Kegan Paul.
Murakami, Yasusuke (1978) 'The Reality of the New Middle Class', *Japan Interpreter*, XII, 1.
Muramatsu, Michio and Krauss, Ellis S. (1984) 'Bureaucrats and Politicians in Policy Making: the Case of Japan', *American Political Science Review*, 78, 1.
Nakane, Chie (1973) *Japanese Society*, Harmondsworth, Penguin.
Narushima, Michinori (1984) 'Administrative Reform: Redefining Japan's Future', *Bulletin of the Socialist Research Centre* (Hosei University Tokyo), No. 6.
Neary, Ian G. (1979) 'Towards a Reconsideration of the Formation of Buraku Communities and the Development of Discrimination Against Them', *European Studies of Japan*, C. Dunn and I. Nish (eds), Kent, Paul Norbury.
Neary, Ian G. (1986) 'Socialist and Communist Party Attitudes Towards Discrimination Against Japan's *Burakumin*', *Political Studies*, XXXIV.
Nee, Brett (1974) '*Sanya*: Japan's Internal Colony', *Bulletin of Concerned Asian Scholars*, 6, September.
Nettl, J.P. (1968) 'The State as a Conceptual Variable', *World Politics*, 20, 4.
OECD (1982) *Economic Outlook*, Paris, Organization for Economic Cooperation and Development, December.
OECD (1985) *Economic Survey: Japan*, Paris, Organization for Economic Cooperation and Development.
OECD (1986) *Economic Survey: Japan*, Paris, Organization for Economic Cooperation and Development.
OECD (1987) *Labour Force Statistics 1966–87*, Paris, Organization for Economic Cooperation and Development.
OECD (1987) *Economic Outlook*, Paris, Organization for Economic Cooperation and Development, December.
Ohmae, K. (1983) 'Management Style: The Mixed Score Card of Japanese Management Abroad', *International Management Europe*, July.
Okimoto, Daniel I. (1988) 'Japan, the Societal State' in *Inside the Japanese System*, D.I. Okimoto and T.P. Rohlen (eds), Stanford, Stanford University Press.
Ono, Akira and Watanabe, Tsunehiko (1976) 'Changes in Income Inequality in the Japanese Economy', in *Japanese Industrialisation and Its Social Consequences*, Hugh Patrick (ed.), Berkeley, University of California Press.
Okamura, Hiroshi (1982) 'The Closed Nature of Japanese Intercorporate Relations', *Japan Echo*, IX, 3.
Osako, Masako (1979) 'Dilemmas of Japanese Professional Women', *Social Problems*, 26, 1.
Ozawa, Masako (1985) 'Consumption in the Age of Stratification', *Japan Echo*, 13, 3.

Ozawa, Terutomo (1985) 'Japan', in *Multinational Enterprises, Economic Structure and International Competitiveness*, J.H. Dunning (ed.), London, Wiley.

Park, Yung H. (1978) 'The Local Public Personnel System in Japan', *Asian Survey*, XVIII, 6.

Park, Sung-Jo (1979) 'Foreign Investment and New Imperialism Theories with Special Reference to Japanese Foreign Investment in East and South East Asia', in *European Studies of Japan*, C. Dunn and I. Nish (eds), Kent, Paul Norbury.

Patrick, Hugh T. (1975) 'Comment', in *Evolution of International Management Structures*, H.F. Williamson (ed.), Delaware, University of Delaware Press.

Patrick, Hugh T. (1977) 'The Future of the Japanese Economy: Output and Labour Productivity', *Journal of Japanese Studies*, 3, 2.

Patrick, Hugh T. and Rosovsky, H. (1976) *Asia's New Giant*, Washington DC, Brookings Institution.

Pechman, J.A., and Kaizuka, K. (1976) 'Taxation' in *Asia's New Giant*, H.T. Patrick and H. Rosovsky (eds), Washington DC, Brookings Institution.

Peck, Merton J., Levin, Richard C. and Goto, Akira (1987) 'Picking Losers: Public Policy Toward Declining Industries in Japan', *Journal of Japanese Studies*, 13, 1.

Pempel, T.J. and Tsunekawa, Keiichi (1979) 'Corporatism without Labour? The Japanese Anomaly', in G. Lembruch and P. Schmitter (eds), *Trends Towards Corporatist Intermediation*, London, Sage.

Pempel, T.J. (1982) *Policy and Politics in Japan: Creative Conservatism*, Philadelphia, Temple University Press.

Pempel, T.J. (1987) 'The Unbundling of "Japan Inc.": the Changing Dynamics of Japanese Policy Formation', *Journal of Japanese Studies*, 13,2.

Pharr, Susan J. (1984) 'Status Conflict: The Rebellion of the Tea Pourers', in *Conflict in Japan*, E.S. Krauss, T.P. Rohlen and P.G. Steinhoff (eds), Honolulu, University of Hawaii Press.

Plath, David W. (1983) *Work and Life Course in Japan*, Albany, State of New York University Press.

Reed, Steven R. (1981) 'Environmental Politics: Some Reflections Based on the Japanese Case', *Comparative Politics*, April.

Rohlen, T.P. (1979) 'Permanent Employment Faces Recession, Slow Growth and an Ageing Workforce', *Journal of Japanese Studies*, 5, 2.

Rohlen, T.P. (1980) 'The *Juku* Phenomenon', *Journal of Japanese Studies*, 6, 1.

Rokumoto, Kahei (1982) 'The Law Consciousness of the Japanese', *Japan Foundation Newsletter*, IX, 6.

Rotwein, Eugene (1976) 'Economic Concentration and Monopoly in Japan', *Journal of Asian Studies*, XXXVI, 1.

Ruyle, Eugene E. (1979) 'Conflicting Japanese Interpretations of the Outcaste Problem', *American Ethnologist*, 6, 1.

Sabouret, Jean-François (1983) *L'Autre Japan: Les Burakumin*, Paris, La Decouveite/Maspero.

Sakakibara, Eisuke and Feldman, Robert A. (1983) 'The Japanese Financial System in Comparative Perspective', *Journal of Comparative Economics*, 7, 1.

Salamano, S. (1980) 'How Mazda was Rotated', *Management Today*, February.

Samuels, Richard (1981) 'Behind Japan Incorporated', *Technology Review*, 83, 7.

Sasaki, N. (1981) *Management and Industrial Structure in Japan*, Oxford, Pergamon.

Sasaki, Takeshi (1987) Review of *The Liberal Democratic Party in Power, Japan Foundation Newsletter*, XIV, 5.

Sato, Kazuo (1980) *Industry and Business in Japan*, London, Croom-Helm.

Sato, Kazuo (1985) 'Supply-Side Economics: A Comparison of the US and Japan', *Journal of Japanese Studies*, II, 1.

Sato, Yoshio (1984) 'The Subcontracting Production System in Japan', *Keio Business Review*, 21.

Saxonhouse, Gary R. (1979) 'Industrial Re-Structuring in Japan', *Journal of Japanese Studies*, 5, 2.

Sayer, Andrew (1986) 'New Developments in Manufacturing: the Just-in-time System', *Capital and Class*, 30, Winter.

Schultze, Charles L. (1983) 'Industrial Policy: A Dissent', *The Brookings Review*, 2, Fall.

Seike, Atsushi (1985) 'The Employment Adjustment in Japanese Manufacturing Industries in the 1970s', *Keio Business Review*, 22.

Sen, Amartya (1983) 'The Profit Motive', *Lloyds Bank Review*, 147.

Sethi, S. Prakash, Namiki, Nobuaki and Swanson, Carl L. (1984) *The False Promise of the Japanese Miracle*, London, Pitman.

Shimada, Haruo (1984) 'Perceptions and the Reality of Japanese Industrial Relations', *Keio Economic Studies*, XXI, 2.

Shirai, T. (1983) *Contemporary Industrial Relations in Japan*, Madison, University of Wisconsin Press.

Shonfield, Andrew (1984) *In Defence of the Mixed Economy*, Oxford University Press.

Simon, Owen (1986) 'Investing in Infrastructure', *National Westminster Bank Quarterly Review*, May.

Simonson, Nancee (1981) 'The Postal Hydra', *The Banker*, 131, 666.

Smith, Beverley (1986) 'Democracy Derailed: Citizens Movements in Historical Perspective', in *Democracy in Contemporary Japan*, G. McCormack and Y. Sugimoto (eds), New York and London, M.E. Sharpe Inc.

Smith, Robert J. (1983) *Japanese Society*, Cambridge, Cambridge University Press.

Smith, Robert J. (1985) 'A Pattern of Japanese Society', *Journal of Japanese Studies*, 11,1.

Smith, Robert J. (1987) 'Gender Inequality in Japan', *Journal of Japanese Studies*, 13, 1.

Steven, Rob. (1983) *Classes in Contemporary Japan*, Cambridge, Cambridge University Press.

Steven, Rob. (1988) 'The High Yen Crisis in Japan', *Capital and Class*, 34, Spring.

Stockwin, J.A.A. (1984) Review of T.J. Pempel *Policy and Politics in Japan*, *Journal of Japanese Studies*, 10, 1.

Stockwin, J.A.A. (ed.) (1988) *Dynamic and Immobilist Politics in Japan*, London, Macmillan in association with St Anthony's College Oxford.

Storey, D.J. (ed.) (1983) *The Small Firm: An International Survey*, London, Croom-Helm.

Sugimoto, Yoshio (1982) 'Japanese Society and Industrial Relations', *Papers of the Japanese Studies Centre*, No. 4, Melbourne, Monash University.

Sugimoto, Yoshio (1986) 'The Manipulative bases of "consensus" in Japan', in *Democracy in Contemporary Japan*, G. McCormack and Y. Sugimoto (eds), New York and London, M.E. Sharpe Inc.

Tachibanaki, Toshiaka (1975) 'Wage Determinations in Japanese Manufacturing Industries', *International Economic Review*, 16, 3.

Tachibanaki, Toshiaka (1982) 'Further Results on Japanese Wage Differentials', *International Economic Review*, 23, 2.

Taira, Koji (1962) 'Characteristics of Japanese Labour Markets', *Economic Development and Cultural Change*, 10, January.

Taira, Koji (1980) 'Colonialism in Foreign Subsidiaries: Lessons from Japanese Investment in Thailand', *Asian Survey*, XX, 4.

Taira, Koji (1983) 'Japan's Low Unemployment: Economic Miracle or Statistical Artifact', *Monthly Labour Review*, July.

Taira, Koji (1986) 'Consumer Electronics' in *Structural Adjustment in Japan, 1970–82*, R.P. Dore (ed.), Geneva, International Labour Office.

Takagi, Tadao (1981) 'Labour Relations in Japan and Italy', *Rivista Internazionale di Scienze Economiche E Commerciali*, XXVIII, 7–8.

Takano, Makoto (1983) 'Japanese Social Democracy: Conflict and Compromise', *Bulletin of the Socialist Research Centre*, No. 3, Hosei University, Tokyo.

Takeuchi, Hiroshi (1982) 'Working Women in Business Corporations', *Japan Quarterly*, 29, 3.

Thayer, Nathaniel B. (1969) *How The Conservatives Rule Japan*, Princeton, Princeton University Press.

Tokunaga, Shigeyoshi (1983) 'A Marxist Interpretation' in *Contemporary Industrial Relations in Japan*, T. Shirai (ed.), Madison, University of Wisconsin Press.

Tominaga, Ken'ichi (1978) 'An Empirical View of Social Stratification', *Japan Interpreter*, XII, 1.

Tominomori, Kenji (1985) 'Unemployment in Japan', *Hokudai Economic Papers*, XIV.

Tsuda, Masumi (1980) 'Will Life-Time Employment Security Practices be Kept in the 1980s?' *Hitotsubashi Journal of Social Studies*, November.

Tsuruta, Toshimasa (1983) 'The Myth of Japan Inc.', *Technology Review*, 86, 7.

Tsurutani, Taketsugu (1972) 'A New Era of Japanese Politics', *Asian Survey*, XII, 5.

Tuffarelli, Nicola (1981) 'The Current International Situation and the National Restraints of Italy and Japan', *Revista Internazionale di Scienze Economiche E Commerciale*, XXVIII, 7–8.

Turner, Louis (1987) *Industrial Collaboration with Japan*, Chatham House Papers No. 34, London, Routledge & Kegan Paul.

Upham, Frank K. (1987) *Law and Social Change in Japan*, Cambridge, Mass., Harvard University Press.

Ueno, Chizuko (1983) 'The Japanese Domestic Labour Debate', unpublished paper presented to North American Women's Studies Association, Ohio.

Vogel, Ezra F. (1979) *Japan as Number One*, Cambridge, Mass., Harvard University Press.

Vogel, Suzanne H. (1978) 'Professional Housewife: The Career of Urban Middle Class Japanese Women', *Japan Interpreter*, XII, 1.

Wagatsuma, Hiroshi (1979) 'Burakumin in Present-Day Japan', in *Nationalism and the Crises of Ethnic Minorities in Asia*, Tai S. Kang (ed.), London, Greenwood Press.

Ward, Robert E. (1968) 'Reflections on the Allied Occupation and Planned Political Change in Japan', in *Political Development in Modern Japan*, R.E. Ward (ed.), Princeton, Princeton University Press.

Weber, Max (1972) *From Max Weber*, Oxford, Oxford University Press.

White, James W. (1974) 'Tradition and Politics in Studies of Contemporary Japan', *World Politics*, 26, 3.

White, Merry I. (1986) Review of *Education and Equality in Japan*, in *Journal of Japanese Studies*, 12, 1.

White, Michael and Trevor, Malcolm (1983) *Under Japanese Management*, London, Heinemann for the Policy Studies Institute.

van Wolferen, Karel (1982) 'Reflections on the Japanese System', *Survey*, 26, 1.

Woronoff, Jon (1983) *Japan's Wasted Workers*, New Jersey, Allenheld.

Woronoff, Jon (1984) *Japan's Commercial Empire*, London, Macmillan.

Yamamoto, Kiyoshi (1981) 'Mass Demonstration Movements in Japan in the Period of Postwar Crisis', *Capital and Class*, 12, Winter.

Yamamura, Kozo (1982) *Policy and Trade Issues of the Japanese Economy*, Seattle, University of Washington Press.

Yamamura, Kozo (1987) 'Shedding the Shackles of Success: Saving Less for Japan's Future', *Journal of Japanese Studies*, 13, 2.

Yoshino, I. Roger (1983). 'The Buraku Minority of Japan', *Patterns of Prejudice*, 17, 1.

Index

References in italics indicate tables or figures.

Okimoto, Daniel, 264
Okinawa, 198–9
omote, 212, 213, 214
 see also practice (substance),
  principle compared
Opposition parties, 126–8,
 139–49, *149*, 263–4
 in Diet, 151–2, 153
 see also Democratic Socialist
  Party; Japan Communist
  Party; Japan Socialist
  Party; *Komeito*
outcasts, 199, 200, 201
overseas investment see foreign
 investment
overtime, 3, 58, 180, 237–8, 239

Pacific War, impact of, 77–8
'parent companies', 34, 37
part-time employees, 237, 238
 women, 190–3, *191, 192, 193,
  196*, 214
participation rates, labour force
 elderly, *205*, 205
 women, 180–2, *181*, 189
'passing', 200–1
patriarchy, public, 194–7
Patrick, Hugh, 88
patron–client democracy, 131
pay see income distribution; wage
 differentials
Pechman, J.A., 166
pensions, 98, 99, 101, 205, 207,
 208
permanent employment see
 lifetime employment
personal evaluations, company,
 74, 83
personal savings see Postal
 Savings system; savings
piecework, 192, *192*, 193, *193,
 196*
pluralist models, Japan compared,
 22–3, 25, 27, 160–1, 261–2
'policy tribes', 153–4
political parties see Democratic
 Socialist Party; Japan

Communist Party; Japan
 Socialist Party; *Komeito*;
 Liberal Democratic Party
political structure see bureaucracy;
 Diet; Supreme Court
pollution, 220–31
 citizens' groups, 144–5, 195,
  220–3, 228–9, 230
 litigation, 215, 222, 225–6
Pollution Diet (1970), 223
Postal Savings system, 49, 104–5
 taxation, 105, 159–60, 236,
  256, 257
poverty, 164–5, 209
practice (substance), principle
 compared, 211–12, 214,
 229–30
prices, consumer, 53–4, 78,
 121–2, 259
 food, 144, 174, 258
 imported goods, 195, 235, 258
primary sector, foreign
 investment, *247*, 248–9
Prime Ministers, 137
 see also Nakasone; Takeshita;
  Tanaka
principle, (form) practice
 compared, 211–12, 214,
 229–30
private/public sector relations,
 20, 26, 27, 108–22, 261–2
 administrative guidance,
  115–16
 amakudari, 112–15, 119
 policy formulation, 116–19
 see also zaibatsu
private schools, 185
production control, by workers,
 78–9
production methods, Japanese
 overseas, 249–50
productivity, 6, 28, 37–8, *38*, 56
 and company commitment, 70
 'cost-down' measures, 238,
  239
'professional housewives', 189,
 190

Tokugawa, 10, 11
Toshiba, 238
Toyo Kogyo Co., 45–6
Toyota, 234, 239, 241, 253
trade credit, 46–7
trade unions *see* unions
trading companies, 39, 244–6
'traditions', 9–10, 72–3, 100,
  103–4
transaction costs, 33, 34, 35
transfer payments, 96–9, *97*
transfers, labour, 237
transport investment, 94

ultranationalism, 14, 15, 130, 140
UN Treaty on Discrimination
  against Women, 213
unemployment, 4, 194, 199, 240
unions, 2, 17, 20–1, 76–87, *260*,
  263–4
  employment conditions, 86,
    141–2, 239
  overseas, 251, 254
  women's rights, 186, 194
  see also Domei; *Rengo*; *shunto*;
    Sohyo
United Kingdom, Japanese
  factories, 249–50
United States
  Japanese investment, 249,
    251–6
  'learning from Japan', 6–8
  wage rates compared, 63, *63*
  see also US Occupation
universities, 5, 112, 168–9, 185–6
unmarried women, 182–3, 190
upper class, 175–6
ura, 212, 214, 230
  see also principle (form),
    practice compared
urban areas
  housing, 173
  politics, 128–30, 149–50
US Occupation, 15–19, 22, 79,
  80, 110, 123, 124

value-added differentials, 38, *38*,
  254
Vice Ministers, 113, 114, 158
victims' movements, 221, 228–9
violence, school, 200, 217, 218,
  221
Vogel, Ezra F., 6–7, 8, 11,
  16–17, 71, 98–9
voter mobilization, 132, 195

wage bargaining, 79, 82, 83, 85
  see also Densan; *shunto*
wage differentials
  blue–/white-collar, 82, 170
  and size of firm, 58–67, *59*,
    60, 61, 63, 65
  women, 165, 177–80, *178*,
    179, 193, *193*, 213–14
Wage Structure Survey, 168
wealth distribution, 164, 165–7
Weber, Max, 24
weddings, saving for, *101*, 102
welfare
  company provision, 59, 73
  state provision *see* welfare state
Welfare Facilities Survey, 59
welfare state, 7, 25–6, 75, 96–9,
  219
  for the elderly, 206–9
    see also pensions
  and savings, 99, 108
  see also social security
wholesale distribution, 52–5
white-collar workers
  blue-collar compared, 79, 82,
    170–1, 172
  women, 183
women, 21, 177–97
  education, 168, 169
  employment, 171, 174, 181–4,
    196, 212–14
  union membership, 76–7, 86
  wages, 61, 64–6, *67*, 165,
    177–80, 213–14
work groups, 74–5, 182, 255
working class, 144, 176

Index by A.R. Crook